Growing businesses sense the expanding opportunities for export and investment in the thriving Pacific Rim market. This practical book, written by an author who has had hands-on experience in helping companies set up Pacific Rim trade and operations, shows how you too can get started in the region.

All aspects of marketing, manufacturing, and investing are covered, from determining whether your company is ready to take on Pacific Rim trade to starting off on the right foot by supporting your market partner and understanding Pacific Rim business cultures. Thoughtful attention is given to each of your options: licensing, franchising, contracting, joint ventures, and wholly owned operations. A chapter on financing covers the key issues of getting paid, financing your exports, taking advantage of government finance programs, and financing direct investment.

A final profiles section surveys each individual Pacific Rim nation and provides a comprehensive overview of the current economic situation, specific trade and investment opportunities, and important developments to watch out for. And the thorough listing of resources includes a critical review of government services and helpful private organizations, books, periodicals, computer data bases, as well as export assistance programs.

It's easy to bemoan the difficulties of international trade, but it requires a little digging to uncover the stories of opportunity and success. Yet those stories are there—by the thousands! How have those companies succeeded? And how can you follow suit? In *Pacific Rim Trade,* Mike Van Horn investigates the experiences of successful companies so that you can learn and benefit from the opportunities they seized—and overcome the obstacles they faced.

The rapidly maturing economies of the Pacific Rim nations provide constant new opportunities for trade and investment. *Pacific Rim Trade* is a timely and trustworthy primer for growing businesses in search of new venues to expanding profit.

Pacific
Rim
Trade

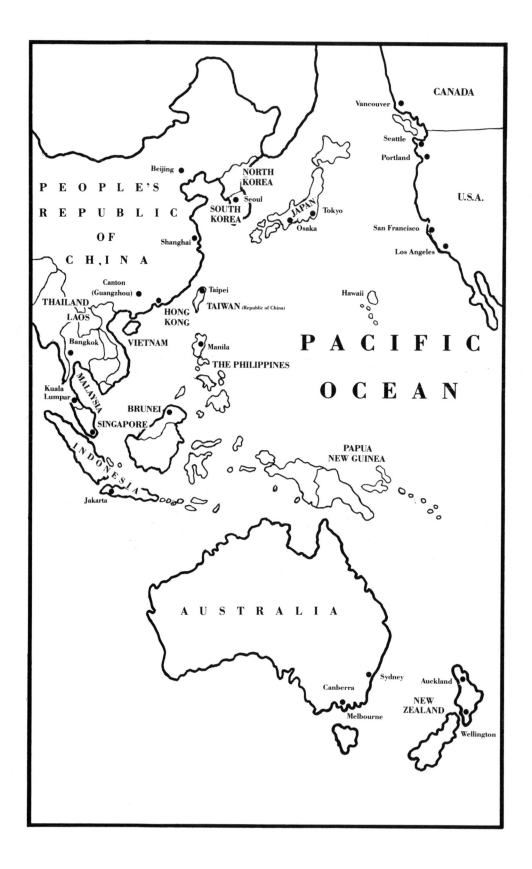

Pacific Rim Trade

The Definitive Guide to Exporting and Investment

Mike Van Horn

amacom
American Management Association

Library of Congress Cataloging-in-Publication Data

Van Horn, Mike.
   *Pacific Rim trade : the definitive guide to exporting and
investment / Mike Van Horn.*
      p.   cm.
   Includes index.
   ISBN 0-8144-5930-7
   *1. United States—Commerce—Pacific Area—Handbooks,
manuals, etc. 2. Pacific Area—Commerce—United States—
Handbooks, manuals, etc. 3. Export marketing—Pacific
Area—Information services—United States—Handbooks,
manuals, etc. 4. Investments, American—Pacific Area—Information services—United States—Handbooks, manuals,
etc. 5. International business enterprises—Pacific Area—
Handbooks, manuals, etc.   I. Title.*
   HF3043.V36   1989
   658.8'48'099—dc19   88-48031
                                                        CIP

Printing number

10   9   8   7   6   5   4   3   2   1

To my wife,
confidante,
sounding board,
editor,
and
Pacific Rim sailing partner—
B.J.

The Mediterranean
  is the ocean of the past,
the Atlantic,
  the ocean of the present,
and the Pacific,
  the ocean of the future.

Secretary of State John Hay, 1898

To understand the future,
you must understand the Pacific.

Secretary of State George Shultz, 1986

Table of Contents

Acknowledgments

To all the people who said, "This book is needed!" and urged me on: my editors, Eva Weiss, Kate Pferdner, and Nancy Brandwein; my typist, Ginny Greenfield; Rick Hanson and Scott Morse; Frank Caffrey, and many others at the Department of Commerce; Diane Lipka of Business International; Susan Catalano of Theos Software; Roger Harker and Steve Riggs of Bently-Nevada; Bob Wells of SpectraPhysics; Ernie Vonderschmidt of Xilinx; Judith Olewine of RAMS International; Tim Olsen of California Energy Commission; Jerry Luftman of California Export Finance Program; Drs. Otto Butz and Hamid Shomali of Golden Gate University; Allen Choate of the Asia Foundation; Norman Solomon of the Center for International Business; Eldridge Wood of Inter-Pacific Capital Corporation; Martin Tang of Hong Kong Venture Investment Fund; Ding-Hua Hu and Ta-Lin Hsu of Hambrecht & Quist; Peter Dietz of Cybeq Systems; Lewis Griggs of Going International; John Sakai of AZCA, Inc.; Remi Ceci of Pan Pacific Energy Development Corp.; John Quinn of First Interstate Bank; Verna Borisenko of Union Bank; John Brinsden and John Draheim of Standard Chartered Bank in Hong Kong and Taipei, respectively; Thomas Jordan of DuPont Japan; Valerie Gaynard of Interior Decor in Tokyo; Yuko Hanada of ACCJ; Mimi Webster of AMCHAM Hong Kong; U.S. Foreign Commercial Service officers Ying Price in Hong Kong and Camille Sailer in Seoul; Stephen Craven of the American Institute in Taiwan; Michael Dubrow of IntelliBanc; Robert Johnson of Strategies Unlimited; Greta McKinney, Bruce Quan, Jim Hume of SPIRIT; Jim Stocker. My thanks also to the several people who took the time to talk with me but did not want me to use their names and asked me to disguise their companies and lines of business.

Thanks to the many Pacific Rim representatives who assisted me, especially Melinda Parsons, Wendy Leung, and Mark Pinkstone for Hong Kong; Jackson Chen and Dr. Yi-Der Chuang for Taiwan; Deputy Consul General Pil Joo Sung for Korea; Dr. Narongchai Akrasanee for Thailand; Consul General Alexander Lolong and Mark Adleson for Indonesia; Ryuichi Hattori of JETRO for Japan; Barry Hain for the Australian Trade Commission; Eng Wei Chong of the Singapore Economic Development Board; C. K. Lee in Seoul; Consul for Investment Tan Ah Yong for Malaysia.

Special thanks to my family, who supported me all the way: my wife, B.J.; my parents, for sending me a constant stream of articles; and my daughter, Becky, for setting a good example for me by how hard she works.

Preface

It's easy to read about the difficulties of international trade; stories about successes and opportunities require a little digging. Yet the successes are there by the thousands. In the midst of the barriers to trade, how do so many companies succeed? And, if *they* can do it, couldn't yours as well? If you don't look seriously at this question, you could be leaving a pile of money on the table. Worse, you could be leaving yourself even more vulnerable to competitors—whether from Taiwan or from the next town—that do take their international trade seriously.

Time after time, business executives have told me that the biggest barrier they have encountered to Pacific Rim trade is lack of information. Without timely, trustworthy, affordable information, they have had no choice but to pass up potentially lucrative business. I first decided to write this book when two consulting clients asked me to investigate Pacific Rim export opportunities for them, and I had a heck of a time finding the information I needed. I eventually discovered that there is a vast amount of information available, but it is spread all over; nowhere is it cataloged or evaluated.

Throughout this book I stress the opportunities for smaller companies. Large corporations now dominate international trade—perhaps because they can afford to conduct extensive market studies overseas. But the opportunities are abundant for small and medium-size companies as well. And you can take advantage of such opportunities *without* spending a small fortune. This book is addressed to the executives of smaller companies. Small in this context could be a half-billion-dollar corporation. Perhaps a small company is simply any business that has felt overwhelmed by the challenge of entering international trade.

Pacific Rim Trade is a starter, how-to book designed to (1) explore the factors you need to consider, using examples from businesses that have been there; (2) briefly sketch Pacific Rim markets; and (3) catalog and evaluate all the resources and sources of information you need. The book covers U.S. trade and investment by American companies with the crescent of Asian Pacific Rim nations (starting from the north): Japan, Korea, China, Taiwan, Hong Kong, Thailand, the Philippines, Malaysia, Singapore, Indonesia, Australia, and New Zealand.

I focus on the Pacific Rim because this is the fastest-growing sector of international trade for American business. Of course, a number of issues covered in the book have application to wider international trade and investment opportunities.

I use the term *trade* to cover both export and investment. In the emerging climate of international business, investment is more and more important—and increasingly within the reach of smaller companies.

Mike Van Horn

Introduction

Although I have had an established business in the Pacific Basin for over twenty-five years, I still found it refreshing to read Mike Van Horn's *Pacific Rim Trade*. Had such a thorough and practical book been available when my company began its expansion in the Pacific, I am confident that the process would have been far more efficient and smooth.

Of course, your key consideration will be, "Should we do business in the Pacific Rim?" No one can answer that for you, but surely the prospect should be carefully considered by any growth-oriented company. Learning the right questions is the first step to take in considering whether or not to expand into the Pacific Rim, and the chapters of *Pacific Rim Trade* follow a logical order in raising the right questions and guiding you through the process that will enable you to find trustworthy and timely answers.

By any normal measure, it would be difficult to duplicate the extraordinary growth already recorded by most of the Pacific Rim nations since the late 1970s. Japan's story is already legendary, and Korea and Taiwan are not far behind Japan. Although it is natural to question the future development potential for a region after such a rapid rate of growth, even a cursory review of the publicly announced plans of Pacific Rim countries, a count of the airlines serving the region, and a look at many of the area's larger companies suggest overwhelmingly that the past truly may be only a prologue. And when you consider the possibility of the Pacific Rim countries becoming outward-looking trading nations again, the picture brightens even more.

In my opinion, and by almost any set of standards, the countries of the Pacific Rim are poised for at least as much growth over the next decade as they have experienced during the past ten years. Needs are changing, however. Japan, Korea, and, to a substantial degree, Taiwan are no longer "developing" countries. Their industrial and commercial expansion has enabled them to become fully integrated and developed economies, with all the problems associated with commercial success. Their infrastructures are being strained across the board. Environmental problems are surfacing rapidly. In short, all the ancillary problems associated with successful and developed economies are beginning to surface in earnest. Thus, if your organization supplies products or services for these markets, you might well consider the Pacific Rim.

Another important component that will drive and sustain growth is the availability of adequate investment capital. Korea, Japan, and Taiwan have large trade surpluses, and all three are under some pressure from the United States to buy more from American companies. New Zealand is prospering under its new government; the Australian economy continues to be robust; and the ASEAN countries all have substantial untapped growth potential. When you add to the picture the possibility of mainland China becoming a trading nation once again, a very compelling case can be made for a long period of sustained growth in the Pacific Basin.

Fortunately, Mike Van Horn's book has come along at the right time for those giving serious thought to expanding into the Pacific Rim. His knowledge and experience in helping other companies enter these markets are evident throughout the book, and they provide a rich source of practical information and advice about entering the markets of the Pacific Rim.

ARTHUR H. STROMBERG
Chairman Emeritus,
Pacific Basin Economic Council *and*
Chairman, URS International, Inc.

1 | Pacific Rim Opportunity

- *Why export when the U.S. market is so big?*
- *Why trade with Pacific Rim nations?*
- *Why reconsider foreign trade if you have avoided it in the past?*

Who sells the most chopsticks in Japan? If it's not a Japanese company, it must be some Taiwanese or Korean outfit, right? Guess again. It is Lakewood Industries, Inc., a small company out of Hibbing, Minnesota. Lakewood was instrumental in creating the market for disposable wooden chopsticks in Japan, where polished wooden or ivory chopsticks have been traditional from time immemorial.

Theos Software Corp. in Walnut Creek, California, a small five-year-old company that produces multiuser operating system software for personal computers, was forced into the European market to protect the rights to its software. After establishing distributors in Europe and Saudi Arabia, it moved into Pacific Rim markets—Australia, Japan, and China. Today, international trade represents 40 percent of its revenue. Even though Theos still employs just two dozen people, its growing network of distributors has a hundred reps working exclusively on Theos products.

"Why should I go to the trouble of getting into foreign markets when my domestic sales are so good?" asked the president of Med-Rite, a medical products supplier. His $50 million company had grown every year. But then he began to feel pressures on his domestic markets, and at a conference he heard a speaker mention the need for specialty medical supplies in Asian markets. He thought to himself, "I could supply that." And now $18 million in sales to Asian markets contribute to 25 percent of the company's gross and 30 percent of its profits. Its Pacific Rim markets are growing much faster than its domestic markets.

Golden Gate University, a private business school in San Francisco, didn't need to go into the Pacific Rim for defensive reasons. But President Otto Butz always keeps his antennae out for opportunities, and during a casual conversation with a Malaysian business executive he came up with the idea of a joint venture business school in Malaysia. He helped set up a program in Kuala Lumpur and has expanded into Indonesia, Singapore, and other Pacific Rim countries.

Molex, a $300 million manufacturer of electrical connectors headquartered near Chicago, had no choice but to go overseas: All its customers were moving to the Asian Pacific Rim to take advantage of cheaper labor. Today Molex has thirty-eight factories overseas, including five in Japan. International business accounts for almost two thirds of its revenues.

H-Tech went to the Pacific Rim because its domestic markets were drying up. H-Tech develops photovoltaic power generation systems—commercialized versions of the solar cells used as power sources in satellites. Photovoltaic power showed promise in domestic markets during the oil crisis of the mid-1970s. But when oil prices declined, photovoltaic systems were no longer competitive. However, in developing nations, including many Pacific Rim countries, photovoltaic systems are a viable alternative for remote areas that are not on the central power grid. H-Tech found a competitive advantage in engineering simple, reliable "turnkey" systems tailored to each situation.

Toys R Us operates in a number of Pacific Rim countries, including Singapore, Hong Kong, and Japan. It sells 80 percent of the same merchandise overseas that it offers in the United States. The company does make some concessions to local taste, such as selling cricket bats in Britain, but it is surprised at what sells well. For example, in Singapore, kids have taken up street hockey thanks to Toys R Us. The company still gets most of its sales growth domestically. However, the international toy market is twice as large as the U.S. market, and the company is staking out its claim overseas for the inevitable day when growth prospects at home slow down. Toys R Us expects to open at least 200 stores overseas in the next decade.

Executives from Loctite, a manufacturer of adhesives and sealants (best known here for Super Glue), traveled to a government factory in China to solve a serious leakage problem in the internal combustion engines produced at the plant. After conducting tests and negotiations for five years, Loctite embarked on a 50–50 joint venture with the Chinese. Today, almost half its $250 million in annual sales come from international operations, and a recent jump in profits resulted largely from strong overseas performance in Japan and other Pacific Rim countries.

These are just a few of the thousands of U.S. companies that are succeeding in exporting to businesses within the Pacific Rim. You'll notice that not one is a multinational industrial giant. They are large and small; they come from all parts of the United States, and they provide all kinds of products and services. They are companies much like yours, with CEOs much like you, that have one thing in common: They have maximized the opportunity for doing business with Pacific Rim nations. Your business could join their ranks.

U.S. Department of Commerce figures indicate that international trade is becoming more and more important to all U.S. industries and that trade with Pacific Rim nations is the fastest-growing sector. As a region, despite recent economic difficulties, it still has the fastest economic growth in the world. Despite barriers, these rapidly maturing economies are always providing new opportunities for U.S. companies.

Many Pacific Rim economies are still roaring along: China and Thailand are among the world's fastest-growing economies; Japan, Taiwan, Hong Kong, and Korea—plus Australia and New Zealand—offer an increasingly affluent market of over 200 million consumers. The other Pacific Rim economies, which faltered after a boom lasting into the early 1980s, have been bouncing back.

Important changes are occurring in economic and political structures. Trade pressures from the United States are beginning to force open markets to American imports. Governments of several developing Pacific Rim nations now realize that their commodity-export-based economies are not adequate to keep pace with the global economy. They see the need for heavy investment in industrial diversification and social infrastructure. Many opportunities are thus created for U.S. companies, which have a large competitive advantage in these areas of business.

Most Pacific Rim governments have always been oriented to the free market, but many of them are becoming even more so by reducing their guidance, protection, and control of local business. They keep getting hammered by the fact that their past economic policies have not provided sufficient economic dynamism to keep pace with the global markets. As more and more control is passed to private industry, doing business with American companies gets easier.

Many American companies have recognized the opportunities in the Pacific Rim and have already taken advantage of them. Nevertheless, the Department of Commerce notes that "a relatively small number of U.S. companies account for most U.S. merchandise exports. A thousand exporters account for more than 60 percent of exports." In the face of continued Pacific Rim growth, the Commerce Department maintains that thousands of U.S. businesses "should" be exporting and are not. With all this opportunity and potential, why don't more companies trade in the Pacific Rim?

Why Trade in the Pacific Rim?

The Familiar Carrots

Why do businesses enter international trade? First, the traditional reasons for exporting are still valid in many cases:

- *To increase their competitiveness.* By going overseas, companies can broaden and diversify their marketing base. They find markets that are complementary to their present business.
- *To hedge against market swings and business cycles by entering countercyclical or counterseasonal markets.* Companies can extend the lives of their products by entering markets in which product lines that are on the downslope of their lives may have new potential.
- *To better utilize their capital investment.* International trade can be valuable if, for example, companies want to expand production to reduce their overhead burden but have too great a productive capacity for their domestic market.
- *To obtain tax incentives.* International investment may offer incentives from the U.S. government or from overseas governments.

Why U.S. Companies Get Into Foreign Trade

- To broaden and diversify their marketing base—to find markets that are complementary to their present business
- To hedge against market swings and business cycles
- To extend the lives of their products
- To expand production in order to reduce their overhead burden
- To obtain lower offshore production costs
- To establish production facilities closer to their main customers
- To penetrate trade barriers—to enter markets they could not enter otherwise
- To establish a presence and to have better market intelligence
- To protect their competitive position
- To make a defensive investment in order to protect their technology in Pacific Rim countries
- To participate in what they recognize to be a global marketplace
- To keep up with competitors that go international

Second, the traditional reasons for establishing overseas operations are still valid.

- *To obtain lower offshore production costs, labor rates, and raw materials costs.* Companies want to establish production facilities closer to their main customers.
- *To break through trade barriers and enter markets that could not be penetrated otherwise.* This is a major factor in increasing foreign investment in all directions. It is the reason many overseas nations, especially Japan, are investing in the United States.
- *To establish a presence in the market.* Customers need to be made more aware of these companies, and the companies need to be able to respond more rapidly.

The Familiar Sticks

In addition to these traditional reasons, there are increasing pressures on U.S. companies to trade in the Pacific.

- Companies need to protect their competitive position, whether from a domestic or from a foreign competitor.

- Businesses may be forced to make a defensive investment to protect their technology in Pacific Rim countries or to enter a new market as early as they can. Otherwise, the Pacific Rim companies will develop in their own protected markets with high prices, learn how to get costs down, and then go to the United States and compete with American companies in their home markets.

• Businesses are competing with other companies that view the world as a global marketplace. To ignore foreign trade today is to say something like, "We sell only west of the Mississippi River." As one executive who has been there said, "As a CEO, you should routinely scan for opportunities for your product or service. Otherwise, you have your head in the sand. You should also routinely scan for threats—incoming competitive threats. When you ponder how you can counter these threats, often you see that the best way involves entering foreign trade."

Companies need to keep up with competitors that go international. A business that engages in foreign trade gains greater leverage and market clout. A company that does not soon finds itself in the position of a mom-and-pop store facing a supermarket chain.

Why Companies Stay at Home

In the face of these potent carrots and sticks, why do American companies stay domestic and fail to take advantage of Pacific Rim opportunities? The following are the reasons I hear most often in informal surveys of companies that "should" be doing business in the Pacific Rim. They reflect many tenets of today's conventional wisdom about Pacific Rim trade. I do not mean to suggest that these statements are false, just that they are *not* the whole truth. There are ways to circumvent barriers and avoid problems.

"We have such a great domestic market, why go overseas?"
"We have all the market here that we can handle."
"Export is only for the big boys. We don't have the resources. We are too small."
"Small companies can't afford to go overseas. Our situation and resources won't
   let us."
"We lack the management depth and experience to give overseas trade the atten-
   tion and commitment it needs."
"We can't take the time required to get established."

Then there is the category called "We would consider Pacific Rim trade, but . . .":

"We're having trouble staying competitive here. The last thing we need is to take
   on a complex new commitment like foreign trade."
"The damned trade barriers are not worth fighting."
"Japan and other Pacific Rim countries are not open to American goods."
"Starting up a foreign operation is just too unfamiliar and difficult for us."
"There are just too many uncertainties, and the added risk factors are too hard to
   evaluate."
"It is very difficult for small American companies to get financing for Pacific Rim
   trade; other governments finance, guarantee, subsidize, insure, and provide
   low-interest loans."
"We have no trade connections or local angles."

"It's hard to get the information needed to make an intelligent decision. It takes
   so much digging. It's too expensive."
"Pacific Rim trade is a West Coast phenomenon."

Throughout this book, I challenge each of these assertions, and show how
companies have circumvented foreign trade problems and succeeded—and how
you can find a way to handle these challenges successfully for your company. The
major differences between the domestic and international trade environments are
summarized in Table 1–1.

The Barriers to Pacific Rim Trade Are Real . . .

We are bombarded daily with news about trade barriers—especially those of the
nations we wish to trade with. We also hear complaints about the technology
export controls of our own government and institutions. Getting an export license
alone can seem like an interminable process. In complying with the Foreign Corrupt Practices Act, companies can get eaten up by paperwork. Tax incentives
come and go and cannot be counted on.

Trade financing is often very hard to obtain—especially for smaller companies. Many banks have pulled back from trade financing, partly because of their
previous bad debts in developing countries. The debt buildup among nations that
have been major trading partners with the United States eliminates many opportunities. We are constantly buffeted by fluctuations in currency exchange rates,
especially in relation to the dollar.

. . . But Barriers Are Just Part of the Story

These are all indeed very real barriers. Yet thousands of American businesses
have succeeded in Pacific Rim trade despite them. Let's look at some success
stories taken from U.S. industries that are often thought to be unable to compete
in domestic markets, let alone to export successfully.

Textiles is one such industry. The head of a trading company noticed affluent
tourists from Southeast Asia attending housewares shows in the United States and
buying towels and linens with rolls of hundred-dollar bills. Investigation showed
that a number of the countries represented, generally characterized as poor, have
affluent urban populations that consider many ordinary American household products to be high-status, prestige items—just because they have "Made in USA"
labels.

A Taiwan retailer asked me: "Why doesn't your textile industry use just part
of the money it spends lobbying for protectionist legislation to promote upscale
apparel in this market? They're leaving the market wide open to the French and
Italians."

Or consider shoes—another U.S. industry decimated by foreign competi-

Table 1-1.   Differences between domestic and international trade environments.

U.S. Trade	*International Trade*
Single currency	Currencies that differ in stability and value
Uniform financial and business climate	Variety of economic climates
Relatively homogeneous market	Fragmented and diverse markets
Uniform legal and accounting framework	Diverse legal and accounting framework
Relatively stable political climate	Political climate lacking in continuity
Cultural mores and values that are relatively well understood	Cultural values and mores that must be identified and understood
Data that are available and relatively easy to collect	Accurate data not readily available and extremely difficult to collect

tion. American shoes have long been shut out of the Japanese market by a formidable, unofficial trade barrier—the inability to wangle an invitation to Japanese shoe industry trade shows. The head of one shoe company in Seattle, with the help of a Department of Commerce trade representative, exerted firm yet polite pressure for several years. At last the CEO did get invited to the major show and brought home several orders.

Many American companies have successfully marketed their products or services in Japan. Today more than 50,000 different U.S. products are sold in Japan. U.S. companies are represented in more than 85 percent of Japan's 126 industrial sectors, and at least 12 U.S. companies hold the number one market position in their fields. Since 1982, sales to Japan of U.S. computers have increased by 48 percent, telecommunications equipment by 38 percent, pharmaceuticals by 41 percent, and electronic parts by 63 percent.

Agriculture, long the mainstay of the U.S. trade surplus, has fallen on hard times in international markets. But positive examples abound. The California Almond Growers Exchange reports that shipments of almonds to Japan have risen 119 percent in five years, confounding the doomsayers. This phenomenal increase was achieved by developing a steady flow of new high-value-added almond products, many of them specifically tailored to Pacific Rim markets—for example, a mixture of slivered almonds and sardines and a snack mix of almonds, rice crackers, and peanuts.

The California Wine Institute reports that in 1986, more than 400 California wines were imported into Japan compared with 150 the year earlier. California now ranks second to France as Japan's major source of wine imports, compared with seventh place two years ago.

With such positive examples, there must be more at work discouraging U.S. businesses than trade barriers. Time after time, traders have said that what keeps American business out of the Pacific Rim is not the trade barriers, but out-of-date attitudes. Companies fail to take advantage of opportunities staring them right in the face. It would appear that the biggest barriers are internal—misconceptions and out-of-date ideas about international trade and about the Pacific Rim in particular. American business clings to two passé images about international trade and the Pacific Rim.

Passé Image 1: The Golden Era of American Exports

In its heyday during the 1950s and 1960s, the United States was the undisputed top dog in trade. After World War II, the United States had the only major economy that was not shattered. Japan—today's leading Pacific Rim economy—was just beginning to recover from a devastating wartime defeat; Korea was still devastated by war and newly divided; and after decades of civil war China had a new revolutionary government consolidating its power. Taiwan was full of refugees from mainland China, and Singapore was a marshy fishing village. Hong Kong, and most of Southeast Asia, was still under colonial status.

We had no competition. We could call the shots. *They* needed *us;* we didn't need them. We helped Asian nations get back on their feet, partly out of altruism and partly out of fear of communism. We saw the Pacific Rim as an export market for our excess or obsolescent goods. From the investment perspective, we saw a source of cheap labor—when the people were trained enough to hold steady jobs.

But these twin U.S. blessings—economic predominance and a huge domestic market—also proved to be a curse. As the world economy began to change, too many U.S. businesses held on to the image of a golden era. Our wonderful domestic market meant we didn't have to rely on foreign trade—unlike our competitors, the Europeans and the Asians. That is, up until recently.

Thus we have too often treated international trade as a stepchild—as indicated by the fact that we see ourselves engaged in "foreign trade," not "international trade." Our commitment to the international marketplace is much lower than that of most Pacific Rim companies, which depend on exporting for their survival.

In the past, whenever things began to go either bad or very good in our domestic economy, we pulled back to our home market and abandoned the overseas business we had built up. As a result, we established the reputation of being inconsistent and unreliable. In the Pacific Rim, where customers put a high value on reliability, if you withdraw once, you are "out." Not only are *you* out, but you hurt the prospects of similar American companies in the same markets.

We became fat and lazy. We failed to apply the lessons that we taught to the Pacific Rim nations. Quality control. Giving customers what they want. Cost control. Productivity. Financial acumen. The importance of building business relationships and cultivating human resources. We put too much emphasis on short-term financial performance.

The education and culture of American CEOs was strictly domestic. They felt discomfort with people who didn't speak English. They were ignorant of foreign values. Executives receiving an overseas assignment often felt derailed from the fast track.

Passé Image 2: The Uncompetitive Yankee

Because many U.S. companies stayed focused for too long on Image 1, they ran head on into the changed reality of the early 1980s. Times got tough throughout the world, and at the same time competition in international trade increased dramatically. Then came the oil crisis and worldwide recession. Debt built up in developing nations that had once been major U.S. trading partners. Even in the miracle region of the Pacific Rim, growth slowed. Protectionism and protected markets became important factors in overseas trade.

At the same time that the United States began relying more and more on international trade, global overcapacity appeared in both industrial and agricultural production. Competition increased. The new competitors included Europe as well as former Pacific Rim trading partners—not just the Japanese, but many smaller Asian economies. Their products were moving up the "value-added curve." They gained engineering sophistication, not just in products but also in manufacturing processes. Thus they began competing in many of the market sectors in which the United States had long enjoyed strong competitive advantage and dominance.

Other factors made them more competitive as well. Because they had long depended on export markets for their livelihood, and because we still had a huge domestic market, they became more aggressive than we were. They often showed more sophisticated marketing techniques than we did, even in our own country. They provided better financing, better quality, better service, and lower prices. U.S. businesses complained—with some truth—that they were being beaten by lower labor costs, an overpriced dollar, and savvy competition subsidized by local governments. But it was just as often true that Asian companies succeeded because they were better at listening to what customers wanted. As a result, their products invaded our domestic markets and started edging U.S. businesses out of lucrative overseas trade as well.

Those we had helped had learned well the business lessons we had taught them—they were applying the lessons of "Yankee ingenuity" better than the Yanks themselves.

As a result, the U.S. trade deficit with Pacific Rim nations ballooned to unprecedented proportions; and many CEOs and government officials began to believe Image 2, that U.S. industry could not hope to remain competitive in world markets. Strong protectionist sentiment grew. The United States started putting pressure on its trading partners to open up their domestic markets. Myriad books, articles, and conferences covered the new phenomenon of U.S. uncompetitiveness. American business is *still* struggling with the image of the Uncompetitive Yankee.

The New Reality of Pacific Rim Trade

This brings us up to the present—and to the near future. The wheel continues to turn. Times are again changing. We learn from our errors, and our trading partners again begin to look merely mortal. Opportunities again begin opening up. Image 2 is also passé.

But too many businesses are still dazzled by one or the other of these passé images and fail to see what is now emerging. Many American companies have difficulty with the new realities of international trade. Because they cling to the image of the tough trade climate, they find it hard to see the new outlines clearly. As a result, many companies that should be profiting from international trade are shying away from it.

Here is the operating reality for the late 1980s and early 1990s.

- Growth *has* slowed from the torrid pace of a decade ago—but it is still good in the Pacific Rim.
- Trade barriers are still daunting—but there are important pressures to ease them, and the barriers are rapidly diminishing.
- Because of trade restrictions, direct investment in overseas operations has become as important as exporting. Companies must often have the "appearance of being local." This takes more attention, commitment, and up-front investment.
- Business has become globalized. No market is safe from the competition of a large international company, whether that company is based across town or across the world.
- Financial and equity markets have become globalized. This means that on top of all your other skills, you must be a "financial engineer."

Easier Access to Pacific Rim Markets

All this makes the new reality sound tougher. But weighed against these factors are others that make Pacific Rim trade more accessible to American companies today.

- Because times have been tough, there has been a shakeout. Many companies have left the market. This means that as Pacific Rim economies regain an even keel, new opportunities become available.
- Market access is improving. Because trade barriers have been stacked against the United States, the pressure to gain access to more markets will open many opportunities to watchful companies.
- As the dollar has declined, American companies have sometimes discovered that they are the low-cost producers, and American exports have again surged. Many companies that formerly manufactured in the Pacific Rim have reopened their U.S. production facilities and resumed exporting.
- Because nations have been gaining on the United States, both they and their citizens are becoming more affluent and sophisticated. They provide better markets for many of the products and services in which U.S. companies have competitive advantages.

- As the United States becomes more of a service economy, the market for exporting services is improving.

Granted, this is the optimistic view. The United States is in the midst of a battle between protecting markets and forcing them open. I believe that the pressure toward opening up markets must gradually prevail, because the alternative is so frightening to everyone—the economic equivalent to all-out nuclear war. A watchful company can be poised to move quickly into profitable new markets as they open up. Later I discuss the "critical issues" and "critical driving forces" to watch for.

On top of these factors, the route to Pacific Rim trade has become easier. Some of the causes are the flip side of the difficulties mentioned above.

- International business is maturing. So in some ways it looks more like domestic operations. It is easier to find qualified and experienced managers and workers in Pacific Rim nations—many of whom have U.S. educations and have already worked for international companies.
- Companies entering Pacific Rim trade need not be pioneers. They can follow trails blazed by others, drawing on their knowledge and experience. Business publications are focusing on both the successes and the horror stories, so you can see what to avoid. Many more reliable and consistent information sources are available, both domestically and in Pacific Rim nations.
- The dollar has declined in value relative to other leading currencies. This has certainly not proved to be the hoped-for panacea for American trade woes, especially since the currencies of many U.S. trading partners are tied to the dollar. But it is helping—the U.S. trade deficit is declining because of increased exports.
- Many governments and agencies—both federal and state—are promoting and assisting Pacific Rim trade. Much support that used to be available only to huge multinationals is now accessible to smaller companies. In addition, U.S. export controls are easing, with many products now removed from the proscribed list. More funding sources are opening up, including both debt and equity sources within Asian Pacific Rim markets.
- More varied forms of operation are available, so smaller companies are more likely to find one suitable to their circumstances. (Chapters 5 and 6 examine the different forms of operation—from lesser to greater commitment of resources.)
- English is the language of international business. Virtually everyone in Pacific Rim trade speaks English as a first or second language.

We *can* learn from the examples of others. All the Pacific Rim nations have been honing their exporting expertise, and we must catch up. However, they have had to grind through and make all the mistakes, so now we can learn from their example and avoid making those mistakes ourselves.

Special Advantages for Smaller Companies

Small and medium-size companies often have special advantages beyond those just described. For example, smaller, privately held businesses are often better able to take advantage of emerging market opportunities. They have the option of taking a longer-term view rather than emphasizing short-term financial performance, a position often forced on large corporations by their stockholders. This is particularly important in the Pacific Rim, where the successful companies are characterized by flexibility and long-term perspectives.

The political and business climate of some Pacific Rim nations is more congenial to smaller American companies than to larger, well-entrenched multinational ones. Developing Pacific Rim nations like China and Malaysia try to create special opportunities for smaller businesses—perhaps out of lingering suspicion of the huge multinationals. In Taiwan and some other Pacific Rim nations, markets are too small to be of interest to huge corporations; but such neglected markets may be very lucrative for smaller businesses.

Why the Pacific Rim?

Many of the ideas presented up to now pertain to international business as a whole. Why focus on the Pacific Rim? As the profiles of the Asian Pacific Rim nations in Chapter 11 demonstrate, those countries are becoming major U.S. trading partners. Trade and direct investment are increasing much faster in the Pacific Rim than in any other part of the world. By the end of this century, if protectionism is contained, the newly industrializing countries (NICs) should equal the present European Economic Community, and the Association of South East Asian Nations (ASEAN) should be where the NICs are today.

4½ Groups of Nations

To clarify business opportunities in this diverse region, we can divide the Pacific Rim nations into five groups. These categories pertain mainly to level of economic development, not to culture or politics. Of course, any broad categorization is dangerous. Each Pacific Rim nation is unique. Lumping together Thailand, Malaysia, the Philippines, and Indonesia is as unrealistic as lumping together Britain, France, Germany, and Italy. Yet grouping them highlights important similarities and distinctions to help you identify markets with the most potential.

Group 1: Japan. Japan stands alone as America's leading Asian trade partner, and has a mature, democratic, fully developed high-tech consumer economy rivaling that of the United States. The Japanese are proud of the superiority of their own products, and although it is still difficult for U.S. companies to break into many markets, the Japanese are importing more and more foreign products and services—especially the artifacts of American culture. Major export opportunities include processed food products, leisure products and sporting goods, jewelry and objects of decoration, furniture for home or business, and hardware for the do-it-yourselfer.

Group 1½: The NICs, or Four Tigers.   The newly industrialized countries consist of Korea, Taiwan, Hong Kong, and Singapore. I call this category group 1½ rather than group 2 to emphasize how rapidly the countries are maturing and closing in on Japan. Through hard work, discipline, and access to American markets, they have, within a generation, developed into major competitors of the leading industrialized nations. They have moved from turning out cheap copies and doing low-cost assembly to high-tech design and engineering. Their people have growing democratic and consumer aspirations. Some of the major opportunities for Americans are shown in Figure 1–1.

Singapore and Hong Kong are affluent, cosmopolitan city-states, open to any product or service. Although the domestic markets are small, they provide gateways into other major markets. Taiwan and Korea, two of the most rapidly growing economies in the world, are just beginning to open up their domestic markets to foreign consumer goods and services. This new openness, coupled with the people's newfound affluence, makes Taiwan and Korea two of the best markets for American companies. The NICs also offer good markets for companies selling to the industries that predominate there: electronics, plastics, toys, and textiles. Companies sell the equipment used by these industries, and specialized components as well.

The NICs are becoming major markets for imported consumer goods. What can we sell them? To see where the NICs will be, look at Japan now. The big question is, Will the NIC markets be as difficult to penetrate as Japan's?

No. The battle being fought now is changing our trade relationships with the NICs as well with Japan. Taiwan and Korea are learning at the same time as Japan to shift from export-driven to consumer-driven economies. These markets are opening up; the only question is, How competitive will Americans be in them?

Group 3: Australia and New Zealand.   It is sometimes hard for Americans visiting affluent, democratic Australia or New Zealand to remember that they

Figure 1-1.   Major opportunities for American Companies in Japan and in the NICs.

Capital equipment
Medical products and pharmaceuticals
American consumer goods and fashions
Products of American culture, such as music
 videos, movies, and records
Franchises
Engineering and construction services

are in a foreign culture. Both countries are turning their attention increasingly toward the Asian Pacific Rim economies. The governments of both nations are reducing their involvement in the business sector, and have further opened domestic markets to foreign business in an effort to force domestic industry to become more competitive. Although both countries rely on exports of agricultural and mining products, they offer markets for the most sophisticated products and services. American companies sell the same kinds of high-tech products in Australia that Australian companies sell in the United States. The levels of consumer services of both countries are close.

Group 4: ASEAN. The Association of South East Asian Nations includes Singapore, Thailand, Malaysia, the Philippines, Indonesia, and Brunei.* These are all unique nations, with different levels of development. Singapore is already a NIC, and Malaysia and Thailand are well on their way to becoming NICs. Besides Singapore, all are resource-rich and technology-poor. They are striving to develop under varying degrees of political autonomy (from democratic to authoritarian) and economic control (from free-market to government-directed).

ASEAN is a favorite site for foreign investment in medium-tech assembly where high levels of engineering skills are not required. There are major markets for American companies able to supply needed social and economic infrastructure. Government-sponsored projects—telecommunications, electrification, port facilities, airports and railroads, hospitals and schools, and the industrial infrastructure—plus related services and training make up the myriad support industries needed for ASEAN's expanding industrial base. Many American companies are building or managing tourist facilities or providing needed services for ASEAN's growing tourism industries.

Group 5: China. Also a developing nation, China stands alone because of its huge size and unique economic background. It needs everything, but can afford little. It is changing so rapidly that the rate of change itself is the biggest threat to stability. When considering China, a company cannot afford to ignore the onrushing economic integration with Hong Kong and Taiwan. China offers opportunities for companies that can:

- Build infrastructure, such as telecommunications systems or electric power generation and distribution grids.
- Build up industries that improve China's technological capabilities. Although China has tried to attract high-tech industry, the companies that have been most successful have manufactured medium- and low-tech products.
- Contract with a Chinese enterprise for the assembly of low- or medium-tech products, most or all of which are re-exported.

China is not yet a place for companies new to foreign operations, but Hong Kong can be used as a gateway for smaller companies to make arrangements to

*Brunei is not covered in this book.

enter China. The two toughest roads into China are exporting products to China and setting up a plant there to manufacture products for the Chinese domestic market.

Some General Observations About the Pacific Rim

Several observations pertain to selling anywhere in the Pacific Rim. These will be examined in more detail throughout the rest of the book.

Go to Japan First?   Japan is by far the dominant Pacific Rim trading partner for the United States. But does this mean that every U.S. exporter goes to Japan? Not at all. Size of market is not everything. Smaller markets frequently offer more opportunity. Even in Japan, foreign companies are beginning to rediscover Osaka, which has long been ignored in favor of Tokyo. Within large nations with diffuse populations, markets are often concentrated. In Australia, two thirds of the population live in an area the size of coastal California. In ASEAN, many markets and services are concentrated in the capital cities.

Selling Services.   The Pacific Rim nations provide markets for a long list of business and consumer services that American companies can offer. Ask Australian, Japanese, or Chinese people who have spent time in the United States what they miss most and you will get a list of consumer services that *could* be provided in their home markets: copy shops and desktop publishing, full-service computer and software retailers, launderettes and parking garages, shopping centers and child care facilities, and training and retraining institutes. These services are in addition to the existing strong markets for all sorts of franchises and entertainment.

The markets for commercial and professional services are just beginning to be tapped by foreign companies as markets open to them. The range of opportunities is suggested in Figure 1–2.

There is also a growing opportunity for smaller companies to sell services in the developing nations of the Pacific Rim. In the service sector, it's not *technology* transfer but *technique* transfer that is important. As every developing Pacific Rim nation seeks to expand its industrial base and develop more sophisticated products, it needs more than just technology; it also needs many types of expertise that are not available within its own borders. Many smaller U.S. companies have been very successful in providing such services.

Companies familiar with the emerging needs of Pacific Rim nations contract to help manage and apply technologies that have been transferred in the following areas: energy and conservation; agriculture, agribusiness, and food processing; minerals and other primary resources; health care; education and training; and transportation. Small companies help develop managers, workers, and local entrepreneurs. They consult on all aspects of management, including systems development, human resources development and labor relations, production processes, operations control, and incentive programs.

Figure 1-2.   Opportunities for selling professional and commercial services in
the Pacific Rim.

Insurance
Finance, commercial banking, venture capital
Investment, merger and acquisitions
Legal and accounting services
Software design, customization, application
Engineering, design and technical services
Construction management, architectural services
Management, professional, or technical consulting
Franchise organization and management
Distribution, retail management
Trade management
Advertising, promotion, marketing
Communications and information handling
Videotex (A newly defined field that includes electronic news, telebanking, and other
  interactive electronics services)
Health care and other medical services
Health care facilities design and management
Transportation and travel services
Tourist facilities design and management
Education and training
Equipment leasing

Many manufactured goods include services. Since these are not broken out
separately in trade statistics, opportunities are masked for smaller companies that
could offer these services. Similarly, many investments include opportunities for
the sale of manufactured goods, as well as services, by a subcontractor.

Selling Value-Added Commodities.   The United States has been a major
exporter of basic resources and agricultural products to many Pacific Rim nations.
Like the other primary-resource providers, American companies are being forced
up the value-added ladder, from selling bulk commodities to selling processed
specialty products. This is true in a wide range of industries, from specialty steel
to processed almonds.

Small Companies Get Engineering Contracts Too!   Large government-
sponsored engineering projects for building health care facilities, educational institutions, agricultural improvements, and communications and transportation
networks are largely the realm of huge engineering companies; but there are also
ample opportunities for smaller companies to provide needed subsidiary services,
hardware, training and ongoing support, and surrounding infrastructure. After
this infrastructure is in place, many other opportunities are created to manage and
maintain it.

Foreign Investment.   Openness to direct foreign investment varies among
Pacific Rim nations. Japan, Australia, New Zealand, Hong Kong, and Singapore

treat foreign and domestic investment almost alike. However, Taiwan and Korea, the other ASEAN members, and China all restrict foreign investment to a greater or lesser extent.

Throughout the Pacific Rim, the trend is toward greater openness to foreign investment. Protection of domestic industries has led to domestic noncompetitiveness. To make domestic industries competitive on world markets, they are being exposed to the heat of international competition, and several of these nations must have direct foreign investment to accomplish their goals.

If you decide to invest in the developing Pacific Rim nations, you will have to play by their rules. That is:

1. Work with local partners. You may be allowed only a minority ownership stake in the investment.
2. Hire and train local managers and workers, and use local resources and services.
3. Be ready to face very strong competition.
4. Channel your investments into sectors desired by the government of your target country, especially when going into high-value-added manufacturing that requires technology transfer.
5. Manufacture products for re-export as well as for sale to domestic markets.
6. Recognize that your ability to get foreign exchange out may be limited.

Export or Invest? In the nations most open to foreign investment, your decision to invest or export will be made on economic grounds. When selling products for use in the developed Pacific Rim markets, the question a company must ask is whether to export from its U.S. plant or to manufacture there. With the declining dollar, drops in tariffs and other trade barriers, relaxation of barriers to foreign investment, and increasing Pacific Rim wage levels, many companies that formerly were forced to manufacture in the Pacific Rim have profitably resumed exporting from their U.S. plants. On the other hand, maintaining a marketing presence is all the more important, as that allows a company to quickly tailor products to industrial or consumer demands.

Direct investments often have a multiplier effect. For example, companies that have set up operations in Singapore or Malaysia—to assemble electronic products for re-export to the United States, Japan, or Western Europe—see their sales spreading to neighboring nations: personal computers in Indonesia, disk drives in India, and add-on boards in Taiwan.

The Key Challenges of International Trade

Despite these opportunities and advantages, there are several key problem areas in international trade—especially for small and medium-size businesses:

- Understanding the cultures of doing business in Pacific Rim nations
- Obtaining trade financing
- Obtaining the market information needed to make sound decisions

- Engendering the commitment and resources needed for distant ventures
- Refining your product or service for export to meet local demands and tastes
- Finding the best strategy to enter a market
- Finding the people who can do the job for you, both in the United States and in the Pacific Rim
- Overcoming or working around the trade barriers

The purpose of this book is to address these major trade issues. The following chapters are built around them.

2 | Should Your Company Trade in the Pacific?

- *How suitable are your products or services for Pacific Rim trade?*
- *Is your company ready to take on Pacific Rim trade?*
- *How do potential Pacific Rim markets compare with your domestic markets and your other foreign markets?*

We have seen the potential rewards of Pacific Rim trade for U.S. companies. Now let's see what it takes to take advantage of the opportunities. This chapter introduces the factors a business must weigh—pro and con—to evaluate its Pacific Rim potential. You can pinpoint any weakness in your company's international organization and see how your products or services can become more competitive in Pacific Rim markets. If your company is already involved in international trade, review these factors to check how you are doing.

Are Your Products or Services Right for Pacific Rim Trade?

The most important factor to consider is whether you have a product or service that can be sold successfully and profitably in the Pacific Rim markets in which you intend to sell it. We will look at several scenarios:

- Your product is fine as it is. You sell it to Pacific Rim markets that are very similar to your domestic markets, or you will sell it for use in the same way that it is used in the United States. The package that is shipped to Des Moines could just as well be shipped to Tokyo or Jakarta.
- Your product is appropriate for the market, but it will be used for purposes other than those of your domestic markets. A classic example is the bicycle—used for recreation in the United States but as utility transportation in many other nations.
- Your product needs to be refined for export, or "exportized," to be made more appropriate for target Pacific Rim markets.
- You want to develop or engineer new products for Pacific Rim markets, or apply your existing technologies to new situations.

These considerations, which may well vary for each target Pacific Rim market, are discussed briefly below. Chapter 3 examines in depth ways to determine how to fit your product to a particular target market.

Selling As Is

Your product may need no change. Your ideal is to sell the same products in the Pacific Rim that you sell in your domestic markets. Sometimes this works. Many American goods sell well simply because they are American. This is particularly true of clothing, fad items, fast food, and other products that represent the popular culture. Examples range from a single product like a McDonald's hamburger to an entire product mix like the toys merchandised by Toys R Us. For many such products, it is the American packaging—despite the foreignness of its language and style—that is eagerly sought after by Pacific Rim customers.

Many commercial and industrial products offered to domestic markets are initially designed for international sales as well. The measurements are metric and the quality meets common international (especially Japanese) standards. As one example, Japanese and European cars are designed so that they are easily adaptable to either right- or left-hand drive.

Seeking Alternative Uses

Research doesn't *have* to be drudgery. Take a working vacation to Pacific Rim countries, and look at the unexpected ways in which many manufactured products are used. This should help you brainstorm ideas about how your company's products or services can be adapted to markets that may or may not exist in the United States. SpectraPhysics, a manufacturer of industrial lasers, discovered an untapped market for its laser products in Pacific Rim discotheques.

A Pacific Rim tour would show you how many ordinary American consumer products are high-status or specialty items in some Pacific Rim markets. For example, towels and bed linens with American labels, which are stacked high in domestic department stores, are repackaged and sold as luxury gifts in Malaysian specialty stores that cater to affluent city dwellers in Kuala Lumpur.

Exportizing to Different Markets

Many American products can be adapted successfully to Pacific Rim markets with a reasonable amount of effort and expense. Without this refinement, they might utterly fail. This process of exportizing, or refining or adapting to different markets, may involve anything from printing the packaging and instructions in a different language to completely redesigning the product. You may wish to refine your product or service to adapt to:

- Features sought by buyers in your target markets
- Products or features offered by your competition
- Quality standards of the target nation

- Market restrictions in the target nation
- Emerging opportunities or market niches

Many American products have failed abroad because they were either not exportized at all or not exportized appropriately. A Nissan "feels" no more foreign than does a Ford. But how many American products still feel foreign to Pacific Rim customers? The ways that U.S. companies have failed to adapt their products to Pacific Rim markets are notorious: inappropriately wired appliances, nonmetric measurements, toilet seats unsuited to Asian toilets, mainframe computers with inadequate local training or maintenance, rugs too large for Japanese living rooms.

Exportizing to Quality Standards. You may have to refine or re-engineer a product to meet product standards, safety standards, or technical specifications. Many U.S. products have been kept out of Japanese and other markets because they did not meet the mandated standards of quality, safety, and reliability. These standards have two sources: (1) standards set by individual governments and (2) standards imposed by the market. Sometimes these standards—or the testing procedures devised to determine how well products comply—are set unnecessarily high by governments in order to keep imported products out of domestic markets. In such cases, a company may or may not be able to fight the standards successfully. But most often the Pacific Rim country's standards *can* and need to be met.

Quality standards are often imposed by the market itself. Some American products don't sell well in Japan because consumers themselves feel that such products (cameras, TVs, and other consumer electronics products) are of inadequate quality. Many Taiwanese and Korean manufacturers prefer Japanese or German components over American ones—because of quality *and* price. In most markets, competitive pressures will force you to change the quality of your products. U.S. companies that once did very well exporting second-quality or obsolescent products have been forced to offer top-rate products or lose their markets.

Bear in mind that quality standards may mean not that *higher* quality is demanded, but that *different* quality is desired. For example, consumer tastes may dictate different degrees of sweetness or spiciness in fast foods or soft drinks. You may have to re-engineer your product for reduced quality so that you can sell it at a more competitive price. Sophisticated high-tech products may have to be engineered downward—simplified—to sell to markets in which users are less skilled.

Exportizing Your Sizes and Measurements. Another way to adapt your product to the new market is to re-engineer it to metric measurements or overseas sizes. For example, when American soft drinks first went into Asia, the can sizes had to be reduced. Why? Did Asian people want smaller portions? No. The vending machines could hold only smaller, metric-measure cans. For manufacturers of industrial products that are the same in virtually any market, exportizing consists primarily of preparing manuals and other written materials in different languages, engineering products in metric measurements, and making products adaptable to different voltages.

American producers of industrial products and components initially design products to international standards, using metric measurements and making adaptations for varied electrical systems. A large part of their product exportizing lies in obtaining different certifications in different countries. For example, Bently-Nevada, which manufactures instruments to measure vibration in high-speed machinery, must ask each nation's version of the Underwriters Laboratory to certify that its products are safe for use with hazardous gases and will not create sparks and explosions.

Exportizing Your Packaging.   Your packaging must conform to the norms of display and distribution in each market. In some instances, your current packaging will be just fine. Many U.S. products sell much better in the Pacific Rim with English labels and slogans than their counterparts would sell in the U.S. with Japanese or Chinese labels. Many consumer products, especially status and fad items, sell well because they have "Made in USA" labels. This fact is not lost on Japanese marketers. The leading brand of cigarettes in Japan is manufactured in Japan from Japanese tobacco and is sold only in Japanese markets, but if you examine the package, you cannot find one Japanese character. All the labeling is in English. The product has been manufactured to simulate American cigarettes—perhaps a bit like having the menus in upscale U.S. restaurants printed in French.

But don't take the effectiveness of American packaging for granted. The colors of packages and the wording of brand names and slogans are crucial elements to examine before sending your products to a new market. Other reasons you may need to repackage your products are:

- *To ship them overseas successfully.* Whether you're shipping by ship or by air freight, you may need to use different types or sizes of cartons to increase strength, lower weight, or fit different-sized containers.
- *To meet the needs of distribution channels.* You must know how your products will be stored and distributed in the new market. Depending on how many middlemen there will be and what size orders they will handle, you may want to change the number of packages you have in a carton.
- *To fit different ways of displaying or merchandising your products.* Will your products be displayed on shelves alongside other, related products? How large are the shelves? How much shelf display space are you likely to get? What will the size of the nearby packages be? How will they be wrapped? The answers to these questions can influence your packaging.
- *To take advantage of a local market niche.* Local markets may differ from those you serve domestically. The repackaging of towels and linens for luxury gift markets in Malaysia is an example.
- *To meet local tastes.* Suppose local consumers consider the lovely green on your packages to be an unlucky color or the white to be a symbol of death. It's best to know this before flooding the local market.

Exportizing for Different Styles and Tastes.   During market tests, Kentucky Fried Chicken discovered that its traditional eleven-spice recipe wasn't right for many Asian tastes. The company adjusted the formula to make it more spicy, and since then the product has succeeded greatly in Pacific Rim countries. The largest Kentucky Fried Chicken outlet in the world opened in Beijing, just across from the tomb of Mao Zedong. Other examples: A wine cooler succeeded when it was made sweeter and less lemony. Dunkin Donuts succeeded in Japan with smaller, less sugary donuts—in a market where donuts had previously been unknown.

In Asia, Gillette sells familiar products in different packages or smaller sizes. For example, Silkience Shampoo is sold in half-ounce plastic bubbles and Right Guard Deodorant is sold in plastic squeeze bottles instead of metal aerosol cans. In other markets, Gillette has developed new products—for example, plastic tubes of shaving cream that sell for half the price of its aerosol.

Exportizing Your Advertising, Promotion, and Slogans.   When Pepsi-Cola entered the soft drink market in Thailand, its slogan "Come alive, you're in the Pepsi generation" was translated as "Pepsi brings your ancestors back from the dead." No doubt this could have exposed the company to serious false advertising claims. This is an extreme example, but it points out the importance of scrutinizing your translations, since advertising slogans are so often idiomatic. To render the sense of idiomatic expressions accurately, the translator must be fluent not only in both languages, but also in both cultures.

Beyond the matter of accurate translations is the larger issue of rethinking your advertising and promotion strategy to meet the needs of the new market. You must refine your advertising and promotion to fit the new market niches and distribution channels. In addition, you must consider the available channels of promotion and advertising in your target market, and develop advertising vehicles that fit the available channels. For example, if you have relied on TV ads in the U.S. market, in Malaysia you may have to recast your advertising for radio or newspapers. If your domestic promotions are aimed at end users, in Japan you may have to recast them to appeal to a key link in the distribution chain. If you push the technical sophistication of your industrial product in the United States, in the Philippines you may have to promote its simplicity of use and maintenance.

Exportizing Your Language.   All manufacturers of technical products face the task of translating their literature, manuals, and specifications into the language of the target market. As used here, *technical product* means any product for which the consumer relies on printed material to learn its use. Such products range from toys to home appliances to mainframe computers.

Failure to exportize printed material properly has been a major cause of downfall for many products and services. To grasp the importance of this idea, look at it in reverse. When many Japanese products were first marketed here, they carried instructions in Japanese that were indecipherable squiggles to Americans. That rarely happens today. But how often do American products head across the ocean with instructions in English or tortured Japanese? Far too often. English may be everyone's second language, and English labels may connote status for some products; but consumers prefer to read instructions and warranty information in their native language.

This is as true for commercial and industrial products as it is for consumer products. Computer and software companies must often translate computer programs as well as instructional materials into the language of the local market. This can be expensive if a company is entering several markets simultaneously. Rewriting English-language programs to accommodate Japanese or Chinese character sets is a very complex task.

Translation is fairly expensive—from $20 to $25 per page—and many companies are unaware of how much they are spending on it. There is more involved than just translating the text. Often companies must redesign art and layout as well because the foreign language takes up more (or less) space. If you are responsible for producing your own translations, you can hire a translation service. Such agencies are available in most major American cities. Hiring an in-house staff for translation may not begin to make economic sense until you reach the level of 5,000 pages per year.

After your material is translated, how can you make sure that the translation is accurate and adequate, even when it has been done by someone in the market (such as your distributor) who knows the culture, the language, and the technology? You may have to obtain a "back translation." That is, once your material has been translated from English into Japanese, you may have to have someone else translate it back into English so you can see how it reads. The indecipherable parts of the back translation show you where to re-examine the translation. Technical terms translate and back-translate much more successfully than idiomatic language. A classic example is the case of "out of sight, out of mind" being back-translated into "unseen idiot."

Is Your Service Transferable to Pacific Rim Markets?

Selling services overseas raises a number of concerns beyond those that apply to products. These issues include:

- The language of likely markets and the difficulty of translating written materials
- Your ability to deliver your service in the market, whether by people you send in, people you recruit locally, or agents or other partners
- The technological sophistication of your likely foreign buyers
- Restrictions on bringing needed hardware, materials, or instruments into your target markets as well as possible restrictions on exporting that hardware from the United States
- Other overseas regulations and restrictions that might hamper the export

of your service, such as limitations on foreign employment, capital remittances, technology protection, and methods of obtaining needed capital
- Local customs, biases, religions, labor practices, and other cultural factors that might jeopardize the sale of your service

For example, when McDonald's began establishing outlets in Pacific Rim countries, its initial concern was to deliver a uniform product. But the company discovered that the biggest challenge was to find people who could ensure the quality of service McDonald's insists upon. It was not just customer service that posed a problem. One of the most difficult things for McDonald's to export was the quality of management that has led to its success in U.S. markets: vigilance over cost control, cleanliness, and hustle. Similarly, when Holiday Inn opened its first hotel in China, it had to hire and train housekeeping personnel who had never before made a Western-style bed or made a porcelain toilet sparkle.

Getting Information on How to Exportize

Properly exportizing your product or service requires that you know what the market wants. Getting input from your target market on whether your packaging, promotion, and advertising are appropriate is essential. How do you get that information? There are several ways. (See the Appendixes for organizations to contact for information on your target market.)

Information Sources

It's best to start with the easiest, most accessible information sources, such as the U.S. Department of Commerce; in particular, get in touch with their country representatives in Washington, D.C., for your target market. The commercial officer at the U.S. embassy or consulate of your target market can also give you general information. Try to get input from others who have been in your target country: U.S. government representatives, U.S. companies with related products, and people from the country who are doing business here.

Talk with people from your target market who are now living or studying in the United States. Their opinions can be very valuable, because they have been sufficiently exposed to American culture to understand the problems you may have in their home culture. On the other hand, be wary: They may have been away from home too long and be out of touch. Imagine the misinformation a French company would get from asking an American who has been living in Paris for the last ten years about the latest trends in American home design!

In these ways you can get feedback on simple but crucial things like voltages, configurations for electrical outlets, and standard sizes for standard items, plus some input on color, styles, merchandising, and advertising and promotion.

The most important advice you can get is probably not on how to sell what is right, but on how to avoid major pitfalls. If you show a mock-up product or package to Chinese students living here, they can point out obvious things that you may otherwise miss: inappropriate colors or packaging, unclear translations, names with negative connotations, and so on.

With consumer items, in particular, you may never know whether a product will sell without customization until you try. This is the shot-in-the-dark method of market entry. You test it in some local markets in a variety of ways and see how it does. While this approach to market entry has a high likelihood of not working, it's also the least expensive, and when it works it can be a very pleasant surprise.

One way to determine how well your domestic product may sell "as is" in Pacific Rim markets is to track what sells through domestic outlets but ends up in Pacific Rim markets. For example, if you exhibit your product in domestic trade shows that are attended by buyers from ASEAN or Taiwan, you should follow up and ask them how well your product is selling in their home markets and what adjustments in product design or packaging would make it sell better for them.

Market Tests

For more specific information, you may need to conduct market tests. If you are working through distributors, assign this responsibility to them. Otherwise, you can hire a consultant experienced in your target market. Such a specialist is most needed when your product must comply with different technical standards or specifications, or pass tests for quality standards. (Chapters 5 and 8 discuss the process of selecting such a representative.)

Market Visits

There are strong arguments for visiting the market yourself to check out what others have told you. You—or one of your top people—should go there personally. If you have a consumer product, you should see the places your product will be sold. How will it be displayed? What do related packages look like? What do competing products look like? If you sell commercial or industrial products, visit potential customers and see how competitors' products are used, supplied, and serviced.

When Dunkin Donuts decided to enter the Japanese market, it initially mocked up a typical franchise outlet in Tokyo and invited hundreds of consumers to come in, try the donuts, and make comments. On the basis of this input, the company discovered that Japanese consumers prefer smaller, less sugary donuts and that the Western-style decor needed to be refined for Japanese tastes. Using the results of this initial investigation, it successfully entered the Japanese market, where previously donuts had never been sold.

If you get beyond the stage of selling through a trading company, you will *have* to go to the market to establish relationships with key customers or distributors. On the same trip, you can gather firsthand intelligence on how your product must be refined to suit the market.

Engineering New Products for Pacific Rim Markets

You may plan to develop new products, especially if you are opening production facilities in your Pacific Rim market. Or you may find that the degree of re-engineering of existing products amounts to developing new ones.

Almost by definition, services must be re-engineered for each market. Golden Gate University, the private business school in San Francisco, developed an entirely new way to deliver an MBA program in order to take advantage of its opportunities in Malaysia and Singapore. Each market Golden Gate entered has required a new program design to fit its particular needs and institutional constraints.

Your "unique technology"—the source of your competitive advantage—must also be appropriate technology. To make sure that what you are selling fits the needs of the target market, you may have to refine or re-engineer it so much that you are essentially developing a new product.

Consider the photovoltaic power generator installed by H-Tech in the Philippines. Initially, the company expected to sell a generator it had successfully marketed in the United States, the Middle East, and elsewhere. When company representatives got to their target market, they found that a combination of corrosive weather conditions, invasions of plants and bugs, and lack of skilled maintenance mechanics would have quickly doomed the system. H-Tech had to re-package the system so that it could withstand climatic and environmental extremes. The company had to simplify its technology to create a more reliable system that could be maintained by less-skilled mechanics. It also had to redefine its marketing concept—away from providing a piece of hardware toward providing an integrated "turnkey" system that included ongoing training, support, and maintenance. Somewhere during this process it became clear that H-Tech was not refining the product but developing an entirely new product.

Campbell Soup successfully introduced canned soups to the Japanese consumer market (which, until the early 1980s, had not accepted canned soups) by developing several new soup flavors tailored to Japanese tastes. Campbell is now well established in this market. Likewise, the California Almond Growers Exchange has been very successful at developing new almond products for Japanese tastes.

Many companies have realized that they are not selling a particular product at all; they are selling their expertise or technological capability. This is much different from selling the technology itself. Although many Pacific Rim nations are eagerly seeking technology transfers from companies that wish to protect their technology, you may satisfy your customers' needs by selling just a particular application of your technology. For example, Loctite worked with a Chinese automaker for several years, using its own adhesive technologies to develop sealants for internal combustion engines. Lakeview Products adapted its technology for producing Popsicle sticks to the manufacture of disposable chopsticks for the Japanese market. Both of these companies, a large one and a small one, developed products for a particular market through on-site research of local problems.

The Cost of Exportizing

U.S. companies often encounter high exportizing costs because they do not consider international markets when their products are first engineered. This short-sightedness has proved to be a major source of U.S. uncompetitiveness in international markets. The best advice comes with hindsight: Eliminate exportizing in the future by designing your new products so that they will either fit a wide range of markets as is or be easily adaptable. To do this, of course, you will need to research a variety of markets to learn what the common elements are and what elements will have to be varied from market to market.

The cost of developing new processes or technologies can certainly make a promising new project vastly more expensive than anticipated. If you have to develop new products or adapt your technologies for new situations in foreign markets, ask yourself how compatible the desired end results are with your domestic products. Even though Lakeview is a small company, it has been able to enter an entirely new market because its chopsticks are a complementary application of its Popsicle stick manufacturing process.

To minimize costs, look for things in your target market that are complements to your products or your manufacturing processes. For example, small American integrated chip manufacturers with strong design capabilities have teamed up with Japanese companies that offer automated chip assembly—a process that is unavailable in the United States.

Figure 2–1 gives a list of some of the factors in addition to exportizing that can increase the cost of selling overseas.

Selling Products That Are New to the Market

If you are planning to sell a product that is already sold in your target market, you can observe your competition and conform to the norms for sizes, packaging, colors, features, promotion, distribution, and so on. But in many cases you will be trying to introduce an entirely new product or service and will have to conduct market research to determine these factors. There are several basic questions you need to answer.

• *Are other products needed for yours to succeed?* When you are investigating the market readiness for your product or service, you must ask, "What other products or services are required for mine to be successfully introduced and used?" If you do not find these prerequisite products, you might conclude that the market is not ready. On the other hand, you might look at their absence as an additional opportunity—for you to supply those products as well. Or you might refine your product or the way it is delivered so that it conforms to existing market conditions.

• *Are new distribution channels needed?* A similar approach must be taken for channels of distribution: Are distribution channels available? How can your product best be distributed? Are there several ways it could be distributed? If the channels are not in place, could you arrange the needed channels? Would that give you a new competitive edge?

• *Can you regionalize your products?* If you are going to have to exportize your product for one Pacific Rim market, you may be able to make additional changes now so that it will fit other markets you may enter in the future. Or your product may have to be refined separately for each market you enter. For example, an appliance manufacturer adapting its smaller refrigerators for Japanese markets should also make sure they are suitable for homes in Korea, Taiwan, and Hong Kong as well.

Your decisions on exportizing will be affected by the competition you face. Depending on the qualities or the characteristics of the market and the competition, you may feel pressure to diversify or to standardize your product or service. There is pressure to diversify when you face a low growth rate in each target

Figure 2-1. Factors that increase the cost of exporting.

Extra inventory (e.g., to build up enough to fill a shipping container
  or to meet greater deviation in the shipping schedule)
Packing for overseas shipment

  · Cost of containers by volume, not weight
  · Package redesign to reduce volume of packing material

Inland transportation charges and loading fees
Paperwork
Financial management strategies (e.g., exchange rate hedging)
Transportation by sea or air
Cost of capital for time of shipment
Storage fees while awaiting customs
Fees to customs brokers
Customs clearance charges
Import duties and related fees
Repackaging for distribution and sale at destination
Replacing lost or damaged goods
Freight forwarder fees
Insurance at each stage

market or when the stability of your sales is low. And finally, competitive lead time is important: The company that introduces a product gains a strong advantage.

On the other hand, there is pressure to standardize when your product or service needs a concentrated sales effort or when you encounter economies of scale and distribution. In addition, if your service or product depends on adaptation to each market's needs, the pressure to diversify a basic product is reduced.

Most likely, your company will not be able to afford to customize products for a number of different markets at the same time. Instead, you will first enter the market with the best potential and create the product that appeals to the most lucrative segment of that market. After you build up a track record and gain experience in that market, you can go after your second-best market and again refine the product for it.

Exploiting Your Uniqueness

The road to success in Pacific Rim trade is to spot the unique features and advantages you have to offer—not just in your product or service itself, but in the way it is manufactured and distributed and how its sales are financed. Each Pacific Rim market has unique qualities and idiosyncrasies, but one element remains uniform—competition. Competing companies from Japan, Singapore, Hong Kong, Korea, Taiwan, and elsewhere are invading market niches that were formerly U.S. economic strongholds. This has forced U.S. companies to look again at the advantages that they do have. Some companies have become a bit fatalistic on this point and have adopted the attitude: "What's the use? Whatever we do, they will just copy it in a few months and sell it back to us even cheaper." Sometimes executives of American companies complain: "They are not playing on a level playing field." But the real problem for many companies is that they see and play on only part of the field.

To maximize your chances for success, you must exploit your uniqueness; and to identify your uniqueness, you must expand your thinking. Figure 2–2 presents a simple tool for this analysis. There are nine squares in the grid. (You can probably extend it even more.) The way to find a competitive product that meets the needs of the market is to seek potential sources of competitive advantage in each of the squares. Ask yourself how you can innovate in each square. This is what your competitors are doing.

You might think that you sell industrial products (box 4) and fail to see the consumer applications (box 1). You may seek to lower your prices by applying new technologies to your product (box 6), yet fail to see that your competitors are lowering costs by introducing high technology into their production processes (box 5). You may be up against a commodity that suffers a worldwide glut, and complain because your competitors receive hidden subsidies from their governments, when you should be seeking ways to add value to your product and market it to a particular niche (boxes 1 and 3).

Figure 2-2. Increasing your competitiveness by exploiting all competitive advantages.

	Expand the markets:	Refine the manufacturing process:	Refine the product:
Consumer product	1	2	3
Industrial product	4	5	6
Service	7	8	9

Consider the export prospects of just one kind of company, a relatively small company with a somewhat individualized technology: H-Tech saw that its competitors were basically selling hardware (box 6), and gained a strong advantage by adding a number of *services* desired by the customer (box 9). The grid suggests the importance of applying innovative technologies not just to the product, but also to the manufacturing process and even to the way the product is marketed. For each of the nine boxes, ask yourself how you can:

- Apply your unique technology or obtain a technology to create a distinct advantage. For example, if you understand the different technological capabilities and needs of Japanese industry, you become aware of niches that offer you a major opportunity. As noted earlier, U.S. chip makers have linked their design capabilities with Japan's automated assembly of chips to establish a strong market position in circuit boards in both Japan and the United States.
- Reconceptualize your marketing, packaging, product mix, distribution channels, and financing terms.
- Apply your financial engineering wizardry to find the lowest cost of capital on global financial markets and to offer your customers the most attractive financing terms.
- Apply the specialized skills of your people to determine what your customers really want, to stick with promising situations, and to provide the needed training and support to sales and manufacturing personnel.
- Apply a global management strategy.

All this is true whether you are going to develop new products or services for Pacific Rim markets, exportize your existing products, or just find new ways to market and distribute your present products.

Is Your Company Ready to Take On Pacific Rim Trade?

Regardless of whether your products are currently ready for Pacific Rim markets, your company must be prepared to tackle Pacific Rim trade. Not only must you be able to invest the needed resources, especially money and time, you must also have an adequate management team with the appropriate level of commitment. These key resources can be summarized as follows:

- Management depth and experience
- Management commitment
- Market experience plus the willingness to learn
- Time
- Financial strength and the ability to raise capital

Even if there are deficiencies in your organization in terms of Pacific Rim trade—and there probably are—you *can* adjust your operations to work around them. So beyond all the resources listed above, you need a willingness to find a way that works, using the resources you have.

Management Depth and Experience

Undertaking an export or overseas investment operation puts tremendous strains on a company's management team and current operations. You must understand this and be ready to commit the needed resources. Administrative complexity will be increased: International operations create stacks of new paperwork—much of it unfamiliar. You must stay on top of bills of lading, insurance, documentation for letters of credit, and myriad tax returns. You must obtain export licenses, permissions to import, and distributor agreements. In addition to the increased administrative burden, you must factor in the effort needed to distribute, service, and maintain your products and to keep track of your remote operations.

Some smaller companies become tripped up by tacking responsibility for international operations onto the job of some already overworked executive. Without sufficient organizational depth and experience, management effectiveness becomes diluted, and both international and domestic operations suffer. Responsibility for international operations should be vested in one person. Even some Fortune 500 companies are lax in this regard. Since responsibilities are divided functionally, they have no single manager with overall responsibility for the success of international operations. Thus no one has an overall picture of the company's international successes, problems, or opportunities.

Along with responsibility must go authority. In the organization, the manager in charge of foreign operations must have the full backing of the company in order to make on-the-spot decisions that will meet rapidly emerging developments.

Having adequate management depth doesn't mean you have to add on expensive layers of managerial talent. It means you must have people who can do the jobs required without stretching themselves too thinly because they have dual responsibilities. Wearing many hats is the norm in smaller companies.

There is no minimum company size needed to trade successfully in the Pacific Rim. The export proportion of the overall business can be any amount. Susan Catalano, president of Theos Software, a company with two dozen employees, travels for half the year to markets on four continents. Theos remains successful despite the length of her absences, because of the quality of her employees and the level of communications they maintain.

Management Commitment

Commitment includes not only an ability to commit the needed resources but, even more important, a willingness to stay committed. As the head of a small company, you can compensate for a shortage of committable resources by the form of international operation you choose. Your willingness to accept the required commitment becomes the crucial variable. You cannot succeed if you treat your Pacific Rim business as a stepchild. Suppose you say you are committed to it, but when things get tough in your domestic operations, you draw back, focus all your attention on home markets, and let your Pacific Rim business slide. Your reputation—based on your ability to perform as you promised—will travel throughout the marketplace. Once you neglect your Pacific Rim customers or distributors, your reputation may be irreparably harmed, and your ability to work in that market in the future may be jeopardized.

You need to find your "comfort zone" in international operations. Good managers learn not to get in over their heads. For some American businesses, this is reason enough to stay out of the Pacific Rim. If you have never ventured out of your domestic market, you may feel that a forbiddingly high threshold of economic and marketing technology must be mastered to succeed overseas. But one message of this book is that Pacific Rim success can be achieved on many different levels of commitment, and you can find a level that is comfortable for you. This message may seem obvious, but since so many companies appear blinded to major opportunities, it needs to be stated again and again.

Market Experience

Many companies, large and small, have blundered in international operations by undertaking a venture that was beyond their skill and experience. Companies that have tried to sell directly to Japanese markets, to negotiate contracts with the Chinese, or to install high-tech equipment in the Philippines have fallen flat on their faces because of inexperience. Their failure shouldn't keep your company out of Pacific Rim trade. The antidote to inexperience is assistance. Prudent companies have evaluated their level of knowledge and experience, obtained as much help as possible, and found a method of operating that matched their abilities. As your skill increases through experience in Pacific Rim trade, your undertakings will naturally become more ambitious.

Time

Establishing successful Pacific Rim operations usually takes more time than does setting up comparable domestic or European operations. Time is money, and distance is also money. One of the key qualities required is patience. It takes time to establish contacts and identify the best market opportunities, to build and nurture personal relationships, to build a viable operation, and to run it long enough to become profitable. These processes may take considerably longer than a comparable expansion into a new domestic market.

Companies become tripped up when they do not allow enough time for market operations to happen. The American business culture says: "Go in, do your business, get your profits, and look good quickly or get out." This is just the opposite of the business approach used in most Pacific Rim cultures. The American effort is 25 percent building relationships and 75 percent talking deals. This is reversed in Asia: Pacific Rim business is 75 percent building relationships and 25 percent talking deals. Many American companies have been shut out of Asian markets because (1) they tried to push the deal making too soon and so alienated their counterparts, and (2) they set an impossible timetable. They said, "We must close this deal in two years" or "We must be profitable in three years"—and such a time frame may just have been unrealistic.

So it is important to allow time for operations to proceed correctly without being governed by strict schedules. When Theos Software expanded into Japan and China, management had to make sure it had absolutely the right distributor. Then it worked closely with the distributor to translate software and user manuals into Japanese. Since quality was so important, Theos made sure the glitches were worked out of the Japanese software versions. It firmly resisted announcing the release of its software in Japan until everything was just right. Despite the fact that Theos was itching to start selling in the Japanese market, the company spent almost a year on the preparatory processes before releasing the software.

Businesses that are trying to open the Chinese market find that a set timetable is impossible. No deadlines. This is a matter of building relationships, looking at the problems that need to be solved, and finding solutions—going at Chinese speed.

You have a lot to learn, and it will take time to learn it. No matter what your level of experience, you learn by trial and error. You are not going to do everything right the first time. So you must factor in the time to learn what you need in order to achieve success and profits. Obviously, your company cannot display such patience if rapid payback on your effort is mandatory. But many small companies like Theos have found ways to make these extended time horizons work to their great advantage.

Financial Strength

You must be able to finance your overseas business in order to become profitable; every aspect of the venture costs money. This is true for domestic operations as well, but it may take longer for Pacific Rim operations and thus may cost more.

If you have stockholders who are interested in your short-term performance, you may have to put on an educational campaign to obtain their support. You may have to convince them that your company's greater success depends not on short-term profit but on building presence and market share in the long run.

The main problem of any new venture is undercapitalization. This is true with domestic operations and with expansion into international markets. Companies get tripped up because they don't consider everything that will cost them money: the cost of exportizing the product, packaging, advertising, production, and marketing. Lack of money forces a company to try to hurry things up: "We can support this effort for two years. Then it must pay its own way."

Since time is money, and distance is money, you might think that these requirements would keep out the little guy who doesn't have the staying power of a multinational. Not necessarily—as demonstrated by the many successful small companies operating in the Pacific Rim. For example, in the mid-1980s, Florod Corporation—a manufacturer of specialized laser instruments—had annual sales of just $1.6 million when it was forced into serious financial difficulty by overwhelming competition from NEC—one of the biggest and most aggressive Japanese electronics companies—in Florod's domestic markets. While NEC steadily eroded Florod's markets over a period of two years, Florod desperately sought new products and new markets, belatedly realizing that to survive it would have to enter the Japanese market. Despite lack of experience and capital, Florod found an appropriate Japanese representative who was able to sell Florod's new industrial laser instruments to Japanese high-tech manufacturers. Florod has since doubled in size to $3 million a year.

Chapter 5 shows how smaller companies successfully enter Pacific Rim markets by taking it one step at a time. Whether by luck or acumen, their first venture succeeds and becomes profitable. Using that as a steppingstone, they move on to a slightly more ambitious undertaking, and when that succeeds they move on to yet another market. The trick is to find a succession of steppingstones not so far apart that you fall into the drink.

Typically, when companies fail in the Pacific Rim, they are tripped up by:

- *Poor estimates of the start-up time and capital needed.* Many companies underestimate the administrative complexity of doing business in the Pacific Rim and often divert their attention from other operations.
- *Lack of commitment.* Many companies see Pacific Rim operations as a stepchild or orphan and do not take them as seriously as they do domestic operations. Often, they do not stay in the market to provide service and support.

- *Poor planning perspective.* Some companies either are not in it for the long haul, or else they fail to appreciate the differences in doing business in the Pacific Rim.
- *Language barriers.* These barriers exist even for companies that "know the language." Companies often fail to factor in the costs of translating written materials, logos, packaging, slogans, and so on.
- *Lack of knowledge and experience.* This is usually coupled with an unwillingness to put in the effort to learn what is needed. Companies don't do their homework as well as their competitors or those they do business with.
- *Timidity.* Some companies just stick their toes in when they should take the plunge. Or they work only through a trading company when they should establish their own distribution network.

Personal Qualities Needed for Pacific Rim Operations

A key factor in Pacific Rim success is having the right people—that is, having people with the right experience, the right skills, and the right personal qualities in key positions.

If you are looking for someone to head your Pacific Rim operation, there are several personal qualities to keep in mind. (You may be the person yourself, you may be sizing up someone already in your organization, or you may be preparing to hire someone from outside.) Many of these qualities are crucial for success in a domestic operation as well, so you will not be asking for the impossible. Here I will focus on why they are particularly critical in Pacific Rim executives.

Willingness to Learn—A Crucial Factor

If your business up to now has embraced only domestic operations, you are in for one heck of a learning experience. So willingness to learn is one of the crucial qualities for you and your key people. You will need to acquire a vast amount of information on conducting business in the Pacific Rim, and on the markets and business cultures in Pacific Rim countries. Your initial lack of knowledge and experience can be compensated only by a willingness to learn and an ability to work with good mentors.

For Florod Corporation, the key to successful entry into the Japanese market was not just finding a Japanese representative, but also having a person on its own staff who could be an effective mentor for Florod's management. Vu Tran, a Vietnamese engineer, had been with Florod for years. Tran had been educated in Japan and spoke fluent Japanese, so he was able to teach Florod's president how the Japanese do business, how to make presentations, and how to handle requests for demonstrations.

Knowledge of the business cultures in the Pacific Rim cannot be mastered by going to a seminar or reading a book. You must go there and find out for yourself. By selecting a level of operation that allows you to succeed initially, you can get paid to learn what you need for your next stage of growth.

Learn to look at expansion into Pacific Rim markets as an educational experience, not just as another part of doing business. There is a bit of a contradiction here. On the one hand, the companies that are successful in international trade are the ones that view domestic and international operations as an integrated whole. They regard it all as "global business." On the other hand, companies that are just entering international operations need to take a "nonglobal" view, at least initially. They need to recognize the differences between international and domestic operations and then take special care to prepare for them. And they must factor in the time needed for learning and for careful planning.

Whenever you begin questioning the need to put in all this time and effort, you must again get in touch with the ultimate gains you will achieve. Remember the guidelines in Chapter 1. Remember, too, that the people you deal with in the Pacific Rim markets will often be more familiar with American business practices than you are with their practices. They will have familiarity with international trade and negotiations. You will be shocked to learn how much they know about *your* business, *your* industry, and *your* costs, advantages, and efficiencies.

Before the president of Theos Software went to China for negotiations, she talked with many people, including Department of Commerce representatives and a Chinese consular official in San Francisco. She said to them, "I am going to China for business negotiations. What are some of the things I need to know about meeting and negotiating with Chinese people?" She then read several books on doing business with China, which gave her a wealth of practical tips: things to do, and to avoid doing; things to watch out for; rules for politeness; what to expect in negotiating sessions.

Other Important Qualities

Here's a boy scout list of other important qualities that you and your Pacific Rim executives should possess.

• *Open-mindedness.* Learn to see things in a new way, to look "newly" constantly. Understand how things are done differently and appreciate the differences.

• *Creativity and imagination.* Think on your feet, come up with new ways to get things done, and make do when all the pieces are not in place.

• *Patience.* Learn to sip tea and talk politely when unforeseen glitches come up. Try to refocus on the larger picture, the overall purpose, and avoid getting thrown off course by the inevitable maddening and expensive delays.

• *Negotiating skills.* Always be polite, yet firm and tough. Take this stance not only with people in your Pacific Rim markets, but also with people in your own organization who get excited about time delays, unexpected costs, and other glitches in the project.

• *Thoroughness.* Know your business thoroughly. Have a grasp of detail. Do your homework. Be a good planner and organizer—work things through beforehand. American businesspeople are sometimes surprised to discover that a Chinese or Japanese negotiator knows their business as well as they do. If you haven't done your homework, you are at a distinct disadvantage. You will also lose respect in their eyes.

• *Stick-to-itiveness.* Follow through. Do what you say you will.

• *Adaptability and flexibility.* Adapt to different paces and styles of doing business. Change plans to fit shifting situations, to function well in an unsettled environment. You will be in so many unfamiliar situations that it will be impossible to predict everything. You must be able to roll with the punches and make appropriate changes.

• *Sensitivity.* Be sensitive to cultural and business differences, to people with different backgrounds. Learn to get along with many different kinds of people. You can't possibly master the etiquette of so many different cultures—what you should say and what you should avoid saying, when to sit and when to stand. The quality that will carry you through the tough times is your basic sensitivity. You must learn to understand people's meaning even when you don't understand their words. You will be surprised at how much you can understand. The people you are dealing with recognize that you are in an unfamiliar situation, and they will appreciate your effort to understand, even when you commit horrible gaffes.

• *Ability to size up people.* Be a good judge of character. In business cultures that stress personal contact, people who promise you entrée to top officials may be exaggerating their influence a bit. It may be difficult for you to check out these people quickly, so it is good to gain a sense of the value of what people are telling you.

• *Tact and courtesy.* Always be courteous, especially when disagreements and problems arise. Saving face is very important in Pacific Rim cultures.

• *Trustworthiness.* Since business in the Pacific Rim is based on personal relationships, trustworthiness is a key quality. If you promise something and you do not deliver, you lose face in others' eyes. You must do what you say you are going to do. If, on the basis of your promise to them, they make promises to someone else, they are putting their reputation on the line. If you let them down, you may damage their reputation as well.

• *Trust.* Learn to trust the people you are working with. This follows from initially sizing them up correctly. In many Pacific Rim nations, business is done on the basis of trusting business relationships, and formal contracts may not specify as many terms as American executives are used to. Many items are left to each party's trust in the fairness of the other. Insisting that every term be spelled out may be taken as a sign of lack of faith in your contacts.

• *Interest in world affairs.* Show an interest in other cultures and other peoples. It's less a matter of knowledge than one of attitude. Will your Pacific Rim counterparts have a larger sense of the global economy, and a larger share of the qualities we have been discussing? Not really. But it is true that Pacific Rim businesspeople have had to live by exporting, so they have been forced to develop a greater appreciation of different cultures. They are not inherently any more tolerant or open-minded, but they may be used to functioning in many different cultures and situations.

• *Watchfulness.* Learn to keep your antennae out. Many American companies first got into Pacific Rim trade because an opportunity dropped into their laps. How did they attract that opportunity? They were looking for it; they had their antennae out; they were putting out the word. They were making themselves known in circles familiar to Pacific Rim buyers.

• *Willingness to travel.* Get up and go there. Since business success grows out of personal relationships, face-to-face meetings between peers are crucial. People want to know exactly whom they are doing business with. Their willingness to do business grows out of their sense of you as a person. During your trips to the Pacific Rim, you will be able to make initial contacts, size up market potential and local partners, monitor your operations, and solve problems in ways that you could not possibly do from home. You will also bring home orders. Your sales reps and engineers cannot do all this. The presidents of your distribution companies want to talk with a *president*. They will not be as open and forthright about problems and opportunities with a sales rep as they will with someone they consider a peer. Travel goes both ways: In many cases, you will want to invite key overseas people to visit your plant, your offices, and very possibly your home.

Executives emphasize the importance of having the resources to spare for a risky venture. Although this is true as far as it goes, remember that there are appropriate ways to get the most from Pacific Rim trade regardless of the size of your company or the time and resources your company is able to commit. If you want to be in Pacific Rim trade (that is, if you have the basic commitment), you don't have to let any particular obstacle keep you out. A way can be found that fits your resources, strengths, and limitations. Just don't try to hack your way through the underbrush; find a road that is going in the right direction and take it. The most important rule of thumb is to get all the help you can from experienced professionals. Much of what you need is free or inexpensive. Following is a success formula for new exporters:

1. Get help—from the Commerce Department, state agencies, Pacific Rim traders, bankers, freight forwarders, and accountants. Find the agency that will help you to:
   • Market and advertise your product

- Identify potential customers and market partners
- Learn the dos and don'ts so that you can avoid pitfalls
- Identify useful events such as trade shows and conventions
- Evaluate potential deals for their viability and appropriateness

2. Get yourself focused. Do one thing well initially. Give a lot of study and thought to what you do best. Determine what has the greater appeal to the target market, offers the greatest competitive advantage and profit potential, and leads into other things.
3. Work through others initially. Look for ways to leverage your effort. For example, licensing may be better than selling through an in-country rep, and that in turn is probably better than direct selling. Find an excellent market partner—for both sales *and* service.
4. Learn, learn, learn.
5. Make sure your product works well the very first time.
6. Make sure each deal is profitable. It is easy for small companies to do business and not make money. Factor in travel costs and time.

Figure 2-3. Management skills needed for success in Pacific Rim trade

To succeed as a global executive, you need to:	At the same time, you must:
1 Provide strong leadership. Give a sense of direction to a far-flung, diverse corporate network. Be decisive and take effective action when the time comes.	Encourage diverse viewpoints. Give incentives for finding ultimate best solutions, not for avoiding mistakes. Be able to assimilate many different types of information.
2 Develop a worldwide perspective. See the entire world as your marketplace and your resource base.	Tailor your marketing approach to the needs and requirements of each nation or region.
3 Balance centralized and decentralized control. Set up and lead a global organization that can run lean—to attain the highest economies of scale, to afford to invest heavily in high-tech R&D, to collect and digest data from all over the world.	Be flexible enough to move into markets that have diverse requirements. Tailor your operation to the needs and requirements of each individual nation or region, such as Brazil, Sweden, China, or Singapore. Hire skilled local managers who understand and can be responsive to local conditions. Motivate them to take initiative in your company's best interest, rather than being obstructive bureaucrats. Give them incentives and authority to develop diverse innovative strategies to succeed locally.
4 Be marketing-minded. Make sure consumer needs, not production needs,	Be production-minded. Focus not just on high-tech products, but on high-tech pro-

drive your international marketing and your technology development.	duction processes and on rigorous quality control.
5 Install the latest technology in your production and distribution to maximize productivity.	Evaluate whether the latest technology will live up to expectations and truly improve your productivity. Procure needed resources globally and buy production capabilities if you can't build them in time.
6 Take the long view. Transcend the short-term "equity viewpoint." Lengthen your strategic planning horizon for market penetration to ten or twenty years when necessary. Have the patience to invest in new markets, such as China.	Adopt a compressed corporate planning cycle: Make rapid and accurate tactical responses when opportunities or problems suddenly appear. Cut deadwood and get profits from every sector of your business. Satisfy equity investors who are looking at short-term performance.
7 Be a "financial engineer." Take advantage of the best financing options, good resource prices, and acquisition opportunities anywhere in world markets.	Be a "people person." Realize that in a high-tech, knowledge-based industry, your people are your key resource.
8 Protect your technology from leaking out and creating your own competition five years hence.	Remain aware that technology transfer and investment in joint ventures are the routes to market penetration and profitable growth in the future.
9 Recognize and exploit your natural competitive advantages.	Be willing to aggressively create new areas of competitive advantage for your company.

Management Skills Needed for Pacific Rim Operations

The management skills needed for a Pacific Rim operation are the same as those needed for any business involving global trade. Figure 2–3 shows the changing mix of management skills that U.S. companies need in order to remain competitive today. The figure is divided into two columns to illustrate the conflicting, almost contradictory nature of the skills required to succeed in global trade. The global executive must balance these skills in ways not called for by traditional domestic markets. As your company becomes an experienced international player, your management team will need to build and strengthen these skills while keeping their balance in a global economy.

3 | Which Market Should You Go Into?

- *Conducting a market study to select a new market*
- *Using a market research company or doing your own research*
- *Comparing different sources of information*

Here's an example of typical Pacific Rim market research:

"Hey, Bob, listen to this! At the conference in Houston, I talked with this guy from Taipei who was interested in our product line. He says they've been buying from Japan, but they need a second source, and he likes the breadth of our line. The initial order would be about 25 grand. I asked Harry to check him out through the bank. What do you think?"

"Well, why not?" is the response.

U.S. companies often cite difficulty in obtaining market information as a major reason for not entering Pacific Rim trade. Market selection and market research are huge topics, and it is impossible to cover them completely here. We can, however, explore the main issues to be considered in making an intelligent business decision about entering a foreign market and how the necessary information can be obtained.

Many companies enter Pacific Rim trade when an opportunity falls into their laps, so that their initial market area is dictated by the source of the "golden opportunity." But those same companies often outgrow their golden opportunity quickly and want to move beyond it, so they need a more systematic approach to subsequent market expansion.

It's one thing to see what your company can offer and how that product or service can be adapted to existing Pacific Rim markets and needs. But in a rapidly changing world market, the real task of market research is to identify emerging needs (obviously the key to success in domestic markets as well). This chapter examines how companies find out where opportunities are opening up and where market needs are being largely ignored. Chapter 4 then details the specific sources of information needed to make market-entry decisions.

Comprehensive Market Studies

Let's start by looking at how several different kinds of companies selected their initial Pacific Rim markets and how their analyses of potential markets related to the kinds of products offered and the resources at their disposal. These examples illustrate (1) how to zero in on an initial target market and the kinds of information needed to do it *and* (2) how companies that cannot afford full-fledged market research can get good information. An analysis of the common factors used in selecting the best markets follows the examples.

Example 1: H-Tech
Selling an advanced technology in a new market.
Comprehensive market study.

H-Tech* is a small California company that develops and manufactures photovoltaic power generation equipment. When sunlight strikes a photovoltaic cell (a thin silicon sheet), some of the sun's energy is converted directly to electricity. Photovoltaic systems, which have no moving parts, are used to power space satellites. A lot of research was done on commercial photovoltaic systems during the 1970s oil crisis. But as oil prices declined, photovoltaic power generation lost competitiveness for most domestic applications, and the companies that had developed the technology began looking around for other markets.

Photovoltaic power has real potential in many developing nations (including some in the Pacific Rim), where remote areas with sunny climates lack central power grids. H-Tech set out to evaluate potential markets. Since there was no one out there clamoring for photovoltaics, the company had no choice but to create its own demand, search systematically for the best potential markets, and decide which ones to go after first.

H-Tech used a four-stage approach:

1. It conducted library research to identify potential markets and eliminate unlikely ones.
2. It made phone or letter contact with specific people to narrow the field to a few promising markets and identify the decision makers and potential local partners.
3. It met with top people in the countries that remained as final prospects.
4. It made a final selection on the basis of market need and a newly discovered competitive edge.

Stage 1: Conducting Research. H-Tech first established a set of criteria by which to judge the general suitability of a marketplace. These criteria had to be based on information that was both available and consistent so that the company could compare apples with apples. So H-Tech looked at three key factors.

1. *General demographic data.* H-Tech researchers focused on the type of population and its distribution. For example, they asked: "What is the size of the off-grid population?" Since the question was not directly answerable, they

---

* H-Tech is the disguised name of a company that did not want the precise nature of its emerging business revealed. The facts have been altered, but the essentials of market selection remain.

found indirect ways to define the size of this population. They first looked at the proportion of rural to urban populations (which they found in World Bank publications) and then at the sales of light bulbs and other electrical appliances that are universally used in areas with electricity.

2. *Climate.* H-Tech isolated a number of nations with sunny climates in which photovoltaics could offer advantages over other power generation methods (such as small-scale hydroelectric plants).

3. *Clients.* H-Tech decided that the most likely buyer would be a government that wanted to provide electrical power to some remote, small-scale facility or community. Purchase by a private company or institution for some remote facility was deemed less likely.

An important factor that emerged from this research was the need to determine the ability of a target government to pay for installation of a photovoltaic system. So H-Tech looked at economic indicators such as gross domestic product, trade balance of payments, national indebtedness, and sources of outside financial assistance available to the government. It also looked at the stability of the government, the absence of rebel groups in the remote areas, and other political indicators. In this way, it went on to develop several yardsticks that were semi-quantifiable and comparable from one country to another. From several such "indicator yardsticks," the company prepared a matrix of countries, rated by each indicator, and ranked each country.

On the basis of this ranking, H-Tech eliminated two thirds of the countries from the list. Others were kept in a "check again later" file, with notes on what factors would have to change for each country to become a good prospect.

The countries that remained viable candidates had (1) a potential market, (2) the ability to pay, and (3) sufficient political stability. Important questions remained unanswered, but each country had clear upside potential. H-Tech's relatively crude research might well have eliminated a good prospect, but this drawback was outweighed by the fact that poor initial prospects were completely weeded out and no further energy was spent on them.

Stage 2: Talking to People. For each identified "good prospect" nation, H-Tech talked with the local Department of Commerce trade specialist—or region-specific expert at the Department of Commerce headquarters in Washington—and gained introduction to the country. Through these people, H-Tech was introduced to the U.S. Department of Commerce representative in each country and received the names of people involved in power generation efforts there. Included were government employees, academicians, and members of power industry associations. H-Tech contacted key people by letter or phone and in this way—without even leaving the United States—was able to identify those who would be most valuable to the success of its effort.

At this stage, the people that H-Tech had contacted were certainly not ready to say, "We need photovoltaics. Here's our money!" Their point of view was broader in scope: "We need to help more of our people in rural areas. We must do many things to build up their infrastructure. One of the things they need is electricity." H-Tech had to find out whether these representatives knew about photovoltaic power and, if so, how they perceived it. Had they ever heard of it? Did they see it as novel and interesting, but merely laboratory technology? Or did they see it as having real potential for their own situation?

As a small company with limited resources, H-Tech had to find out how far along the learning curve these officials were. It had to decide how much time and effort it could afford to take to educate them—a process that could involve several years and still not lead to any business.

H-Tech questioned local authorities about the environment in order to make informed judgments about the real functionality of photovoltaics. H-Tech executives did not want to pursue any situation in which some other option—such as hydroelectricity or diesel power generation—would beat them out. They needed a cold, hard look at the edge that their technologies had over the alternatives. They probed to find out which other technologies (if any) had been considered in the country in order to identify possible competition.

During these discussions, it became clear to H-Tech executives that to do business in virtually any of the prospect countries, they might need a local partner. So they began to identify businesses within each country that would be qualified to act in that capacity.

In light of this new factor, H-Tech again shortened its list of prospect countries. The company reviewed the candidates and began to rank them on the basis of much more subjective judgments, trying to answer the question "Are our prospects in that country good enough to warrant a trip there?"

Stage 3: Traveling to the Markets. After identifying the top few prospects, H-Tech realized it could not proceed further without traveling to the countries involved. The trips had a dual purpose:

1. Final assessment of market potential
2. Final assessment of potential business partners

H-Tech hoped to cover part of the cost of these trips by selling a small demo project, which would include installation and training of local people. This goal proved to have three valuable by-products. First, purchase of the demo revealed which candidate country was most serious about the project. Second, the tangible demo made the later sale of a larger installation much easier. Third, the process of "getting our hands dirty" in the country provided invaluable insights into the requirements for a later full-scale installation, including the functional deficiencies of H-Tech's engineered-for-the-USA technology.

Most important, H-Tech discovered its true competitive edge: The company would offer to sell, not just a piece of high technology, but an entire turnkey system. As H-Tech representatives got to know the local community, they discovered that the real concern was *not* whether H-Tech's technology would be cost-efficient, but whether H-Tech could make the technology work at all! The company found out that several competitors were attempting to sell equipment on a "commodity" basis and wanted to rely on a local partner to install and maintain it. H-Tech saw that its path to success would be to put together a systems group to handle all aspects of building facilities and roads, installing the system, providing spare parts, and training people to run and maintain the system.

Stage 4: Making the Final Selection. By the time H-Tech had completed this process, the initial market had all but selected itself. Because H-Tech had seen the importance of providing a turnkey system, complete with follow-up support and maintenance, its product won out over the competition. This was no mean feat for a high-tech product in a developing economy, and the success gave H-Tech a firm base from which to approach other potential clients. It also provided a way to minimize the "copycat syndrome," since the specialized knowledge underlying H-Tech's services was very difficult for a competitor to duplicate.

But what if H-Tech's research had eliminated *all* countries? What if nobody had fit the bill? That possibility was always there, and H-Tech was prepared to accept it. Moreover, in a sense H-Tech executives *did* determine that all potential customers were unsuited for the product they initially wished to sell. They did not identify a viable market for their equipment as they set out to sell it. They actually ended up discovering another market—for integrated systems—that they filled by re-engineering their product and their service mix. They exportized their package to fit the market needs they discovered.

Researching and Selecting Pacific Rim Markets

Following is a set of questions that you too must get answers to if—like H-Tech—you are bidding on a contract with a Pacific Rim government.

- Are potential buyers serious? Or are they just using your bid to become educated?
- Are potential buyers knowledgeable about your product or service? How much groundwork must be laid before buyers can make a decision about your product?
- Is additional infrastructure required for the use of your product?
- Do local businesses or third-country companies have an inside track? Have they ignored anything that you can provide? Do you have a strong advantage over them on which you can capitalize?
- What is the means of getting business?
- If business is obtained through competitive bidding, to what extent is the bidding process open and decided on merits? Are there special advantages you could have in the bidding process?
- If business is obtained through contacts, do you have those contacts—or can you get them?
- What is the timetable?

- Can you arrange to have governments invite you to provide your product or service?
- If you get a contract, does the government have the means to pay you?
- Regardless of whether or not you can sell your product, is it a "good deal" for the government in question?
- Can you sell to need?
- Can you provide or ensure the required training, maintenance, and follow-up presence?

From the answers to these questions, a fixed procedure emerges—a general set of steps your company must go through to select the best market. This process is similar to developing a marketing plan for domestic expansion. It involves developing selection criteria, gathering and evaluating information, narrowing down alternatives, and making a final decision.

Determining the Ideal Market for Your Product

There is really a "prestep," something that every company should already have done (but that many neglect) in its domestic markets. You need to define the ideal market for your product or service. This may not be at all obvious, and in many cases your understanding of what you are selling will shift midway through the market selection process. Draw a profile of the market you look for when you are considering expanding: Who wants what you offer? How much will buyers pay?

Now your task is to find which Pacific Rim markets most closely resemble this profile—or, conversely, to determine which of the opportunities you have spotted best fit with what you already do. Which markets have these characteristics? Set your market selection criteria, being aware that in many cases they will be refined or amended as the selection process continues.

Decide what you need to find out about each market to determine whether it meets your criteria. Here's where an experienced consultant can be of great benefit. A market researcher can tell you what information is available and how you might apply it to your situation in innovative ways in order to reach the decision you need. A competitor of H-Tech, one that built small-scale hydroelectric dams, selected prospective markets by examining maps of tree cover and terrain. It figured that heavy forests meant a lot of rain and that hilly areas were more suitable to hydroelectric installations.

Finding Markets That Look Initially Promising

It is often said that almost every American company first goes to Japan. If this was in fact true at one time, it is becoming less true as other markets mature. The same factors that once pointed to a "Japan first" approach now indicate other initial markets.

To clarify your target market, you need information that will help you narrow the field. Build a profile of prospective Pacific Rim markets. Obtain market information on products by countries. Identify the most important factors, and prioritize them for your product or service. Use this information to narrow the field initially.

From the *supply* perspective, ask these questions for each potential market: Is your product or service already sold there? Is it needed? Can it be imported? Is there a way you can supply it (or is the market locked up)?

Then approach the issue from the *demand* side and determine what you can sell to whom: What do governments buy that you can supply? Is it defense, infrastructure, roads, health care, education, agricultural improvements, communications, transportation, business services, tourist facilities? What does business and industry buy? How can you meet those needs? What can you sell to consumers? Through whom?

Making the First Cut of Promising Markets

The first step in identifying promising markets is to eliminate unpromising ones. At this point you should already be ready to make your first cut. Determine which markets should be eliminated from consideration for the time being and select a handful for further investigation. For each of the latter, get more detailed answers to your questions.

At each remaining stage of your decision, continue to eliminate markets that look unacceptable, but don't forget about them completely. Keep them filed away with some notations on what factors would have to change to make them good prospects. These factors just might change. Whoever spots the coming changes first will have the best shot.

Narrowing Your Alternatives

Narrowing alternatives requires that you ask more penetrating questions. What is the market potential for your products or services in a particular market? How many can you sell? What market share can you hope to secure in the existing market? In the potential market? Do appropriate distribution channels exist? Who are your competitors, and what advantages would you have in that market for your products or services?

Compare the strengths of the Pacific Rim competition with those of your domestic competitors. What are your chief competitive advantages and weaknesses? (Chapter 10 presents a framework for evaluating competitive advantage.) If your products or services are not available in the market, how is the need you satisfy currently being met? What would it take to induce buyers to change their current behavior and buy from you?

• *Entry barriers.* What barriers to entry would affect your products and services in each market? (Chapter 7 describes political and regulatory environments in the Pacific Rim and barriers to market entry.) Are the barriers insurmountable? Are they tough and expensive? How can these barriers be reduced or circumvented? Is it worth the effort?

• *Political and economic risk factors.* What are the economic and political risk factors in this market? Can you protect what you sell from your competition? Can you protect trade secrets and technology in the market?

• *Aids to entry.* What are the incentives and assistance to entry? (See Chapter 6.)

• *Market fit.* How close is the match between what you offer and what is needed? How much must you refine your product or service in order for it to sell in that market? What are the costs of exportizing a product or service, including re-engineering, resizing, repackaging, and translating literature into another language?

• *Operating environment.* Does the success of your product or service require the availability of other products or services? Are these available? How can you maintain a presence? Can you service your products in the market (training, maintenance, spare parts, troubleshooting, and so on)? Identify the critical issues for success in each market.

• *Distribution channels.* How appropriate are the existing means of distribution for your product or service in this market? Are there suitable agents, distributors, or joint venture partners? The answers will differ depending on whether you have an exported product or service or a product to be manufactured there (more on this in Chapter 6). What is the extent of domestic production? What major foreign companies and U.S. companies compete there?

• *Special costs of operating in the market.* What are your likely start-up costs? How long will it take to hit your stride? How do the costs of operation compare with the price you can charge (Chapter 10 shows how to evaluate potential profitability)? How stable and predictable will the market be?

Making the Final Decision

List three or four of your most viable alternatives, and rank each market. To go further, you will need to contact people in those markets. Before making a final decision, you will likely need to visit the markets in person, as discussed later in Chapter 4. Even if only one market seems viable, you must travel there to finalize agreements with distributors or agents. Once you have seen the markets and spoken with contacts, you can make a well-informed decision.

Market Studies Tailored to Your Needs

H-Tech's example shows a small company sponsoring an entire market research project by itself and suggests how much a comprehensive project would entail. For many companies, the answers sought at various stages of the research project are so obvious that they need conduct only those parts of the research that are critical for them. In so doing, they can significantly shorten the market identification process for their initial Pacific Rim market.

In the following example, a small company conducts its own market study and gathers firsthand information in the market without undertaking a large, expensive research effort.

Example 2: Bowlin Frozen Unbaked Croissants
Consumer product new to market.
Survey of consumer tastes.

Bowlin Bakers,* a supplier of baked goods and breakfast pastries in the San Francisco area, was offered a "golden opportunity." A representative from a Japanese trading company saw an appealing ad for Bowlin's croissants, contacted Bowlin, and suggested that there might well be a market for the company's products in Japanese specialty shops. He then indicated that his company would be interested in handling them. Bowlin had never before considered exporting and decided not to accept the offer as extended. But the seed for Pacific Rim export had been planted, and Bowlin began its own market research.

Bowlin knew that croissants would be a virtually new consumer product in Japan. Its own plan was to sell frozen unbaked croissants to a distributor that supplied Japanese tea and coffee shops. The shops would bake them and serve them hot and fresh.

In the beginning, Bowlin did not consider international expansion a high priority. The company simply hired an MBA candidate to do some market research. The researcher got help from the Department of Commerce library. The Commerce Department trade rep convinced Bowlin executives to take the opportunity seriously and linked them with the department's trade specialist in Japan. The trade specialist helped Bowlin get data on the Japanese market and identify several trading companies as potential distributors.

Bowlin contacted the distributors by letter and then by phone and found two that were very interested—interested enough to do some initial research into the best markets. It was the distributors, then, that came up with answers to the key questions: Was there a market for this new consumer product? Could Bowlin link

* Not its real name.

up with suitable distribution channels? Could it produce the product in the United States, airfreight it to Japan, and still sell it profitably? How vulnerable would Bowlin be to competition if it did establish a market?

Bowlin learned, among other things, that it would be better to enter Osaka first, before Tokyo. Osaka was deemed a more innovative market than Tokyo for consumer products—perhaps like Los Angeles compared with New York.

Bowlin's is a more likely scenario than H-Tech's for smaller companies first entering Pacific Rim markets, especially with consumer products. Bowlin didn't need to investigate every possible market. It knew initially that there were only a couple of potential ones—and the company needed only one to start with. It did not need to hire a market research company because of the help it obtained from the Department of Commerce specialist in Japan and from potential Japanese distributors.

Why did Bowlin decline the initial offer from the Japanese trading company? After some investigation, it discovered that it had the resources to handle part of the distribution process. Instead of leaving everything up to a large trading company, Bowlin made its arrangement with smaller local distributors. By cutting out one middleman, the company obtained a higher profit margin and retained greater control over the quality of the distributed product.

Bowlin did enter the Osaka market, but its products proved so popular that they almost immediately began selling in Tokyo. This is bringing Bowlin new headaches: How should it set up its own bakery in Japan to meet the demand? And should it set up franchise outlets there to fend off sudden competition from a much larger European company?

Market Selection of Consumer Products

The following questions regarding market selection pertain particularly to consumer products or services:

- Is there an existing market? How is the need for your product now met?
- Are there entry barriers to your product?
- What advantages can you capitalize on? Are American products particularly desirable for reasons of style or status?
- Does your product have alternative uses in that market?
- How much re-engineering, repackaging, or translating is required?
- How can you reach intended consumers? Through promotion? Advertising?
- Are existing distributors appropriate for your product?
- Can you set up your own distribution channels? Are there good local partners for distribution or production?
- Can you provide any needed maintenance or customer support?

Example 3 shows how a small company minimizes expensive market research by having potential distributors prove that there is a market.

Example 3: Theos Software
Commercial product and service sold through distributors.
Getting potential distributors to prove there is a market.

Theos has a different kind of product: operating system software for personal computers. Its market includes businesses and institutions that need to link together several personal computers but that don't have a full-scale mainframe or minicomputer system. Thus its criteria for selecting a target market were quite different from Bowlin's:

1. Theos had to find overseas markets where personal computers were used in the way described above.
2. As a small company, Theos had to service customers through distributors. Thus identifying suitable distributors to work with was critical.
3. Since the company's software and instruction manuals would have to be translated for any non-English-speaking market, Theos needed to find a way to have the translation done in the market country.

It was very easy for Theos to eliminate most Pacific Rim nations as potential markets: There just weren't enough personal computers used. This was determined through armchair research—just by analyzing the software industry literature. Theos also had a second rough measure of potential interest for its software in various markets: inquiries received from all over the world after articles written by Theos employees appeared in software publications, including a magazine published exclusively for Theos users.

Theos did not want to take on more than it could handle. It had recently entered markets in Europe and Saudi Arabia. It didn't want to enter every market, just the best Pacific Rim market. The two Pacific Rim markets that showed the most promise initially were Australia and Japan. Theos first went into Australia because expansion would be easier there—no translation required. Also, Australians use a lot of American computer and software products, and experienced distributors are available.

As soon as the Australian operation was on solid footing, Theos turned its attention to Japan. Japan was potentially a much larger market than Australia, but it obviously required much more preparation. Because the Japanese market was so critical and competitive, and so unfamiliar to Theos, the company had to proceed carefully and meticulously. It couldn't afford a consultant-directed, customized market study and had to rely on its own efforts. Theos found two key ways to get the needed information: from the Department of Commerce and from potential distributors. Theos also got help in identifying some potential distributors through the Commerce Department trade specialist in Japan. The company's president and top software engineer traveled to Japan several times before making a decision on which distributor(s) to work with in which Japanese cities.

The ideal distributor was a company that was already established in the market for the kinds of customers Theos wanted and one that had the technical capability to translate the material, sell it, and answer customer queries. Part of the screening process involved having a distributor demonstrate that the potential market was adequate (one criterion for selecting distributors). Furthermore, Theos limited its risk by having the distributor cover the cost of translating the software and manuals into Japanese.

Market Selection for Consumer or Industrial Products

Here's a principle for smaller businesses: Since market research is expensive and time-consuming, do only what is necessary and consistent with getting the results you want in the marketplace. At each stage, you need to ask: "Is there a way that we could get by without doing this, or by having someone else do it for us inexpensively?" Here are the market selection questions you would focus on for a commercial or industrial product:

- How much re-engineering, repackaging, translating, and other exportizing is required?
- How will your intended customers or distributors view your company?
- What are the import restrictions?
- Are existing distributors qualified to handle your product? What are their technical qualifications and stature in the marketplace?
- Can distributors provide the service and customer support required for your product?

The following are questions to ask for commercial or industrial products that are new to the market:

- What is the potential demand? Are there similar markets elsewhere with comparable characteristics?
- How is the need being handled currently? Are there alternative products?
- For your product or service to be accepted:
  —What related products and services must be available in the market?
  —What level of consumer knowledge or sophistication and other cultural preconditions need to be present?
  —What distribution channels need to be available?

Selecting a Market for Investment

If you are entering international trade for the first time, you are probably not planning to establish an overseas operation on your own; most likely, you plan to use a distributor that is already there. But there *are* some circumstances in which you might go it on your own; or you may wish to select your initial export market with an eye toward eventually establishing your own operation there. The next example shows several additional factors a company must consider in its market study of potential locations for its operations.

Example 4: Gary Industries
Investment in a factory.
Hiring a consulting firm.

Gary Industries,* a midwestern manufacturer of pumps, saw the handwriting on the wall. Although it had sold its pumps—which are used as components in a variety of industrial products—to companies in various parts of the world, it saw that its market share was slipping because some of its major customers were so far away. It recognized the need to build a manufacturing plant in the Pacific Rim to supply its major Asian customers as rapidly as its Korean and Australian competitors could. But where should it locate the plant? The manufacturer hired Business International, a consulting firm with extensive experience in the region, to help it identify the best plant sites. Business International helped narrow the choice down to three sites, first by doing an economic analysis of the cost of supplying customers from each of the sites, and then by evaluating other critical economic and political factors. Two of the most likely sites were in Taiwan and Thailand, each of which had its own advantages. Thailand had lower labor costs, but Taiwan had more available skilled engineers and managers. Facilities and finances were readily available in both nations.

After all factors were considered, one site stood out. Business International then arranged for company executives to travel to that nation to meet potential joint venture partners and representatives of the appropriate government agencies and ministries. Below are some of the critical issues the executives had to consider before making an investment decision.

- Government investment policies (which industries are welcomed, and which are tolerated?)
- Attitude of local government toward foreign investment and toward foreign company's profitability (is foreign investment welcomed or seen as a necessary evil?)
- Limitations on foreign equity and ownership
- Investment incentives from the government
- Efficiency and stability of local bureaucracy
- Approval procedures (e.g., for purchasing or building a facility, obtaining a licensing agreement, importing a new product)
- Taxation policies and practices, and tax rates
- Availability of investment finance
- Barriers to the repatriation of capital and profits
- Legal structure and how consistently it is applied
- Ease of gaining legal redress for patent or trademark infringements
- Proximity to customers
- Availability of suitable facilities
- Labor costs (is the pool of low-cost labor drying up?)
- Skilled labor and management pools

* Not its real name.

- Supply of entrepreneurial skills
- Adequacy of inland transportation, port facilities, communications network
- Availability of needed support industries and services
- Resource base and the ease of developing resources
- Quality of the infrastructure, and its breadth across the country
- Threatening forces (ethnic or religious divisiveness, unresponsive leadership, and other factors)
- Profitability of similar companies operating in that country

Gary Industries built its new plant in Taiwan. Higher labor costs were outweighed by the availability of skilled engineers and local support industries such as foundries and machine shops. Taiwan's proximity to major Japanese customers offset Thailand's labor-cost advantage for products as heavy and costly to ship as pumps. And finally, Gary now anticipates that its Taiwan subsidiary will be able to establish an assembly plant in mainland China within a few years and thereby regain the advantage of low-cost labor.

Market Research Rules of Thumb

Let's draw together a few rules of thumb from these examples.

• *Can markets be selected without market research?* Yes, they can be. The question is how good a job you can do. The answer might be "Good enough." You might decide, "We are going to Japan," and base that decision on things you have learned bit by bit over a period of time. The golden opportunity might drop into your lap, and you say, "Let's go for it." You might sell to or through a trading company. (See Chapter 5.) You might throw a dart at the map.

• *When should you worry about market research?* You need to worry about researching markets for your products when the outcome of your international sales makes more than an incidental difference to your operations. If you are selling through a trading company, why not just let it worry about the market? It will have its own market insights or contacts, or will do its own market studies. So initially you *can* leave it up to the trading company. But very soon you will need to start making independent soundings. You cannot rely on what is reported back to you. You will be unaware of the movement of the competition, of emerging opportunities, and of needed product refinements. You need to find out who your customers are and follow up with them directly. Find out why they are buying from you and how you can better serve them. You can ride their interest into new markets.

• *What if you find no market?* Suppose you conduct a market study and find no obvious market for your product or service. It is very important for a smaller company to be ruthlessly honest with itself. Hope is probably the greatest trap for entrepreneurs in such a situation. Put a placard on the wall above your desk that reads "Be not self-deceived, yet not overcritical." At the same time, you don't want to be so conservative that you miss out on a deal that will make $10 million for your competitor in a couple of years.

• *What if you find too much market?* Conversely, suppose you conduct an initial market study and discover a handful of markets eagerly awaiting what you offer. Should you go for all of them at the same time? The answer depends on your resources, of course. But many smaller companies overextend themselves, generally because they underestimate the difficulties in getting established in promising Pacific Rim markets. Walk before you run: Find the single best market and go for it. Remember, though, that it's a sound principle of business to spread your risks and not tie up too much of your business in one market. So as soon as you are solid in one market and have some experience, begin looking around for the next one.

Different companies focus on different parts of the market research process, depending on the characteristics of their products. They shortcut many of the steps. In the case examples, not every company completed every step.

Market research is a very expensive undertaking for smaller companies, so it seems obvious to do the least amount you have to, consistent with making a good market decision. Your goal is to find the best sources of information for the least cost to you and do maximum pruning at each step before proceeding to a more expensive one. Many smaller companies have relied on other sources in addition to private market research firms.

In general, the more precedents there are for entering the market, the easier it will be for you to get easy and inexpensive help, and to eliminate some of the expensive steps. On the other hand, the more unique your situation is, the more likely that you will have to undertake a complete market study. Of course, if your unique opportunity pans out, it points to a greater market opportunity as well.

4 | Obtaining Information to Select Your Markets

- *Conducting and commissioning a market study*
- *Comparing different sources of information*
- *Determining when to travel to your new market*

For many companies, the difficulty of obtaining needed information is a major factor in the decision not to enter international trade. The world is awash in information, but what you need is often proprietary, expensive, scattered all over the world, or published only in Japanese.

A Pacific Rim market study prepared by a consultant costs $100,000 and up. Small and medium-size companies often cannot afford to commission or carry out full-fledged market research themselves. If you are one of those companies, the question becomes: How can you obtain the market information you need to make an intelligent decision?

You can get assistance from trading companies, the Departments of Commerce and State, local chambers of commerce, trade organizations, target country trade reps, and many other sources (see Figure 4–1). In this chapter, I describe the best sources, compare them, and summarize the pros and cons for each.

If you are new to international trade, you should first gain general background information by keeping abreast of world events that influence the international marketplace. Focus on learning how political events lead to the opening or closing of economic channels. Also, get specific information related to your industry and potential Pacific Rim markets. Scan announcements and watch for overseas projects that may present opportunities for your company.

Talk to the Department of Commerce and your industry or professional associations. Talk to successful exporters of similar products or services. Review prepared or off-the-shelf reports on your industry and potential markets overseas, and then get focused help from the Commerce Department and its country reps. If necessary, work with a market research professional who is experienced in your product areas and likely markets.

Market Studies

Sometimes, you can get enough information and guidance from informal sources to point you toward definite markets and potential distributors. In other instances,

Figure 4-1.   Sources of market information.

Business publications
Market research
Sources in the target market itself
U.S. government agencies

  · Departments of Commerce and State
  · Small Business Administration
  · Overseas Private Investment Corporation
  · U.S. Agency for International Development
  · U.S. Export-Import Bank

State and local governments and development agencies
World Bank
Private U.S. consulting firms specializing in the target market
Banks, shipping companies, and accounting firms
Industry or trade groups in your line of business
Chambers of commerce
Trade shows
Foreign trade organizations
Cultural organizations
Pacific Rim government representatives of target markets
  (e.g., consulates, embassies, development agencies)
Noncompeting companies from target markets that are doing
  business in the United States

---

you will need a complete market study. Basically, there are four ways to obtain one:

1. Do it yourself.
2. Work with the Department of Commerce.
3. Commission a market research company to carry out the study.
4. Buy a prepared, off-the-shelf study.

Whoever prepares the market study should follow the general approaches outlined in Chapter 3. The final report should cover the following topics:

The Industry
- Definition of the industry: products, services, technologies. Important distinctions among products and applications. Descriptions and technical specs.
- Components of the industry: companies that comprise it.
- Background and history of the industry. Trends and development.
- Baseline production volume and trends.
- Typical uses and applications of the products, services, or technologies.
- Characteristics of this particular product or service that affect its exportability: need for patent protection, export licenses, intellectual property protection, particular resources or manufacturing processes.

Supply

- Structure of the industry. Leading suppliers and market share by region and applications.
- Competition: major players for each segment. Where are they from (United States, third country, the local market)? Do any of the competitors have "captive markets"?
- Other products or services that serve the same needs.
- Market-share trends for each type of competitor.
- Basis of competition: price, service, local supply, quality; hardware versus turnkey; government subsidy to competitors.
- Ease of protecting competitive advantage.

Demand

- Applications of this product or technology in markets being investigated. Are they the same as they are in the United States? Are there any unusual applications? (What is secondary in the United States may be primary elsewhere and vice versa.)
- Demand forecasts.
- Driving factors in the market. What stimulates market growth? How can you take advantage of these factors?
- Segments of the market. For each market segment or application of your product, service, or technology, determine who the buyers are (consumers, industry, government). How fast is each segment growing? What about future market growth? How does the size of market at present compare with its potential? (A current small segment may have very great growth potential.)
- Geographic distribution of potential customers within the target market.
- Regional market opportunities—that is, starting in the target market and expanding outward.

Marketing Environment

- Distribution channels available in the market compared with those ideally needed. What is the availability and quality of agents, distributors, marketing, or production partners? What synergies are available for marketing or production?
- Advertising and promotion channels available.
- Educating the customer. What types of promotion and advertising are needed? How can you increase awareness, especially of the benefits of the new technologies? (Customers may not be aware of this product or may have misconceptions about it. Can you educate them without giving up your secrets?)
- Market-entry strategies available. How easy is it to enter?
- Assistance and incentives available in the target market—for example, tax breaks, demo projects, subsidies by host government to stimulate commercial demand.

- Barriers to market entry:
  —Within the target nation or market
  —Within the United States
- Pricing and cost analysis:
  —For this product, service, or technology; for a competing one
  —For supply from a given location
- Available financing:
  —For customer
  —For company doing the exporting or investing

Conducting Your Own Market Study

Large companies have the resources to have their own people investigate potential markets, but smaller companies normally cannot afford to do so. Instead, they have to rely on information that is already published, or hire people experienced in that market who have trustworthy and pertinent information.

Sources of Information.   It is usually easier to identify the suppliers in a market than it is the potential demand. But supplier information—knowing the characteristics of the industry that provides your products—can give you important clues about existing and potential markets. There are many sources you can research on your own (if you hire a market research company, it will tap the same sources):

- Journal articles on your industry, products, or services. Check the *Guide to Business Periodicals*. Search computer data bases as well.
- Published books on your industry or products. Check the library, catalogs, data bases, and *Books in Print*.
- Reports prepared by relevant industry or trade associations, or by associations in related fields.
- Existing studies, as described later in this chapter. A study that is even partially relevant can save you time and money.
- Commerce Department data on imports and exports of your product or of competing products.
- Data on your industry from such sources as *Standard & Poor's Industry Surveys* and *The Census of Manufacturers*.
- Tearsheets on your competitors' advertisements, from services such as Packaged Facts in New York City.
- Reports on the industry or individual companies prepared by Wall Street investment houses.
- Data on advertising expenditures by companies in your industry, in both

the United States and other nations. Leading National Advertisers, Inc. in New York City and similar commercial information services conduct such surveys. Knowing how much other companies spend on advertising can give you some indication of the size of their operations.

- Consumer audit companies such as A. C. Nielsen and SAMI (for consumer products).
- Catalogs from other companies in the industry that contain technical specifications and product descriptions.
- Annual reports of companies in the industry or Dun & Bradstreet reports on privately held companies.

If you checked all these sources, you'd have quite a stack of information and could develop a very thorough picture of the industry. The market leaders and innovators would become apparent. You would also have the names of experts to contact and interview over the phone about emerging trends, problems, and opportunities. The search would give you a list of other important contacts: manufacturers, wholesalers, retailers, and customers in your industry.

Difficulties in Researching Pacific Rim Markets. It is tough enough collecting market research information in the United States. If you need to collect market data in the Pacific Rim nations, it is even tougher. Even though a lot of information is available, it isn't gathered in one place. Moreover, data won't be comparable from one nation to another, so it's hard to find apples to compare with apples. It's often difficult to find information that pertains directly to your questions, so you may have to impose "creative" interpretations. The information that *is* available is often much more politicized than similar U.S. data: It's hard to get negative information, for one thing. Some of the data won't be translated into English, and some of what is translated will be old. Finally, some of the data you need may not be available at all to outsiders.

In Japan, you will run into the opposite problem—too much information. Japan is an extremely leaky society, and sometimes it seems impossible to keep a business secret there. An immense amount of published information is available from government and industry, trade associations, research organizations, and commercial magazines and newspapers. The problem is not finding the information, but screening and evaluating it so that you can make good business judgments.

Of course, most of it is in Japanese, and indiscriminate translations will yield little of value to you. Much of the material that is in English comes from secondary sources, which you will find too general, too specific about the wrong thing, or of questionable accuracy. Because, in order to gain an edge or to protect themselves, people eagerly watch for leaks of the latest happenings. So much information is leaked that some information leaks are often intentionally misleading or untrue. All this argues for getting assistance from someone familiar with the market.

Working With the Commerce Department

You can supplement your own efforts by using the Commerce Department as a major resource. It won't do your report for you: You will do it yourself with the department's guidance and assistance, drawing from a large number of sources. The Commerce Department has many of its own information sources—in particular, libraries, standard reports, and special reports.

The Country Trade Specialist. You can start working with the Department of Commerce in one of two ways. You can either go to the trade specialist at the closest district office of the Commerce Department or call the department's country desk officer in Washington, D.C., for the country you are interested in. (Addresses and phone numbers are listed in the Appendixes.)

The country specialists in the Department of Commerce (and in the State Department) can give you background on many important questions, including investment climate, attitude toward business, trade barriers to export, and political risk factors. In addition, they will be able to refer you to market research companies that operate in a particular market and to potential distributors, agents, or joint venture partners. They will give you the names of the commercial representatives in the U.S. embassies and the names of people working for U.S. businesses in the country. This is all telephone work.

If you can, make an appointment with a trade specialist at one of the Commerce Department's regional offices. During the meeting, you'll get the best overview of what the Commerce Department can do for you, given your specific needs. Many of the trade specialists are former country reps and are very knowledgeable about the needs of American companies in international trade. They will also point out reports and pertinent statistics on file in the Commerce Department's marketing library, suggest books you can buy from the U.S. Government Printing Office, and explain reports that country reps can research for you in the overseas offices of the Departments of Commerce and State.

The trade specialists will also contact the commercial officer of the U.S. embassy in the country you are investigating and ask for the information you are seeking. And when the time comes, they will provide help in planning your initial trip to that country. This assistance is either free or very inexpensive.

The Commerce Department's commercial officers in each country are familiar with business, political, and economic conditions there. The officer keeps in touch with the U.S. business community in that country, with economic and business policy, with officials from the government, with financial institutions, and with major local business interests. The commercial officer can check up on people and companies you may wish to do business with—whether as customers, as representatives, or as joint venture partners.

Pros and Cons. For a company that is new to international trade, the Department of Commerce offers unbeatable advantages. It maintains offices all over the country and has representatives in every Pacific Rim nation. Many of the reps are knowledgeable specialists who have spent a lot of time in their host nations aiding U.S. businesses by cultivating contacts with local businesses and the government. They are accessible and inexpensive compared with other sources.

Commerce Department information is readily available and is quite reliable in providing general background on commercial activities in each Pacific Rim country. All the data and reports strive to be free of political bias. Furthermore, all the statistical data are in a standardized form. You won't realize the value of this until you start trying to collect data on your own from other sources!

Yet there are several drawbacks to working with the Commerce Department. The information may not be as current as you need. It may not be gathered for the product or service categories you want, so you may have to do some fancy interpretation to get the kind of information you are seeking. Next, as with all such information, the statistics are essentially backward-looking, describing what has already happened. If you have a new product or service, are trying to penetrate a new market, or are seeking a new market niche, it may be difficult to find directly relevant data.

Most Department of Commerce trade specialists are hardworking, conscientious, and experienced. Although many are very good, some are better than others. For one country, you may work with someone with twenty years' experience; for a neighboring country, you may encounter a newly hired staff member who can do little more than help you look things up. It is hit or miss, depending on which office you go to. Many staff positions change after a new U.S. President takes office, so it can be hard maintaining continuity.

Finally, the amount of information available from the Department of Commerce can be overwhelming. Most local Commerce Department libraries suffer from serious understaffing. They can do little more for you than point you toward the type of publication that *may* contain the data you seek. You will be confronted with a numbing mass of reports, with little idea of how to extract and interpret the precise data that you need.

Market research companies often disparage the value of the Commerce Department data and services—and, unfortunately, many smaller businesses believe them. But it should be pointed out that there *are* problems in doing market research with these data: Your product or service may not fall into the standard industry classification (SIC). If you are "piggybacking," i.e., selling subsystems or support services, these may not be separately tracked in the Commerce Department data.

However, if you are just starting out, it is very unwise to pass by the wealth of information and assistance available through government agencies. They may not have everything you want, but they have a great deal to offer. Go with them as far as you can, and then move on to the next source, whether it's doing your own research or working with a consultant or a market research company.

Like the reports from the Department of Commerce, State Department surveys and the CIA's situation reports offer solid, reliable information. They are professional, display consistent quality, and have relatively little political bias. Reports produced by other government agencies and departments are of uneven quality. Some reports are available at low cost and are superficially very attractive. But they may have been *prepared* at low cost as well, often by a consultant who contracted to prepare them.

Hiring a Market Research Company

The effort required to collect, boil down, and interpret research data is a major argument for hiring a market research company. Whether you choose one in the United States or one in your target market, it's essential that the company have experience in your industry and your intended market, so that it is not learning at your expense. You have many other options besides sponsoring a $100,000 field survey that culminates in a customized report.

A market research company with solid experience in the Pacific Rim can help you identify your best markets and detail the restrictions on trade or investment, the incentives, and the market entry strategies open to you. It can put you in touch with people you should talk to and work with, such as potential agents and distributors. It may or may not conduct market tests, but it can put you in touch with the best test marketers and then help you evaluate the research and develop a market strategy.

Forms of Assistance.   You can work with market research companies in a variety of ways:

- *Buy their existing reports.* These contain good current data based on some fieldwork.
- *Sponsor semicustomized research.* They will prepare a report by drawing on their existing reports and general knowledge of the market and by doing some additional fieldwork. They will help you identify and compare potential distributors.
- *Commission a customized study.* The final report will include forward-looking analyses on critical issues and forces influencing future directions of the market; it will also relate them to your product or service. The best consulting companies are attuned to this need.
- *Obtain operational assistance.* Some companies will help you set up your marketing operation, advising you on establishing a local presence, negotiating with the distributor or joint venture partner, and launching your operation.

Cost of Market Research Services.   You can pay anything from $1,000 to $100,000 or more for a market study, as shown:

Type of Study	Cost
Off-the-shelf report	$1,000-$2,000
Multiclient report	$3,000-$10,000
Individual customized study:	
With little travel	$10,000-$50,000
With more travel and fieldwork	$100,000 and up

Finding the Right Company.   Whether you hire a company that is based in the United States or one that is based in your target market, you must make sure it has experience pertinent to your needs and in your target markets. There are any number of market research companies; the trick is finding the best one for your needs. Look in the *Findex* catalog, described below, which lists hundreds of research companies that publish off-the-shelf reports. Many of these companies also conduct customized market research. By seeing what types of reports they have produced, you can gain some idea of their skill and relevant experience.

In many Pacific Rim markets, you can hire an in-country research company. The more mature the market is, the easier it is to find appropriate researchers and the more reliable they will be. It's easiest to find good research companies in Australia, New Zealand, Japan, Hong Kong, and Singapore. It's toughest in China. The other Pacific Rim nations lie in between.

You may have the greatest difficulty finding a market research company that can conduct studies for consumer products or services across national or cultural boundaries. A company in Singapore, for example, may prove inadequate for studies in nearby Malaysia. And in-depth studies of emerging consumer preferences are much rarer than in American markets.

You can obtain a list of qualified organizations from the U.S. embassy in your target market. You must screen candidates carefully to make sure of the following:

- They have a track record, a good reputation, and widespread knowledge of your industry.
- Their final report will be based mainly on primary field data.
- Their report will contain very specific recommendations, not broad generalizations.
- They have a proven ability not just to gather basic data, but to analyze and interpret them and apply them to your specific needs.
- They will provide you with a locally based contact.
- They will give you access to the raw data underlying the final report.

Most U.S. companies that have succeeded in Japanese markets have used outside market research companies to analyze their market and their competitors and to report on their competitors' motivations. In Japan, competitive aims often differ greatly from what we are accustomed to in the United States. The booklet *Sources of Information in Japan,* by David Baskervill of the American Electronics

Association office in Japan, summarizes the sources of information that are available in English. (See the Appendixes.)

Advantages of Market Research Over Commerce Department Data. The Commerce Department can point out alternative markets or distributors for you, but it cannot make direct recommendations. It can give you a list of distributors and some basic evaluative information, but you will need to make the final evaluation yourself before selecting a market.

The primary mission of the Commerce Department is to promote exports, not direct investment overseas, so you will find it easier to get information on exporting products or licensing than on establishing a joint venture or building a factory. Traditional government policy has been that promoting exports does more for the U.S. trade balance than does promoting overseas investment. However, since investment is becoming so important, even for companies just entering international trade, the government is being forced to change this stance. It is becoming increasingly possible to get government assistance with setting up overseas operations.

Even so, if you are interested in a form of Pacific Rim trade that involves direct investment, you are more likely to get better results from a private consultant or marketing organization that is skilled in locating sites for facilities, finding suitable joint venture partners, negotiating agreements, and uncovering sources of investment capital.

Even if you work with a consultant or market research company, it's wise to do some initial research on your own, just so you will know what to ask the paid consultant for. You get the most from a consultant if you know exactly what you need. Ask a general question, you get a general answer. Ask a specific question, you get a specific answer. Work first with the Commerce Department to get answers to your general questions so that when you need an expensive consultant, you can request specific results. You will be better able to evaluate the consultant's proposals and recommendations and the primary information that is ultimately provided.

Buying an Off-the-Shelf Study

A report tailored to a company's specific needs is usually the most desirable and valuable research tool. But many smaller businesses don't want to pay for an individualized research report. As a result, a new industry has sprung up—companies that produce market studies ahead of time and then offer them for sale at prices ranging from $1,000 to $2,000. These off-the-shelf reports are often prepared by the same companies that do customized research, using the same methods and with the same high-quality results. But since the reports are sold to a number of buyers, they cost much less.

The best type of off-the-shelf report is the multiclient study. A market research organization approaches several companies in an industry and proposes to perform a top-notch, in-depth market study for them at a cost of, say, $100,000. If ten companies sign up for the report, each of them pays $10,000. Subsequently, the report may be sold to other companies for a higher price. Off-the-shelf reports are also available from Wall Street investment houses, market audit organizations, trade associations, and various government agencies.

There are also several services and directories that can help you find the report that best meets your needs. One is *Findex: The Directory of Market Research Reports, Studies, and Surveys,* which describes nearly 10,000 report titles from over 350 U.S. and foreign sources. This directory is available in many Commerce Department offices and other libraries.

There is a spectrum of report quality. At the low end are the "grad student" reports, based on armchair information. Next are reports containing good current data, based on some fieldwork. The best ones contain proactive research that identifies and analyzes data on critical issues and drivers of future events and relates the information to your product or service.

There are two main hazards to buying low-cost reports, whether they are government reports or ones produced by private companies. First, you get what you pay for. People who are preparing reports on a low budget cannot invest much time in obtaining meaningful, firsthand information. Their reports are often based solely on published information available in libraries, and they contain a lot of general demographic data. Be aware, in particular, of these pitfalls:

- Information that pertains only indirectly to your needs. You will have to do a lot of creative interpretation.
- Lack of timeliness. Events change rapidly. Even year-old information can be obsolete, especially information about a competitive environment and economic policies.
- Inaccuracies or gaps in the data that may not be obvious without close scrutiny. Stay alert, too, to incompleteness, especially with negative information.

Second, low-cost reports may be biased or politicized. Some are written not just to provide reliable data to private business, but to serve a particular purpose or to advance some particular country's or agency's objective—such as fostering trade with a certain nation or promoting a new technology or commodity. Such reports often paint a slightly rosier picture than they should.

Despite these drawbacks, off-the-shelf reports can be useful—if they are inexpensive enough. They can bring together data that will save you many trips to the library. The risk is that if they do paint too rosy a picture and you believe them, you may invest a lot of money before discovering the downside. You must find ways to double-check the report. If the data seem very tempting, find another confirming source before taking the leap. If you can, check out the background of the report. Find out what its purpose was and what methods were used. This is phone work.

Secondary vs. Primary Data

Plus for Secondary Data—Minus for Primary Data

- Prepared reports are quicker to obtain than customized research.
- Secondary data are much cheaper than primary research.
- Off-the-shelf studies often cover most of the information needed.
- Prepared reports are a good way to start. Pay for only the incremental primary field research you need.

Minus for Secondary Data—Plus for Primary Data

- The data you need may not be available or published.
- Off-the-shelf reports are not precisely targeted. Customized studies can be tailored to your specific needs.
- The information may be out of date. The data in an off-the-shelf report will be less timely than primary data.
- Everyone else has the information. Many other companies are seeing the same data as you are.

After evaluating the report, double-check everything, since every single source is likely to slant information. Even trusted agents and representatives or managers of subsidiaries are likely to tell you what they think you want to hear or to slant the information in a way that will help them.

Act now! To the extent that you rely on published reports to make marketing decisions, remember that you must be prepared to move quickly to take advantage of opportunities you spot. Companies all over the world are reading those reports at the same time that you are and are geared up to respond rapidly.

Unconventional Market Selection Processes

Many, many companies select markets without conducting a full-fledged market study. I reiterate this point to make sure you are not frightened away from overseas expansion by the prospect of conducting or paying for a regular market research study. This section includes a few more examples of companies that identified markets in informal or unorthodox ways without the expense of a full market study.

Keeping Your Antennae Tuned

Chapter 1 describes how Golden Gate University in San Francisco identified an opportunity to establish an MBA program for managers of corporations in Malaysia. President Otto Butz emphasized that he wasn't looking at any overseas market in particular, but that he always kept his eyes open for opportunities. The idea for the Malaysian MBA program came out of a casual conversation he had with a Malaysian banker at a reception.

For Golden Gate University, the market research was limited to testing that particular opportunity to see if it was feasible and could be initiated with minimum cost and risk. Golden Gate accomplished this by having its customers—a group of Malaysian corporations—use their influence to obtain the needed approval of the Malaysian government and to guarantee a certain number of students at a specified tuition.

Once the Malaysian program was under way—and successful—Golden Gate used more formal market studies to check out Pacific Rim opportunities in Singapore, Indonesia, and Australia.

Keep your own eyes open to opportunity by scanning relevant publications. You already read trade and professional journals with an eye to spotting domestic opportunities. Subscribe to publications that cover Pacific Rim opportunities as well—for example, *Asian Wall Street Journal Weekly, Asia Week, Commerce Business Daily,* and *Business America. Business America* has a section called "Trade and Investment Opportunities" that lists what are, in essence, want ads from companies around the world wishing to do a particular type of business with the United States. Here are a few entries.

> Indonesia. P. T. wishes to contact U.S. firms interested in establishing a licensing arrangement and/or providing technical assistance for producing cosmetics products or pharmaceuticals preparations for human use. Terms of interest will be negotiated. [*Followed by contact.*]

> Taiwan. The American Institute in Taiwan has been informed that the China Steel Corporation, Coal Tar Project, has been given preliminary approval by the Taiwan authorities to invest $20 million, including $4 million in foreign equipment purchases. The project needs foreign engineering design assistance.

> Australia. Joint Venture Opportunity. Australian company is looking for joint venture partners to develop diatomaceous earth deposit covering 200 hectares.

> Australia. Licensing Opportunity. Company seeks technology to manufacture fireproof plaster using a combination of gypsum and vermiculite.

By the same token, since American technical publications are distributed internationally, people all over the world will see any ads and articles you place in them. You can gauge potential demand for your product or service by tabulating and responding to inquiries from various sources. Whenever you get an inquiry, reply promptly. Don't be put off by poor print quality, inaccuracies, or grammatical errors. Send complete information on your products or services, including technical specs, pricing, terms, and delivery. If a pro forma invoice is requested, include one. Respond by airmail, to a post office box if given. It is not uncommon to ask for payment for any requested samples. If you have distributors for that area, send the lead on to them.

Using Your Customers for Market Research

Once you are established in a Pacific Rim market, a major way to keep your finger on the pulse of that market is through your customers. Electrical South of Greensboro, North Carolina, a manufacturer of solid state AC motor controls, works closely with all its overseas customers to stay in touch with what foreign competition is doing. This gives the company opportunity to meet any competitive features that will soon be introduced into the United States. Its policy is to follow up any lead or query within twenty-four hours. The company has installed telex and fax equipment to speed overseas communications, thus eliminating the delays of several weeks characteristic of traditional overseas correspondence.

Some companies find imaginative ways to obtain market information through customers and thus avoid expensive market research studies. Tracom, Inc. of Fort Worth, Texas, sells pretested used components for heavy machinery. The president of this small company became interested in exporting and chose Australia as a first market because it seemed similar to Texas. To anticipate the needs of potential Australian buyers, he examined his domestic buyers to pinpoint similar needs and conditions in Australia. Through the Commerce Department, he then got names of 400 potential customers and sent them telexes outlining his company's products. Tracom answered the first query instantly and received an order for $8,000. The president of the client company invited Tracom's president to Australia, where Tracom obtained several more orders. Within six months, it had received $470,000 in business from Australia.

Tracking Critical Factors

The greater your potential commitment to a market, the more you need to keep an eye on a broad range of factors that can affect your performance in that market. If you are selling through a trading company, you have little concern about the threat of expropriation or a national monetary crisis. But if you have resources and investments directly committed to a market, you need to pay attention to factors that lie outside a strictly economic market study. Let's call these "critical factors." Besides the obvious market factors, these critical factors include:

- Political factors in each of your market areas (changes in national leaders; major policy shifts)
- Competitive factors, especially broad changes in the competitive environment
- U.S. economic and political factors (new trade legislation enacted by the U.S. government; shifts in exchange rates)
- Global economic factors that affect all international trade, including yours; for example, the outcome of the GATT negotiations, or the impact of the 1992 economic integration of Europe

Your Early Warning System

Whether you are considering entering a market for the first time or monitoring a market you are already invested in, you need to track these critical factors, both to get an early warning of impending problems and to spot opportunities before your competition does. If you are seriously evaluating Pacific Rim markets, you must confront questions like these: How do you evaluate investment opportunities in the Philippines under the measures taken by the new government? How will potential ethnic and religious strife in Malaysia affect the stability of that economy? Will the political liberalization of Korea and Taiwan affect the openness of the economies of China and Indonesia? How will Hong Kong's reversion to Chinese control in 1997 affect doing business there?

You will need to become an avid watcher of the outcome of trade negotiations and the fate of protectionist trade legislation. If legislation goes one way, it means opportunity. If it goes the other way, it may mean a setback—or a different opportunity. Watch the effect of U.S. pressure on Asian nations to open up their markets to American goods; if those nations begin making concessions to that pressure, look for the opportunities for you.

Tracking critical factors requires an ability to make judgments with only fragmentary and tangential information. Thus you must seek corroborative reports, and double- or triple-check whenever possible. Much of this process is just one step removed from gazing at a crystal ball!

Adopting a contrary approach can be valuable. Whenever the media start spouting the same conventional wisdom and "administration spokespeople" all get on one bandwagon, begin to suspect that the opposite position has more than a grain of truth in it. In the hue and cry over failing American competitiveness, many businesses are quietly establishing lucrative, competitive market share in Japan. As national leaders complain about increasing foreign investment in the United States, several U.S. governors fly to Tokyo to seek companies to invest in their states.

A Look Beneath the Surface

One pitfall in tracking these critical factors is being swayed by the superficial. Media reports are often full of doom and gloom. During crucial negotiations, many national leaders make extreme statements of the "all is probably lost" variety. But this may just be a form of jockeying for negotiating advantage, and such pessimistic, alarming statements often come just before a breakthrough.

The superficiality of most TV news stories can also be deceiving. We see the riot police and the tear gas on prime time newscasts, but we have a hard time sizing up the desire for continued growth and stability in the hearts of the people. Yet through all the upheaval, four major Asian nations—China, the Philippines, Taiwan, and Korea—have moved decisively toward less authoritarian regimes.

You must learn to look beneath the surface. There is no formula, but keep several things in mind. You must ask yourself: Are the players involved serious negotiators who will get the best they can while maintaining a commitment to the smooth operation of the system? Or are they ideologues who are willing to lose a lot in order to make a point, save face, or preserve principles? As long as pragmatists are running nations, reaching mutually acceptable agreements will remain a priority in spite of all the bluster and dire warnings. Also, regardless of the goals and statements of national leaders, their powers are limited, and you must look at the quality and motivation of the forces behind them as well—for example, the U.S. Congress and the Diet in Japan. Finally, you need to keep an eye on the interests of contending forces and special interests. Just as in the United States, the final outcome of U.S. trade negotiations with Japan and Korea will represent a balance between the internationalist and the isolationist forces within each country.

Having an economic stake in a distant market gives you wonderful focus, and you will soon understand the inner workings of the government of your Pacific Rim market. If you are not used to keeping your finger on the pulse of distant economic events, or if you don't have the time to do so, you may want to get some expert help. In any overseas operation there is an important, but as yet unmentioned player whom I will call the global information specialist. The role may be filled by you or by someone else in your company, or you may want to rely on the market research consultant you worked with initially. If you are the decision maker for Pacific Rim trade, you cannot totally delegate this function. You must hone your ability to spot and interpret pertinent items as you are scanning publications or watching the news. Your info specialist and others will feed you key facts, but you will make the decisions on what moves to make in your markets, how to avoid trouble, and so on.

Traveling to Your New Market

Every export business that does more than sell through a trading company needs to travel to its new markets before making final decisions. There are two maxims for your travel:

"Lay groundwork from afar. When you are onto something, go in person."

"Once you have something established, your periodic personal presence is imperative."

Obtaining Firsthand Information

Take your first trip to the country only after you have narrowed down the choices and have obtained all the information you can without being there. Lay as much groundwork as possible so you don't waste time and money on markets that don't pan out. Then turn to the crucial information that can be obtained only by traveling to the market. Here are the things you need to do or find out firsthand:

1. *Solidify contacts.* When you make your initial trip to your target country, one of your main purposes is to meet with potential joint venture partners, distributors, government officials, and major customers. You need to size up the people you are going to deal with and enable them to size you up as well. Conduct discussions and negotiations with an agent or distributor and perhaps make the final selection of a business partner.

2. *Meet face to face.* Because personal relationships are so important for doing business in Pacific Rim nations, you are unlikely to find anyone who is willing to work with you in any substantial manner without a face-to-face meeting. (The corollary is that you should be wary of anyone who *would* do business without meeting you.)

3. *Double-check information.* Verify the information that you have gathered at home. Check out your potential distributors or joint venture partners by talking with local bankers, American foreign service officials, representatives of other American companies, and other contacts.

4. *Check out the market.* See for yourself what conditions are, how your product or service will be received, and what modifications will be required. See how your product or service will actually be delivered to the customers. If you can, talk to people who might be potential customers. If your product will be sold commercially, go into local stores, look on the shelves, and see how your package will compare with the competition. Even if you hire experts to do your exportizing for you, you will want to check the physical surroundings yourself during your visit.

5. *Get needed "area information."* If you are selling to a government, find out how easy or difficult it is to obtain the needed approvals and licenses from the government. Find out what procedures and fees are required and, if you can, begin to obtain needed approvals and licenses. If you are bidding on a project, size up the on-site conditions in order to make a meaningful bid. Talk with the people who will be responsible for project management to see how capable and committed they are.

If you are busy running your domestic operations, can you delegate this job to someone else? Not really. The top person or people should go, as well as the people who will routinely service the market. Top people will spot more things—and peer negotiation is important.

Getting the Most From Your Visit

Visiting a Pacific Rim country is very expensive, in terms of both time and money, so it's important to make the most of your trip. This means you must:

1. *Make thorough preparations.* Line up appointments ahead of time. Identify the people you need to see beforehand and contact them by phone, letter, or fax to arrange appointments. Or at least let them know that you will be in the country and would like to meet with them.

2. *Seek government assistance.* In many circumstances, you will know ahead of time who the people are that you need to meet, and will have had correspondence and conversation with them beforehand. If you are uncertain about what people you should contact, the Departments of Commerce and State and the Overseas Private Investment Corporation (OPIC) can provide valuable help in identifying and setting up face-to-face meetings with various contacts. This is true whether you're going on your own or as part of a sponsored trade mission. Read carefully through the next section for these and other sources of relevant market information and assistance.

3. *Allow more time than you think is necessary.* Things won't move as quickly as you expect or want them to. Appointments may not take place on schedule; information you thought would be available won't be. If you schedule yourself too tightly, you'll have to leave before you get everything done—and that may mean a second trip.

4. *Defray costs.* To help defray the cost of travel, find a way to make your visit pay for itself—for example, by making an initial sale. If you conclude an agreement with an agent or a distributor or with a joint venture partner, you may actually contract for an initial sale. If you are investigating the feasibility of a major contract with a government or a development bank, you may be able to sell a demonstration project.

Other Sources of Market Information

There are a number of other sources of information you can draw on, in addition to the Commerce Department and market research companies, to identify the best Pacific Rim markets for export or investment. The ways to contact all these sources of information are listed in the Appendixes.

Federal Agencies

The Department of Commerce is only one of many sources of market-related information available from the federal government.

U.S. Department of State. The State Department publishes "background notes" on close to 200 countries and territories. Short (six- to ten-page) pamphlets give an overview of the society, history, geography, government, and economy of foreign states. For these and other State Department resources, contact the department's Office of Commercial Affairs.

U.S. Embassies and Consulates Overseas.   One of the prime responsibilities of U.S. embassies and consulates is to help exporters. The Foreign Commercial Service of the Commerce Department and agricultural attachés from the Agriculture Department handle export assistance programs and market research projects through the embassies and consulates. They do company credit checks, gather leads for trade investment and licensing, identify and check out potential distributors, help companies participate in foreign trade fairs and missions, advertise and promote new products and services, and assist U.S. companies in any trade complaints against foreign businesses.

It's important to realize that all the economic and trade information collected in the U.S. government's Pacific Rim offices is not necessarily sent back home to some central trade data base. The most complete and up-to-date information is likely to be available in the U.S. embassy or consulate located in a Pacific Rim nation.

If you are planning to visit a Pacific Rim country, you should contact the U.S. commercial officers there first. If you visit the embassy, you can get help from its staff in arranging meetings with government and business officials, building a list of prospective customers, and analyzing the market potential for your product or service in that country. They will give you practical information on business culture and practices, regulations, and standards that can affect your product or service, and can show you how to use their library and market research resources.

U.S. embassies will help you find local partners for licensing, joint ventures, or other direct investment. You can publicize your product, service, or technology through the magazine *Commercial News USA* and through embassy newsletters. To find a suitable partner, you can work directly with the embassy in your target nation. Commercial officers will do a customized search for contacts. For products, they will help locate potential agents or distributors as part of the Agent/Distributor Service (ADS), for which there is a nominal charge. They will conduct a similar search for a licensee or investment partner for no charge. Caveat: You will receive a list of potential contacts with no comments or recommendations.

OPIC.   OPIC offers several kinds of information and assistance. Its primary mission is to make loan guarantees for investments in designated developing economies. (See Chapter 9.) OPIC prepares reports on investment climates and investment opportunities in the countries it works with, so its services are less relevant for companies interested only in exporting.

OPIC can help you arrange contacts with private investors and top officials in your target market. When you are ready to travel to the country, OPIC can help set up meetings with local businesspeople who are potential joint venture partners or distributors. If OPIC is active in one of your target countries, you should contact the nearest representative.

If your first trip to a country is part of a trade mission, keep in mind that OPIC as well as the Commerce Department sponsors such missions. OPIC's trade missions help participants identify and size up particular investment opportunities in the target market. For such a trip you can expect to spend several thousand dollars, which is a very reasonable cost.

Agency for International Development (AID).   AID administers most U.S. foreign economic assistance programs through grants and loans to foreign governments to procure products and services from U.S. sources. Each year, AID buys millions of dollars' worth of consulting services, social services, building and construction equipment, and engineering designs from overseas suppliers. Opportunities are publicized in *Commerce Business Daily,* published by the Commerce Department, and in AID information bulletins, which are available on request.

U.S. Department of Agriculture—Foreign Agricultural Service (FAS).   FAS is one of the most effective exporter service agencies in the U.S. government. Its agricultural commodities specialists analyze foreign market data and advise agriculture exporters on international trade. They are linked to the agricultural attachés in the U.S. embassies abroad. They can advise you on selecting and entering any Pacific Rim markets that handle agriculture-related products or technologies. FAS agricultural specialists work closely with companies that sell technology and consulting skills applicable to agriculture—for example, genetic crop development, food processing, irrigation, and animal breeding technology.

U.S. Department of Transportation.   The Federal Highway Administration (FHA) and the Federal Aviation Administration (FAA) supply overseas opportunities to U.S. service companies, manufacturers, and engineering firms. Contact the FHA for technical assistance in programs involving highway planning, contract administration, design, construction, maintenance materials, traffic and safety, surveying, photogrammetry, management, and computerization. The FAA has overseas contracts for avionics, aeronautical and civil aerospace products, and related services.

U.S. Army Corps of Engineers.   The Army Corps of Engineers contracts for engineering, design, and construction of various military and infrastructure projects.

Department of Housing and Urban Development (HUD)—Office of International Affairs.   Businesses involved in construction, engineering, city planning, and architecture should contact HUD and request the pamphlet *Selected Publications Checklist, Department of Housing and Urban Development,* which has sections on basic utilities, country profiles, design, international business, planning and land development, and other topics.

Development Agencies

World Bank. The World Bank makes loans of billions of dollars each year. Most procurement is based on international competitive bidding. There are opportunities to sell many different kinds of products, as well as consulting and engineering services, to projects financed by the World Bank. To find out about opportunities, ask to be put on the mailing list. If you wish to register with the World Bank, request a copy of its *Guide to Completing the Consulting Firm Registration Form.* The standardized registration form provides the data for the DACON computer data base, which is also used by the Asian Development Bank. Registration forms should be sent to the DACON Receiving Center at the World Bank.

Companies wishing to sell products or services to the World Bank can learn of opportunities by subscribing to the biweekly *Development Form Business Edition,* which has information on the World Bank and the Asian Development Bank. Order it from the United Nations Publications Sales Office.

International Monetary Fund (IMF). IMF monitors the economies of over a hundred member nations. Any company needing a comprehensive risk analysis of an overseas market should contact IMF's Public Affairs/Public Relations Office.

Asian Development Bank (ADB). ADB works in a way similar to the World Bank. (See Chapter 9.) For information on opportunities for U.S. companies, request *Guidelines for Procurement Under Asian Development Bank Loans* and *Guidelines on the Use of Consultants by the Asian Development Bank and Its Borrowers.* For registration and general information, contact the Office of the U.S. Director.

State and Local Government Assistance

Most states and many cities have established their own offices or agencies to help promote exports and overseas investment. These offices vary widely by the types of services they offer and how much help they have actually provided to companies in overseas Pacific Rim trade.

Export Promotion Agencies. As of early 1988, thirty-six states offered full-service export education and promotion programs, thirty-two states maintained offices overseas, ten states had export finance programs, and nine states had export trading companies. (See Chapter 9.) In addition, some states have set up special programs to assist particular industries—for example, the California Energy Commission's energy export program.

Superficially, the services of state agencies may appear to duplicate those of the Commerce Department. (For example, many states sponsor trade missions.) However, state agencies can offer a greater depth of information on the particular industries and products important to that state, and if your products fit into the categories they emphasize, your company may be able to get much more directed assistance than it can from the Commerce Department. Also, state agencies may have more local offices and thus be more accessible.

Companies that have used state offices make several observations. These offices promote the importance of foreign trade and match up companies with similar interests. But the knowledgeability of staff members varies tremendously. Further, many of the agencies focus on particular industries, and if yours falls outside those industries the agencies will be of limited help to you. State agencies are strong in their lobbying efforts and in trade missions, but weak in providing assistance with obtaining trade finance.

State services offer a great deal of information—some of it valuable and hard to obtain in any other way. Yet there are important gaps in the information they can provide, and the information they do have is often dated. They seem to focus more on studies done by government and academia than on studies commissioned by private organizations. For example, the California World Trade Commission does not subscribe to the information update services of Rand Corporation, Business International, or SRI International—which, by the way, are all located in California.

Nonetheless, state and local programs are becoming more sophisticated and more serious every year and are providing more comprehensive services, including assistance in obtaining financing (even loan guarantees), as described in Chapter 9. A new relationship is emerging, with the Commerce Department as the wholesaler of trade information, and the states as its distributors.

So contact your state export promotion agency. Even if that agency is not the most dynamic, make sure it knows you exist. Get your company in its files. Question staff people very closely about the results they have produced for other companies in your industry. What deals have they actually helped put together?

Chambers of Commerce.   Many chambers of commerce in larger cities have international trade sections. Besides offering general trade information, they are often a good resource for making contact with other companies involved in international trade.

Foreign Government Assistance

Pacific Rim Consulates and Trade Offices.   Every Pacific Rim nation except Taiwan and Hong Kong has an embassy in Washington and consulates in other cities. Since Hong Kong is politically a British colony (until 1997), its trade affairs are handled through the Hong Kong Economic and Trade Office of the British consulate. And since Taiwan (Republic of China) was "derecognized" by the United States in favor of mainland China, it has no consulates. In the United States, the Coordinating Council for North American Affairs (CCNAA) and the Far East Trade Service perform the same trade and political functions for Taiwan.

Consular officials from Pacific Rim nations will refer you to organizations in the United States that specialize in trade and investment activities. The biggest drawback to working with these organizations is that their trade offices are located in just a few cities, mainly on the East Coast and the West Coast. However, a number of Pacific Rim nations have sent their own trade delegations on tours throughout the United States to seek out companies that wish to trade with them or invest there.

The basic job of these trade offices is to increase U.S. imports from Pacific Rim nations and U.S. investment in those nations. So they are not your first line of help for exporting to Pacific Rim countries, but they provide a valuable complement to the Commerce Department. If the type of overseas business you intend to operate involves direct investment, they will probably be a better source of information than the Commerce Department. If you're interested in exporting, stay with the Commerce Department. Regardless of your goal, a Pacific Rim trade office can provide a wealth of information in many areas: the general background of the country, the culture and infrastructure, demographic and economic facts, the business climate and business conditions, rules and regulations for doing business, trade regulations and restrictions, economic policy that affects foreign business, and potential government and industry contacts in the country. The office may be able to refer you to bankers, potential distributors, and other local business contacts as well.

If you are interested in investing in the country, the trade office will become interested in you. If you have something of value, wheels will begin turning. Trade officials can tell you what types of investments are being sought, what the requirements and restrictions are, where you can locate, and what resources and incentives are available. They will also help you set up appointments with potential joint venture partners, bankers, and government officials.

Keep in mind, however, that—as in all government bureaucracies—you are getting the official line, which might differ somewhat from real life. Trade officials may be more attuned to macropolicies than to individual businesses and industries. You will be less likely to hear about ways to work around trade barriers. But if the officials are forthright about ongoing economic policy debates and you listen carefully, you may pick up some clues about future opportunities.

External Trade Organizations.   Japan, Taiwan, and Korea—which have big trade surpluses with the United States—maintain external trade organizations in the United States to help American companies locate markets or investment opportunities in their countries. These organizations are interested in attracting

U.S. exports, and they can provide valuable assistance in linking you with trading companies or distributors in their countries. This will help you break into their markets, *if* your products or services may be imported there.

Foreign Government Officials.   If you are home and wish to contact an official of a Pacific Rim government, by all means go through its embassy or consulate in the United States. If you're in that country, you may do better to contact an official directly. If you know the person (or office) you need, contact him directly to save time. However, if you are not certain, contact the highest-ranking person you can. In contrast to the diplomatic etiquette of some countries, the rule for contacting officials in the government ministries of the Pacific Rim is, "Start at the top." Even though the top official often will not see you personally but will refer you to some lower official, you're more likely to get needed attention if the referral comes from the top down rather than from a receptionist at the front door. Again, U.S. government agencies can be of value here in arranging for you to meet the highest official of the appropriate ministry.

Trade Association and Private Industry Assistance

Industry and Professional Trade Associations.   Professional and industry trade associations are extremely valuable sources of information for the early stages of market research. These associations can often obtain confidential, unpublished data from their members. The larger associations maintain an international staff and collect their own trade data. They may have contacts with counterpart organizations in foreign nations. You should check not only the association from your own industry, but also associations that have strong representation in a Pacific Rim market sector complementary to yours. This could be important if you apply your technologies or business concepts to market niches that are different from those you pursue in the United States. For example, a company selling an industrial product may see an opportunity to sell it for entertainment purposes and thus wish to affiliate with another trade association. Through trade associations, you can:

- *Identify potential Pacific Rim buyers or distributors and obtain commercial leads and market information on Pacific Rim markets.* Trade publications and newsletters are sources of valuable information and leads. Check the articles, advertisements, and inquiry cards.
- *Make contacts with people from other companies who have differing types of experience in international trade.* Get expert advice. Some members will be experts in international trade and be willing to assist the novice. Associations with a heavy interest in international trade often sponsor seminars or conferences for companies that are interested in entering those markets.
- *Participate in domestic trade shows that attract overseas buyers and join*

trade missions to Pacific Rim countries. Many trade events are jointly sponsored by the Department of Commerce and a trade organization (for example, the American Electronics Association).

- *Contact foreign trade organizations and associations.* Link up with members of parallel trade associations in Pacific Rim markets. (Membership directories include lists of overseas members.) You may be able to find a business in your field that is interested in carrying your line along with its own.

Trade associations with large international memberships (such as electronics, software, and engineering) can be valuable sources for potential overseas business partners. Through meetings or directory listings you may identify a company that would be interested in handling your product or service in its market. If your association is not large enough to have an international division or affiliates, it can still help you identify a relevant association that does. You should also check the publications listed in the Appendixes for relevant associations and organizations in the United States.

Export Seminars.   There has been a proliferation of seminars on export and international trade, many of them focused on the Pacific Rim. They fall into four general categories:

1. Seminars and conferences aimed at executives and managers of multinational companies.
2. Seminars focusing on cultural contacts and the business culture of an overseas nation. These seminars focus on areas covered in Chapter 8: styles of communication, appropriate and inappropriate behavior, selling and negotiating, and so on. They are aimed at executives who are about to travel to the country on business for the first time.
3. Seminars aimed at people who would like to start an export business out of a "spare room." These seminars focus on packaging products, shipping and documentation, and preparing a package in order to obtain a bank loan.
4. Seminars for the entrepreneurial heads of going businesses who are considering international trade.

Seminars aimed at entrepreneurs are by far the hardest to find. (That is one reason I have written this book.) The majority of seminar leaders are managers of multinational companies who are unfamiliar with the concerns of smaller entrepreneurial businesses. Nevertheless, these seminars can provide a valuable introduction to many of the topics and concepts of overseas trade and can be a valuable source of contacts. This is particularly true of seminars sponsored by trade or professional associations, at which you can meet executives of companies with similar concerns.

Seminars for companies new to the export business are sponsored regularly by the Commerce Department, the Small Business Administration, and various state export promotion agencies. In many cases, these will be your best bet for an initial exposure to international trade.

Banks.   In Chapter 9 I talk about getting information on trade finance from banks. Banks can also be sources of information pertinent to selecting markets: Many provide market research information, supply source contacts in Pacific Rim markets, and help in identifying and checking out potential distributors or joint venture partners. Banks involved in international trade should also have information on available financing programs.

Start with your own bank. If you are a good customer, your banker will readily introduce you to his counterparts in Pacific Rim banks, and these bankers will be among your best sources of information. Even if your bank is not a large one, you may be surprised to learn that it has overseas correspondent banks in the markets you are investigating. Then seek out banks with Pacific Rim operations and banks from Pacific Rim nations, especially Australia, Japan, China, Taiwan, and Hong Kong. Some of these banks are truly global financial institutions. They are used to doing business all over the world, so you need not limit yourself to questions about doing business in their home country.

Accounting Firms.   Increasingly, the largest accounting organizations are getting into international trade and are publishing reports and guidebooks for their clients. These reports are very good at technical analysis but are often weak on human and cultural factors.

Freight Forwarders and Shipping Companies.   Freight forwarders and shipping companies provide invaluable information to businesses that are intending to export their products. They have much information that can help you answer your market study questions.

Trade Missions.   Trade missions are in vogue. Participating in one can be very useful, especially in the later stages of your market selection process. They are sponsored by the Commerce Department, various state export promotion organizations, industry trade organizations, cities, and universities. They are also sponsored by some Pacific Rim nations, especially Taiwan, Japan, and China.

Trade missions are valuable for companies interested in exporting as well as for companies interested in establishing a facility in a country. Some trade missions go to only one country; others may tour several countries. As a first exposure to business conditions and opportunities in the Pacific Rim, trade missions can be invaluable—even in the relatively open nations where it is easy to do business. In China, participating in a trade mission may be the only feasible way for a small company to break into a market. The contacts you make by participating in a trade mission provide the entrée to further investigation that you may have no other way of obtaining.

During your trip, a government agency—the State Department, the Commerce Department, or a state agency—may be able to line up meetings with local businesspeople and government officials that would be difficult for you to arrange by yourself. Some people have suggested that Pacific Rim government officials feel more comfortable working with their counterparts in the U.S. government than they do with representatives of business, so having a government agency intercede on your behalf can help your cause. Trade missions are designed to stimulate trade, and if you lay the proper groundwork, you may be able to make enough sales during the trip to pay for it.

To find out about upcoming trade missions, contact a regional office of the Department of Commerce, your industry or trade organization, or your state export promotion agency. Typically, trade missions are announced nearly a year in advance. The Commerce Department will probably have listings of trade missions sponsored by Pacific Rim nations, since many are cosponsored by the Commerce Department.

If it's appropriate for your product or service, you can multiply the impact of attending a trade mission by coordinating the visit with an international trade show or exhibition, particularly one sponsored or promoted by the Department of Commerce in your target nation. The Commerce Department publishes information on upcoming fairs and exhibitions in its *Overseas Export Calendar.* The department will help you arrange an exhibit space and will advise you on designing your exhibit, displaying your products, and shipping them to the exhibition.

American Chambers of Commerce in the Pacific Rim (AMCHAMs). Most Pacific Rim nations have chamber-type associations of American companies doing business there. If you are investing in the Pacific Rim, you will undoubtedly want to affiliate with these associations. They are a community of like-minded people and are probably far more valuable to you than members of your chamber of commerce back home. Contact the chambers of commerce for business leads in the Pacific Rim. When preparing for your first visit, making arrangements to meet with AMCHAM members should be a top priority. The AMCHAM may put together a special meeting for you, perhaps a "briefing breakfast," attended by local people in your industry, bankers, U.S. commercial officers, and other key people.

These offices often work very closely with the U.S. embassies to promote U.S. products or services and investments in licensing opportunities. The Appendixes list the Pacific Rim American chambers of commerce and business associations. For a free listing entitled *American Chambers of Commerce Abroad,* contact the U.S. Chamber of Commerce's International Division.

Other U.S. Companies.   You will find that representatives of American companies operating in your target markets can be very helpful in providing background information on pitfalls, difficulties, and business climates. Prime sources include U.S. managers of the overseas operations of manufacturers, banks, accounting companies, and consulting firms. These managers will share your perspective and background and be able to see things through your eyes. Of course, they often will not be familiar with your line of business, and they certainly won't give you competitive information—but their background information on doing business in the market can be invaluable. Identify them through the Commerce Department country rep or the American chamber of commerce in the country.

Target Market Companies Doing Business in the United States. If you were in Japan and a Japanese company needed some general information on doing business in the United States, think how valuable your insights would be. Turn this around to see the potential value to you of talking with noncompeting Pacific Rim businesses operating in the United States. Most Pacific Rim nations have business associations in major U.S. cities—for example, the Korean-American and Japanese-American chambers of commerce. Members include overseas companies doing business in the United States as well as some American companies doing business overseas. Many of these associations are listed in the Appendixes.

Ranking Sources of Information

Here's how experienced international managers rank the relative importance of various information sources. Note that experienced managers view the sources differently from executives of companies new to international trade, who tend to favor sources offering more basic or general information.

Information Source	Percentage Importance
1. Subsidiary managers	74.6%
2. Regional managers	68.9
3. Corporate headquarters personnel	64.8
4. Banking community	44.6
5. External consultants	28.0
6. Business periodicals	24.9
7. Other companies	22.8
8. Agents and outside counsel	22.3
9. U.S. embassies	17.6
10. U.S. government domestic agencies	16.6
11. Professional journals	14.5
12. Trade associations	13.0
13. International organizations	10.9
14. Newspapers, radio, and television	10.4
15. Academia	9.3
16. American chambers of commerce	8.3
17. Journalists	8.3

Needed: An International Trade Data Bank

The biggest problem in finding the information you need is not a shortage of data, but the fact that nobody catalogs and analyzes all the latest data from all the sources. No one source has everything. Often government agencies will not have the reports published by private market researchers—such as Business International and SRI International—and vice versa. This holds even for reports that are not proprietary. And private organizations too often disparage the quality of Commerce Department services and reports, perhaps viewing them as low-priced competition.

Many university libraries will eventually have the broadest spectrum of data, but it takes them a long while to obtain and catalog it. By the time it is available to you, it is out of date. Also, some data are cataloged to meet the needs of the academic researcher, not the executive decision maker. Periodicals are not indexed by the subjects that global traders are looking for. Titles of articles are misleading. More often than not, the publications you need are checked out or missing. It is all so time-consuming. And, of course, a library may be inaccessible or have limited facilities. After you've lost out on a few opportunities because of the difficulty of obtaining data, spending five figures for a semicustomized research report doesn't seem so bad!

What's needed is a computerized data bank for international trade and investment, one that contains up-to-date information on trade barriers, policy changes signaling trade opportunities or problems, available contracts, news on who entered what market, and other valuable information. On-line data bases accessible to anyone with a personal computer and a modem are just beginning to appear.

Needed: The Global Information Specialist

I have mentioned the need for a financial engineer to help you deal with global financial markets. You also need an "info conjurer" to help you track information that is pertinent to your marketing decisions. This information specialist should have responsibility for obtaining data from varied sources, synthesizing it into a coherent whole, and putting it into a form useful for business planning and decision making. The specialist would stay tuned to events in all your present and potential markets, tracking information on all the political, economic, market, and competitive factors discussed in this chapter.

There are many ways to identify your markets, but regardless of which track you follow, be sure that you:

1. Obtain all the free or inexpensive information you can.
2. Go to multiple sources and double-check everything.
3. Get professional help for specialized research. Seek advice from a consultant with proven experience in the area before making a key decision.
4. Use the information you obtain. After buying expensive market research, you must react quickly to the opportunities identified, especially those in published studies. Remember, your competitors are looking at those published reports too.

5 | Trade or Invest: Exporting

- *The available types of Pacific Rim operations*
- *The easiest ways to enter Pacific Rim trade*
- *Direct and indirect exporting*

California almond growers, who separately lack the clout to market their products internationally, now successfully sell their almond products to Japan and other Pacific Rim markets through a cooperative—the California Almond Growers Exchange.

Xilinx, a manufacturer of specialized microchips, licensed its unique technology to a larger Japanese manufacturing company in return for access to that company's efficient manufacturing process technology.

Video Update, a successful St. Paul franchiser of video rental stores, was approached by several Asian companies wanting to establish franchises in the Pacific Rim. Video Update has licensed a joint venture for a hundred Video Update stores in Malaysia.

Adaptek started a small plant in Singapore's version of the Silicon Valley to assemble personal computer add-ons for re-export to the United States, then discovered it had a growing market among other ASEAN nations.

These brief examples suggest the variety of operational forms suitable for initial entry to Pacific Rim trade.

A Progression of Commitment

The types of overseas operations listed below are a sequence of options that represent a progression of commitment, from sticking your toe in to plunging all the way. There is a spectrum of choices available to you—from "least commitment" to "most commitment"—with gradations of attention and resources required. Basically, they fall into a handful of categories, as follows:

1. Export of your products without your knowledge or involvement
2. Indirect exporting
   - Trading company that buys your products and resells overseas
   - Foreign buyer or export broker that buys for overseas clients
   - Export management company that buys outright or works on commission
   - Confirming house that purchases your goods on behalf of foreign buyers, then ships and arranges payment

3. Direct exporting
   - Overseas company that buys directly from you, with goods shipped from your factory
   - Overseas distributor that buys and sells on account
   - Overseas agent working on commission
   - Overseas broker (for commodities primarily)
   - Organization that makes agency purchases for governments
4. Licensing or franchising
5. Contracting
6. Joint ventures
7. Wholly owned affiliates

This chapter examines the forms of exporting that you can do without having to set up your own operations in the Pacific Rim. Chapter 6 explores the types of operations that require a greater level of commitment, including direct investment in the overseas market. In both chapters, I assess the pros and cons and trade-offs for each type of operation, suggest which form might be appropriate for a particular kind of product or service, and show how companies know when it is time to change from one form to another.

Indirect vs. Direct Exporting

It is important to clarify the distinction between indirect and direct exporting. An *indirect exporter* sells to a trading company or some other organization in the United States and thus does not have to worry about export documentation, foreign exchange or overseas market research. A *direct exporter* sells to a distributor in a foreign market and therefore takes greater responsibility for documentation and currency transactions.

Indirect exporting has definite benefits if you are new to international trade, even though in the long run your profit margins are lower. Consider the cost of establishing even the smallest exporting department. If you set up your own international division, it must have one sales rep at a minimum, plus one or two backup staff members. This will cost you at least $200,000 a year in salaries, travel expenses, and communications. Your sales rep, if you get a good one, will probably come from a larger company and will be used to going first class. That's the kind you need for success. This level of overhead can be difficult to recoup.

As the CEO of a growing company that has no experience in international business, you may be at the mercy of a fast-talking deal maker from a Pacific Rim country. You may be very sharp in dealing with domestic buyers and yet fail to make a good deal in a Pacific Rim market.

As you gain experience, you reach a point where it pays to take more direct control of your exporting. Things that initially seemed so daunting, such as paperwork—often called the single greatest trade barrier—begin to settle into a routine. You learn how to use the specialists: freight forwarders for shipment and documentation, credit companies for insurance coverage, and packaging companies to meet package and label specifications.

You also grow to understand the advantages of establishing a local presence in your overseas markets, advantages that cannot be provided by middlemen. You need to have someone on the scene who understands your technology in depth and who is selling, dealing with the political climate, following up with leads and customers, and providing service and support.

The pros and cons of indirect and direct exporting are summarized below.

Indirect		Direct	
Pros	*Cons*	*Pros*	*Cons*
No capital needed	Less contact	More control	Paperwork
No experience needed	with markets	Higher profit	Greater risk
	Less control	Better exposure	Greater effort
	Lower profit		

Remember, however, that with direct exporting you can get help from freight forwarders, banks, insurance companies, and packaging companies.

The "Trade vs. Invest" Issue

Conventional wisdom dictates that small businesses just entering international trade should do so by exporting—perhaps through trading companies and then later through their own distributors. Only as they gain experience and resources would they begin to invest directly in their best overseas market. *Direct investment* means establishing an overseas operation that requires capital outlays (as opposed to investment for purely financial purposes in another business or in securities). Although this is still true for the most part, recent developments make direct overseas investment in manufacturing or distribution—whether joint venture or subsidiary—much more important from the very beginning, even for small companies.

Pacific Rim countries still restrict many imports, and more sophisticated and competitive markets demand a level of product design and service that is impossible to provide across the Pacific Ocean. Repeatedly this axiom is heard: "Appear to be local." Many Japanese executives have echoed this sentiment: "Whoever is successful in Japan has factories here. That commitment is important to Japanese customers." As a result, there has been a pronounced shift from export to investment.

Indirect Exporting at the Entry Level

Many companies are already international traders and don't know it, and are surprised to learn that their products are exported without their knowledge. Buyers from foreign companies may purchase the products from a wholesaler, or a domestic company may purchase the products to use in an overseas project. You may be unaware of such exports of your products until you begin to receive unsolicited inquiries and even orders from overseas customers. Follow them up!

Many U.S. companies are unaware of the extent to which foreign buyers are familiar with their products through advertising and articles in domestic journals. These journals, although published for the domestic market, are distributed and read avidly all over the world. Many companies have initially entered overseas markets after responding to an unexpected and unsolicited inquiry from a foreign buyer who read a domestic ad.

If you are aware of this potential, you can shape your ads and articles to attract overseas as well as domestic customers by saying something like "Inquiries from domestic or foreign representatives are welcome," or "For the name of our nearest domestic or overseas distributor, please contact us." You should also pay attention to how your ads or articles may be perceived by someone who is unfamiliar with your product line and product jargon, with the U.S. market, or with many other things that you take for granted in your domestic operations.

Trade Shows in the United States

If you attend domestic trade shows for your own industry, you will probably notice a number of Pacific Rim buyers and representatives. You may receive several inquiries. These buyers are often either export *brokers,* buying specified products in the United States for clients back home, or export *merchants,* buying products on their own account for closely guarded market opportunities. These brokers often specialize in a particular type of product—whether electronics components, cosmetics, or dry goods—and they are skilled purchasers.

For many United States companies, casual conversation with overseas buyers has opened the door to Pacific Rim opportunities. Overseas buyers know their markets—they know who wants your products and why—and they can tell you how to refine your products to make them fit those markets better.

The astounding thing is that many companies fail to follow up on overseas inquiries, thinking they are not worth pursuing, and thereby turn down potential markets of considerable size. So the inquiries are made, instead, to a Japanese or German company that, five years later, is making a strong entry into the U.S. market. For many companies that followed up on such leads ten and twenty years ago, Pacific Rim trade now accounts for over half of their sales volume, so you can grasp the potential being passed over every year by U.S. companies.

U.S. Buying Sprees by Pacific Rim Nations

One way to do some armchair exporting is to sell your products to buying missions from Pacific Rim nations, especially from Korea, Taiwan, and Japan, when they take one of their periodic swings through the United States. On a recent Buy American mission from Korea, a group of executives from large Korean corporations toured the United States and spent $2 billion on everything from aircraft to oil to electronics parts. These missions are largely public relations events designed to defuse criticism of a country's trade surplus with the United States. However, if your company sells a product they are shopping for, take advantage of it. The trips are publicized well in advance, and you can find out about upcoming trips by contacting the Commerce Department or a nation's trade reps in the United States.

Piggyback Selling

Manufacturers of technical products are often introduced to international markets when their products are specified for use by the principal contractor in an overseas project. For example, suppose you manufacture medical testing equipment, and your instruments are specified by an engineering company that is building health care facilities in Thailand. The contractor, whether U.S. or foreign, is purchasing your instruments in the United States, so your company has little involvement with exporting. Yet you can receive valuable feedback on how your instruments perform in foreign facilities and how they stack up against the international competition. The contractor becomes an informal market adviser, telling you how you can take advantage of overseas market opportunities. This arrangement is less common now than it used to be, however, since more and more contracts require competitive bidding on all components.

Indirect Exporting Through a Trading Company

A typical way for a small manufacturing company to enter overseas trade is to sell to trading companies. Initially, the company sells its products to a buyer in the United States that ships and sells to Pacific Rim markets. The company thereby avoids the hassle and expense of setting up a Pacific Rim operation and does not need to have a depth of experience to be successful.

What a Good Trading Company Does for Its Clients

Trading companies provide invaluable services, especially for smaller businesses that are new to export. Since most trading companies buy goods for cash and sell on terms, they effectively finance overseas sales. (Some trading companies do take goods on consignment, paying the manufacturer only after the goods are sold; others act as manufacturers' agents.) Trading companies provide entrée to markets and distribution channels that you may otherwise have great difficulty penetrating—especially in Japan and Korea. They have the resources to service your products in the new markets, to alert you to new opportunities, and to provide you with market research and intelligence on how to exportize your products for their new markets.

Some trading companies bring together complementary product lines, so that the appeal of your products, as part of a more complete line, is increased. They also handle much of the hassle of export: packing, freight forwarding, storage, and customs clearances. Even some larger companies with their own overseas distribution will use a trading company for a new market if the demand is not great enough to justify setting up a new distribution system.

Overseas Trading Companies

The largest and best-known Pacific Rim trading companies are those in Japan and Korea, followed by Taiwan and Hong Kong. The Japanese trading companies, or *sogoshosha,* handle close to half the imports of Japan. They were set up to sell the products of Japan's huge industrial cartels to the rest of the world and to bring in the raw materials needed.

Some *sogoshosha* handle many different kinds of products for sale in varied overseas markets. Others specialize in one industry or product line, such as dry goods, machine tools, hardware, or electronics components.

As the giant Japanese manufacturers have begun to handle their own worldwide marketing, the *sogoshosha* have moved into manufacturing, banking, and venture capital in the United States and other countries.

The largest Japanese *sogoshosha* include:

C. Itoh & Company	Mitsui & Company
Kanematsu-Gosho	Nichimen Corporation
Marubeni Corporation	Nissho Iwai Corporation
Mitsubishi Corporation	Toyo Menka Kaisha
Sumitomo Corporation	

Many Pacific Rim trading companies make it very easy for American companies to do business with them. They go shopping in the United States for specific types of products. This is different from the "shopping spree" buyers that are looking for onetime purchases. Trading companies seek to set up ongoing relationships with U.S. businesses. Japanese trading companies, in particular, are very sophisticated at this. The Nichiryu Group, which represents sixteen Japanese supermarket chains, made a tour of six U.S. cities (Portland, Chicago, New York, New Orleans, Denver, and San Francisco) to find new food products for supermarket shelves. In each city they sponsored a display of food products from local U.S. producers, ranging from dried prunes and granola to cookies and cheese puffs. The products they selected were featured in a major American Food Fair in 840 stores across Japan.

U.S. Export Trading Companies

American trading companies could not legally be structured like the *sogoshosha* until 1982, when Congress enacted the Export Trading Act to allow American banks to invest in American companies that perform the same functions as their Japanese counterparts. The Act was designed to help U.S. manufacturers develop overseas markets for their products and to become more competitive internationally. It broke the longstanding American taboo against letting banks engage in nonbanking activities. These trading companies, owned by a bank holding company, can jointly offer their goods for export. The Export Trading Act removed any uncertainty about the application of U.S. antitrust laws to the export trade.

Besides brokering and trading, an export trading company (ETC) can offer a number of other services to its members: market research, legal assistance, insurance, transportation, communication, and warehousing, as well as regulatory and legislative research for the domestic and foreign markets. ETCs enjoy economies of scale because they export large volumes of products from many sources, at lower per unit costs, through established networks of overseas offices, transportation facilities, and warehousing.

Export trading companies were soon set up by Bank of America, Sears Roebuck & Co., and other financial giants. However, their success was limited. They were hurt by the strong U.S. dollar, which made American exports less competitive. More important, they were set up, funded, and directed by large, highly structured parent corporations. To be successful, a new trading company needs to be very entrepreneurial and must act quickly to take advantage of emerging opportunities. The parents did not allow them to do so. Furthermore, the ETCs were competing with the past masters of international trading from Japan, Hong Kong, and Korea, and many of the "new kids on the block" did not have the trading acumen to succeed.

Finally, the ETCs were not set up to service the needs of small and medium-size exporters. They set overly demanding criteria for clients. Privately held companies feared, probably with little justification, that the bank holding company would release confidential data to a trade competitor and that, because of the bank's government-imposed reporting requirements, crucial information would be disclosed by the Department of Commerce as public domain. However, some U.S. trading companies are still operating successfully and are gaining experience. New ones should be able to learn from the mistakes of the pioneers.

A new breed of American trading company is emerging: smaller, more entrepreneurial companies that have multidisciplinary teams able to provide a comprehensive set of services. They focus on satisfying markets, not just buying and selling goods. They look at the investment opportunities that go along with trade flows and are thereby better positioned to help small to medium-size American companies penetrate Asian markets.

An example of such a trading company is Washington, D.C.–based Beijing Trade Exchange, Inc. (BTE). It recently put together a countertrade transaction to secure a supply of latex gloves adequate to meet the suddenly surging demand for use by health workers. BTE identified manufacturing facilities in Asia, secured raw material sources, oversaw the supply of equipment, and provided the needed production techniques. It works closely with Asian manufacturers to ensure the highest possible product quality by controlling the production of the latex gloves from beginning to end.

Another example is U.S.-China Industrial Exchange, Inc., with offices in Beijing, Guangzhou, and New York. It provides a whole package of needed services: market analysis, financial planning, trade facilitation, import/export coordination, negotiation, translation, equipment repair and maintenance, teaching and training, and day-to-day problem solving. In a typical deal with China, it packaged medical equipment, high-tech medical training, and health care services provided by several of its client companies; then it arranged for after-market support to the end users. In the process, it helped the Chinese government define some of the medical technologies most suited to China's needs.

For exporters that sell similar goods, the ETC arrangement makes it easier and cheaper to obtain essential export services such as trade financing and finance management. For example, a group of small agricultural producers could pool its resources. But the ETC arrangement is a particularly valuable way for a group of cooperatives to pool its resources—as has been done by Zenoh, the large Japanese trading cooperative. An ETC cannot engage in production and qualify for the antitrust exemption, while a single agricultural cooperative is restricted to the products of its member producers and can do only first-stage selling. So to market and sell a broad range of products overseas, a group of related cooperatives must work through—or form—an ETC. The two organizations are complementary. By joining forces, they enable smaller producers to respond to large central buyers in Pacific Rim countries.

Many different kinds of companies are taking advantage of the ETC: small and large manufacturers, export agents, shipping associations, trade associations, banks, service companies, and agricultural producers and processors. Here are some ways ETCs have been used.

• *Shippers' associations.* The International Shippers Association—a group of fourteen suppliers of fish and agricultural products based in Washington State—used the antitrust protection of its certificate to negotiate joint transportation contracts for exporting its members' products.

• *Agribusiness.* Agribusiness companies that form ETCs have achieved significant economies of scale by shipping and marketing their nondifferentiated products together. Products include rice, prunes, and raisins from California; sweet cherries from the Pacific Northwest; lumber from Alaska; and pecans from the Sunbelt states.

• *Technology licensing agreements.* Two or more competing U.S. companies can benefit by pooling their efforts to remove the antitrust uncertainty that often surrounds licensing agreements. (See Chapter 6.) The licenser must be able to grant the licensee exclusive rights for a particular application or territory and must prevent the licensee from competing in territories reserved by the licenser.

• *Trade association ETCs.* Trade associations play a vital role in bringing companies together to share the risks of international business and achieve economies of scale. The National Machine Builders Association acts as an ETC for its 268 members, preparing joint bids, establishing export prices, allocating markets, and disseminating information. Similar associations include the Industrial Equipment Manufacturers Association, the American Film Marketing Institute, the Millers National Federation, the U.S. Hides and Skins Association, and Southeastern Fisheries.

A company wishing to participate in an ETC must apply to the Commerce Department's Office of Export Trading Company Affairs for a Certificate of Review—a legal instrument that provides antitrust protection for specific activities. The office will assist you in setting up an ETC, will help you identify other companies that might be interested in working with you, and will list your products or services in its directory. In addition, the Commerce Department sponsors seminars in cities all over the country to explain ETCs. Two valuable guides, *Partners in Export Trade* and *The ETC Guidebook,* can be purchased through the U.S. Government Printing Office.

State Trading Companies

North Dakota, Virginia, and several other states have formed ETCs to promote their exports or their port facilities. Other states are showing interest as well.

The Port Authority of New York and New Jersey has set up XPORT, an export trading company that specializes in export services for small to medium-size businesses. One New York City company that worked through XPORT to break into a Pacific Rim market is American Beverages, Inc., which markets a "natural soda" in Japan. XPORT provided assistance that allowed the company to successfully enter a tough Japanese market in which a variety of less expensive soft drinks were available. The market approach stressed features attractive to "juppies"—or Japanese yuppies—emphasizing all-natural ingredients, giving the soda a trendy Art Deco packaging, and using the slogan "Taste of New York."

XPORT, in turn, worked through Japan External Trade Organization (JETRO) to identify one Japanese importer that would bypass the multilayered Japanese distribution system and sell the soft drinks directly to restaurants, upscale supermarkets, and department stores, thus cutting costs and keeping prices competitive. With this experience under its belt, American Beverages is ready to go after the Hong Kong and West German markets as well.

How to Find the Right Trading Company

There are trading companies for many types of products: consumer goods, industrial products, electronics supplies and components, value-added agricultural products, and so on. For the most part, it is a buyer's market. Many trading companies are eagerly seeking good clients. So even if you are new to the game, you can afford to be selective.

Questions to Ask. Below are some of the questions you must get answers to—by talking with the companies themselves or by asking third parties. At first you may feel presumptuous even asking the questions, but you will quickly begin to notice the differences among trading companies and learn to spot the ones that you would entrust your products to.

- Which of the services mentioned above will they actually provide?
- How experienced are they in your product area? Will an experienced specialist be assigned to it?
- What competing products will they handle, and how will yours be distinguished?
- How well established are they in the markets for your products? What solid contacts do they have with distributors or potential customers?
- How will they promote your products, and what will the promotion budget be?
- Can they provide the technical support and service your products require?
- How well can they advise you on needed refinements or exportizing for their markets? Can they provide translations of your printed material?
- What is the cost of their services?
- Will they agree to a limited market, for a limited time period?

Large vs. Small. Should you work with a large or small trading company? For smaller exporters, there are advantages and disadvantages to each. Here are the pros and cons.

Larger Trading Company	
Pros	*Cons*
Marketing clout	May lose your product in the shuffle
Wide distribution	May demand an exclusive contract
Prestige	May be resistant to making changes
Part of "old-boy network"	

Smaller Trading Company	
Pros	*Cons*
Flexible response to new opportunities	May lack clout or visibility in the market
Specialized market knowledge	May focus only on one type of market, or one nation
Personal attention, strong focus on your product	May have limited budget for promotion
Key contacts in right markets	

It is crucial to find a trading company that shares your goals and outlook and has the same level of aggressiveness in its marketing and promotion. To identify trading companies that operate in particular Pacific Rim nations, talk to trade officers at the nation's embassy or consulate, or contact the Department of Commerce. The major trading companies in Japan, Korea, and elsewhere are regional in scope. Addresses of trading company associations are listed in the Appendixes.

Advantages and Disadvantages.   If your company is new to export, there are several advantages to working through a trading company. You will be able to ease into international operations, and thereby help your own people gain experience while limiting your risk and exposure. Your products will be introduced into many more markets than you could enter on your own. When you gain sufficient experience and knowledge about your international markets, you can begin to handle your own distribution.

You should consider replacing your trading company with an agent or a rep when you see that your profit margin could be increased by taking over the function of a middleman.

There are disadvantages as well. Attention to your product may be diluted. It may never get the focused attention it needs to succeed. Especially in the beginning, you must pay close attention to what your trading company is doing, since the reputation of your product may suffer from its missteps.

Further, you will not establish any personal presence with your customers—a factor that is increasingly important in current markets. Since you have to rely on secondhand information about your customers, you may have more difficulty gauging your market, your market share, emerging opportunities, and how your product could be refined to perform better. In fact, some trading companies may want to keep the buyers of your products secret from you so that you can't approach them on your own and cut the trading company out.

However, good trading companies are willing to share this market information. They know that if your products have increasing market potential, you are not going to stay with them indefinitely. They know that the more they help you and the more satisfied you are with their performance, the longer you are likely to stay with them—and to refer them to up-and-comers. Information disclosure should be one of your selection criteria. Have a clear understanding up front of what information you must have from a trading company and what the scope of your Pacific Rim involvement will be.

Indirect Exporting Through an Export Management Company

Many smaller manufacturers use an export management company (EMC) to handle their exports. An EMC often does the exporting for several businesses with related, noncompeting product lines. An export management company is somewhere between a trading company and an agent or manufacturer's rep.

EMCs specialize in a narrow range of products (often high tech), whereas trading companies usually represent a more general line. A trading company is more likely to buy your goods and do what it wants with them; an EMC normally works more closely with the manufacturer, whether it buys the goods or sells on commission.

What an EMC Does for Your Company

Like a trading company, an EMC handles all the details of documentation, packing, shipping, customs, and storage. It may also provide trade financing, buying your products with cash and then reselling them on terms. Typically, the services of EMCs make them suitable for product lines that require more attention than most trading companies provide.

An EMC will often research new markets or niches and develop new ways to distribute your products, whereas a trading company is more likely to stick with existing contacts and channels. An EMC may also help you to exhibit your products at international trade shows or to work your way through the bidding process for an international contract.

Since an EMC sells to wholesale distributors in the overseas market, not to the end user, it will find overseas distributors for you. After markets and distribution channels are selected, the EMC will help you develop appropriate marketing materials and arrange for needed translations. It will also advise you on obtaining patents, trademarks, and other protection.

An EMC can act as liaison and translator between you and your customers—for example, by handling correspondence. The EMC will negotiate deals for you with customers and will take responsibility for obtaining payment. Some EMCs are paid on commission, so they have an incentive to expand the sales exposure of your product. If appropriate, an EMC will also keep on top of the published bidding lists for international projects and seek to sell your product to the governments sponsoring these projects. The EMC will handle the competitive bidding for you.

In short, with an EMC, you gain feedback on your markets and customers and some exposure to the process of selling and marketing, so you develop your own export skills. This is important if you intend to have a long-term commitment to Pacific Rim markets. Keep in mind, however, that the distinction between a trading company and an EMC is blurring as competitive pressures force many trading companies to take a much more active role in performing middleman functions.

Who Should Work With an EMC

EMCs are ideal for many smaller start-up businesses and for rapidly expanding companies that are going into export for the first time and are not equipped to handle export on their own. An EMC saves you the cost of setting up your own export department, especially at the beginning of your entry into Pacific Rim markets. Using an EMC is a low-cost way of exporting. Since the EMC is exporting for several companies, the export overhead costs and shipping costs for each company are reduced.

On the other hand, EMCs want to handle products with expanding sales potential, fully knowing that manufacturers will sooner or later want to take over exporting their own products. Some EMCs may be tempted to act more like trading companies, buying your products and reselling them under their own name. The best EMCs recognize that clients will be with them for a limited time but still offer full assistance. To evaluate an EMC's performance, talk with past and present clients.

EMCs can be somewhat secretive because they are concerned about competing EMCs. Also, an EMC may discourage you in subtle ways from learning more about overseas operations because it recognizes that if you learn how to handle your own Pacific Rim operations and your market gets big enough, you're likely to leave.

If your company's product requires technical support, you should not work through an EMC. Whenever your product is sold, your company's name is on the line, so it's imperative that whoever sells your product has the capability to provide the required technical support. EMCs do not.

Work with an EMC if your product:
- Can be sold as is to your customer base
- Requires no special training or service to be used successfully
- Is packaged for the end user
- Has too diffuse a market for you to service efficiently

Don't work with an EMC if your product:
- Must be modified for different customers
- Requires training, service, and follow-up
- Requires technical support
- Requires training and demonstrations to educate users or to create a market

EMC Discounts or Commissions

An EMC may either buy your products and resell them or sell them on commission. If the EMC takes title, it will buy at a discount from your wholesale price, sell to distributors overseas, and bill them the appropriate wholesale price for that market. If you give your domestic distributors a 40 percent discount, then you should give your EMC a 45 percent or even 50 percent discount, since the EMC's costs are higher. In addition, the EMC must be able to compensate for the Pacific Rim trading company buyers that will seek to circumvent the EMC and buy directly from a U.S. distributor. Giving this larger discount is justified, since you don't have to apply as great a proportion of your advertising and promotion burden to sales through your EMC.

However, if you do give a greater discount to the EMC, make sure you have a written agreement that the products will not be sold in your domestic markets.

You may even want to mark the serial numbers of export products with the letter E so that if they begin showing up in your domestic markets, you will know where they are coming from.

If your EMC sells on commission as your exclusive agent for a particular market, you will invoice your customers directly. Even so, the EMC may help you with problem collections. Typical commissions range from 7.5 to 20 percent of your overseas wholesale price.

How to Find the Right EMC

There are EMCs located all over the United States. They specialize in various industries. You can identify appropriate candidates by contacting the Federation of Export Management Companies (FEMCO) or the Export Managers Association. However, many EMCs do not belong to these national organizations, so you may want to talk with local freight forwarders, foreign trade associations, and trade reps from the Commerce Department or the Small Business Administration. The biggest and best-known EMC is not necessarily the best for you. Word of mouth is also important. Talk with other companies in your industry to find out if they have worked with an EMC and what their experience has been.

Once you identify several candidates, how do you find the right EMC for you? You select an EMC the same way you select any other professional organization, such as a freight forwarder or a consulting firm. Of course, it's best if you understand your needs clearly so you know what to ask for. But if you are new to export, you may not know, so part of the selection process is judging how well the EMC understands what your company and products need for the latter to be exported successfully.

Talk with EMCs about the kinds of companies they work with, the markets they work in, and the distribution channels they use. Are they the right size for you? How many companies do they handle, and how closely related are the products? Find out what services they can provide for you and how much attention your lines will receive. Find out what they expect from you as well. For example, if they sell on commission, will they insist that you be responsible for problem collections? Ask each EMC for references from companies it has worked with in the past, particularly ones that have left. Do a credit check on each prospective EMC—as you would on any other customer—to assess its financial status.

When to Move On

The time will come when your company should stop exporting through an EMC. You have gained the needed experience, and your market density is great enough that you can provide the same services and increase your profit margin. The next step for you may be to work directly with distributors or agents in the market or, in some cases, to hire your own people there. When you take over operations in one market, you may assign an EMC to initiate efforts in another market you intend to move into.

An EMC recognizes from the beginning that the company it represents successfully is eventually going to leave it. The more successful the EMC is in selling the company's products, the sooner the company will take over its own overseas operations. Even so, a good EMC knows that it does not pay to withhold information or hold down sales in order to hold on to a company, since the EMC's future business comes from word of mouth.

Direct Exporting at the Entry Level

We have examined the main methods of indirect exporting—that is, selling your products in the United States to a company that then takes responsibility for shipping and selling them overseas. This contrasts with direct exporting, in which you take responsibility for overseas sales: shipping, preparing documentation, dealing with customs, arranging terms, and collecting payment overseas.

Pacific Rim Trade Missions

The best entry-level method of direct overseas selling is to go on trade missions. Most are sponsored by government agencies: the Commerce Department, state export promotion organizations, Pacific Rim governments, and sometimes even city chambers of commerce. Trade missions are generally organized around a particular industry or type of product.

The sponsoring organization will make all the arrangements: travel to one or more Pacific Rim cities, accommodations, and meetings with government economic officials, bankers, potential customers, distributors, or agents. The mission will often be coordinated with a trade exhibit, in which each participating company displays its products. Costs are shared among the trade mission members. Each one may pay from $5,000 to $10,000—a relatively inexpensive and painless way to get introduced to overseas markets. Very often, sales made during the trip will more than cover the cost.

The Department of Commerce puts together several types of trade missions that can help you test interest for your product in the markets, increase awareness of it, and make sales. Typically, the department selects particular product lines and markets that have high potential for increased export sales from the United States. The department's agenda is to increase overall U.S. exports, so its shows may or may not coincide with your products and targeted markets. But if they do, they afford you a valuable opportunity to make contact with potential customers, agents, and distributors. *Business America,* published biweekly by the Commerce Department, lists the dates and locations of all its trade promotion events, both in the United States and overseas.

Trade missions are also organized by industry and professional trade groups.

For example, the American Electronics Association sponsors weeklong trade missions to Pacific Rim countries, often in cooperation with local chambers of commerce or other organizations. Generally, these trips are organized with the support of the Department of Commerce.

Trade Fairs and Exhibitions

One of the easiest ways to enter international trade is set up an exhibit at an international trade fair or exhibition. Hundreds of these are held each year—some general, some specialized by industry. Most of them are open for participation by any company in the industry.

The Department of Commerce can assist you in attending any of these exhibitions, which are also listed in its *Overseas Export Calendar.* The department will promote your products before the show, help you design your exhibit area, give you advice on shipping your products to the show, and provide basic logistical support, such as arranging for electrical service and maintenance. You must have a qualified representative at the show to demonstrate your products, give information, and make sales.

If no exhibition is planned in a product area with promising sales potential, the Commerce Department will put together its own exhibits of products manufactured by U.S. companies.

Catalog or Videotape Shows

There are ways to take advantage of overseas trade shows, even if you do not want to attend them directly. Each year, the Commerce Department puts on a number of overseas catalog or videotape shows. Each one is for a particular range of products and is designed to cover a small cluster of countries. You send the department your catalogs, which are displayed at a trade show in each country.

Some shows are set up to run videotapes as well. If you have a product that needs to be demonstrated in action in order to attract interest, a videotape can be a very valuable way to promote it.

Your exhibit will be staffed by a Commerce Department trade rep or someone from your trade association who is qualified to explain the products in your catalogs and in those of other participating companies. Catalog and videotape shows are well promoted by the Commerce Department and are attended by local business reps and potential agents and distributors. If these people are interested in what you have displayed, they will contact you directly.

A catalog exhibition of U.S. plastics machinery and equipment toured major markets in Asia throughout 1988. The show featured plastics packaging machinery, plastics production machinery, resins and materials, instrumentation, and controls. It visited China, India, Pakistan, Korea, Malaysia, Thailand, New Zealand, and other countries. Cost to participants was $1,000.

One drawback to these shows is that your catalog and price lists will be displayed right alongside those of your competitors. So it is essential that you review your catalogs or videotapes beforehand, checking to see how clear they are, how well they promote the benefits of your products, and how well they communicate your advantages over your competitors.

You may have to develop new versions of your product literature, including translations, to effectively participate in a trade show. This can be the most expensive part of the show, which is why some companies resist redoing their literature until *after* the show. Their thinking goes like this: "We don't want to invest in a Japanese translation unless we see that there is enough interest in our products there." So they rely on their English version. And sure enough, there's not much interest in their products. All the Japanese buyers pass by and go on to the next booth where all the brochures are in Japanese.

Before you participate in any trade show, it's important for you to clarify what you intend to get from it and to plan your exhibit and staff, your promotional material, and your expenses accordingly. Trade shows can promote several objectives for you at a very low price. They are valuable for gauging interest in your product in particular markets; for contacting potential customers, agents, or distributors; for identifying potential new markets or applications for your products; for seeing how your products stack up against your competitors', especially overseas; and, of course, for promoting and actually making sales. It is essential to follow up on all inquiries generated at a show. If you ignore inquiries completely or put them on the back burner, you are damaging your future reputation in these markets.

Trade Center Shows

The Commerce Department maintains trade centers with exhibition facilities in a number of cities around the world. The Pacific Rim centers are in Tokyo, Sydney, Seoul, Singapore, Taipei, Beijing, and other cities. A center may put on up to ten shows a year, each devoted to a particular type of product or industry.

You or a representative must attend the show. If you have an agent in that country, this is a very good way to supply support for your agent. Having the agent staff your booth will extend the agent's ability to reach customers. Participating in a U.S. trade center show can cost up to $6,000.

Some state agencies also sponsor trade shows. For example, the World Trade Commission of California displays products from California manufacturers in trade shows worldwide, and these companies share the space and the cost. The World Trade Commission has offices in Tokyo, London, and elsewhere, and has practical information on marketing products and services overseas. It actively seeks to match buyers and sellers.

The governments of Pacific Rim countries also sponsor trade shows—for example, the Expo HiTech Shanghai '86 Fair. This weeklong event, organized by a company in Washington, D.C., had about 250 exhibitors and was held in the former headquarters of the Chinese–Soviet Friendship University.

Made in USA Fair '87, sponsored by the JETRO (Japan External Trade Organization) office in San Francisco, was held in Osaka. The fair helped U.S. producers of health care products link up with Japanese importers and distributors. The Japanese government sponsors such events in order to lower the trade deficit and lessen trade tensions with the United States.

A 1988 exhibition in the Westin Chosun Hotel in Seoul displayed U.S. high-tech products in the fields of analytical and scientific instruments, laboratory instruments, electronics equipment, energy-saving technology, and telecommunications and broadcasting equipment. Twenty-eight U.S. companies participated, exhibiting 500 different types of equipment, technology, and services. They reported sales of over $2 million and more than 500 sales leads.

On many trade missions for U.S. businesses, companies seeking to import to the United States outnumber those seeking to export to Pacific Rim countries. Yet it is the exporters who are the most popular, because the nations to which these trade missions go are usually eager to buy products from the United States.

You will get the most from attending the small, specialized trade shows jointly sponsored by a U.S. chamber of commerce and the chambers of commerce of one or more cities in the Pacific Rim. For example, you might go from Indianapolis to Canton. At these shows you will have a chance to talk one on one with a number of trade officials and representatives of manufacturing organizations. The big, flashy trade shows with dignitaries get lots of publicity, but they will probably afford you less opportunity to meet one on one with people you can really do some business with.

Host Country Invitations

Getting invited to invest in a Pacific Rim nation may seem like a serendipitous event that cannot be planned for—and sometimes it is. A small furniture manufacturer in Michigan was sought out by the Chinese government to help set up an office furniture factory near Beijing. The reason? A Chinese student intern who had worked at the plant while studying at Michigan State University happened to be the daughter of a high-ranking Chinese official—and she liked the company.

You don't have to be a wallflower waiting at the dance. You can make your company known, and you can keep your antennae out. The companies that are noticed and invited are the ones that have something unique to offer. What appears as a valuable and unique resource to others may seem ordinary to you. Not only governments but also private companies may notice you and contact you—if you have a good reputation, have something they want, and make yourself visible. The president of Golden Gate University had no particular intention to expand overseas, but he was always alert to opportunities. Then, shortly after a conversation with a Malaysian banker at a reception, he was invited to investigate setting up a professional MBA program in Kuala Lumpur.

Japanese trading companies and financial institutions are particularly eager to connect American businesses that have strong design capabilities with Japanese firms that are strong in automated assembly. Japanese manufacturers are continually scanning American technical journals for articles on technical or design breakthroughs. They may contact the executives who submitted the articles—an overture that could lead to an offer to form a joint venture or licensing agreement. An American company can gain a very strong entrée to the Japanese and other Pacific Rim markets in this way. Many companies have used such an opportunity as a springboard into international trade.

But beware. You are likely to be flattered when you are approached directly by a company, and the offer may not be right for you. You should check out the company like a prospective suitor. And, as I discuss later, do not bargain away your most important resources.

Piggyback Distribution

Small businesses that cannot afford to set up their own overseas distribution can sometimes piggyback on the distribution of a larger company. General Electric and other large American corporations that have extensive Pacific Rim distribution are willing to represent complementary products from smaller companies just to broaden their own product offerings. But the distributor does not have to be a behemoth. Theos Software, as small as it is, works with many even smaller companies that develop applications software for them. These companies piggyback on its distribution network. They follow the path blazed by Theos and link up with Theos distributors, who are known quantities.

Direct Exporting Through a Local Representative

U.S. companies selling services internationally for the first time often sell through a local representative, agent, or distributor. In the Pacific Rim, the local seller might be a single individual or a multinational company. Small U.S. companies selling management, engineering, or technical services or engineering will often find a respected local consultant, engineer, architect, or programmer to represent them in that market.

When to Use a Local Seller

Let's distinguish a few terms. *Agent* and *representative* are sometimes used interchangeably. Most often, *representative* means a manufacturer's rep who sells products, whereas an agent represents the seller of services. Agents and sales reps usually work on commission, assume no risk or responsibility, and sign a contract for a specified period of time. A *distributor* buys goods on discount and resells in the local market. The difference between a distributor and a trading company is a fuzzy one, especially since smaller trading companies often specialize in one market and one product line and provide a range of services and assistance. Distributors offer some of the same benefits as trading companies. Since they purchase from you and then resell, they are financing your trade. They carry inventory and so finance your inventory. They provide technical assistance and servicing for your products. They assist you in making needed refinements for the market, including translations of literature. They may market your brand or sell under their own private label.

The customers you wish to reach may be less likely to buy from you, an unknown, than from reps or distributors they already do business with. So you can often penetrate the market much more rapidly by using an existing rep or distributor than by hiring your own salespeople and developing your own means of distribution.

But what if appropriate reps or distributors are not available in the market? If your products or services are new to that market and market research has convinced you that there is a demand for them there, you may have to establish your own sales force and channels of distribution. As discussed later, it may well be worth your while to do so.

An example of a company using overseas distributors is POM, Inc., of Russellville, Arkansas, which sells parking meters. It began a serious exporting business in 1979 and now exports equipment to fifty countries, including three in the Pacific Rim: Malaysia, Australia, and Taiwan. POM sells through distributors that are based in the foreign countries. Since it is selling a concept as well as a product, it must make sure its distributors have outstanding entrepreneurial skills. POM undertakes a strong communications effort to ensure that foreign distributors understand the successful elements of its program. To find distributors with the needed entrepreneurial and communications skills, POM worked through the Commerce Department's Agent/Distributor Service and the Foreign Commercial Service officers in U.S. embassies.

You should use a rep or an agent instead of a trading company if you sell a service or if your product has a large service component—namely, technical support or service. Use an agent or distributor instead of licensing when your key information cannot be adequately protected in a licensing agreement; when you have adequate domestic productive capability to manufacture products for your Pacific Rim market; and when you *may* export U.S.-produced products into that market.

Agent or Rep vs. Distributor

Whether you select an agent/representative or a distributor depends on your circumstances and the marketing needs of your service or product. An agent or a representative is an independent seller comparable to a manufacturer's rep in the

United States. Like domestic reps, they sell products on commission, do not take title, and accept very little risk or responsibility. A distributor, on the other hand, purchases goods at a discount, takes title, and assumes responsibility for marketing merchandise. Although some agents will work exclusively for you, you will most likely want to link up with one that already has an established business in the market. In this case, your products will not receive exclusive attention from the agent. However, do make sure that the agent can give you adequate attention.

Finding the right agent is a matter of seeking a balance. You want one that has the necessary contacts and is big enough to be recognized yet small enough to be hungry and to put out the needed effort to sell your products. An example is Remington Shaver's entry into the Japanese market. As its agent, Remington selected a well-established consumer electronics company that had recently lost some important business and was in danger of being forced to lay off some key sales agents. The company had a vacuum that Remington filled very well. In turn, Remington gained an agent with solid contacts and reputation, one that gave the company the concentrated attention it needed to break into a very difficult market.

In some markets, you may have a choice between an agent or a distributor. Table 5–1 shows the trade-offs you should consider in making a choice. With an agent, you retain greater control and initially invest less money and fewer resources. You control the price, promotion, and quality of service. The commission you pay an agent is likely to be less than the discount you give a distributor. On the other hand, the distributor needs less financing and takes responsibility for in-country storage, transportation, distribution, and payment collection. Whichever one you choose initially, be sure to structure the agreement so that it can be changed if your situation changes.

Table 5-1. Agent or representative vs. distributor.

Market Factor	With Agent or Rep	With Distributor
Your involvement with customers	Mostly direct	Mostly indirect
Learning reasons for lost sales	Firsthand	Secondhand
Analysis for new products or improvements	Firsthand	Secondhand
Control over selling price	You	Distributor
Name on the package	Yours	Yours or distributor's
Identity of prospects	Forwarded to you	Possibly hidden from you
Finger on sales potential	You	Distributor
Payment collection	You	Distributor
Order consolidation	Difficult	Very easy
Maintenance and support	You	Distributor
Import problems	You	Distributor
Initial setup cost	High	Low
Cost of sustaining operations	Moderate	Low
Establishing direct sales force	Relatively easy	Quite difficult

Agent or Distributor vs. Direct Sales Force

Establishing your own sales force in a new market may sometimes be the best means of penetration. Larger companies that are experienced in international operations often have staff members living in each of their major foreign markets. You have more control over your employees than over an agent. They are hired to serve your interests exclusively. They will work to establish a solid, positive image for your company and its products. The personal contacts they establish are for the sole benefit of your company. Employees are likely to know your products better than an agent and be able to provide technical support and maintenance to your customers. They can take a more active role in identifying opportunities or even help create opportunities for you.

Some independent distributors may adopt practices detrimental to your market penetration strategy. For example, an American appliance manufacturer wishing to gain a strong share of newly opened markets in Taiwan may contract with a local distributor. But the distributor may decide to maximize short-term profits by selling the appliances for premium prices. The American company may thereby gain a much smaller market share than Japanese or European competitors, who retain control of their pricing strategy and offer lower prices.

There are several disadvantages to establishing your own sales force. Initially, at least, it will cost more to position your own people in a market—even people you hire locally—than to use an agent who is already established there. Second, you may have difficulty finding, recruiting, and training qualified local people to represent your company, and some countries place severe restrictions on using foreign employees. Also, even if you can hire U.S. salespeople, they probably will not know that market, the culture, or the language. It may take them years to establish business relationships and become accepted by customers.

In some situations, you may be unable to find a qualified, reputable agent in the market who is willing to take on your product. This is especially true if you are offering a somewhat specialized product or service that lacks an established pool of experienced sellers. There may be just a handful of qualified agents in that market, and the competition for their services will be very great.

In most Pacific Rim nations, you will find a growing pool of local professionals and other skilled people who have business experience in their own culture and in the United States. This is true in Australia, New Zealand, and Japan, and in the overseas Chinese cultures—especially Hong Kong, Taiwan, and Singapore, where many professionals have received business or technical training in the United States (many companies market in China through reps from Hong Kong or Singapore). In these nations, you will likely have your choice. Your problems will be identifying the best people and competing for scarce services.

Finally, in some markets, no qualified agents or employees are available *and* the restrictions on American salespeople are prohibitive. These are not the markets to enter first.

How to Select the Best Representatives

Although there are differences between agents and distributors, I discuss them together in this section, since the methods of locating, evaluating, and coming to agreement with them are quite similar.

The aim of selecting a foreign representative is to create a solid working relationship of mutual benefit to both parties, one in which each has a stake in the success of the sales effort. A representative in a Pacific Rim market will operate much more independently than a domestic rep, so you must be doubly careful in selecting one that will do the job you want. Identify candidates and check their reputations to see if they are appropriate for your products or services. Give them a chance to see whether you are appropriate for them before you negotiate an agreement.

Most of the following suggestions for identifying, evaluating, and selecting the right distributor or agent pertain just as well to finding a licensee, franchisee, or joint venture partner. They are summarized in Figure 5–1. I refer to this section several times in Chapter 6.

Figure 5-1.   How to find a good market partner overseas.

---

1 Set your criteria for:

- Ease of communication (no language barriers)
- Technical knowledge and skills for selling, supporting, and servicing your products or services
- Contacts with local governments, banks, and other institutions
- Proven track record with the customers you want to reach
- Reputation (trustworthiness, no payment hassles)
- Facilities and people who fit your product and desired image
- Ability to cover the territory you wish to cover or to expand as needed (regional or local representation)
- Strong motivation to work hard on your behalf

2 Identify and investigate candidates through:

- U.S. Commerce Department's country reps, Agent/Distributor Service, Foreign Trader's Index, and WTDR series
- OPIC
- Trade publications for reports on the company, its advertisements, and articles by its key people
- Trade associations, freight forwarders, commercial banks—especially banks in that country—and accounting firms
- Local customers
- Government officials and members of the local business community
- Business associations in that country, especially AMCHAM
- U.S. companies operating in that country

3 Evaluate likely candidates by getting detailed information (plus a third-party double-check) on:

- Interest in working with you
- Size and number of employees
- Track record in your type of product
- Financial resources
- Availability of suitable facilities
- Manufacturing facilities and processes
- Reputation in the market
- References from current clients
- Names and background of principals
- Current sales territory
- Range of products handled
- How new products are introduced
- Range of customers
- Size and capabilities of sales force

4 Pay a face-to-face visit to assess:

- Corporate goals that are complementary to yours
- Policy on handling competing products
- Exclusive or nonexclusive distribution
- Technical capabilities for management, service, user training, maintenance, and language translation
- Willingness to provide feedback

5 Sell yourself by:

- Showing samples, technical data, and marketing data
- Presenting a pro forma agreement
- Supplying references
- Suggesting a reciprocal visit

Establishing Your Criteria. How do you choose distributors or agents? Some obvious criteria (you will have others specific to your circumstances) are given below.

- You can communicate with them. They speak English or there's a strong person in your company who speaks their language.
- They have the technical knowledge, specific skills, and capabilities needed to sell and service your products.
- They have contacts with local governments, banks, and other institutions.
- They have a proven track record with the kinds of customers you want to reach.
- They have a solid reputation (trustworthiness, no payment hassles, and so on).

- They have the kind of facilities and people that fit your product and the image you wish to project.
- They cover the territory you wish to cover or can expand to cover that. (Do you want regional or local representation?)
- You have something that they want, so they are motivated to work hard on your behalf.

Identifying and Investigating Potential Reps.   To identify potential representatives, check a variety of sources. Contact the Department of Commerce's country trade rep, and check the department's Agent/Distributor Service and *Foreign Trader's Index*. Also contact the American Chamber of Commerce there. Check trade publications in the appropriate industry for reports on a company; read its advertisements and articles by its key people. Check with trade associations, freight forwarders, and commercial banks.

You may be contacted by a company that wishes to act as your agent or distributor in a given market. You should evaluate such an offer just as thoroughly as any other, and you should probably identify other agents so you have more than one to choose from.

The Commerce Department's *World Trader's Data Report* (WTDR) series contains key data on overseas companies that might serve as your representatives. Each inexpensive, two-page report summarizes the latest information on a foreign trader, including:

- General background and reputation
- Product line
- Level of annual sales
- Number of employees
- Companies it presently represents
- Bank references

The reports also give U.S. embassy recommendations on the appropriateness of establishing business relations with foreign companies.

The Commerce Department maintains a file of thousands of WTDRs. If you request a report on a previously researched company, you can receive it in a week or two. If no current report is on file, the company will be researched by the U.S. embassy staff in that country. The investigation can take from one to three months. Dun & Bradstreet provides credit reports that focus more on a company's financial standing than on its overall business background. These reports are based on unaudited response questionnaires, so you may have to double-check the data before you reach any final decision.

Evaluating Likely Candidates.   After you have narrowed the initial list by applying your criteria, you must follow up more closely with the most likely candidates. First, contact each company by letter and find out whether it is interested in representing you. Send it all the relevant information on your company: the products you wish to market, who your customers are, and what you want from a representative. Point out that you would like to visit in person before making a final selection.

Those companies that respond favorably to this inquiry become your final candidates. You may need to request additional information from them. (At the same time, they will likely want additional information from you.) You should request these details from each candidate:

- Size of company and number of employees
- Track record in your type of product
- Financial resources
- Qualifications
- Names and addresses of companies it currently represents
- Names and background of the principals
- Facilities available (such as warehousing and distribution)

You will also need specific information on the company's marketing efforts: current sales territory, range of customers, range of products handled, size and capabilities of sales force, methods of marketing and promotion, and the way new products are introduced.

At the same time, check a company's reputation and performance with third parties. The Department of Commerce will help you evaluate your possible representatives. If you are working with a department trade specialist, give the specialist the names and addresses of these candidates; the U.S. commercial officer in that country will check their reputation, financial and trade references, the kinds of products they handle, and the territory they cover. More specific information on them can be obtained in their country through banks, other companies that have been customers, government officials familiar with the business community, the American Chamber of Commerce in the country, and noncompeting U.S. companies operating in their country.

Visiting the Top Candidates.   Nothing replaces personal contact. Even for a small company, the cost of visiting a home market before making a final selection is well worth it. It is very risky to make the selection without a personal visit. For each candidate, you must double-check all the information you have received and examine the physical facilities, the methods of operation, and the personal characteristics of the principals and of the sales force. You should always talk in person with customers, bankers, and others in the business community who are familiar with the candidate. These appointments should be arranged before departing.

When you meet the top candidates, chemistry and style will be important elements. In addition, there are a number of tangible factors to explore. You will need to confirm their size and facilities, track record in your type of product, and reputation in their market. Also assess their corporate goals. You want a partner whose goals are congruent or complementary with yours. Evaluate their experience in handling your type of product and complementary products. (What about handling competitive products?)

Determine their technical capability—their ability to service, to train users, to conduct maintenance, to translate documents into their language, and to correspond in English. Also determine their willingness to give you feedback on markets, customers, and emerging needs or problems. Can they tell you what customers are asking for and what competitors offer that you should too? You want them to be your source of intelligence on economic and political shifts in the country—for example, tariff barriers that are easing or getting stronger, political rumblings that could affect your operations, economic policies that are being debated, and rumors about the balance of payments and currency exchange rates.

Inspect their facilities, talk with their people, and view firsthand how they package, deliver, and promote other products and services. They will be sizing you up as well. When you hold the first face-to-face meeting with the final few candidates, it's as important for you to sell yourself and your product as it is for them to convince you. This is a courtship. If you are a smaller business talking with very large overseas companies, you may be tempted to put too much emphasis on selling yourself and not be careful enough to check them out and make sure they're right for you.

On your end, provide information about your products, your goals, and your resources. Show samples and technical and marketing data. Present a pro forma agreement so that candidates can see in detail the type of relationship you desire. Give them references (your bank, your suppliers, your customers) so that they can check out your reputation in the United States. Before finalizing an agreement, they may want to visit you, examine your factory and headquarters, and talk with your key people. (See Chapter 8.)

Selecting Your Representative.   After all the above criteria are satisfied, you and the rep will select each other on a handshake and then work out the final details of the agreement.

In most Pacific Rim countries, interpersonal relations are a much more important basis of working agreements than written contracts that spell out every contingency. This is just the opposite of most U.S. arrangements. Trying to cover too much detail in a written contract may suggest a lack of trust and may actually kill the proposed working agreement altogether. On the other hand, you want to have everything nailed down, so that when disputes do arise you can fall back on the impersonal document rather than fighting with a valuable associate. This is an argument for having an experienced person help you craft and negotiate the agreement at the outset.

Outlining the Agreement.   An agreement with an agent or distributor should cover the items summarized in Figure 5–2. The agreement should be made in writing—not only to limit the damage in case things go wrong, but also to outline the way that the two parties will work for their mutual benefit when things go right. There is a temptation to enforce a very restrictive contract, yet good performance by an agent or distributor requires a mutuality of interests and ben-

Figure 5-2. Terms of the agency agreement.

Parties to the agreement—specified in a legal sense to ensure that the agent is not a shell company without resources.

Products or services covered by the agreement.

Sales territory. Is it exclusive or not?

Sales quotas or minimum levels.

The time period covered by the agreement. What happens at the end of that time period in the case of termination of the agreement or extension and expansion of the agreement?

For an agent: when and how commission rates and schedules will be paid.

For a distributor: discounts and resale prices.

Price-setting authority and how prices will be set and changed.

Form and method of payment. In what currency and when will it be made?

Responsibilities of each party for all required activities, including training, selling, advertising and promotion, technical support, and shipment and transportation.

Procedures for handling shipments and claims.

Use of trademarks.

Warranty terms and responsibility for repairs made in and out of warranty.

Responsibility for clearing customs and paying tariffs, taxes, and insurance.

Inventory levels to be maintained.

Facilities to provide service and maintenance.

Policy on dealing with competitive or complementary products.

Agreement to refer all inquiries received from outside the designated sales territory to the U.S. client company for appropriate action.

Agreement not to reveal confidential information or enter into agreements binding on the client company.

Rights of inspection and audit.

Legal jurisdiction over the contract, the means of resolving disputes, and the language to be used.

Circumstances or location at which title to the goods passes from the client company to the buyer (for tax purposes).

Limits of liability.

Rights of assignment.

Procedures for cancellation or termination of the agreement: conditions under which the agreement will be canceled by either party, and rights and duties upon termination.

---

efits, and the agreement should spell those out. If an agreement is done right, it can help cement a long-term relationship and protect your associate's investment in building a territory.

Nevertheless, the relationship should proceed like a trial marriage, because if the agent or distributor turns out to be wrong for you, you could be stuck in a hard-to-cancel agreement. Some of the terms should be limited at first, with the understanding that after a record of success the terms will be renegotiated or expanded. Initial limitations may be placed on the territory to be covered, the products or services to be handled, and the time period.

Keep your options open. You may want to enter a joint venture or establish your own operation in that market in the future, either with your present agent or with another. Point out the circumstances in which you may wish to sell directly into the agent's market—for example, to a prior customer of yours that subsequently begins operations in the market. For tax purposes or to limit your exposure, you may wish to set up a subsidiary as your legal entity and partner to this agreement.

Negotiating the Agreement.   Once the initial relationship is established, you may be able to complete the final details of the agreement by mail, phone, or fax. Details can take time. Negotiating an agreement with an agent or a distributor is similar to negotiating a contract with a customer. Pay close attention to local laws regarding the termination of agency agreements. In some countries, this process is weighted toward the agent and can be very expensive for the exporter if it is not done correctly. Avoid provisions that may be contrary to U.S. antitrust laws. It's essential to have competent legal review of the agreement. I discuss negotiating in more detail in Chapter 8.

6 | Trade or Invest: Pacific Rim Operations

- *Licensing, franchising, contracting, joint ventures, and wholly owned operations*
- *The type that is best for you*
- *When to switch from one type of operation to another*

This chapter continues to explore the different forms of operation that U.S. companies can adopt when entering Pacific Rim markets. The forms considered here—licensing, franchising, contracting, joint ventures, and wholly owned operations—require a greater commitment of effort and resources than the ones outlined in Chapter 5. The costs and risks are undeniably greater, especially for companies new to Pacific Rim trade, but the payoffs are greater as well. On the one hand, market barriers and competitive pressures force businesses that would rather stick to exporting to adopt one of these forms. On the other hand, evolution in the markets makes it easier for less experienced companies to enter Pacific Rim trade at deeper levels of commitment.

These forms of operation are often referred to as *direct foreign investment,* which means the establishment of an overseas operation that requires capital investment. (It's called direct investment to distinguish it from an investment in securities for purely financial purposes.)

Licensing Agreements

Licensing is easy enough to understand: Your company sells another company the right to manufacture and distribute some unique product, process, or service within a specified market. In return, your company receives a royalty based on sales and perhaps an initial cash payment. As an overseas operation, licensing doesn't require a lot of setup effort. So it may be a very desirable track for a smaller company.

A word of caution: *Any* licensing venture should be considered a sophisticated form of operation appropriate for experienced players in international trade. Since the unique, proprietary knowledge you are licensing is the lifeblood of your business success, the risk is substantial. Once you sell access to it, you no longer have complete control. If you are naïve or careless, the licensee will use your specialized knowledge to compete with you, perhaps even in your home markets.

In terms of the level of commitment required, licensing lies somewhere between working with a trading company and running your own operation. Although you are not investing directly in the market, you must closely monitor the operations of your licensee; obviously this requires much greater levels of attention, expense, and time than selling through a trading company. On the other hand, it's much less costly than developing your own channels of distribution. For that reason, licensing is often the most attractive market entrée for smaller companies whose resources are limited but whose technologies, processes, or proprietary information is in high demand *and* is protectable. If done properly, licensing is a tremendous boon to the rapid growth of small companies that lack the productive capacity to manufacture enough to sell in all promising markets.

Licensing has often been done haphazardly or poorly. In the 1970s many American high-tech companies eager to enter Japanese markets licensed their proprietary technology to Japanese companies, with very little control and for very little in return. Small start-up companies that were desperate for cash were enticed by the offer of a large infusion of capital from certain Japanese or Korean companies. Then, to their distress, they discovered that they had created their own competitors.

Despite the risks, these alliances can be very valuable to a small company that is willing to learn from past lessons. The key is savvy negotiating. Cordata Corporation in Thousand Oaks, California—a manufacturer of computer add-on boards—negotiated a workable agreement with Daewoo of Korea despite Cordata's desperate need for capital. Cordata granted Daewoo a license to manufacture a private Daewoo label for the Korean market while Cordata retained first option for other overseas markets. In return, Daewoo gave Cordata a sizable infusion of cash, a substantial line of credit, and leverage to purchase materials in large quantities. Cordata's president, Daniel Carter, does not fear being knocked off by his new partner, and the chairman of Daewoo sits on Cordata's board and thus has a fiduciary responsibility to the company.

Discussions of licensing often emphasize the terms of the licensing agreement. They are indeed important. However, equally important is the process of selecting the licensee, maintaining a relationship, and making sure you get something equally valuable from the licensee in return. Cash may not be enough. You should also obtain knowledge, which is equally valuable. Xilinx, for example, traded its specialized knowledge of the design of programmable gate arrays to a Japanese company in return for the latter's knowledge of efficient manufacturing processes for microchips. Such a transfer of technological data benefited both tremendously—and made them equals in the exchange.

When to License

Let's look at some situations for which licensing is appropriate. You sell a service or intellectual property that is in great demand and that meets one or more of the following criteria: It has a valuable patent or trademark or involves a trade secret; the technology is exclusive, intensive, or complex; your production processes are

---

When Licensing Is Appropriate

- You have a valuable patent, trademark, or trade secret.
- Your technology is exclusive, intensive, or complex.
- Your production processes are exclusive or complex and hard to duplicate.
- Your service is unique or widely recognized and requires specialized inputs of knowledge or management.

---

exclusive or complex and hard to duplicate; your service is unique or widely recognized and requires specialized inputs of knowledge or management. The common denominator here is protectability. You can protect the property you want to license from being easily duplicated or improved upon through legal means and careful controls.

If your product or service meets one or more of these criteria, several situations may induce you to license your technology to another company (one with similar products or technologies) that will manufacture products appropriate to the market.

- *The market is so diffuse or spread out that you cannot afford to service it.* Or at least the volume in that market does not justify the cost.

- *Your product is not suitable for export without expensive refinements.* You cannot afford to export, but the technology upon which the product is based can be used to develop products suitable to the market.

- *You want to protect your technology or your patent, but the potential sales volume in the market is too low to justify setting up distribution or exporting.* If you license a local company to produce your product for you, you get much more protection from that market than if you just register your patent or trademark, since the technology may have to be used in order for the protection to remain valid.

- *The licensee has something you want.* For example, you can obtain a needed infusion of cash through the initial licensing fee.

- *Licensing one technology may help you sell something else.* This is a variation of the "services sell products and products sell services" rule. For example, if you have a technical services company and you also sell a proprietary product, you can license the product as an entrée to sell your technical support services. Each one leverages the other. Many service companies find it difficult to sell services by themselves because their customers view services without hardware attached as being somehow intangible and hard to value. On the other hand, selling products without support services is often inadequate, so the licenser of hardware or technology may create a competitive advantage that better fits the market by offering the needed support services and tangential products.

Licensing vs. Exporting.   In some circumstances, licensing your technology may be more attractive or more feasible than exporting your product or service to international markets. For example, trade restrictions or barriers may prevent you from exporting directly to a market or from selling your services in that market. Or foreign exchange problems may prevent you from getting revenues out of the market.

Sometimes, even if you can sell your product in a country, it is difficult to find a sales rep or distributor capable of selling and servicing your product. A local business sophisticated enough to handle your products wants to be more than a distributor. For example, a small company that develops specialized software to control industrial processes cannot find a distributor skilled enough to provide the needed installation and customization for customers. Instead, the company licenses its software to a Taiwanese manufacturer of industrial process controls.

Licensing vs. Direct Investment.   Licensing may be better for you than establishing your own operations in an overseas market when the cost of direct investment required to succeed in that market is more than you can afford. You may lack the capital, the management skills, and the experience to enter that market directly. Or you may have invested heavily in research and development and so lack the resources to invest in manufacturing facilities in that market. Some companies faced with this situation opt for a joint venture.

Licensing vs. Joint Venture.   Some companies form a joint venture with their licensee, as described later. Yet, initially at least, licensing is often the only route for a smaller company that has a valuable or desirable technology but cannot afford direct investment in a country, even in the form of a joint venture.

Licensing vs. Going Out of Business.   Many small companies that have sunk most of their capital into the development of promising new products or processes find themselves too strapped for cash to mount an effective marketing and expansion campaign, even domestically. If, as is often the case, they are unable to obtain additional venture capital in the United States, they will license their technology to a larger company in exchange for a critical infusion of cash. Because of the current status of U.S. capital gains laws, it is often easier for a business to obtain venture financing from an overseas company than from a domestic venture capital group.

Pitfalls of Licensing

Let's review the licensing risks you must protect against.

   • *Giving away too much.* Many small U.S. companies, lured by the promise of large initial licensing fees, have given up valuable technology to larger companies for relatively little in return. The small companies were eager and needed the money badly, and the other companies, so large and attractive, seemed to be in a strong negotiating position. As a result, too much was given away in the licensing agreement. The U.S. companies soon found themselves unable to compete with their licensees in worldwide markets or even, in some instances, in U.S. markets.

• *Creating your own competition.* A major pitfall to licensing is the risk of losing your technology, your trade secrets, or your patents and actually creating competition in your own domestic market. This has been called the *copycat syndrome.* If you fail to protect your intellectual property, crucial proprietary information, patents, or trademarks may be used against your interest. This can happen whether the licensee is a small local business or a multinational. If the license expires and you do not renew it, the licensee may continue manufacturing and selling your product in the initial or other markets. Or the licensee may reverse-engineer your product and develop competing products.

• *Poor performance by the licensee.* The licensee may not sell enough of your product or service to justify the cost and effort of the licensing agreement. Poor performance manifests itself in two ways:

1. Lower than expected royalties—you fail to realize the expected revenue from the licensee.
2. Dilution of product quality—the licensee sells inferior products in your name. Your key concern as a licenser is to ensure that your quality standards are upheld, whether for a service, a consumer product, or an industrial product. If you pick inappropriate licensees that lack the reputation or the capabilities in the market, if they do not manufacture your product to your quality specifications, if they apply your technology in inappropriate ways, if they market the product inappropriately, or if they fail to train users or to service the product appropriately, your reputation can be badly tarnished.

If your licensee fails to respect your wishes (even if those conditions are spelled out in the agreement), your technology may be incorporated into products without your company and its contribution being acknowledged. In this case, you basically become invisible and do not gain the exposure you want in that market.

How to Protect Your Property

Protecting yourself means that you select the right licensee in the first place, negotiate a sound agreement that makes it in the interest of the licensee to protect your interest, and remain vigilant against misuse and breaches of confidentiality.

Finding the Right Licensee.   If you are attempting to identify a potential licensee, you can use the same resources described in Chapter 5 for identifying agents and distributors. However, in many cases, the choice of potential licensees is severely limited, and the issue becomes whether to accept a company you are already in contact with as a suitable licensee. You can investigate that company's physical facilities, financial condition, and market standing, but face-to-face meetings will be required to evaluate trustworthiness and congruence of goals. Through those face-to-face talks, inspections, and discussions with third parties, you should get the following questions answered to your satisfaction:

- If the potential licensee will be manufacturing your products, *does it have the production facilities, skill, and experience required?*
- If it will be marketing a service, *is its personnel capable of delivering that service and maintaining your standards?*
- If it will be distributing, *does it have access to the distribution channels? Does it sell to the customers that are best for your products?*
- *If the licensee is a manufacturer, does it also have the capability of marketing and servicing the goods, or does it have access to the right distributors?* Suppose you license your technology to a company that has advanced manufacturing processes but lacks appropriate marketing channels for your products. Your licensing agreement may require that it link up with a specified trading company or distributor.
- *Does the licensee have the financial resources to take on your operation?*
- *Can the licensee obtain the needed licenses and permissions to manufacture and distribute your product in a particular market?* Remember that in some nations certain markets or products are reserved for specified companies.
- *Does the licensee have something as valuable to you as your license is to it?* Since proprietary knowledge is probably at least as important as money, it may be more important to you to obtain valuable knowledge of techniques or manufacturing processes from the licensee in exchange for your licensed knowledge.

Maintaining the Quality of the Relationship. Besides a strong licensing agreement, the best way to protect your proprietary knowledge is to make sure the licensee is benefiting more by working *with* you than against you. Work hard to maintain a good relationship with the licensee and provide the technical assistance, management support, and quality control that the licensee needs to be successful.

The licensing agreement, of course, is designed to protect you, but it is also a framework for the way that you and the licensee will work together to your mutual benefit. Therefore, the agreement should spell out the items that you will provide for the licensee throughout the term of the relationship—for example, training for the licensee's people, backup technical assistance when needed, assistance with advertising and promotion, and provision of the latest technology and design changes.

Making Sure the Licensee Has a Stake in Your Product. Why does the licensee want to work with you? Most likely because access to your technology or proprietary knowledge gives the licensee a competitive advantage. If the licensee is truly not interested in gaining your secrets and then going out on its own, it will seek an ongoing relationship with you in order to retain access to your latest technology.

The desire to maximize competitive advantage provides a strong incentive for the licensee not only to sell well but to provide you with intelligence on the actions of competitors, on emerging market opportunities, and on ways to make your product, service, or advertising better fit the market. Incentives for the licensee may include rights to an expanded territory, special fees it can charge for providing corollary services, access to more technology, and in some cases expansion of the licensing agreement to joint venture equity sharing.

Put the burden on your licensee to enforce the agreement. If the licensee buys your technology to produce a component that will be used in products manufactured by other companies, then you want to make sure that those products are not subsequently sold in markets reserved for you. You must require your licensee to enforce such limitations with its customers, and you must impose penalties if you discover products with the licensee's components sold in your market.

Maintaining Control of Key Elements. To protect against creating your own competition, you may retain control in several ways:

1. Supply key components, materials, or expertise that the licensee cannot obtain elsewhere. This, of course, works less well in markets with strong engineering and technical capabilities.
2. Make sure you have a strength that the licensee lacks (such as the ability to continue developing the latest technology). The licensee will then continue to need you, since the technology that the licensee holds will rapidly become obsolete if your licensing agreement terminates.
3. To thwart reverse engineering, consider putting in a high-tech-looking component that actually does nothing. Engineers can be slowed down a long time trying to figure out what such a piece does.
4. Register your patents or trademarks in the foreign country.
5. Negotiate separate agreements to cover new services, products, or techniques you develop.
6. Require the licensee to put up a performance bond, with the money to be held in escrow outside the country.

Being a Savvy Negotiator. Since knowledge is the basis of wealth, market share, and competitive advantage in a global economy, it's often a bad bargain to trade irreplaceable proprietary knowledge for mere cash and resources. The way you turn a royalty arrangement into a good bargain is to have an exchange of technologies as well.

You can also negotiate for more than one source of revenue. Here are three ways to get paid for licensing:

1. *The up-front license fee*—paid by a larger manufacturing concern to a smaller high-tech company. This can amount to millions of dollars.

2. *Fees for related services*—often provided by a strong licenser for a smaller marketing licensee.
3. *The royalty rate*—can vary depending on what you are providing. A typical range is from 3 to 7 percent of net receipts from sales.

In some markets, it is difficult to guarantee the receipt of your licensing royalties over time. Local laws may provide you with virtually no protection if the licensee doesn't pay you. In that case, instead of licensing, you may want to sell your technology outright for a specified amount—perhaps the current value of your estimated royalties over the lifetime of a licensing agreement. Make sure that this amount is paid up front and in hard-currency funds from a major bank in a third country. Your technology should be held in escrow pending this payment; then exchange title.

To make licensing more lucrative, there are several things you can do: You may sign a separate contract along with the licensing agreement to provide essential equipment or some other input to the manufacturing process. You may sign a contract to provide an essential service, such as the design, construction, or management of the production facility. You may contract to provide engineering, technical support, service, or maintenance. You may require that the licensee purchase certain key components, special equipment, or machinery from you.

When you obtain revenue from offering a supplementary service to the licensee, you should make that contract separate from the basic licensing agreement. The services or components you provide may need to be changed while the basic licensing agreement remains in force. For example, if the licensee gains experience and no longer needs your contracted management services, you won't necessarily want to renegotiate the entire licensing agreement to amend the management terms.

Negotiate a strong agreement. Structure a licensing agreement that allows you to do all these things.

Policing the Agreement.   A strong agreement is of little value unless you police it to ensure high-quality production of your products or timely delivery of your service. On the one hand, you will want the right to inspect the licensee's plants and facilities to observe manufacturing, promotion, and distribution, and you will want to retain the right to cancel or terminate the licensing agreement if quality standards aren't maintained. On the other hand, you must provide all the training and support that the licensee needs to offer the best product.

If your technology is misused, don't count on obtaining legal redress against the licensee. Of course, if all else fails you may attempt to do so, but you should make a strong agreement from the outset to do everything else possible first.

The legal environment for protecting intellectual property is improving. More Pacific Rim nations—often under U.S. pressure—have enacted laws protecting foreign patents and copyrights. Larger U.S. companies that can afford to wage legal battles have won a few fights. Thus the atmosphere is brighter even for smaller companies. Licensees that would have once considered misusing trade secrets may now feel constrained. Once the tide begins to turn against misappropriating technology, the business community becomes self-policing to some extent. If Company A can't get away with it, then it wants to make sure that Company B can't either. U.S. companies have become aware of the pitfalls of licensing and are becoming better negotiators; companies that depend on licensing American technology do not want their reputations damaged by allegations of misappropriating the technology of a licenser.

Terms of the Licensing Agreement

A number of important terms should be covered in a licensing agreement. These include the territory covered by the agreement, the payments made by the licensee to the company, how trademarks and patents will be protected, and how commercial operations will be conducted in the market. In addition, there are some special terms that pertain to manufacturing technology and proprietary know-how. Figure 6–1 shows the issues you must have settled in your own business plan before entering negotiation with any potential licensee. The figure can serve as a planning and negotiation guide for any company considering licensing.

(*text continues on page 126*)

Figure 6-1.   Terms of the licensing agreement.

Parties to the Agreement

1 Precisely identify the legal entities.

What Is Covered

1 Define clearly what is being licensed: know-how, secret ingredients, patents, trademarks, or specialized equipment.
2 Specify the quality standards for all aspects of the agreement: products, services, management, marketing and promotion, and follow-up support.

Territory Covered

1 State the geographic territory for which the license is valid.
2 State the type of operation permitted by the licensee.
3 Specify whether the license is exclusive or nonexclusive. You should retain the right to convert the license from exclusive to nonexclusive or vice versa.

Expected Levels of Performance

1 Tie an exclusive license to a certain level of sales, or establish a minimum royalty payment regardless of sales.
2 Specify the accounting methods used and reports to be submitted by the licensee; retain the right to audit accounts and reports.
3 Specify uncontrollable circumstances under which either the licensee or the licenser can be exempt from responsibility for not performing (acts of God, political upheaval, government interference).

Figure 6-1.   Terms of the licensing agreement (*continued*).

Term

1 List the effective date, duration, and termination date of the agreement.
2 Specify terms of renewal and how the rights of the licensee may be extended to additional territories or for an additional period of time.
3 State the conditions under which the license may be modified, canceled, or terminated by either the licensee or the licenser (for example, changes in key personnel or ownership of the licensee). Take into account the laws of the country.

Intellectual Property Protection

1 State the rights and privileges of the licensee in using the intellectual property, how it may be used, and the restrictions on its use. Specify what constitutes misuse and how such misuse may be penalized. (The property here includes all patents, trademarks, and copyrights.)
2 Specify what proprietary information requires confidentiality by the licensee and list remedies for breach of confidentiality.
3 Describe the patent marking required on manufactured items.
4 Fix the licensee's responsibility for protecting against infringement by competitors.
5 Specify that the licensee must protect the secrecy of the information being transferred for the duration of the licensing agreement and for a number of years thereafter.

Payments by Licensee

1 State the amount of any initial payment and the royalty rate as a percentage of specific factors.
2 Specify any payments by the licensee for other items, including transfer of technical information, training, promotion and sales programs, products, parts or services to be provided by the licenser, and warranty or guarantee services.
3 List the taxes that must be paid, how they relate to the royalty agreement, and who pays them. Take into account customs, duties, business taxes, payroll taxes, and insurance.
4 State the currency in which royalties and other fees will be paid. Specify payment by the licensee for future services or upgrades, including cost of product improvements, manufacturing process improvements, and new patents, trademarks, or copyrights.

Services Provided by Licenser

1 Describe how the licensee's personnel will be trained initially and throughout the term of the agreement.
2 Describe the marketing and promotional assistance to be provided to the licensee.
3 Specify how continuing assistance and technical information will be provided to the licensee and the licensee's responsibility to incorporate new information.
4 List the research and engineering to be carried out by the licenser for the licensee.
5 Describe the access of the licensee to future patents by the licenser.

For a Technical Assistance Licensing Agreement

1 Specify the technical information covered by the agreement and what is not covered. In particular, how will future improvements or developments in technical information

be treated? (Here the intellectual property is proprietary knowledge or know-how rather than a patent or trademark.)

For a License to Manufacture

1 State how proprietary manufacturing processes may be used, and for what products. Specify the range of products that are to be manufactured, quantities, and schedules of production.
2 Describe what competing or other products the licensee may or may not manufacture.
3 Establish standards of quality that must be maintained, and state how compliance will be checked and ensured.
4 Specify the source and quality of raw materials, components, and spare parts, and state how changes or improvements in products will be handled.
5 Reserve the licenser's right to inspect and review the licensee's operation to check compliance. Specify when and how the licensee's books may be audited and the selling and advertising efforts to be surveyed.
6 State the conditions under which the licensee will be required to discontinue a particular product or process.

Optional Provisions

1 Reserve the licenser's right to technological improvements developed or discovered by the licensee.
2 Specify how technical information and patent rights will flow from licensee to licenser in a two-way mutual assistance licensing agreement.
3 Enumerate the licensee's rights for sublicensing and subcontracting and assignment of the original license. Specify limitations and any required prior approval.
4 State the conditions under which the agreement may evolve into an equity agreement (joint venture), since the licenser may want to buy into the licensee's operation.

Other Factors

1 Specify where the agreement will be executed. Designate the legal system that covers the agreement, including the governing law for the resolution of disputes. Specify whether the English- or other-language version is predominant in cases of discrepancies between translations.
2 Define the required communications for both parties (how notices will be sent).
3 Specify all regulations of the U.S. government and foreign governments that must be complied with.
4 State that the licenser will be held blameless and free of liability for any actions of the licensee.
5 Enumerate the rights and obligations of both parties after the licensing agreement is terminated.
6 Specify how disputes with the licensee will be handled and when and if arbitration will be used. Specify what happens for each term of the agreement that isn't met.

Make sure the intended provisions of your agreement are legal in the country you are licensing in. For example, the government may wish to limit agreements that drain capital from the country or restrict its exports. If government policy seems to be a problem, you or the licensee candidate may be able to resolve the matter ahead of time by demonstrating to the government that the benefits outweigh the cost. For example, perhaps the local company will be gaining experience and skills, technology will be transferred, or the need for imports will be reduced.

Franchising

A franchise is a right to market goods, services, or trade secrets (rather than technologies) in a particular territory. It normally includes product specifications as well as merchandising, quality factors, and supply requirements. Franchising in international markets relates as much to joint ventures as it does to licensing, because often the only way to get a good franchisee and to retain adequate control is to take on an equity partner.

An increasing number of small U.S. franchisers are taking their concepts abroad, following the trail blazed by McDonald's, 7-Eleven, and many other large chains. Pacific Rim consumers are as receptive as Americans to a standardized format that offers a known level of service and quality. Many of the success stories in Pacific Rim trade have been in fast food and hotels and motels. Today, franchises are also available there in photocopy marts, children's exercise centers, and other services. Video Update, Inc.—a franchiser of video rental stores based in St. Paul, Minnesota—has licensed a joint venture in Malaysia to open a hundred Video Update stores over two years. It is negotiating a similar venture in Singapore.

Areas of Opportunity

Most existing franchises are in consumer products or services. Are there other areas that have been overlooked as having potential for franchises? One way to judge is to look around the domestic markets and see what's opening up. Prime areas include professional services and business services; training, education, and industrial services; and medical and health care. Some of these are franchises and some are wholly owned chains.

As of the late 1980s, over 500 U.S. franchisers held over 30,000 overseas franchises. Most of the growth has come from small and medium-size franchisers that market a wide variety of services and products. Over half of the new franchisers are in business services, as companies all over the world go outside to fulfill many functions previously performed internally. Franchising is rising rapidly in accounting, collection services, mail processing, advertising, message taking, package wrapping and shipping, business consulting, security, business rec-ordkeeping, tax preparation, and personal services.

The personal-service franchises popular in the United States are spreading to the Pacific Rim as well: weed control centers, hair salons, temporary-help agencies, printing and copying services, medical centers, and clothing stores. Japan still has the most U.S. franchises in the Pacific Rim, including restaurants, ice cream parlors, donut shops, and convenience stores. But U.S. franchises are spreading rapidly throughout the region. The following table shows the distribution of U.S. franchisers in the Pacific Rim in 1985.

Nation	Number of U.S. Franchisers
Australia	75
Japan	66
New Zealand	22
Rest of Pacific Rim	74

For many of these franchisers, marketing has been easy. They have been deluged with unsolicited inquiries from other countries. Their problem lies in making sure that they select the best available franchisees. The key to franchises in the Pacific Rim—as in domestic markets—is keeping adequate control to ensure a standardized product. Maintaining that control with an independently owned franchise requires that somebody be there—a key person who can monitor operations closely, give adequate direction, provide technical support, and supply essential ingredients that can be controlled. The franchiser must specify and control the advertising and promotion and offer assistance to maintain quality, ensure operating procedures, and oversee marketing and promotion.

Some small franchisers sell a master franchise to a well-capitalized local company with experienced management, giving it the right to establish all future franchises in that country. This ensures the small franchiser that someone in the country has a financial stake in its investment, knows the local market, and can provide needed support to local franchisees.

Pitfalls of Franchising

Many new, smaller franchisers encounter several problems as a result of their inexperience and lack of overseas clout. The major pitfalls in franchising are similar to those in licensing: the possibility of losing control and of creating competitors. These risks also hold in the domestic market and are potent pressures for having an equity joint venture partner or for converting a franchise into a joint venture or a wholly owned subsidiary. To avoid these pitfalls, you must check potential joint venture franchisees initially, making sure they have adequate capital and business acumen.

Another pitfall for inexperienced franchisers is failing to take into account the need to exportize a product or service for a Pacific Rim market. One franchiser that initially ignored this was Yogurt Tree, Inc., a Baltimore chain of frozen yogurt stores. It spent nearly a year preparing for the opening of its first overseas store in Tokyo. A major reason for the delay was the discovery that its yogurt did not suit Japanese tastes. Yogurt Tree then conducted taste tests with Japanese people living in the United States and reformulated its product.

Regardless of how well written the franchising agreement is, when things do go wrong the parties will get through, not by legal recourse, but by the quality of their relationship. This means not only that the parties think they can get along together, but that there's something of benefit in the agreement for each one so that it's worthwhile to fight to maintain the relationship.

Companies interested in franchising can get information and assistance from the sources listed in the Appendixes.

Contracting

Overseas contracts are often thought to be the province of huge engineering companies like Bechtel. The contract may involve the construction of a railroad or a highway, an electrical grid or a hydroelectric dam, an airport or a hotel, a hospital or a university campus. The customer may be a national government, a local government or agency, or a private company. Such a large contract requires the diversified resources and capabilities of a major company that has tentacles all over the world to seize opportunities, the patience and clout to negotiate contracts, access to huge sums of working capital, the craftiness to outbid hungry competitors from all over the world, and the staying power to weather innumerable delays and changes in direction. What to a contractor is just a project with limited scope and duration is to the client government a major investment in its infrastructure, one that must be closely monitored by government watchdogs or international financiers.

But for every large contract there are hundreds of smaller overseas contracts and subcontracts, and many of these provide opportunities for smaller U.S. businesses to enter international markets. Many projects in the Pacific Rim go to large Japanese, Korean, and European companies, but some of the subcontracts go to alert American entrepreneurs.

Money Left on the Table

Going after Pacific Rim projects is an area in which many U.S. companies leave lucrative opportunities on the table. Caught up in the crush of domestic business, such companies are often surprised to discover that the know-how they take for granted is in very high demand in many developing nations and can provide the basis of very lucrative Pacific Rim business. This holds not just for engineering and manufacturing services, but also for professional and management skills that are sorely needed in developing nations. Following are the range of needs:

- Feasibility studies
- Engineering and design services
- Site preparation and layout
- Facilities selection or construction
- Provision and installation of specialized equipment or components
- Construction of needed infrastructure: roads, utilities, housing, schools, shops
- Management services
- Hiring and training of workers
- Project or subproject management
- Professional services
- Project design
- Provision of technical support or maintenance
- Ongoing project management

There are two ways for smaller companies that lack an extensive track record and resources to obtain contracts: (1) bidding on jobs financed by development banks and (2) piggyback contracting.

Bidding on a Development Project. How do U.S. companies without prior Pacific Rim experience tap into such opportunities? The first step is to subscribe to *Commerce Business Daily,* published by the Department of Commerce, which lists all international bidding opportunities. When developing nations obtain funding for projects from international sources such as the Agency for International Development (AID), the World Bank, and the Asian Development Bank (ADB), they are often unable to perform the work themselves. They then award contracts under international competitive bidding. When the United States provides the funding, the contracts must go to U.S. companies. A range of projects is available for both prime contractors and subcontractors. For large projects, whether government or private, there is advance notice of a year or more.

ADB supports two types of projects: loans and technical assistance grants. ADB announcements are made a year or two in advance, often when projects are in the tentative stages, and names of contacts are supplied for each project: potential contractors, equipment suppliers, and consultants.

For loan projects, the primary responsibility for selecting suppliers rests with the executing agency in the borrowing country. The best way to establish contact is through the appropriate U.S. Foreign Service Commercial officer. For technical assistance projects, there is little opportunity for contractors or equipment suppliers, but consultants are often needed. It's important to respond quickly, since ADB selects consultants as they are needed. Get in touch with ADB through the U.S. Director's Office. Express interest in specific technical assistance projects, and put your credentials on file.

Some recent Pacific Rim projects sponsored by ADB include:

- *Korea.* Construction of sewage treatment plants.
- *The Philippines.* Development of Tago River irrigation projects, including

related civil works, pilot demonstrations, rural water supply, and public health services. Rehabilitation of the North Harbor in Manila for domestic container handling and provision of cargo-handling equipment. A preliminary technical assistance project.

- *The Philippines.* Technical assistance in project preparation. Feasibility study for the rehabilitation and expansion of selected steel mills.
- *Thailand.* Project preparation for building 1,000 kilometers of secondary and provincial roads.
- *Indonesia.* Advisory and operational technical assistance for improving the operation and maintenance of government-run irrigation systems. Assessment of current operation and maintenance, procedures, practices, organizations, and budgets.

Development banks are not in the business of promoting exports. They don't buy directly; they work through agencies in the developing nations. However, small companies can work through them to sell professional or technical services or sometimes a demonstration project. Consultants are hired to perform feasibility or engineering studies. Equipment manufacturers that cannot sell their equipment directly to a project may be able to get paid to install a demo program. Some companies hired to conduct a feasibility study have written their own hardware into the final design.

Consultants can register with ADB by forwarding a completed copy of the DACON 1600 form, which can be obtained from ADB's Consulting Services Division. This is the same form used by the World Bank and by other development banks and international financial institutions. (See the Appendixes.)

The major drawback to relying on published bid notices is that the time between publication of the bid list and the closing date is often quite short. You must send in a letter saying what bid you are responding to, what equipment or services you have, and what your price is. That is why it's important to identify projects long before the tender announcements are officially made in *Commerce Business Daily.* You would do well to make a personal visit to the executing agency to demonstrate your expertise and experience on similar projects. Visit the Pacific Rim nation or the bank offices. (The World Bank is in Washington, and both AID and ADB are in Manila.) Don't wait for the computer to pop your name out. Make your presence known initially and keep up correspondence. Through such contacts, you will learn of projects in the early talk stage and thus be prepared to respond more quickly to tender announcements.

One of the functions of an export management company is to represent its clients on appropriate bidding lists. All you can do is register with such a company and gain representation on the lists. If you get no response on a particular bid after a year or so, forget about it. You may well win a bid eventually, and in any case, participating in the bidding process is an important discipline for you to learn.

You can also work through the growing number of U.S. or state agencies that help contractors find appropriate opportunities. For example, under California's energy export program, the California Energy Commission helps link up small California companies in the energy field with overseas contracting opportunities and assists them in working through the bidding process.

One of the major pitfalls to bidding on overseas projects is that bidding often takes place in two stages. The first round is usually just for the purpose of feeling out the market. Agencies solicit bids that they have no intention of accepting in order to get an idea of what contractors will offer and for what price. Then they refine their tender offers and put out the real requests for bids. Sometimes project requests for bids are written with one company in mind and are stated so that only one company can qualify. This is the old "sole source" stratagem, very common in the United States. In fact, all overseas practices are familiar to companies that make bids in the United States.

In some countries, the bidding process is simply not fair. Despite the published list, the bid is awarded on other grounds. It can be very difficult for small companies to bid on certain ASEAN projects because of the level of corruption. More often than not, the parts of contracts that are accessible to small companies—such as providing the carpeting in a series of new hotels—are awarded to the cousin or uncle of a chief decision maker. The only way to get in is to know the key decision makers and to make them feel it is worth their while to give the contract to you.

American companies are at a disadvantage as a result of the Foreign Corrupt Practices Act, which makes it illegal to make payments to influence the award of a contract. Unfortunately, competitors from many other nations face no such limitation. This provides a competitive disadvantage that effectively shuts American companies out of many projects.

Some small companies put too many of their eggs in one basket. You should never depend on or wait for any one project. The fact that bidding and negotiating can go on for years means that you must have an ongoing stream of other business.

Piggyback Contracting. Many smaller businesses have used subcontracts as a springboard to successful international operations. For example, Bently-Nevada first entered Pacific Rim trade as a subcontractor, riding on the coattails of a larger Korean company that had a contract to build fertilizer plants in China. Bently sold instruments to the prime contractor and also contracted to train the Chinese to monitor the equipment.

It is tempting for a company just to sell its equipment to a prime contractor and then wash its hands of the project; but this is a very dangerous approach. To protect your name in a given market, it is important to retain control over the installation and maintenance of your equipment.

Bently-Nevada felt it was essential not just to sell its instruments, but also to service them and train people to use them. The company knew that if the instruments broke down or were used incorrectly, the whole project would falter and its reputation would suffer irreparable damage—both in that market and throughout the region. The prime contractor realized this as well and made service part of the specs of the job. Of course, going with the larger company was invaluable for Bently-Nevada in another way: It was able to leverage its market-entry capabilities much more than it could have on its own. It used the subcontracting arrangement as a springboard for establishing a permanent presence in the region.

Creating Your Own Opportunities

If you read the bidding announcements in *Commerce Business Daily,* you soon discover that one of the qualifications is prior international experience. However, even if you are new to global trade, you can still use this route to break into the Pacific Rim. Here's how.

1. *Offer something unique.* Offer a unique service that a Pacific Rim nation is having trouble finding elsewhere. This is where many U.S. companies miss golden opportunities. They fail to realize that the organization offering the contract must put together a complete package of services to execute a project successfully. Their particular technical or professional know-how may be a hard-to-find key element in that project.

2. *Keep your antennae out.* How can you gain a broadened perspective? It is a matter of keeping your antennae tuned. Talk with the people directly engaged in a project, either clients or contractors. Talk to knowledgeable people not directly connected—people the project is meant to serve. Read published commentaries on the difficulties major projects are facing. You will find yourself saying, "I know what they need! I could provide that."

Contact the people who are in a position to understand what you are saying, and to make a decision. By offering to solve a small piece of the puzzle, you can sometimes avoid the competitive bidding process and be hired directly by the project sponsor or contractor. In fact, your real customer base may not be project sponsors at all, but a limited number of major engineering companies that win most of the bids. Your strategy should be to keep in touch with those companies. A huge multinational may seem like a "whale" to you, but your role may be simply to act as "pilot fish." The whale needs the pilot fish and vice versa.

3. *Become part of the problem-solving process.* With experience, you learn that a key to success in contracting for overseas projects is to become part of the problem-solving process rather than responding to request for bids. For example, Loctite worked for several years with Chinese automakers to find a solution for a leakage problem in automobile manufacture. The company was subsequently awarded a joint venture contract to manufacture sealants in China.

4. *Do a good job.* When you get a contract, whether it's a feasibility study, a demonstration project, or a subcontract, make sure you do an outstanding job the first time. Your performance on this one will greatly affect your ability to get future jobs.

Negotiating Turnkey Contracts

A valuable way to establish presence in a market is to turn a contract to supply a particular service or piece of hardware into a turnkey arrangement. H-Tech discovered that its key to success lay in providing a complete, "walk in" project. Its turnkey system included hardware specially adapted to the circumstances and the environment, site preparation, construction, training, ongoing technical support and maintenance, and all other services needed to ensure that the facility would work as promised.

Turnkey service is very important to developing nations, which often lack the skilled personnel to operate and maintain sophisticated equipment. Again, turnkey contracts may be negotiated with the project sponsor or with the prime contractor. Sometimes, such projects are undertaken with a local joint venture partner selected according to its ability to provide the ongoing technical, maintenance, and management services.

There are drawbacks to turnkey contracts as well. On a turnkey project, you play or share the role of prime contractor. You will be held responsible for the successful completion of a project and for its successful operation thereafter. Thus you face two main hazards:

1. You can be held liable for the impact of events beyond your control; for example, a typhoon wipes out the work of a subcontractor, delaying the project beyond the contracted completion date.
2. You take on too much and fail to perform adequately.

Ironically, some small companies are defeated by too much success. Suppose you are in the final stages of negotiating a project with the Chinese. They like you, and you are very convincing. They keep suggesting other services, and you find yourself saying, "Yes, I can do that. Yes, I can do that too!" All of a sudden, your $2 million company has a $5 million contract—bigger than anything it has ever done before. With the dollar signs looking bigger and bigger, you may promise to do things you are unable to deliver. Now the smart thing would be to go home and start putting together a group of companies to help you out. Instead, you may say to yourself, "I worked hard to get this. Why should I share the wealth?" Because the option may be to default. You may put yourself in better shape for future contracts by demonstrating your skill at assembling a consortium of contractors and managing them successfully.

Forming a Joint Venture

A joint venture is a new business enterprise that is legally separate from either of the parent companies. Two companies agree to set up a new venture and share in its ownership, management, and control; each parent has equity in the new enterprise according to the resources it has put in. Entering a joint venture in the Pacific

Rim means making a significant commitment to the market. The risks are the same as those inherent in any partnership, but in addition, your partner is a distant foreign company!

Range of Joint Venture Partnerships

A joint venture partner might be a small local distributor, a huge multinational, or even a foreign government. There are as many types of partners as there are reasons for making joint venture agreements. The key reasons that a joint venture may be the preferred method of operation, especially for a small or medium-size company, are described below.

Local Requirements.   Many companies that would prefer a wholly owned operation are forced into a joint venture because the foreign government requires local ownership in direct foreign investment. Joint ventures are becoming increasingly common in the Pacific Rim. Import controls and trade barriers may make the import of your products difficult or impossible, and the limitations on foreign ownership may prevent you from setting up a wholly owned subsidiary. In these cases, a joint venture may be your only way to gain access to the market.

Synergism.   Two companies with complementary strengths may form a joint venture—for example, a strong manufacturer with a strong marketer, or an innovative design company with an efficient manufacturer. Small businesses often form joint ventures with larger companies to gain financial clout, market access, and manufacturing capacity, whereas the larger companies seek to gain the latest technology. Williams-Sonoma, a San Francisco-based specialty retailer with eighty-six U.S. stores and $140 million in revenue, teamed up with Tokyu Department Store Co., one of Japan's largest retailers, with seventeen stores and $4 billion in sales. Williams-Sonoma provides retailing and mail order marketing expertise, while Tokyu handles site selection, operation, and finance. Williams-Sonoma is majority owner.

In some markets, especially in Japan, you may form a joint venture with a company that has complementary technical resources. For example, your company may have design and engineering capability, while the Japanese company has manufacturing process knowledge and capabilities that you lack. Together you can undertake a project that neither one of you could handle alone. Forming a joint venture may require less capital or other assets from you than paying for the entire operation yourself.

SpectraPhysics sought a synergistic combination by teaming its laser technology with the strong materials-handling technology of its Japanese partner. SpectraPhysics did not want so large a partner that it would be overwhelmed. The key here is that instead of a technology transfer the two companies made a technology exchange, so that no matter what happens in the future, they are going to get as much out of the joint venture as they put into it. When it comes to high-tech knowledge, cash and market share can often be less valuable in the long run than access to that knowledge.

A consortium of companies may form a joint venture so that they can offer a complete-package bid on a project for which none of them alone has all the required capabilities. Shearson Lehman Hutton and Tishman Speyer entered a joint venture with Chinese partners to finance and build the million-square-foot Beijing American Express Center, a project involving land assembly and construction companies, law firms to deal with three languages and three legal jurisdictions, and forty financial institutions.

Greater Local Control.   Some companies upgrade a local distributor to a joint venture partner because they feel that a business with equity in the venture will have a greater stake in its success. A larger company may form a joint venture with a smaller distributor in order to gain greater control over the distributor's efforts in the local market. Franchisers may form joint ventures with their franchisees in order to gain more control over the quality of service or production.

A local joint venture partner knows the local market, has a general knowledge of the local business and political environment, and knows the language and the culture. The ideal local partner is one that knows customers, has a good reputation, has access to the marketing channels, and knows the competition. Such a presence and experience might take an outside company years to build up—if, in fact, it could do so at all.

Access to the local business community, including bankers and government officials, has two great benefits: Through your joint venture partner, you get an earlier warning than you might otherwise of impending changes in policies, whether for the better or for the worse. Also, if part of your enterprise is locally owned, it is protected (relatively speaking) from the ill winds occasionally directed against foreign investment.

Market Penetration or Expansion.   You might form a joint venture with another U.S. company or even with a company from a third country in order to enter a local Pacific Rim market, either for a specific project contract or for an ongoing enterprise. For example, Bechtel has found little market for its services in Japan or Korea; however, it has had success in working with Japanese engineering companies that operate in other Pacific Rim countries.

Forming a joint venture with a company from a developing nation might be a way to become competitive in one of the fields in which American industry has lost ground in recent years—for example, construction, hotel management, or engineering. You may form a joint venture with a local company in order to manufacture and market products or services both in the local country and in other countries as well. U.S. electronics manufacturers in Singapore have formed joint ventures with local agents to distribute to other ASEAN markets.

An American company wishing to set up assembly plants in China often joint ventures with a Hong Kong company experienced in arranging and managing Chinese operations, rather than going into China on its own. The Hong Kong company expects to gain access to the American technology and thus upgrade its technical capabilities.

You might enter or build a market by forming a joint venture with a government-run enterprise. In China this is often the only option, the only way of doing business. An example is Loctite's joint venture with a Chinese automobile manufacturer. Another joint U.S.–China project involves importing tens of thousands of American cattle, raising them in China under U.S. agricultural methods, and then exporting the beef to other markets in Asia. Government-sponsored joint ventures are also common in Indonesia and Malaysia.

Advantages and Drawbacks to a Joint Venture

A joint venture is often a logical progression from some other form of operation. A company may enter international trade selling through a trading company, gain experience and move on to an agent or distributor, and then form a joint venture with the agent or distributor for that market. A company that licenses its technology to a manufacturer may later form a joint venture to work more closely with the manufacturer, exchange techniques and processes, and create a more unified image. Making such a progression has advantages as well as drawbacks (see Table 6–1).

Lower Risk, Higher Profit. If you have been exporting your products, there are several advantages to shifting to a joint venture: You are sharing the risk, you are gaining more control over operational decisions than with a distributor or contract manufacturer, and your profitability and return on sales are likely to be greater.

A joint venture combines the benefits of using your own trusted employees and having good local support. Since you are teamed up with a company that has

Table 6-1. Forming a joint venture vs. selling through a local distributor.

Advantages of a Joint Venture	*Drawbacks of a Joint Venture Compared With Distributor*
· You "look local" and can circumvent some market-entry restrictions.	· It is harder to find a good partner than a good distributor.
· Your joint venture partner has a major stake in having you succeed in the market.	· It's like getting married: If you choose the wrong partner, it's hard to change.
· You gain some protection from competitors.	· You are committed to the market and face big penalties for early withdrawal.
· You have more recourse against unfair treatment in local courts.	· There may be political limits on your ownership and control.
· Action in local courts against patent or copyright infringement may be easier.	

equity, your partner shares your interest in the success of the venture. A joint venture also means a significantly larger involvement in the market on your part. Since, at this stage, you are investing your equity and exposing yourself to liability and the possibility of losing assets, you have a much greater responsibility for the management of the operation and for marketing in unfamiliar markets.

Danger of Losing Control.   In addition to the problems inherent in any partnership, the major drawbacks to a joint venture relate to losing control of the remote operation to a partner with divergent interests. Many companies opt for wholly owned subsidiaries over joint ventures in order to retain control, ensure high-quality management, and guarantee product quality. The key question is: How do you retain adequate control to get what you want from a joint venture? If you own the majority share, the problem is lessened. But in some nations, you'll be prevented from retaining majority ownership.

The two most important areas over which you risk losing control are financial decision making and the quality of your product or service. A joint venture may not work if you can't control pricing, production processes, and the ways in which profits are used. These pitfalls can best be avoided by selecting the right Pacific Rim partner, negotiating a strong agreement, staying in constant communication, and keeping on top of operations.

You can maintain effective control even if you're a minority owner by retaining some key function or essential component—for example, design or engineering capabilities, production process technologies or equipment, technical or management expertise, access to financing for sales, or access to international markets, especially in the United States. In each of these cases, effective control is maintained because you have the key resources without which the joint venture would fail. Of course, this cuts both ways. If your joint venture partner is supplying a key factor, it has great control even if it is only a minority owner.

Another common strategy is to find an inactive partner or passive investor, such as a banker or venture capitalist. If you are forming a joint partnership simply to gain access to a market, you may seek a partner that will benefit but has no interest in making operational decisions. Or you may seek a partner whose role is limited to providing an important local resource such as raw materials, land, or production facilities. The key to success in a joint venture is not retaining control or having an ironclad agreement, but finding a partner that shares your goals and has as much to gain from a successful operation as you do.

Finding the Right Joint Venture Partner

Compared with an agent or licensee arrangement, a joint venture agreement is much harder to undo if it doesn't work out to your satisfaction. So it's more important to spend time making sure you have the right partner before negotiating a final agreement. Identifying a potential joint venture partner is similar to identifying potential agents or distributors, a process described in Chapter 5. You first need to define the criteria for an ideal partner. Profile the joint venture partner that you want in terms of complementary resources, financial clout, access to marketing channels, production facilities, technical capabilities, quality of management and work force, and political, business, and financial contacts in the nation.

Identifying Potential Partners.   In most countries, there are fewer options for joint venture partners than for distributors or agents. In fact, there may be only one possibility. You may quickly identify the one company that is a potential joint venture partner for you; or perhaps that company has identified you and approached you with a tentative offer. If you are already operating in the market, you probably know all your potential joint venture partners, or you may be considering a joint venture agreement with your agent or distributor. If you need help in identifying potential partners, the Department of Commerce, OPIC, and AMCHAM can provide referrals. You can also use the other sources described for distributors in Chapter 5.

Again, if you are going into China, you may have no choice in the matter. In many situations, you either form a joint venture with a designated government-run enterprise or get shut out of the market. Many companies just stay out. The ones that do enter, do so after years of negotiation.

The normal channels of identifying a suitable joint venture partner don't work in China because few organizations will have the background you need. Patience and persistence are required, but they can pay off very well. Ederer, Inc., of Seattle, a crane manufacturer with a hundred employees, spent seven years exploring business possibilities in China before signing a contract. After traveling widely in China, company executives finally decided they could work well with the managers of a factory in Szechuan Province under the Power Ministry. For an initial joint venture project, they signed a $6 million contract to build a dam that involved $5 million worth of U.S. exports. Ederer provided engineering, technology, and technical equipment and helped the Chinese build some of the basic equipment for the project.

Today Ederer technicians live in China, and a Chinese official works at the company's factory in Seattle. Ederer's premise is that the enterprise must be mutually beneficial. The company has nothing but praise for the performance and quality of work of its Chinese partner. A positive attitude plus painstaking preparation is the key to Ederer's long-term success in China. On the basis of this experience, it is investigating opportunities in Korea and India, and in Taiwan, where Ederer hopes to sell cranes for nuclear power plants.

Meeting Face to Face.   After you have selected a potential joint venture partner, you will need to set up several face-to-face meetings before saying yes. During the initial meetings, your purpose is not to negotiate a contract but to get to know the other party. It is important to hold extensive discussions early on. Explore the goals and priorities of your prospective local partner and make sure they are congruent with yours. Key issues include rate of growth, product areas to expand into, allocation of revenues and profits, marketing and promotion, and strategies for dealing with the competition. When joint ventures founder, the cause is less likely to be personality clashes than diverging interests.

You must be willing to back out of a promising venture if it becomes apparent that there is a misalignment on basic policy issues. And if you do come to terms, these basic policy decisions must be incorporated into the joint venture agreement.

Ironing Out the Agreement.   Financial issues can be particularly knotty. Negotiating the percentage share of equity for each party can be tricky, since the contributions most likely involve things other than cash. A value must be placed on technology, manufacturing processes, access to distribution and markets, equipment and facilities provided, and ongoing management of operations.

To meet Taiwan's requirement for majority local ownership, a Connecticut manufacturer of surgical sponges set up a corporation with a Taiwanese "silent partner" producing the sponges. However, the local partner took advantage of its official majority share and claimed the right to redistribute profits. The ensuing litigation forced the manufacturer out of business. This debacle was caused by a poor understanding of Taiwanese law, poor documentation of negotiations, and poor chemistry between partners.

The agreement must recognize the fact that the relative contributions of the partners may change over the life of the joint venture. For example, if one partner makes major contributions of cash and facilities up front and the other partner manages the operations, develops products, and markets over a period of time, then the second partner's equity share in the enterprise should increase over time. These are very difficult factors to quantify, yet the effort must be made in order to have a workable and lasting agreement.

You should also pay close attention to operational issues. You must make sure the new entity is properly incorporated, capitalized, and licensed to do business—in every nation involved. Then come the issues of decision making and control:

- Who is responsible for decisions on new products or services, new markets, competitive strategy, pricing, purchase of facilities or capital equipment, and advertising or promotional strategies?
- Which partner will be responsible for making which management decisions?
- How will managers and other key people be selected?
- How much autonomy will the ongoing venture have? That is, will it operate more like a division or an independent subsidiary? To the joint venture's managers, the enterprise is a subsidiary with two parent companies. Thus all the potential problems of any parent-subsidiary arrangement become doubled (at least) if there is not a smooth working relationship among the three entities.
- How will earnings from the joint venture be allocated? For example, will they be reinvested or returned to the parent companies?

Local laws may influence your decisions in many of these areas. You may be limited in your ability to take profits out of the country, and most of the joint venture's managers and other personnel may have to be local people. Some nations not only limit foreign ownership but also require an increasing proportion of local ownership during the life of the venture. Figure 6–2 presents ten important guidelines for setting up a successful joint venture.

Sustaining the Partnership.   Successful operation of a joint venture requires continuing communication between the partners. Two operating principles are at work here:

1. *Flexibility.* You must be willing to roll with situations and problems as they emerge.
2. *Continuity.* It is important to avoid constant turnover of key people, either within the joint venture or among involved divisions of the parent companies. Turnover is often much greater in U.S. companies than in Asian ones, and your Pacific Rim partner will resent the resulting lack of continuity.

If you are just starting out, avoid making an agreement with a joint venture partner for exclusive worldwide representation. As with licensing, do it first for a

Figure 6-2.   Ten guidelines for creating a workable joint venture.

---

1 Don't waste time negotiating points that aren't really important. Don't become involved in detailed considerations of worst-case scenarios so that you neglect to discuss how the venture will actually operate or what each company expects to get from the venture.

2 Be patient. Like all new businesses, joint ventures can take years to become profitable.

3 Let those who will be responsible for running the operation be among the architects of the deal. The operating managers must be involved from the beginning.

4 Let the CEO of the venture run it with as little interference as possible from the two parents.

5 Keep joint venture operations well defined and of relatively short duration—perhaps even on a project-by-project basis.

6 Specify triggers for reevaluation or renegotiation. Specify events and milestones that will automatically trigger reassessment of the joint venture, at which time the partners can restructure or even pull out.

7 Consider nonequity ways to cooperate with other companies—e.g., cross-licensing agreements, cooperative development projects, and research consortiums.

8 Remember that a successful joint venture depends on friendships among top people, hard work, openness, a sense of humor, and mutual trust.

9 Be willing to take a little bit of risk.

10 Be flexible about cross-cultural contacts. Be aware of different business styles. Typically, U.S. companies want everything specified from the start, a demand that Pacific Rim companies may take as a sign of mistrust.

SOURCE: Adapted from Kathrine Rudie Harrigan, *Managing for Joint Venture Success: Strategies for Joint Ventures* (Lexington, Mass.: Lexington Books, 1986).

limited area or even for a specific project. Start with a "trial marriage" and see how you and your partner perform together in a venture of limited duration and scope. Then decide whether to make the joint venture permanent. If you are small and your partner is big, and that partner ties you up, you will never get big. No matter how great the venture looks to you in the beginning, you may later regret doing it. If you set up a joint venture with a local distributor and your partner performs poorly, your reputation will suffer and your competition will overtake you.

Establishing a Wholly Owned Subsidiary

Companies first entering Pacific Rim trade rarely opt to establish their own facilities overseas. However, any company that is committed to doing business in a number of international markets will eventually want to establish subsidiaries in its major markets. Some companies may leap directly from domestic manufacturing to building a factory in a Pacific Rim nation if the process is made easy for them in that market.

In several Pacific Rim countries—Australia and New Zealand, Singapore, Hong Kong, Taiwan, and Japan—investment is so easy that a relatively small company new to international trade may profitably create an operation there. Taiwan and Singapore, for example, have a number of new high-tech industrial parks. Their governments are so eager to attract U.S. high-tech companies—and certain other companies—that they offer important assistance to smaller businesses. It's a seller's market.

In some other nations—Korea, Malaysia, Indonesia—the governments are more selective about which direct investments they will allow, or to whom they will offer assistance and incentives. Potential investors must pass through many hurdles and bureaucratic delays.

Setting up a wholly owned subsidiary means having your own overseas operation, running your own show, as a branch or subsidiary of your U.S. company. Some U.S. businesses pull up stakes and move their whole operation overseas. A number of smaller service companies owned by Americans—from consulting firms in Jakarta to furniture stores in Tokyo—are well established in Pacific Rim markets. These businesses are not subsidiaries, but much of what is said here pertains to them as well.

Your wholly owned operation can be for any type of business—manufacturing, distribution, service, or all three. It can range from a major factory to a one-person sales office. It may take on new operations as your overseas business matures. For example, many computer component manufacturers that initially set up in Singapore to re-export to the United States now distribute to other Pacific Rim markets from Singapore. They have set up a service center to train their regional distributors and users and maintain their products. U.S.-owned fast-food companies find themselves providing training for hotel operators in China.

Why Run Your Own Operation?

Most companies that enter Pacific Rim markets in a joint venture or a licensing arrangement eventually discover compelling reasons to establish a wholly owned operation. You may wish to regain full control of your operation rather than having to share it with even the most accommodating joint venture partner. You may seek managers and engineers who are 100 percent on your team. In many cases, that team will not be Americans sent there from your home office but local people who have been hired there and trained. Or they may be people from that country who have gone to school and have worked in the United States, whom you hire to run your operation in their home country. You may want to have full authority and responsibility for planning and maximum flexibility to move rapidly into new markets. You may need to be absolutely confident that you are protecting your new technology and keeping your trade secrets secret.

Reasons for Setting Up a Subsidiary

Compared with a joint venture, companies prefer 100 percent ownership in order to:

- Maintain complete control of their operations
- Have managers who are 100 percent on their team
- Have full authority and responsibility for planning
- Protect their technology
- Maximize flexibility to move into new markets
- Maximize return on investment

The two traditional reasons for establishing a wholly owned manufacturing facility in the Pacific Rim are often still valid: to reduce production expenses by using lower-cost labor for assembly, and to gain access to markets that cannot easily be penetrated by exporting from the United States. Today, there are two other key factors that persuade U.S. companies—even small ones—to set up their own Pacific Rim operation.

1. *To establish production facilities near major customers.* In-country production is particularly important in Japan, but is of growing importance throughout the Pacific Rim. Japanese companies prefer doing business with other Japanese companies. Japanese manufacturers rely on just-in-time delivery of components, and thus have a strong preference for nearby suppliers. But if your business operates in the Japanese market for a few years, it may come to be treated like a Japanese company by its customers.

2. *To establish facilities near needed resources.* Today, "needed resources" include not just raw materials but also knowledge and research. Japan, Taiwan, Hong Kong, and Singapore all have versions of Silicon Valley and are seeking to

Figure 6-3. Examples of host-country investment incentives.

Income Tax Incentives

Corporate income tax holidays (exemptions from income tax)—may be limited or unlimited in time and amount
Accelerated depreciation
Investment tax credit
Tax exemption or rebate on funds used to acquire public bonds
Increased deductions for business entertainment in connection with export sales
"Double deduction" of export promotion expenses
Waiver of income tax withholding on royalty or fee income of a foreign transferor of technology
Favorable formulas for determining a foreign contractor's taxable income
Reduced personal taxation of foreign managers and technicians
Reduced income tax withholding on dividends to foreign shareholders from approved investments

Other Tax Incentives

Exemption from excise taxes on imported machinery and equipment
Exemption from registration duties, stamp taxes, or capital taxes upon incorporation
Exemption from property taxes
Exemption from sales, value-added, and excise taxes with respect to export sales

Tariff Incentives

Waivers on import tariffs for machinery, equipment, and raw materials
Access to regional common markets
Tariff-free foreign trade zones

---

attract U.S. companies and their technology. This is a benefit to the United States as well. In Japan, U.S. companies can gain access to the latest research and most advanced manufacturing processes of Japanese companies—information that is often not available domestically. In Singapore, Taiwan, and Hong Kong, companies can hire engineers, designers, and computer programmers at a much lower cost than in the United States.

A major factor to consider in selecting a location for direct investment are the incentives offered by the target country (see Figure 6-3). However, since many multinationals have "gone shopping" for the best available overseas package, the various nations seeking to attract investment have all adopted similar incentives. The major difference is often the "perks" offered to companies that are willing to locate in special areas that the nation is trying to build up.

For a smaller company inexperienced in Pacific Rim markets, the drawbacks to setting up a wholly owned operation are the flip side of the benefits to using a joint venture, a licensing arrangement, or some other, more limited type of operation to first enter a Pacific Rim market. Most of these drawbacks cut across location and include:

- The high cost of establishing a wholly owned operation
- Ignorance of local markets and business culture
- The time it takes to become an effective player
- Bias against foreign ownership from both customers and the government
- Difficulty in obtaining needed financing to begin operations
- Difficulty in finding and hiring managers, sales staff, and technical people

There is another argument against establishing an overseas factory to sell into that market: It may again be cheaper to export from the United States. Some companies that formerly manufactured in the Pacific Rim have recently drawn back to their domestic plants. In many instances, American domestic factories have become the low-cost producer, even for products sold in the Pacific Rim. This is due primarily to three factors: (1) The dollar has declined against other currencies, especially the yen, the new Taiwan dollar, and the Korean won; (2) many tariffs and other barriers to imports have been dropped, often under pressure from the U.S. government; and (3) labor costs in Japan and the NICs are sky-rocketing, and many needed skills are becoming scarce.

For example: Avon used to manufacture cosmetics in Taiwan for the local market, which was protected against imports by high tariff barriers. Then tariffs were almost eliminated, and the new Taiwan dollar appreciated 40 percent against the U.S. dollar. Avon found that it was cheaper to manufacture in the United States and export to Taiwan than to manufacture there. Likewise, U.S. auto manufacturers, which had been manufacturing in Taiwan under license, found it was more profitable to export cars from the United States. The United States is now Taiwan's largest source of imported cars.

There are several ways to establish overseas facilities. In the least restricted nations, you can simply rent space, hang out a shingle, and open a branch sales office. At the other end of the spectrum, you may build your own factory in an industrial park or establish a subsidiary corporation to manufacture for re-export. You may even enter the market by buying a local company—perhaps a former distributor.

Let's look at some examples of where, why, and how U.S. companies have successfully set up their own operations in the Pacific Rim.

Example 1: SpectraPhysics
Setting up a local office for marketing and technical support.

SpectraPhysics manufactures laser products for a variety of markets—from industrial applications to discotheque light shows—and sells around the world. When it first entered the Japanese market in the late 1960s, SpectraPhysics realized how difficult it would be to approach intended customers directly, since it had not built up the personal and business relationships required to succeed in Japan. So the company used a trading company as a distributor, one that was well respected and that knew local customers well.

SpectraPhysics worked very closely with the trading company to provide technical support, training, and follow-up service. Even so, the distributor put just one more layer between the company and its customers. As a result,

SpectraPhysics became less responsive to end-user requirements—particularly in the original equipment manufacture (OEM) area, where products must be modified or custom-designed to meet specific needs.

Because of the diversity of its products and markets in Japan, Spectra-Physics needed a variety of marketing channels. No single distributor could address all its needs. For this reason, in 1981, it established a small office in Tokyo—a combination liaison office and service center—to keep a finger on the pulse of the Japanese market. Initially, the liaison office consisted of one man reading the local papers and monitoring the activities of the trading company as it worked with customers.

After the office was set up, the relationship with the trading company changed. The distributor continued to sell for the company, but the SpectraPhysics country manager took over responsibility for follow-up service. SpectraPhysics set up a service center in the overseas office and hired its own service engineers. From the center, the country manager and service engineers worked very closely with OEM customers. In addition, SpectraPhysics trained its Japanese employees to go after markets neglected by the distributor.

By maintaining a local office, SpectraPhysics has been able to spot emerging trends more rapidly, and thus to enter new markets and gain stronger market shares than it might have otherwise. For example, it now sells an argon ion laser to companies that create lighting effects for discotheques. The original distributor had overlooked this market segment because it did not fit into the company's scientific instruments business.

Because engineers in Japanese companies prefer working with Japanese manufacturers, an American company—even one with Japanese employees—must be more aggressive in establishing a reputation and building business relationships with its potential customers. SpectraPhysics keeps in constant contact with scientists in Japanese industrial research labs so that when the labs develop a product five years from now, SpectraPhysics components will be specified. This is one of its most important tactics for maintaining and expanding its position in Japan.

Before SpectraPhysics established an overseas liaison office, Japan represented only about 50 percent of its Pacific Rim business. OEM currently represents about 85 percent of its Pacific Rim business. The company eventually replaced its country manager with a Japanese engineer. At present, all the personnel in that office are Japanese.

Many Japanese companies—with an injection of government R&D funds—have developed into real competitors of SpectraPhysics. To counter this, the company decided to team up with a Japanese partner—an unusual example of moving from a wholly owned operation to a joint venture.

Example 2: Garrett Automotive Products Company
Wholly owned factory in Japan.

While many manufacturers have found it best to set up a joint venture to enter Japanese markets, others have succeeded with a wholly owned manufacturing operation. Garrett Automotive Products, a wholly owned subsidiary of Allied-Signal Inc., initially entered Japan as a sales and warehouse operation. It slowly expanded its customer base to the point that, in 1985, building a wholly owned factory became feasible. Garrett now makes 25 percent of the 500,000 turbo-chargers bought annually by Japanese manufacturers of truck and car engines. Garrett was able to succeed in spite of stiff competition from nine Japanese companies because it provided its Japanese customers with technology they wanted but could not easily obtain in other ways.

Garrett encountered several unique problems. The Japanese engine manufacturers would have preferred doing business with Garrett in the United States—to protect the confidentiality of their own product development. In order to gain the confidence of Japanese manufacturers, and to recruit a labor force, Garrett had to find the right Japanese manager to run the operation. It hired Hideo Matsuoka—a well-known design engineer and professor who had worked at Mitsubishi Heavy Industries. Relying on old-school ties and word of mouth, Matsuoka recruited the local managers and assembly work force for the Garrett plant. He had to convince potential employees that Garrett was a permanent organization and would provide the same benefits—personal well-being, challenge, and growth—that a Japanese company would.

Garrett made changes in its California headquarters as well. A separate operating group was created to solve overseas problems immediately—such as flying parts 6,000 miles in eleven hours. Overseas customers expected Garrett to react just as quickly as their Japanese supplier next door.

Today, Garrett brings its key Japanese people to California for six-month training periods. The training and the basic manufacturing components come from the United States, but in every other way Garrett is a completely Japanese operation. Parts are designed to meet Japanese quality standards, and the company meets the expected just-in-time delivery patterns and aftermarket demands. In short, Garrett has succeeded by adapting to the commercial practices of Japan—from price negotiations to formal supply relationships to the support it gives to assembly workers.[1]

Branch or Subsidiary?

For a wholly owned operation in a Pacific Rim nation there are two basic modes of organization: (1) a branch office of a U.S. corporation and (2) a subsidiary of a U.S. corporation incorporated in the new market under the laws of that nation. Functionally, the two are about the same—they can be as independent or as tightly controlled as the parent wishes. But you must carefully consider a number of factors—especially the tax ramifications—before deciding which form to use for expansion. In addition there are pros and cons for each form.

1. Gail Bronson (ed.), "Just-in-Time—American Style," *Forbes,* March 9, 1987, p. 132.

Benefits of Opening a Branch

- It is easier and quicker to open—no minimum capitalization requirements.
- It is easier for a smaller company to do.
- There is no need to form a new corporation under foreign laws.
- Parent company can write off initial losses of a branch against taxes.
- It may be easier to obtain domestic financing for the branch, through the parent.

Drawbacks to Opening a Branch

- Parent company is legally liable for the actions of the branch. (A locally incorporated subsidiary is liable only to the extent of its own assets.)
- A branch is harder to sell.
- It is often difficult to transform a branch to a subsidiary later.
- It may be hard to obtain financing in the market.
- Government incentives are not available to a branch.
- A branch can't be part of a joint venture.
- Parent company may have to open the records of its entire operation—including U.S. and other foreign branches—to scrutiny by the local government.
- Net income of the branch is taxed in the United States when it is earned. (A subsidiary's income is not taxed until it is repatriated in the form of dividends. If earnings are reinvested in the subsidiary, U.S. taxes may be deferred indefinitely.)

One way to minimize some of the drawbacks of a branch is to establish a U.S. subsidiary whose sole asset is the overseas branch.

As noted, before choosing between a branch and a subsidiary, you should carefully compare the tax ramifications of each. These vary from country to country, and even within countries. Many nations will waive or defer taxes for companies that transfer technologies or invest in special development zones or industries. You must carefully study the nation's tax codes and its tax treaties with the United States. This is fertile ground for specialists. Get help from a U.S. accounting organization experienced in your markets. Tax factors influence not only whether you establish a branch or a subsidiary but also which market you choose for your operations.

The major tax factors to consider in Pacific Rim nations include:

- Foreign tax credit
- Tax deferral of foreign corporate income
- Taxation of foreign earnings of U.S. individuals
- Policy on tax losses
- Corporate tax rates, capital gains taxes, and individual tax rates
- Sales, consumption, or value-added taxes
- Taxation of dividends
- How taxable income is determined (How are certain items treated—for

example, depreciation, interest, royalties or licensing fees, loss carryforward, entertainment, investment credit for R&D, new subsidiaries?)
- Withholding taxes on dividends paid by subsidiaries
- Treatment of transactions between overseas and home offices (How can expenses and income be allocated? Can home office overhead be allocated to the branch or subsidiary overseas?)

Which Form of Operation Is Best for You?

There are many different forms of overseas operation. For most companies, however, the feasible choices will be quite limited—perhaps to only one choice. The pro-and-con discussions throughout Chapters 5 and 6 compare the most likely pairs of choices. To sum all this up, here are seven criteria to apply in evaluating your overseas operations.

1. *Characteristics of your product or service.* Industrial and commercial products usually have greater worldwide consistency. Thus it is much easier to produce them in a centralized plant. However, you may have to manufacture locally to meet unique production or safety standards.

Some consumer products can't be imported. To be in that market at all, you must produce locally—and perhaps work with a joint venture partner. The more your product needs to be adapted to local tastes or needs or requirements, the more likely it is that you'll want to produce in the local market. Yet even with consumer products, there are significant exceptions. The only way to find out is to do some market research locally.

2. *Allocation of your company's resources.* Obviously, you want to select a mode of operation that is consistent with the amount of resources available and the amount of risk that is prudent for you. You can rank your options by the resources they require: money, effort, information, and commitment. Smaller companies generally don't launch a worldwide market-entry strategy, but enter one market at a time. When you feel comfortable in one market, enter another one. Select a mode of operation that requires fewer resources initially and strengthen your operation as you gain experience and exposure.

3. *Compatibility with your long-term goals.* Select a method of operation that is consistent with your key international marketing objective—whether that goal is getting the greatest return on investment, achieving the greatest market penetration, or maximizing exposure of your products and your company name.

American companies are often criticized for looking at short-run profit maximization rather than market penetration. But the long-run goal is to make a profit. So even if you're looking initially at market share and gaining a toehold, do so within the longer-term strategy of maximizing your profitability. Look at each potential option in terms of how it will contribute to your ultimate profitability.

This is true even if you enter a market for strictly defensive reasons—to prevent the long-term erosion of your profitable markets by stopping a competitor now.

4. *Characteristics of the market.* Your decision will be influenced by the size of the market, by the level of competition, by the market location in relation to your other facilities, and by the local infrastructure. If the distributors for your product or service are inadequate (or perhaps tied to the competition), you may be forced to invest in your own distribution or marketing subsidiary. If the market is small, you'll want low-cost entry through exporting or licensing; but if transportation costs are high, it might be cheaper to produce locally. If your market is an entrepôt to other markets, that may tilt you toward producing there.

If price competition is a factor, you want to select a production location (or locations) that gives you the lowest overall cost and then export to higher-cost areas. If economies of scale are important, you'll want to produce in a centralized location. If responsiveness, flexibility, low transportation cost, low labor and materials costs, or proximity to customers is important, you will probably want to establish production facilities in the country.

5. *The competitive environment.* The more distinctive your product is, the more options you have. If your product is clearly distinguished from those of your competitors and is in high demand, your customers are likely to be more willing to pay the high cost of shipment from the United States. If your markets are more competitive, finding the lowest-cost method of production and distribution will become very important to you.

If your product or service can easily be duplicated in the market by a local company, you'll probably want a local presence to give you market intelligence on how to adapt the product for the greatest competitive advantage. Growing competition may even force you to take a local joint venture partner that has a stake in your success and that will fight to protect the local market from new competition.

6. *The political and economic environment.* Select a method of operation that is consistent with the economic and political risk factors in the local country. If there is a significant potential for economic disruption, you may well select a form of operation that entails less exposure and risk for your operations. Even if you can set up a wholly owned subsidiary now, it may prove more prudent to have a joint venture in which you share the risk with a local business. Or you may decide to enter into a licensing agreement in which the most you can lose is your license, not an investment in expensive facilities.

On the other hand, if the sector of the economy you sell to is growing rapidly, and the demand for your product is likely to increase, you may invest sooner than you would otherwise. Even if it's not strictly justified right now, you may want to select a form of operation that will prevent you from being shut out of a market in the future. For example, even if you are exporting successfully now, you may want to make a direct investment in a subsidiary or joint venture because of the possibility that you will be unable to export in the future.

7. *Learning opportunities.* Select a mode of operation that will allow you to learn the most about your markets and about other potential marketing opportunities. An example is the experience of Bently-Nevada, an electronics manufacturer that operates in most Pacific Rim markets. Bently has successfully used different forms of operation to meet different conditions in each market, and has changed the way it operates when market conditions change or when its goals or resources change.

Example 3: Bently-Nevada
Electronics manufacturer.
Different operations for different markets.

Bently-Nevada is a $60 million company headquartered near Reno, Nevada. It manufactures electronics instruments that measure vibration in high-speed machinery. Its major markets are in petrochemicals and power generation. Bently has worldwide operations and does about 15 percent of its business in the Pacific Rim. It operates in almost every Pacific Rim country, with a different form of business in each market:

- *In Japan.* A trading company has represented it for seventeen years, but Bently is now setting up a factory office.
- *In Korea and Taiwan.* Agents have represented the company for over ten years.
- *In Beijing.* Bently established a liaison office with its own people, after working for years through agents.
- *In Singapore.* Bently has had a wholly owned subsidiary for five years.
- *In Australia and New Zealand.* Bently has given up its own reps and now works with agents.
- *In Thailand, Malaysia, and Indonesia.* Bently has "sponsors" who do not aggressively sell but who lay the groundwork for later sales efforts. If the sponsors do discover a worthwhile opportunity, they contact Bently, which then handles it.
- *In the Philippines.* Bently has had too few sales to justify a permanent presence; it handles each sale as a special situation.

Bently's is a technical product that requires a great deal of engineering support, so each form of operation is structured not only to meet the demands of the local market but also to ensure a way to service the product. For Bently, service strategy is just as important as selling approach. Three factors influenced its strategy for each country:

1. *How much control it could have, legally or practically.* For example, in Singapore, it was able to set up a wholly owned subsidiary. But when Bently initially set up in Japan, the Japanese business culture made working through a trading company the only approach that had any financial sense.

2. *What size presence was justified for the size of the market.*
3. *The ability to find and recruit local people who could sell and service for Bently.*

Bently entered China soon after the United States and China reestablished diplomatic relations. Because of the bureaucratic complexity and the Chinese government's desire to obtain transfer technology, it was very difficult to establish a wholly owned operation. So Bently made arrangements with Chinese agents. These middlemen did fine in finding customers initially, but it soon became apparent that they lacked the technical capabilities to service the accounts. So Bently had to replace the Chinese agents with its own office for engineering and technical support. All Bently employees in Beijing are local Chinese, except for one Chinese man from Singapore, and they have received extensive training with the products.

To protect its technology from local Chinese competition, Bently is working with the Chinese to build fertilizer plants and is showing them how to apply the technology and service it, but not how to design and manufacture it.

Today, competitive pressures are forcing Bently to open a factory in Japan. Bently's initial competition was in the United States and in Europe, but smaller competing companies have begun to emerge in Asian countries, especially Japan. Thus Bently's market strategy has to take into account the need for maintaining as strong a presence as possible in Japan. Ironically, because of strong local competition, its Japanese trading company has worked mainly in markets outside of Japan, buying Bently instruments manufactured in the United States, installing them in equipment in Japan, and then re-exporting them to other nations, particularly in Southeast Asia.

Each Bently agent is an established company, and none is exclusive—all handle a few other products. No doubt Bently is a big piece of their action. A major criterion for agents is that they understand the business of potential customers for Bently products.

Both agents and reps are given tours of Bently factories. In addition, Bently people regularly visit all the reps and agents in the field to monitor how they are doing, make sure that Bently is being represented properly, provide training and support and other needed assistance, and get feedback from customers. Bently's factory people work closely with customers as well. Jointly with the field reps, they put on demos and training programs and help solve technical problems.

Whenever it must start with agents, Bently upgrades to factory representatives as soon as is justified by the market and as soon as appropriate people can be found and trained. Sales knowledge and training can be controlled much more rigorously among field reps than among agents. As a result, Bently's financial return has increased dramatically whenever it has shifted to reps.

There are two exceptions. In Taiwan, Bently has stayed with its agent for over ten years—because the agent is doing such a good job. The same is true in Korea. But if the latter market becomes of greater strategic importance, Bently may change to another form of operation over which it has more control.

Figure 6-4. Typical progressions for different types of businesses.

High-Tech Products

1 Domestic manufacturing and export
2 Licensing to overseas manufacturer
3 Joint venture with overseas producer, with cross-licensing
4 Wholly owned overseas assembly production
5 Overseas R&D and engineering, with local market strategies

Consumer Products

1 Indirect exporting through trading companies, export management company, or agents
2 Direct exporting through local agents or distributors
3 Hiring of local sales force
4 Joint venture with local distributor
5 Local distribution network
6 Local production, market research, and R&D

Services

1 Overseas services provided from domestic offices
2 In-country technical assistance contracts
3 Licensing or franchising to local providers
4 Finding, contracting, and training local service providers
5 Joint venture with local distributor or superfranchiser
6 Services for local markets tailored by overseas subsidiary

Commodities or Agricultural Products

1 Commodities brokers or trading companies
2 Marketing cooperatives and export trading companies
3 Value-added products for particular markets tailored by overseas market research

In Australia and New Zealand, Bently has gone in the other direction. At one time, it had its own factory offices there. However, because of the relatively small market and widespread customer base, the cost of selling and maintaining a local office became too high. So Bently turned the business over to a local distributor (one that handled complementary products) to reduce the overhead burden on each product sold.

From Domestic to Global

From these examples, several generalizations can be drawn. You should change from one form of business structure to another when:

1. You have learned enough to handle the greater level of commitment required and your internal resources are adequate;
2. Needed resources (distributors, marketing infrastructure, financing) become available in the market;
3. Market or competitive pressures make change essential; or
4. You can better achieve your goals—profitability, cost minimization, market penetration, local visibility, access to customers or resources—without unduly increasing your risk.

Your judgment must often be based on trade-offs among these factors. This may mean moving "backward"—for example, from your own operation to a joint venture, from your own sales force to a distributor, or even from overseas manufacture to domestic production. Figure 6–4 shows some typical "forward" progressions for various types of businesses. The degree of commitment increases as you read down each list.

There is no best way. The most experienced and successful companies shift back and forth regularly as conditions dictate. In general, however, as companies gain experience, they become more involved in overseas operations. Or perhaps, more accurately, they become more involved in *global* operations, in which the distinction between "domestic" and "overseas" loses meaning. Many experts, such as Kenichi Ohmae, agree that companies typically follow a five-stage sequence of increasing commitment to overseas operations as they move from being domestic to being global entities.

Stage 1: The company keeps management, production, and marketing in the United States and uses overseas distribution.

Stage 2: The company establishes its own sales units abroad.

Stage 3: The company establishes local overseas production, plus sales and service in key markets. It seeks low-cost labor and operations, and other specialized resources. It sources its components from low-cost suppliers worldwide. It locates near key customers and markets.

Stage 4: The company establishes complete, autonomous businesses overseas responsible for all their major functions. It diffuses risk from volatile currency fluctuations by "financial engineering" (Japanese: *zaitech*)—for example, through currency trading and hedging. It neutralizes the impact of any currency flux by matching costs and revenues in major currencies. (For example, many multinationals—even Japanese companies—are minimizing their "yen exposure" by moving operations and purchasing to the NICs.) The company changes models to raise prices, and pressures suppliers to share currency gains. This is the stage where many U.S., European, and Japanese multinationals are now.

Stage 5: The company achieves worldwide production, and adopts global strategies for finance, R&D, and personnel. Local plants are dedicated to products and components in accordance with worldwide production plans. Ownership and financial decisions are made to take advantage of differences in tax rates and accounting rules. The company seeks ways to control assets without ownership and exploits new developments in financial markets. It builds low-breakeven plants in locations determined by flexibility, labor relations, presence of major customers, quality of local work force, protectionism, and likely shifts in local inflation and currency values. The operation uses worldwide suppliers. Just a handful of advanced multinationals have achieved this stage.

7 | Dealing With Trade Barriers

- *U.S. barriers to exporting overseas*
- *Pacific Rim barriers to trade and investment*
- *How to succeed despite the barriers*

American companies seeking to export or invest are faced with a variety of tariff and nontariff barriers in almost every Asian Pacific Rim country—as well as in the United States. This chapter surveys the trade barriers that arise when you export to *or* invest in the Pacific Rim, how to deal with them, and how to take them into account in your business planning.

When you stand back and look at Pacific Rim trade, several facts emerge:

- The trade policies of the United States create some of the most formidable trade barriers in the Pacific Rim.
- Although some generalizations can be made about Pacific Rim trade barriers, each nation has its own peculiarities. It is of vital importance to look at each potential market individually.
- The informal barriers to trade are often more difficult to work with than the formal, "on the books" barriers.
- The trade environment is continually changing. There are signs that the climate for trade and investment in Asian Pacific Rim nations is opening up—just as the United States is threatening to become more protectionist.

The most commonly encountered barriers to trade and investment cause a variety of problems for U.S. businesses. However, companies do succeed in Pacific Rim markets despite these barriers. So this chapter also examines the ways U.S. companies have adjusted their policies or strategies to work with various types of trade barriers.

U.S. Export Barriers

Two of the stiffest trade barriers you will face are home-grown: (1) U.S. government policies that impede overseas trade and (2) the attitudes of U.S. businesses themselves. As the U.S. International Trade Commission has pointed out: "While foreign trade barriers remain a significant impediment to U.S. exports, and a very important trade problem, they are not the major cause of the rapid growth in the U.S. trade deficit in recent years." This is borne out by the fact that the United

155

States has had a deficit problem only since 1982, yet many foreign trade barriers far predate that time.

Much of the problem lies with U.S. companies themselves. They hurt their own cause in the following ways:

1. They are slow to commercialize the fruits of research and development.
2. They are unable to respond quickly enough to the changing demands of new markets for manufactured goods.
3. They have a short-term planning bias.
4. They lack international marketing expertise.

Let's examine the major U.S. government policies that impede trade.

Currency Exchange Rate Fluctuations

When this book was started, the dollar was high. Exporters were hurting. They found the high dollar made it tougher to be competitive in traditional markets. By the time the book was finished, the dollar had fallen precipitously. U.S. exports were booming, but the costs of establishing an operation in Japan were keeping many American companies out of that market. One thing that you can count on is that currencies will fluctuate. So in your business planning you must take into account the impact of the dollar increase or decline on the currency of your target market. This is not a simple task. The impact of wide fluctuations in exchange rates has been difficult to predict, and the decline of the dollar has held many surprises. More and more companies—both American and Asian—are moving toward establishing manufacturing operations in their target markets to avoid currency problems, among others. But as long as currencies fluctuate widely, exchange rates remain a barrier to smooth trade.

The Foreign Corrupt Practices Act

The U.S. Foreign Corrupt Practices Act of 1977 makes it "unlawful for any domestic firm, directly or indirectly, to pay money or make gifts to a foreign official . . . for the purpose of influencing the foreign official to assist the issuer to obtain, retain, or direct business to any person." Although this rule has not been applied to the many little "bribes" that smaller companies pay to have routine tasks done in foreign countries, it does prevent U.S. companies from making larger expenditures that competitors from other nations—including Japan—can routinely write off as "entertainment."

Export License Requirements for Technology

U.S. companies wishing to export certain products or services must obtain permission to do so from the U.S. Department of Commerce in the form of an export license. For the most part, these controlled items are ones that the government deems harmful to the national security should they pass into the hands of adversary foreign governments.

What Exports Need a License. Since most exports require some kind of export license, you should assume that you need one until you find out otherwise. You need an export license for most kinds of manufactured goods, for technical information, for components, and for repaired products. An exported component used in the manufacture of another product requires a license for re-export.

There are two different types of export licenses: general and validated. Most U.S. exports are shipped under broad general licenses that do not require specific applications. There are over twenty different types of general licenses. A validated license is more restrictive. You must submit an application for each transaction, and it is considered on its own merits. You will probably need a validated export license for the following:

- A *strategic* product that is "capable of contributing significantly to the military potential of any adversary of the United States"
- A *short-supply* commodity that is scarce in the United States
- *Unpublished* technical data—that is, data not generally available to the public—related to the design, production, or use of a product
- Any product to specified destinations where there are *foreign policy* concerns

How to Get an Export License. A good first step in getting through the export license maze is to read a copy of the U.S. government's *Export Administration Regulations* (see below), which describes how to obtain a license, what documentation is required, how to deal with re-exports and technical data, and many other special circumstances. In this way you can discover which type of export license may be appropriate for you.

To determine the type of license you need, visit a regional office of the Commerce Department. The department's determination will be based on the destination of the product, according to the seven country groups contained in *Export Administration Regulations;* on what you are exporting, as checked against the Commodity Control List; and on whether any special restrictions apply to your intended transaction.

If you need a validated license, you must complete the Commerce Department's Application for a Validated Export License. You'll discover it's best to be thorough. Explain the domestic use of the product and how it will be used by the foreign purchaser. Include any technical manuals and specification sheets and state how the product might be altered for special uses. Send all applications to the department's Office of Export Licensing.

How to Use the License. After you receive your license from the Commerce Department, you must write your export license number on the Shipper's Export Declaration and record on the back of the license all shipments you make under it. After the license has been used up or has expired, return it to the Commerce Department for renewal. In many cases, you will have to get the buyer and the buyer's government to sign and return documents as well—in particular, the International Import Certificate, certifying that the exported products will be disposed of responsibly in the foreign country, and the Statement of Ultimate Consignee and Purchaser, on which the purchaser certifies not to resell or dispose of the goods in a manner contrary to the terms of the export license.

Keeping on Top of Policy Changes.   If you are trading in goods that require validated licensing, you must keep on top of the latest policy shifts, whether they tighten or liberalize regulations. The best way to do so is to purchase the U.S. government's *Export Administration Regulations,* which is updated periodically. The regulations explain the Commerce Department's level of control on specified commodities to certain destinations. They also identify the countries for which a validated export license is required to export each commodity, the reason the product is controlled, and any special licenses that might be required for exporting that commodity. These regulations also list the seven country groups to which exports are controlled for national security and other purposes. Included in your subscription will be periodic issues of *Export Administration Bulletin,* which explain recent policy changes and provide replacement pages to keep your set of regulations up-to-date.

Problems Caused by the Export Licensing Process.   There are many uncertainties and delays involved in obtaining all export licenses. For example, companies must negotiate a maze of procedures for licenses to export "dual use" products—those having military as well as civilian applications. Conflicting guidelines from the Departments of Commerce and Defense may make it almost impossible to determine beforehand whether an export license will be approved. Even if it is approved, the license may include unilateral restrictions that were imposed when the license application was filed.

In 1985, the Commerce Department approved 32,500 export licenses and denied only 49. Regardless of the outcome, the licensing procedure creates a mountain of unavoidable paperwork. Most licenses *are* granted, but the process may take up to four months, as indicated below. (COCOM refers to fifteen Western trading partners that belong to the Coordinating Committee on Economic Controls, which regulates trade with communist countries.)

Applications to export to COCOM member countries (in the Pacific Rim, this includes Japan)	5 days
Applications requiring no referral to an outside agency	15 days
Applications requiring interagency review	60 days
Applications requiring interagency and COCOM review	120 days

U.S. companies may even find it difficult to export commonplace products that are widely available from other sources. UltraTech Stepper applied for a license to sell obsolete equipment to China, equipment of a type it had sold there previously. The Chinese could easily have obtained more sophisticated equipment from Hong Kong. The U.S. Defense Department examiner agreed that the equipment was obsolete but failed to pass on the request. (The Defense Department can essentially veto some license requests by failing to act on them in a timely manner.)

Impact of Export Restrictions on U.S. Trade

In the 1970s, forbidding the export of American high tech meant that foreign countries got no high tech. In the late 1980s, it means that countries buy high tech elsewhere. Complex U.S. regulations attempt to cover far too many technologies, including ones that are widely available elsewhere in the international market. At the same time, according to a study by the National Academy of Sciences, these regulations deprive U.S. industry of $9 billion a year in exports and 200,000 jobs.

As a result, the United States loses many markets to countries that do not operate with the same restrictions. Suppose an American company promises to deliver an item to a customer and then discovers that export restrictions prevent it from doing so. To the customer, the U.S. company looks unreliable. Foreign competitors use this forced unreliability as a marketing tool to take away business. Often, foreign manufacturers design out U.S.-made semiconductors from their end products to avoid the uncertainties caused by our export licensing requirements.

Those regulations have created substantial burdens for both U.S. semiconductor manufacturers and their foreign customers. They limit the ability of U.S. companies to engage in joint high-tech R&D projects with other countries. Fortunately, the regulations have begun to ease.

The U.S. political winds have shifted toward more openness and relaxation of restrictions. Under new U.S. law, many items are being removed from the controlled list—in particular, low-technology goods and medical instruments. The U.S. government now concentrates on controlling a small number of items that are genuinely critical to national security and has lifted licensing requirements on goods exported to U.S. trading partners that belong to COCOM. For COCOM members, the United States shortens the average license processing time to as little as a week.

In 1988, the Commerce Department began using an optical scanner to read typed export license applications and enter the data into a computer. This cuts the approval period by at least a day or two, and by much more for the one out of twelve applications for which erroneous data were typed into the computer manually.

These changes make foreign electronics manufacturers far less likely to design out U.S.-made semiconductors. They also make it easier for U.S. companies to enter cross-licensing and joint venture agreements with Pacific Rim countries in order to develop high-tech devices. For example, the development of commercial versions of superconducting microchips may now include Silicon Valley technology, Japanese manufacturing know-how, and international venture capital.

American Protectionism

Regardless of the controversy over the need for legislation to restrict the entry of foreign goods and investments into U.S. markets, it's hard to dispute the damage they cause to U.S. foreign trade in promoting retaliatory trade restrictions. For example, the Common Market Commission published a lengthy list of U.S. trade barriers to counter American criticism of European trade practices. The EEC has threatened retaliation if Congress adopts legislation limiting European imports. In trade negotiations, a flurry of threats and counterthreats often arises just before a resolution is negotiated. However, the mere threat of such restrictions hanging over the head of an exporter can severely hamper overseas business.

Some experts contend that U.S. markets are so important to Pacific Rim nations that they can't threaten retaliation. However, if Pacific Rim nations have trouble selling their products in the United States, they are also restricted from buying U.S. products. Quotas and other trade barriers often hurt the countries that can least afford restricted access to U.S. markets. Retaliation can take many forms, all with the same result.

In 1987, the United States enacted retaliatory tariffs of 100 percent or more on Japanese printed circuit boards, despite a 1986 agreement that dropped U.S. tariffs on computer parts to zero. Although this legislation was enacted to punish alleged dumping by Japanese companies, it turned out to hurt American computer makers even more because the affected circuit boards were vital components for the U.S. personal computer industry.

The other side of this argument maintains that threatened U.S. trade restrictions are forcing the leading Pacific Rim traders to improve access to their domestic markets for a wide variety of U.S. goods and services. To the extent that this happens, American companies will benefit.

Pacific Rim Trade Barriers

Now let's take a look at the different types of trade and investment barriers that U.S. companies encounter in Asian Pacific Rim nations. (See Figure 7–1.)

Tariff Barriers

Tariffs are the taxes imposed on imports by the customs authority of a country. Through multilateral agreements, the average tariff rates among the developed countries have been reduced substantially over the last decade; however, most

Figure 7-1.   Pacific Rim trade barriers.

Tariffs

Nontariff Barriers

Import licensing
Inadequate protection of intellectual property; inadequate and poorly enforced laws
Restrictive government procurement practices
Government subsidies to domestic industries
Product certification as delaying tactic
Forced technology transfer
Technical and industrial standards used as barriers
Exchange rate or financial restrictions
Restricted products
Government monopolies
Countertrade or offset requirements

Barriers to Services

Local content requirements
Closed bidding procedures
Time and expense

Barriers to Foreign Investment

Local content requirements
Foreign investment restrictions
Inadequate legal structure
Restrictions on equity ownership by foreigners

Informal Trade Barriers

Economic nationalism
Corruption

---

developing countries still maintain high tariff rates in order to raise revenues and protect domestic industry.

All the Pacific Rim countries except Hong Kong, Singapore, and Japan have significant tariff barriers to manufactured imports, especially high-value-added products such as pharmaceuticals and chemicals, plastics, paper products, telecommunications equipment, computers, semiconductors, and medical, scientific, and control instruments.

Nontariff Barriers

In some nations in which tariffs are not a barrier to trade, nontariff barriers are used to restrict or keep out imports of particular products. These nontariff barriers are more difficult to eliminate or regulate by international agreement.

Import Licensing. Korea, China, the Philippines, Indonesia, and New Zealand require local importers to obtain government licenses to buy foreign products. This practice gives government officials discretionary authority to regulate imports, and the licenses are often used to restrict manufactured products.

Inadequate Protection of Intellectual Property

Intellectual property is the most important resource of a "knowledge business" whose competitive position depends on its ability to innovate and commercialize innovations. There are two classes of intellectual property:

1. *Industrial property*—including inventions, patents, industrial designs, trade secrets, technologies and techniques, and trademarks and service marks
2. *Copyrights*—protecting written, programmed, literary, musical, artistic, photographic, and cinematographic works

Adequate protection of intellectual property is essential to preserve market competitiveness, yet many Pacific Rim nations fail to offer such protection. You will encounter three different problems in Pacific Rim countries:

1. The laws differ, and if you are not careful you will get tripped up and lose the protection that *is* available to you.
2. The laws are weak in protecting intellectual property.
3. The laws that are on the books are poorly enforced, sometimes by tacit design and at other times because of lack of resources.

The United States itself does not conform to international standards, so American companies used to American rules may run into problems in nations conforming to international standards. In patent protection, there are several important differences, as follows:

United States	Other Nations
• Patent awarded to first inventor, even if another files first.	• Patent awarded to inventor who files first.
• One-year grace period allowed after making invention public—by selling, publishing, using it—before filing patent.	• In nations with "absolute novelty" rule, there is no grace period. You must file before invention is made public anywhere.
• Patent doesn't have to be used to be valid.	• Must be "worked" locally, e.g., by commercial-scale manufacturing.

However, intellectual property protection is improving in most Pacific Rim nations in which American companies have had the biggest problems. The impetus comes partly from international pressure, but more so from the fact that their domestic companies are beginning to develop comparable products, technologies, and other intellectual properties that need protection.

The Cutting Edge. Even among nations whose intellectual property protection matches international standards, there remain several areas of disagreement and issues that have not yet been settled:

- *Chemicals, pharmaceuticals, and other patented substances.* Some nations protect only a particular application or method of production, not the substance itself. There is disagreement about how innovative a variation of a patented substance must be in order to qualify for a new patent.
- *Microorganisms.* Some leading nations have ruled that living entities cannot be patented, but that would deny protection to important products of bioengineering—from recombinant DNA to a strain of mice with the human immune system genetically engineered into it.
- *Copyrighting new media.* New media include satellite broadcasts, cable TV telecasts, and software.
- *Software copyrights.* Can companies copyright the "look and feel" of the software to the user, as distinct from the actual software programming code?
- *Integrated circuits.* ICs with software built in need both patent and copyright protection. What is protected? The particular chip design or the function performed?
- *Trademarks and service marks.* If you enter a nation where a local company has been using your unregistered trademark (or one very similar to it), you can force the company to desist if your mark is "generally known in international trade." But what about protection for the marks of smaller but rapidly expanding companies?

Restrictive Government Procurement Practices

Some Pacific Rim countries have policies that discriminate against foreign suppliers for major government purchases, such as telecommunications. In addition, Japan's corporate procurement practices favor Japanese businesses, and in many industries there is consumer resistance to foreign products.

Government Subsidies. A number of Pacific Rim governments offer subsidies to their export-oriented industries in the form of low-cost loans, cash payments, tax breaks, and provision of goods at below-market prices. For example, Australian businesses can receive government subsidies that enable them to discount their own prices, thereby giving their products an advantage over imported manufactured goods. This is particularly true with robotics, computers, and agricultural machinery.

Product Certification. Many Pacific Rim nations require certification of the safety of foreign products, a procedure that can intentionally delay their import. In this way, pharmaceuticals products, for example, can be copied and marketed by local companies before the importers can get through the certification process.

Forced Technology Transfer. Pacific Rim governments may require licensing of products to local companies. This is, in effect, a forced transfer of technology.

Technical and Industrial Standards. Standards designed to ensure systems compatibility are also used to discriminate against imports. For example, Japan's technical and industrial standards are barriers to imported telecommunications equipment, medical and scientific devices, chemicals and pharmaceuticals, and biotechnology products. Meeting Japanese standards—which differ from most international standards—can be prohibitively expensive and time-consuming, especially for smaller companies.

Exchange Rate or Financial Restrictions. In some countries, only a certain amount of foreign exchange is made available for banks to back the letters of credit needed by your customers to pay for purchases. If customers cannot obtain this payment guarantee, you may not be able to obtain the financing you need to produce the goods for them to buy.

Restricted Products. Some Pacific Rim countries ban certain consumer and industrial products in order to promote development of domestic industry. China bans imports of many consumer goods, such as washing machines and air conditioners, in order to conserve foreign exchange.

Government Monopolies. Some developing countries bar foreign business from entering a particular industry or service that they wish to preserve for domestic companies.

Countertrade Requirements. Some Pacific Rim governments require that foreign companies accept part of their payment in local goods. These goods must then be sold in other international markets to obtain full price. For example, because China is short on foreign exchange, it often requires partial payment in textiles or paper goods, particularly on large orders. If these items had a strong market, China would sell them itself. Indonesia also requires countertrade payment for large orders. Even Australia requires 30 percent offsets for large government and civilian procurement contracts.

Barriers to Services

Local Content Requirements. Foreign governments often require that local people be hired for certain services. For example, in several Pacific Rim countries, producers of TV commercials must use local crews or else pay a high duty, sometimes up to 150 percent. Victor Kiam, president of Remington Shaver, encountered this barrier in the Philippines, Taiwan, Korea, and Australia.

Closed Bidding Procedures.   In many Pacific Rim countries, it may be difficult or impossible to learn the bidding requirements and procedures for a particular project in time to develop a competitive bid. This practice, of course, is not unknown in the United States.

Time and Expense.   Companies that lack the deep pockets of the multinationals are often effectively shut out of markets by the time and effort it takes to make necessary official contacts, gain official approvals, find suitable business partners, conduct reliable market research, and so on. This makes it very difficult to penetrate a market in countries with a high level of government involvement in foreign trade, such as Indonesia or China.

Barriers to Foreign Investment

Many Pacific Rim countries require that some benefit be provided to the country—such as forming a joint venture with a local business, providing technical training, or licensing technology—in exchange for permission to operate in their market.

Local Content Requirements.   In developing countries especially, specific amounts of local materials, labor, or products must be used for local production of a foreign product.

Foreign Investment Restrictions.   Some Pacific Rim countries limit the movement of capital or the repatriation of profits.

Inadequate Legal Structure.   The legal systems of Japan, Australia, New Zealand, Singapore, and Hong Kong are sound and relatively graft-free. Graft is a very dangerous game for any official in China. However, the legal systems of several developing Pacific Rim nations are weak and inadequate in the following ways:

- Different jurisdictions may have conflicting laws or differing enforcement policies.
- Laws are poorly written and fail to cover all contingencies.
- Existing laws are enforced inconsistently.
- Economic laws and regulations have political motivation.
- New laws contradict existing ones.
- Constant changes in a legal system make it difficult to keep up with government policy. In some nations, government officials have a vested inter-

est in maintaining a murky legal system because it's a major source of power for them.

Restrictions on Equity.   Several Pacific Rim nations still require or strongly encourage partial local ownership. These rules change over time: They tend to become more liberal when foreign investment is needed, and more restrictive when government development goals are met. Also, they tend to be more liberal in industries targeted by the government for development.

Informal Trade Barriers

Common practices that are not "on the books" can raise formidable barriers to foreign businesses.

Economic Nationalism.   Economic nationalism lies behind many government policies. As in the United States, laws and regulations that ostensibly promote some legitimate social or economic concern are actually passed at the urging of some pressure group for a special protection or advantage. Such laws include limitations on foreign ownership or equity, requirements for local content in manufactured goods, exclusion of foreign companies from certain markets and means of distribution, requirements for having a local partner, and limitations on hiring foreign citizens. Nationalism also manifests itself in informal ways, especially in a preference for doing business with local companies.

Developed Pacific Rim countries—for example, Japan and Korea—often discriminate against foreign businesses that are new to their markets. In Japan in particular, complex distribution networks make it very difficult to break into some markets. Occasionally, antagonism and even violence may erupt against foreign investors, but this is more prevalent in countries outside the Pacific Rim. Efforts of central governments to make their countries more attractive to foreign investment are often thwarted by such nationalistic impulses.

Corruption.   In many Pacific Rim countries, you may be faced with a request for anything from "tea money" (a gift or favor) to large sums of cash. The request may be in exchange for something the government would normally do anyway, or it may be in exchange for special treatment, such as getting a form expedited or getting goods through customs. Covert payments may also be required to secure a government order or to obtain approval for a distribution license or direct investment.

How to Deal With Nontariff Barriers

Nontariff barriers often have the greatest impact on small to medium-size companies, for two reasons:

1. Smaller companies are less experienced in international markets and in dealing with trade barriers. They don't have the savvy, experience, and connections to maneuver around them.
2. Smaller companies have fewer resources—particularly, internal staff experts—to deal with nontariff barriers. Often they do not want to spend the time or money to work through lengthy processes, such as product certification periods of up to one year.

The first step is to be aware of any barriers to your product or service in your target market, and to plan accordingly from the very beginning. If it's going to take a year for you to get your product certified, or if you're going to need a joint venture partner, it's best to know at the start so you can factor this effort in. If you find that you can't overcome certain handicaps, it may be best just to walk away from the market.

Working With Local Bureaucracies.   Small companies often have limited experience in dealing with the bureaucracies of foreign governments. To succeed, you need to get the right kind of help. Here are several guidelines.

1. *Be prepared.* Research the trade barriers first by talking with local American companies or with the American chamber of commerce to find out what steps you must take, what the danger spots and pitfalls are, and how to avoid them.
2. *Select the right local partner.* One of your criteria in selecting a local distributor or joint venture partner should be a proven ability to work with the local government and business community.
3. *Pave the way at home.* Make your initial approach through U.S. State Department or Commerce Department representatives, or through the country's trade and investment representatives stationed in the United States. Then make contact in the target market itself.
4. *Know whom to approach abroad.* In some countries, it is better to approach low-level officials first, because they are the knowledgeable ones who do the work; the top-level officials may just be government appointees. In other countries, it is best to go to the top-level officials first because lower officials have a narrow perspective and apply rules inflexibly. Keep in mind, however, that there may be adverse consequences to bypassing low-level officials.

Protecting Your Intellectual Property.   Review the points that were discussed in Chapter 6. When licensing your technology, make sure you negotiate good agreements up front. When you work through agents or distributors, make sure you supply them with incentives to help you protect your property rather than to use it illegally. In any technology transfer agreement, make sure to get as much value as you give up so that even if you lose some technology, you are still in good shape.

1. *File correctly in each nation.* Remember that U.S. patents protect you only in the United States. When you first file your U.S. patent, decide in which

other nations you will need protection, and file in those nations as soon as you can. In many nations, a product must be patented locally within a year after the first patent application; otherwise it is not regarded as a new product and thus is not patentable. Be very careful here: Foreign patents may not cover the same protections as your U.S. patent. Work through local patent attorneys, whom you can contact and check out through AMCHAM.

2. *Don't let abuses go unchallenged.* Let the word get out that you will vigorously challenge all infringements. If infringements do occur, use publicity as well as legal challenges. In some instances, political pressure may be more effective than legal sanctions. Taiwan tightened up enforcement of its copyright laws after Grolier raised a ruckus about the instant pirating of its latest edition of the *Encyclopædia Britannica.* Work through your joint venture partner or distributor to obtain redress. Find out which local officials can have an impact, and cultivate positive relationships with them. Learn from the experience of other American companies that have faced similar situations.

3. *Protect your patents through litigation.* Companies that develop high-tech products and patent them in international business are becoming more willing to go to court to protect their rights. To cover the high cost of their research and development, they charge high licensing fees and sue any competitors that use their property without permission.

It's easier to bring suit successfully since the Copyright Act of 1976 clarified software copyrighting and the Semiconductor Chip Protection Act of 1984 created a new form of protection for IC designs. In 1982 the United States Court of Appeals for the Federal Circuit—with sitting patent specialists—was created to hear all patent appeals coming from the district courts.

Several examples show the successful outcome of such litigation:

- Texas Instruments sued eight Japanese semiconductor companies over TI's DRAM (dynamic random access memory) silicon chip patents. These companies are being forced to pay TI licensing fees of up to $300 million.
- IBM has obtained payment from Hitachi and Fujitsu for unauthorized use of IBM technology.
- Zilog, Inc., in Silicon Valley got the U.S. Customs Service to stop the import of a chip from Japan's Sharp Corporation on the grounds that Sharp was using technology it had licensed from Zilog in versions of chips it was not licensed to produce.

Dealing With Ownership Restrictions.   The most common way to get around the limitations of foreign ownership, of course, is to form a joint venture with a local entity. As noted in Chapter 6, it is possible to maintain effective control of a joint venture even with minority ownership.

Dealing With Corruption.   Many customs that are accepted practice in various Asian nations are defined as corrupt under the U.S. Foreign Corrupt Practices Act of 1977. So do your research. Find out what is expected by talking with other American companies operating locally. See how they have dealt with bribery problems and what the repercussions were in taking a stand. In many countries, low-level corruption flourishes despite high-level programs to wipe it out. In some circumstances, threats of exposure can sometimes be helpful. Also, simply stating that your hands are tied by the Foreign Corrupt Practices Act may reduce the expectation that your company will pay certain bribes.

Recognize that there are other types of compensation besides money, many of which are *not* illegal. For example, access to information or assistance in a needed project may be more valuable to a government official than a token amount of money. However, if a payment is demanded, examine exactly what it is for. Some claims are artificial and cannot withstand scrutiny—that is, you can get what you need in other ways. Once the official making the request realizes you know the ropes, your bargaining position improves tremendously. When making a payment appears unavoidable, many companies leave it to their local partner or distributor.

Trade Barriers for Each Pacific Rim Nation

Trade and investment barriers differ from country to country, so it is essential to look at each Pacific Rim nation individually. This section summarizes the formal and informal barriers—to trade, services, and investment. Things have been changing very rapidly in this area. Most Pacific Rim nations have been liberalizing trade and investment policies, dropping tariffs, and tightening protection of intellectual property.

Australia

Since 1987, in a dramatic change in direction, Australia has liberalized many of its restrictive economic policies, away from protecting domestic markets and towards opening Australian companies up to foreign competition, thus forcing their greater competitiveness on global markets. This liberalization process will continue into the 1990s, so some of the barriers mentioned here may be diminished or eliminated. Even though Australia is one of the most developed nations in the world, it still retains some tariff and nontariff trade barriers that are more common to developing countries.

Tariffs. Tariffs—which ranged up to 50 percent into the late 1980s—have been drastically cut, but they still affect imports of a number of items, including such products as plastics, paper goods, machine tools, computers, telecommunications equipment, semiconductor devices, scientific and medical measuring and controlling instruments, domestic appliances, broadcasting and receiving equipment, and lab equipment. Most tariffs are designed to protect domestic producers and are often waived for products not produced in local markets.

Government Procurement. The Australian government gives domestic companies a 20 percent discount over foreign bids. On top of this, many Australian provinces give preference to local companies bidding for state contracts. This means an Australian company's bid can be, say, 25 percent higher than yours and be viewed as the same price.

Countertrade. The government requires offsetting purchases of 30 percent of the contract price for military contracts, for Qantas Airline, and for telecommunications transactions that exceed 2.5 million Australian dollars.

Government Subsidies. Australian manufacturers receive subsidies that allow them to offer substantial price discounts in both domestic and international markets. The major industries affected are metalworking, machine tools, industrial robots, computer systems, agricultural equipment, steel products, motor vehicles, and injection molding equipment.

China

Since 1977, China has moved steadily toward decentralization and is opening up to foreign trade. Its provinces, special economic zones, and cities—and even certain individual enterprises—have some authority in foreign trade. Nonetheless, the barriers to trade in China remain daunting, and as important as foreign trade is to the nation's development plans, the path may well take unexpected twists and turns along the way. This uncertainty in itself can be a major barrier, especially for smaller companies.

Tariffs. China's tariffs range from 15 to 100 percent on such products as pharmaceuticals, plastics, paper goods, agricultural machinery, computers, telecommunications equipment, semiconductor devices, medical and scientific measuring equipment, laboratory equipment, radio broadcasting and receiving equipment, vitamins, antibiotics, machine tools and parts, electrical machinery, and domestic appliances.

China has raised duties on items that compete with budding domestic industries. It has also raised tariffs on popular high-priced consumer products like automobiles and microcomputers in order to limit the drain on foreign exchange reserves. At the same time, China has reduced tariffs on such items as electronics parts and components in order to encourage development of its industries.

Bans and Quotas. To conserve its foreign exchange reserves, China has banned or limited the import of such consumer goods as televisions, washing machines, and air-conditioners.

Intellectual Property Protection. Protection for pharmaceuticals and chemicals is limited to process patents and is not extended to the products themselves. China is now seeking to improve its property protection of trademarks and patents. It has joined the Paris Convention for the Protection of Industrial Property.

Import Licensing.   One of the greatest barriers to doing business with China is its complex import licensing system, which is managed by the Ministry of Foreign Economic Relations and Trade (MOFERT). MOFERT divides product lines into two groups: restricted and unrestricted. China's state-owned trading companies must have import licenses only for the restricted products, but private trading companies must have licenses for both restricted and unrestricted product lines. Individual provinces can approve licenses for products, with certain exceptions. MOFERT itself must approve licenses for such products as computers, televisions, motor vehicles, and home appliances. Furthermore, MOFERT can cancel a license that has already been issued if it decided that the transaction would be detrimental to national interests.

Hong Kong

The Hong Kong government exhibits a classic laissez-faire attitude. With a minimum of controls on finance, trade, and capital, its free-trade policy and demand for manufactured products make it one of the most accessible Pacific Rim markets.

Hong Kong's intellectual property protection complies with international standards, and enforcement has been tightened over the last few years. This situation should not change after China resumes sovereignty in 1997, since Hong Kong will retain economic autonomy. Since Hong Kong will no longer be covered by the laws and international agreements made by the United Kingdom, Hong Kong's officials are currently reworking agreements with several international regulatory bodies. For Hong Kong to have membership separate from China, some organizations that currently limit membership to sovereign nations will have to designate a new category for "autonomous economies."

Indonesia

In 1987, Indonesia began liberalizing, in a piecemeal fashion, a number of its import and foreign investment policies. More changes are coming, so some of the barriers mentioned here may be further diminished.

Tariffs.   Tariffs ranging from 20 to 60 percent are levied on plastics, paper products, computers, communications equipment, domestic appliances, radio broadcasting equipment, and scientific and medical measuring and controlling equipment.

Counterpurchase.   Indonesian regulations require foreign companies to purchase nonoil commodities in an amount equal to the contract amount for any transaction over 500 million rupiah. In practice, the government has often modified or waived this requirement. In any case, this requirement mainly affects companies supplying large-ticket items such as aircraft to the Indonesian government.

Import Licensing and Sole Agenting.   Only state trading companies or licensed importers may import such crucial items as computers, chemicals, heavy equipment, and consumer products. In addition, Indonesia grants the rights to distribute specified imports to a sole local agent, with a specified length of contract and conditions of contract termination. Products covered include heavy machinery, automotive components and equipment, consumer electronics, textile machinery, industrial machinery, chemicals, plastics, and metal products. These restrictions have been relaxed or waived on industrial capital goods and on products and components of re-exported manufactured goods.

Intellectual Property Protection.   Indonesia adopted its first patent law in 1987. Enforcement of penalties against patent and copyright infringement has improved—as much to protect domestic producers as foreign. Of major concern are the resources Indonesia is able to commit to enforcing its provisions.

Product Registration and Certification.   Administrative regulations are designed to force the transfer of technology and to aid the development of local industries. For example, local companies can register new pharmaceuticals much more quickly than can foreign businesses; thus they can market the products earlier. Other regulations force products to be licensed to local companies. These policies have limited the introduction of new products and technologies into Indonesian markets.

Japan

Japan continues to reform laws that tend to block consumer access to foreign goods and services. A major turning point in Japanese policy was the 1986 Maekawa Report, which spelled out the actions needed to stimulate domestic demand, increase overseas investment, and improve market access for foreign goods.

It is slowly becoming easier to open large retail stores in Japan, and these have become major outlets for imported goods. Other services are being deregulated: trucking, telecommunications, finance, energy, agriculture, and new-business formation. Japanese "commodity" taxes have been reduced on many consumer products in which American companies can establish a strong market: golf equipment, watches, furniture, luggage, electrical appliances, and larger cars.

Tariffs.   Tariffs on manufactured products are quite low and are not in themselves a major barrier to competitive trade.

Technical and Industrial Standards. Japanese standards differ from other international standards, and meeting them is sometimes prohibitively expensive and time-consuming for smaller companies. For example, in certain industries, rules require that companies keep a qualified person on staff to be responsible for materials classified as toxic by the Japanese government. To become qualified, this person can either pass an exam—which is given only once a year—or take a certain number of chemistry courses. For a large company, it is no problem keeping such a person on staff. For a smaller company, it can be a barrier. The company must either hire a chemist or wait a year for the test. Such regulations tend to favor large, established domestic companies over small overseas companies.

Japanese industrial standards—the well-known JIS mark—are set by the Ministry of International Trade and Industry (MITI) and the Agency for Industrial Science and Technology (AIST). Products with JIS certification are often given preference by Japanese consumers, much as Americans look for products with the UL seal of the Underwriters Laboratory. Foreign companies must make products according to Japanese standards and obtain factory inspections and product tests.

Nondomestic producers are still denied effective access to Japan's procedures for setting standards. However, Japan is liberalizing this system by (1) reducing the number of items covered by the standards; (2) granting foreign businesses greater access to standard-setting councils; and (3) letting U.S. testing companies, rather than Japanese companies, conduct initial inspections of U.S. factories.

Government Procurement Restrictions. Under government policy, Japanese companies can be effectively precluded from buying foreign high-tech products (for example, communications satellites). Japan's strategy is to import American technology and at the same time protect emerging industry until it can compete with American counterparts. If U.S. high-tech companies were allowed to compete, they would likely receive a significant share of many expanding markets.

Japan's *dango* (designated bidder) system is not open and transparent. Qualified potential bidders decide among themselves who will respond to bid tenders.

Intellectual Property Protection. Japan's copyright laws are adequate, but not effectively enforced. Illegal copying and sales of videotapes and motion pictures still occasionally occur.

It can take six years for Japan to issue a patent. But eighteen months after patent applications are filed, the information they contain is published. Thus Japanese companies can copy a U.S. industrial process and commercially exploit it before the U.S. patent is registered. Similarly, it can take four years to register a trademark in Japan—a time period that discourages many foreign businesses from introducing their products there.

Subsidies. Targeted domestic industries—including microelectronics, fiber optics, supercomputers, satellite communications, biotechnology, and chemicals—are subsidized through market protection, financial assistance, tax incentives, and cooperative R&D programs.

Informal Barriers. All of Japan's cigarette factories are run by Japan Tobacco, Inc., which has a national monopoly. The company resists buying foreign tobacco because it is required by law to buy all the leaf produced by Japan's 100,000 tobacco growers—a politically powerful group. Even though Japan Tobacco no longer has a monopoly in distributing cigarettes, American companies have so far found it difficult to set up their own distribution networks.

Japanese farmers use their political clout to win protection and subsidies. The Japanese government pays rice growers a dollar a pound—almost ten times the world price—because farmers are a major political force in Japan, and their influence has increasingly led to protectionist policies at the expense of open markets.

Korea

Tariffs. Korea's average tariffs are dropping—from an average of 13 percent to below 8 percent by 1993—similar to the levels of other major industrial nations. Duties on cars have dropped to 25 percent; on whisky, to 70 percent; on raw materials, to about 5 percent.

Korea levies tariffs (of from 5 to 25 percent in 1988) on such products as pharmaceuticals, plastics, paper goods, agricultural machinery, computers, telecommunications equipment, semiconductor devices, and medical and scientific measuring and controlling instruments.

Intellectual Property Protection. In 1988, Korea passed a series of laws to bring the protection of foreign patents, trademarks, and copyrights up to international standards. Copyright protection—for printed material, sound recordings, videotapes, computer data bases, semiconductor chips, satellite and cable TV telecasts—now conforms to the Universal Copyright Convention. The new patent law covers chemical and pharmaceutical products, as well as new uses for such products. Patent protection is extended to new microorganisms. Korean companies can no longer register trademarks that are identical or close to those registered by foreign companies. Trademark licenses are no longer linked to technology inducement; thus they continue beyond the life of a company's technology inducement agreement. Technology licenses no longer require re-export.

Public administrative rules and regulations have been formalized, and law enforcement agencies give high priority to enforcement of intellectual property rights.

Subsidies. Targeted domestic industries such as microelectronics, computers, and chemicals are subsidized through market protection, financial assistance, tax incentives, and cooperative R&D programs.

Korea knows it must increase market access for foreign products. Although tariffs have been greatly reduced, the many remaining nontariff barriers tend to weaken or cancel out these benefits—especially the "buy Korean" preference of the government, business, and consumers.

Korean currency is still undervalued. The won has begun to climb against the dollar, but only slowly. And as much as the United States would like Korea to increase the value of the won, it is unlikely to push very hard—for political reasons. Korea is the showcase story of capitalism and the United States wants very much for it to succeed.

Malaysia

Tariffs. Malaysia has tariffs ranging from 15 to 50 percent on such products as plastics, office machines, telecommunications equipment, semiconductor devices, paper goods, agricultural machinery, machine tool parts and accessories, radio broadcasting and receiving equipment, electronics parts, lab equipment, and scientific measuring and controlling instruments. For many other products, including some electronics parts, the tariffs are low or zero. The tariffs are designed to protect infant industries. For example, to help launch Malaysian auto manufacturing, imported components are duty-free, whereas parts for other locally assembled makes of automobiles face very high tariffs.

Intellectual property protection. Malaysia has enacted laws to protect copyrights and patents, but so far it has not been able to enforce them effectively. Thus, just across the channel from Singapore, pirated videotapes, software programs, and publications are widely available.

New Zealand

Tariffs. As part of its late-1980s about-face in economic policies, New Zealand in 1987 and 1988 drastically cut many of its tariffs, which had ranged up to 65 percent. Tariffs are still a factor in the import of several types of products, including control instruments, office machines, radio broadcasting equipment, and domestic appliances. However, the requirement to obtain import licenses has been eliminated.

Countertrade. Certain sales to the New Zealand government—such as aircraft—that are greater than 1 million New Zealand dollars may require an offset or counterpurchase. However, this requirement has so far not been imposed. New Zealand's intellectual property protection meets international standards.

The Philippines

Tariffs. The government has been hotly debating the liberalization of tariffs and other trade barriers. On the one hand, it has eliminated many quotas; on the other hand, it has increased duties on some products and imposed a temporary tariff increase on others. Tariffs ranging from 15 to 50 percent are levied on measuring and analytical instruments, semiconductor devices, laboratory equipment, radio broadcasting equipment, pharmaceuticals, plastics, paper products, welding equipment, electrical machinery, and domestic appliances.

Intellectual Property Protection. The government is inconsistent in enforcing laws protecting such products as pharmaceuticals and apparel designs. The Philippines Transfer Board tries to link intellectual property protection with transfer of technology or other economic benefits.

Singapore

Singapore promotes itself as a free-trade area. There are few tariffs or restrictions on companies doing business or investing there.

Intellectual Property Protection. Until recently, Singapore's enforcement of its copyright protections was so lax that pirated recordings and videotapes produced in Malaysia and Indonesia were readily available from Singapore's vendors. A few widely publicized bonfires of pirated cassettes communicated the onset of tougher enforcement, which now has real teeth.

Taiwan

Tariffs. In 1987 and 1988, Taiwan drastically cut tariff rates and product restrictions as part of its basic policy shift from encouraging exports and protecting domestic industries to encouraging imports and consumer purchasing. As a result, it is economically feasible to import into Taiwan a number of foreign products, from cars to cosmetics, that were formerly kept out. Although tariff rates have been greatly reduced, they remain a consideration in the import of many products and components, including pharmaceuticals, machine tools, computers, telecommunications equipment, laboratory equipment, medical equipment, measuring and analytical instruments, office machines and parts, radio broadcasting and receiving equipment, vitamins, plastics, electrical apparatus and machinery, welding equipment, and domestic appliances.

Subsidies. Taiwan subsidizes targeted industries, including computers and chemicals, through market protection, financial assistance, tax incentives, and cooperative R&D programs.

Intellectual Property Protection. Long notorious for pirated recordings and counterfeit products, Taiwan passed a series of laws in 1987 and 1988 to bring its intellectual property protection much closer to international standards. Stronger enforcement was announced by well-publicized crackdowns by the Anti-Counterfeiting Committee on behalf of Apple Computer and Eveready Batteries. Taiwanese pop singers toured the country urging consumers not to buy counterfeit products.

Trademarks and service marks take only seven months to register. If your well-known mark has been registered by another Taiwanese company, you can file for an invalidation. Trademarks of companies not yet operating in Taiwan can be registered. However, your trademark must be put to use within two years; even selling your trademarked product through a trading company qualifies.

Patents can receive full protection within one year of filing. After filing but before publication, the information is confidential. Foreign companies without Taiwanese presence must file through the Asian Patent Attorneys Association. Under a 1987 law, the composition of pharmaceuticals is protected. Microorganisms per se cannot be protected. However, the process for producing them can be; so can any process for which they are used. Some patent issues remain to be resolved, such as whether integrated circuits should be protected through patent, copyright, or both.

In addition to the changes in Taiwanese law, the government has cleaned up some of the procedural problems confronting U.S. companies seeking redress in Taiwanese courts and tightened enforcement methods used by customs and police officers on such procedures as conducting investigations and detecting counterfeits.

Thailand

Tariffs. Thailand has had a chronic current account trade deficit for many years and has maintained relatively high tariffs in an effort to conserve foreign exchange and produce revenue. Tariff rates range from 5 to 15 percent on raw materials, 15 to 35 percent on semimanufactured goods, and 35 to 60 percent on finished products. Included in the last category are medical measuring and analytical instruments, automatic data processing machines, office machinery and parts, semiconductor devices, laboratory equipment, radio broadcasting equipment, vitamins, antibiotics, vaccines, plastics, paper products, agricultural machinery, machine tools and parts, electrical apparatus, welding equipment, and domestic appliances.

Barriers to Investment in Pacific Rim Nations

The most common problems encountered by companies that invest in Pacific Rim countries are bureaucratic delays and red tape; policies that are inconsistent with their stated goals and erratically and inconsistently applied; economic nationalism and resultant limitations on market access; limitations on hiring, equity, and ownership of land and facilities; bribery and corruption; legal structures inadequate to protect intellectual property and enforce contractual obligations; and limited access to local capital. This section surveys the barriers in each Pacific Rim nation. Remember that policies can shift quite rapidly, so it is essential to check for the latest rulings.

Australia

Traditionally, Australia has required majority local ownership and control of major foreign investments (though many exceptions have been made). Areas such as banking, media, and transportation have been closed to foreign investment entirely. However, the government is undertaking a major liberalization of restrictions on foreign investment, and many Australians now seek joint ventures with foreign businesses to develop resources and overseas markets.

As in the United States, Australia has three levels of government—national, state, and local. The Australian states have greater autonomy in setting investment policy than their U.S. state counterparts, so it is very important to research regulations in any target market carefully.

You must obtain permission from Australia's Foreign Investment Review Board to establish a new business in restricted industries if (1) your investment is more than A $5 million or (2) you intend to buy real estate. The board considers the impact on existing competition.

Indirect barriers to investment are insignificant. Once businesses are set up in Australia, they seem to be accepted as well as domestic enterprises.

China

The government of China recognizes the importance of foreign investment to transfer technologies and managerial skills and to develop its infrastructure. But one of the biggest barriers to doing business in China is the multilayered bureaucracy. Agencies have overlapping jurisdictions, are unwilling or unable to move quickly, and are often staffed by people who are unfamiliar with the demands of business decision making. As economic development proceeds, special offices and ministries are being established to cope with the demands of foreign traders and investors. Sometimes this compounds the problem. Horizontal communication between government offices can be more difficult than communication up and down the hierarchy.

Centralization and decentralization proceed simultaneously. Many provinces, cities, and NEAs (new economic areas) have some degree of authority in making trade and investment decisions. It can often be to your advantage to work directly with these local entities, many of which are more entrepreneurial than Beijing. Yet the balance of power is always shifting, and it's hard to predict which agency will be required to rule on any particular matter.

Local participation is required in most direct investments. A local partner often provides land and facilities. Local labor is required—often at unrealistic, noncompetitive rates.

Hong Kong

A potential barrier to investment in Hong Kong is the uncertainty about what will happen when China resumes sovereignty over Hong Kong in 1997. Even though Hong Kong will become a special administrative region of China, a status that will preserve its present social and economic system for fifty more years, uncertainty over how that system will be implemented may dampen Hong Kong's allure for investors. On the plus side, government officials in Hong Kong are among the easiest to work with. Corruption is rare, although you may still be asked to pay various "fees" for services rendered.

Indonesia

Indonesian investment policy has required a high level of local participation. New projects must have 51 percent local equity ownership, although this provision is not uniformly enforced. Companies encounter increasing pressure to divest equity to pribumis (ethnic Indonesians). To some extent, these rules are being relaxed to stimulate foreign investment.

Several industries are closed to foreign investment, and foreign companies are excluded from retailing and distribution. Raw materials must be obtained locally. Expatriates may be hired only in positions that can't be filled by Indonesians, and positions held by expatriates must be transferred to Indonesians after a specified period.

Corruption manifests itself in two ways: (1) favoritism towards those who have the right contacts and (2) pressure to make small payments to expedite matters through the bureaucracy. Public officials are expected to supplement their low incomes with under-the-counter payments, so such requests from them are commonplace. It is often necessary to make payments to obtain what you should expect as a matter of course: getting goods through customs, having your phone repaired, obtaining a work permit for a foreign employee, and so on. The cost of government-financed projects often includes substantial sums for influential people and middlemen.

Personal ties to those with influence in the Indonesian government are of tremendous importance. Companies without such connections find themselves at a serious disadvantage. Because of the centralized political system, final approvals must be made by high-ranking officials—sometimes even the national president, for whose attention and approval different factions compete. That approval may conflict with existing law. The multilevel bureaucracy produces a high burden of paperwork, and the workings of the legal system are often uncertain.

Japan

Japan's restrictive foreign investment law was repealed in 1979, and since that time, foreign investment has mushroomed. U.S. companies are among the major investors. Under the new law, foreign direct investment is authorized unless specifically prohibited. The government promotes investment—especially in less-developed parts of the country—by offering financing, special depreciation allowances, and subsidized R&D projects. Investment has been restricted in certain industries, but a few (such as telecommunications) are opening up to foreign businesses. There are no official limitations on acquisitions and takeovers, yet unofficial barriers, such as interlocking directorates and stock ownership, make them rare.

A major barrier to investment in Japan by smaller companies is the very high cost of doing business there. The high yen and low dollar of the late 1980s have forced many small businesses to close operations in Japan. It can cost from $10,000 to $20,000 a month to maintain an American employee in Tokyo, yet the companies that remain there affirm that the cost is worth it.

Another barrier is the high individual tax rate for foreign employees, a rate that increases geometrically after a few years. U.S. companies complain that by the time American employees finally become accepted by the Japanese business community, the sliding tax rates make it prohibitively expensive to keep them there. Current government proposals would lower these tax rates.

Korea

The Korean government encourages foreign investment, but tight controls have resulted in a selective attitude toward foreign operations. The main barriers to foreign investment are informal:

- Delays and inconsistencies abound in the application of government policies.
- Pressure may be placed on foreign companies to reduce their equity in domestic joint ventures and to increase the domestic content of manufactured products.

- Traditional bureaucratic red tape and corruption are being steadily reduced by government reform, but they are still encountered in many areas.
- Competitive advantage is often obtained by those who cultivate contacts and grant favors.

Malaysia

Under Malaysia's New Economic Program (NEP), by 1990 the nation's corporate assets must be at least 30 percent owned by indigenous Malays (Bumiputras) and 40 percent by other Malaysians (mainly ethnic Chinese); the remaining 30 percent may be owned by foreigners. Since these goals are not supposed to be met by forced divestment of existing facilities, it may be difficult for new foreign companies to obtain permission to invest.

NEP rules also apply to employment. Foreign investors are required to train Malaysians for all positions whenever possible. Since skilled people will be in greater demand in the 1990s, foreign companies may find it difficult to obtain all the skilled local managers and workers they need.

Foreign investors may be given protection from outside competition if they manufacture in Malaysia. This can be good or bad, depending on which side of the fence you're on. If your company is already there, it's a plus. If you're trying to get in, it's an added barrier. Another barrier is the paperwork involved in dealing with the many levels of bureaucracy. Bureaucratic delays are often the result of the slower pace of the culture.

As in Indonesia, corruption manifests itself in two ways: favoritism to those who have the right contacts and pressure to make payments or give gifts to expedite matters through the bureaucracy. Despite strong government drives to wipe out corruption, you may still receive requests for payments to customs officials or kickbacks to purchasing officers.

New Zealand

The New Zealand government encourages foreign investment, particularly in industries that apply new technologies or managerial skills and in areas that will strengthen New Zealand's economy and open up new products for export. To establish new business in New Zealand, you must obtain prior government consent. Under a new liberalization program, a number of industries that were formerly government-controlled have been privatized, with new opportunities for foreign investment. Because of the rapidity of change, it is wise to check with the New Zealand investment authorities in the United States before planning any project.

The informal barriers to investment are insignificant. Foreign businesses operating in New Zealand seem to be accepted and treated as well as domestic businesses—by government authorities, by the local labor force, and by customers.

The Philippines

The Philippine government has attempted to reduce bureaucratic delays for investors, yet companies still encounter annoying red tape, especially in customs.

Currently, local ownership must be 60 percent or greater.

Political upheaval in the Philippines poses one of the greatest barriers to investment. If the turmoil gets settled in a way that allows the economy to stabilize, excellent investment opportunities may appear.

Singapore

Many companies choose to invest in Singapore because its bureaucracy is the most helpful, consistent, and efficient of all the nations in the Pacific Rim. Yet even here, occasional shifts in policy direction can create problems. There is virtually no corruption. Even entertaining a government official is risky.

The major barriers to investment are the limitations on expatriate hiring, coupled with local labor shortages. At the same time, there has been a rapid rise in labor costs, including government-mandated fringe benefits. The issue here is whether the high labor cost will be justified by the skill and productivity of the labor force. Also, the government has set a long-term goal of replacing labor-intensive manufacturing with high-tech, high-capital industries. For a new company, the risk lies in committing to investing in a Singaporean facility without ensuring that the needed workers are available.

Taiwan

The Taiwanese government carefully screens prospective foreign investments, allowing only nonpolluting industries that do not compete with domestic industries in home markets. The major informal barrier is the bureaucratic style of lower- and middle-level government officials, which many American managers find difficult to deal with. Corruption in the form of payments to speed customs and obtain licenses or approvals has been prevalent. But as salaries increase and government reforms take hold, these practices should be reduced.

Thailand

Thailand's rapid economic growth has been fueled by foreign investment, and many foreign companies have achieved great success. They appreciate the free-wheeling entrepreneurial spirit of the nation. Yet for smaller companies new to Thailand, the atmosphere may seem too freewheeling. Investors are plagued by inconsistent government regulations on taxation, importing, and investment.

Thailand's style is to muddle through without developing a consistent, coherent policy. Worse, inconsistent policy is coupled with strong penalties for noncompliance—including possible imprisonment.

Many government offices and ministries are run as almost autonomous entities, seemingly free to ignore policy changes dictated from above. This factor is at odds with Thailand's reputation as a free-trade economy. Investors are also put off by the burden of paperwork found in the many levels of bureaucracy.

Corruption (in the form of favoritism and bribes) is widespread and similar to practices in Malaysia and Indonesia. Laws and regulations are often intentionally vague so that government officials can retain the opportunity to demand payments for desired judgments. This system is unlikely to change in the near future because the government coalition has a vested interest in it.

8 | Starting Off On The Right Foot

- *Supporting a market partner*
- *Handling your own sales*
- *Understanding Pacific Rim business cultures*
- *Business cultures in the Pacific Rim by country*

Congratulations! Your company is ready to enter the market. You have chosen your market, you know what you will be selling there, and you have selected your selling partner. The marriage is complete. Now you must see how you and your partner get along together. It is very important to start off on the right foot. As you prepare to initiate operations, first impressions and first efforts are critical. Regardless of what you are selling and who you're selling to, your initial aims are to build a presence and a favorable image and to solidify your market position, with both your distributors and your customers. You must also monitor your initial transactions closely to make sure that you are on target, that your product fits the needs of the market, and that it is priced correctly.

This chapter examines the market-entry tactics and actions that accomplish these aims. If you are new to Pacific Rim trade and are not exporting indirectly through a trading company, you will most likely find yourself in one of the following situations:

- Someone else will be doing your selling in the market: a distributor, an agent, a licensee, or a joint venture partner. This is your market partner, and you must give that partner the support it needs to do a great job for you. Initially, you will need to focus your energy more on your partner than on the end users of your service or product.
- You will run your own Pacific Rim operation, perhaps through a sales office in the selected market.
- You will sell directly to customers, such as large businesses or governments. In this case, you need to know how to build relationships and negotiate deals. If you are going to bid for contracts, you need to understand the bidding process and how to maximize your own chances.

The way you enter a market will affect the way you advertise and promote your product or service, as shown below.

If you enter the market by:
- Working through a market partner: distributor, agent, licensee, or joint venture partner
- Selling to major end users yourself

- Negotiating contracts with corporations or government; bidding competitively on projects

Your marketing and selling will require:
- Supporting your market partner and advertising and promoting your product in the new market
- Understanding the business culture of that market
- Learning how to negotiate in that market; maximizing your chance to get the job

Supporting Your Market Partner

Most companies new to Pacific Rim markets do not sell directly to the end user, but work through an intermediary. This intermediary—whether a distributor or an agent, a licensee or a franchisee, a joint venture partner or a prime contractor—is your partner in entering the Pacific Rim market. When you enter a new domestic market on your own, you have control over the situation; when you enter a Pacific Rim market, you have to rely on your market partner. You might feel very helpless. Yet the support you provide can have a great impact on your market partner's success. For you to succeed, your market partner must succeed. Even if you will be dealing directly with the end user to some extent—through advertising and promotion, technical support, or market research—you will do so in the context of supporting your market partner.

Support for a market partner can take many forms, depending on what you are selling; but in each case, you must give your partner what it needs to look good to your ultimate customers. Only in this way can you make yourself look good, build a reputation in the new market, and lay the basis for a successful long-term relationship. Let's look at the steps involved, along with examples of how U.S. companies have supported their market partners (see Figure 8–1).

1. *Prove yourself to your distributor.* When Theos Software entered the Japanese market, it was careful to select a key distributor that knew the requirements of intended Japanese end users and how to work with them. To demonstrate its substance, Theos Software invited the distributor to the United States to visit its offices. While there, the distributor talked with and interviewed virtually all Theos employees—not just the executives, but the secretaries, the shipping clerks, and the engineers. This was very valuable, because it showed the market partner that all Theos employees supported the corporate purpose wholeheartedly and knew their business.

2. *Help your distributor validate you with customers.* The distributor made a videotape of the Theos facility, starting with an outside view of the offices and then moving inside to interview employees as a visitor might for the first time. The distributor used the video to introduce Theos to its Japanese customers, for whom the qualities of the company were as important as the qualities of the

Figure 8-1.   Ways to support your market partner.

---

1 Prove your company and its products or services to your partner.

2 Help your partner validate you to customers.

3 Help your partner to develop selling, promotional, and technical materials appropriate to the market.

4 Be patient. Allow the time needed to lay the groundwork for product introductions and negotiations.

5 Provide impeccable technical support and the backup needed to work with customers.

6 Provide the models, styles, sizes, or colors needed for that market.

7 Respond to questions and requests as rapidly as possible, even on very short notice.

8 Visit your market partner and put in personal appearances together to major customers.

9 Have your market partner visit your U.S. facility and meet your other distributors so all can see that they are part of a substantial operation.

10 Build your reputation for excellence in the market.

11 Make early adjustments or refinements in your product or service to correct problems, improve market fit, and meet competitive responses.

12 Provide the latest models, technology, and styles as soon as they are available.

13 Promote and advertise.

---

product itself. The video allowed customers to "meet" a distant company they were to do business with.

Remington Shaver supplies another example. Initial visits to key potential customers were made jointly by Remington's president, Victor Kiam, and the company's Japanese representative. As important as these meetings were to Kiam, it was also essential to the representative to have the added status of having the president of Remington along during initial contact. Theos too accompanied its distributor during many initial visits to customers, in part to handle any unanticipated technical questions that the distributor was not experienced enough to field.

3. *Provide materials tailored to the market.* You must train your partner or key distributor not just to sell the product, but to be expert in its use and maintenance, in troubleshooting and repair, and in training customers and other distributors on how to use and maintain the product. To do this, you must give your distributor the materials it needs and assist in developing whatever new materials become necessary. It should go without saying, but I'll say it again: The materials you have prepared for your domestic markets may be inadequate for your overseas markets. Domestic customers are likely to be familiar with similar products on the market, with technical jargon, and with common phrases used in promotion and advertising. Overseas distributors, even those who speak English, will not be.

In some cases, you will have to completely rewrite your literature; at other times, all you will need is a supplement to your domestic sales material that clarifies any ambiguities from the point of view of your Pacific Rim distributors and customers. Since you have selected a partner or key distributor on the basis of its ability to prepare and develop these materials for you, you should oversee the work to make sure that the materials are accurate and appropriate from your point of view as well as suited to the needs of the Pacific Rim market. If you have several Pacific Rim markets, you will have to repeat this process with the distributor for each market.

Your published materials can be supplemented very well by videotapes that demonstrate your product or service in use.*

4. *Allow enough time*. Your market-entry period may last from a few months to several years. You must have the patience to allow your key distributor time to lay the groundwork before introducing products or concluding negotiations. Theos Software spent a year laying the groundwork to announce its product. During this time, it worked very closely with its distributor, a Japanese trading company, to translate all the sales and technical literature into Japanese.

The trading company was responsible for this task, yet Theos had to ensure its accuracy. In order to obtain permission from the Chinese government to sell its technical products, SpectraPhysics had to complete testing and certification that took over a year. If your company is trying to obtain a contract to sell products or services in China, you may well spend several years negotiating before you come up with a final agreement. New-to-export companies often become tripped up by underestimating the time required by "time eaters" such as:

- Obtaining financing
- Getting a U.S. export license
- Exportizing products or services
- Negotiating with customers
- Shipping and storage
- Obtaining approvals in the new market
- Getting operations up and running
- Building relationships
- In-country distribution

5. *Back up your distributor's promises to the customer.* After your distributor makes sales, it is essential for you to back up the distributor's promises to your customers. The distributor is primarily responsible for providing technical support in the Pacific Rim market. Theos has a policy of answering any question that its Japanese distributor can't answer within twenty-four hours. No technical inquiry is left unanswered. This type of support is essential, because distributors put their reputations on the line by recommending your product to their customers. If you let them down by failing to follow up on questions, they lose face and reputation in their home markets.

*The VCR is common throughout the Pacific Rim. However, you must check the format of VCRs in your target market. It may not be VHS or Beta. Another common format—PAL/SECAM—is used throughout the world, except in the United States.

6. *Provide technical support.* Lawson-Hemphill, Inc. is a Rhode Island manufacturer of instruments that test the quality of yarn or fiber. The greatest fear of its customers is that they will not receive needed technical support. Sales reps can reassure them, but Lawson-Hemphill must back up the promises of its reps without fail. So Lawson-Hemphill gives swift service. An urgent Friday night call to Rhode Island can get an engineer from headquarters to a customer's plant in Hong Kong by Monday morning.

During initial talks with a newly selected market partner, you must extensively examine what support it needs for your market and be prepared to provide that support. If your partner is selling consumer products for you, you must be able to supply it rapidly with the styles, models, and colors that the market is demanding. If it is distributing your components or materials to manufacturers, you must be prepared to ship certain orders on very short notice and to supply engineering backup when problems arise in the manufacturing process. If you have an agent representing you in sales to a government, you must supply the agent with needed specifications and estimates within a very short time frame, since governments often request bidding information on very little notice and require it to be submitted in the official language.

These factors all go beyond price. Price, of course, is very important in Pacific Rim markets, but for a small company new to international trade, the comparative advantage lies in other factors. Theos Software's distributor knew that the customers for its software package would demand not just an excellent product, but also convincing evidence of the company's substance and ability, since follow-up technical support was so important.

Looking beyond price builds your reputation as a market leader. Until 1982 Lawson-Hemphill exported very little; by 1988 its exports had grown to over 60 percent of sales and extended to fifty countries, including several in the Pacific Rim. The company set out to build its reputation as a market leader and as the best in the industry—a company that offered something unique and did so better and cheaper. This message has been reinforced by Lawson-Hemphill's impeccable customer service.

7. *Make frequent visits, both ways.* Travel to your new market on a regular basis, not only to check up on performance and to conduct market research, but also to emphasize how important your distributor's efforts are to you. Lawson-Hemphill's vice-president for overseas sales and marketing and the president of Theos Software both travel six months a year to visit customers and recruit agents.

Have your partner or key distributor visit your plant to see your operation and meet your other distributors. This is particularly important during the initial phase of your operation. Regardless of your partner's reputation and experience in the industry, you cannot take for granted that it knows how to demonstrate, sell, and service your product. After it gets its feet wet contacting initial customers, have your partner return to your plant for debriefing and evaluation. You can gather early feedback on needed modifications, marketing approaches, prices, and the features of competitors' products.

8. *Promote camaraderie among your distributors.* If you have distributors in several markets, make them feel as if they are part of one large team. In competitive industries where size and clout confer an advantage, your distributors will be heartened to see that they are part of a network larger than just their own markets.

POM, an Arkansas manufacturer of parking meters, works very closely with its distributors in each of its overseas markets. It creates momentum by establishing camaraderie and support among its various distributors, bringing them together to share mutual experiences that make them collectively stronger. In addition, POM's stringent communications standards keep its telex, fax, and telephone systems in constant use. Agent newsletters and other mailings ensure that the distribution network is informed of market trends and competitor activity.

9. *Make early course corrections.* You must be able to make rapid adjustments and refinements in your technical specifications, your formulas, your labeling, and your advertising materials. If your market partner is selling a service for you, you need to be able to refine that service to better match the demands or customs of the local market.

You selected your market partner in the first place because it had its finger on the pulse of the market; but once you begin operating in the market, things come up that cannot be anticipated. You must respond rapidly to problems that need correction, to opportunities that emerge (on which you must move rapidly to take advantage of), and to the reactions of your competitors to your market entry. Competitive responses must be countered as soon as your market partner informs you of them.

If you are licensing a technology, you must provide your market partner with updates and refinements to keep it on top of the competitive marketplace. Many American companies damage their chances in Pacific Rim markets because they look at the region as being so distant that they do not provide the responsiveness that they give to their domestic markets.

10. *Promote and advertise.* A primary way to support your market partner is through promotion and advertising. Even if your partner has major responsibility for these activities in its market, you must still give it the input and raw materials it needs to select the best media and messages and to develop effective campaigns.

Be aware of the impact of your other advertising—especially in U.S. media—which will often be seen in Pacific Rim markets as well. The purpose of your advertising and promotion—through media messages and personal contacts—is to build image and presence and to initiate and maintain awareness. Use U.S. trade journals to promote your image of excellence: Bently-Nevada identifies customers in a potential new market by advertising in and writing articles for trade journals that are distributed and read all over the world. The company gets inquiries from potential customers in markets where it does not operate. Timely follow-up with those customers can lead to identifying new markets. Bently stresses the importance of trade journals as a means of establishing presence and credibility with potential customers all over the world.

Handling Your Own Marketing and Sales

Let's assume you are making direct contact with your customers, whether they are end users, large corporations, or governments. You may be approaching them by yourself or in conjunction with a local agent. If you are selling on your own, many of the points already discussed pertain to your situation. The way you present yourself, your company, and your products or services is of crucial importance. You must provide yourself with the same things you would provide to a partner. In addition, there are several other points to keep in mind.

1. *Find an intermediary.* Once you have identified a likely market, your success in obtaining contracts will depend on more than just having the time, resources, and patience to see the project through. You will also have to decipher the local business requirements, negotiate through the bureaucracy, find out who the real decision makers are for your project, determine how an agreement will ultimately be reached, and master the proper negotiating procedure. Since you are new at the game, you will need an intermediary to brief you on these issues. The intermediary should be someone working closely with you—whether a staff member or a consultant—who knows the language and culture, the government regulations, and the local business community. You may use your agent or distributor as an intermediary when you meet with major customers or government officials.

An intermediary is different from a market partner in that he is not doing your selling for you, just assisting you in identifying the right people to talk with and in making introductions. He is not negotiating for you, just assisting you in doing a good job negotiating. He can make sure you make the appropriate type of presentation, have the right materials and information, observe the proper formalities, and avoid making disastrous mistakes.

2. *Appear local.* In many Pacific Rim nations, it is easier to do business if you are perceived to be local—even when you are not required to have a local partner. This is particularly true in Japan. Japanese companies, and the Japanese government, prefer working with Japanese companies. Yet many U.S. companies have gained acceptance in the Japanese business community by setting up operations in Japan. In addition to working through local distributors, these companies have used a variety of means to appear local. One U.S. company recruited an eminent retired Japanese professor and executive as its intermediary. He lent his prestige to the company's approaches to banks and customers and helped to attract top-quality managers and professionals.

Teradyne, a U.S. manufacturer of electronic testing equipment, established a lab in Japan. It has gained acceptance in Japanese markets by being a chameleon, looking and acting as much like a Japanese company as it can. It has steadily reduced the number of Americans at the Japanese facility, and most of the Americans who remain speak Japanese well enough to conduct business. This "Japanization" is paying off. Over a period of several years Teradyne has cultivated relationships with its major customers to the point that it has become accepted as a full-fledged R&D partner and supplier. After working for four years with Mitsubishi Electric Corporation, one of Japan's major semiconductor makers, Teradyne helped design a system to check computer chip memories.

3. *Fill a need*. The goal for many companies is to make the "local or imported" distinction irrelevant. 7-Eleven has established 1,000 local stores in Japan, competing successfully in a very traditional market while retaining the same formula that made it successful in the United States and elsewhere. This is not because shopping at 7-Eleven seems a prestige act, but because its stores offer something that customers want and can't get elsewhere. The chain has been successful: Japanese students I talked with during their first trip to the United States were surprised to learn that such companies as 7-Eleven and McDonald's are American. These companies are so familiar, the students thought they were Japanese.

4. *Become a part of the problem-solving process*. The Teradyne example demonstrates another important principle. Working with the Sony Corporation, Teradyne developed a machine that tests the image sensor used in Sony's 8mm videocamera. Since this device has potential applications in photocopying, industrial robots, and toys, sales could become astronomical. Richard Dyke, director of Asian operations, noted in May of 1987: "We are testing it only because we are in Japan. If we were just a U.S. manufacturer, we would have been left out forever, because by the time it got to the United States, it would be too late." Teradyne became part of the problem-solving process.

5. *Refine your local niche*. To successfully challenge the giants, smaller companies must be creative and nimble and must emphasize personal service. This approach is as important in Pacific Rim markets as it is in domestic markets. Aggressively go out and meet current and prospective customers, wherever they are. Get their feedback on your service, adjust it to meet their needs, and develop added refinements.

Because you are there on the spot and can respond rapidly, you can meet needs that larger companies cannot. You can identify lucrative niches that are too small to be worthwhile to larger companies. And as I've said before, you can find a lucrative niche by offering a product or service that complements what a much larger company sells in the market.

This approach is particularly important when you enter markets in developing nations. Loctite succeeded in China by working closely with the managers of an automobile manufacturing plant to help solve a serious leakage problem in high-pressure cylinders. Loctite applied its technology to develop a sealant that solved the problem and then negotiated a joint venture to provide the sealant and other products to Chinese industry. So, again, Loctite became part of the problem-solving process and made itself needed.

6. *Provide turnkey packages.* Services sell products. You may be able to give your product a competitive advantage by making it part of a package of services that satisfy a broader need of the customer. H-Tech worked with the governments of several Asian nations to identify the best technologies for electrical power generation in remote areas, and then helped design the packages they needed. H-Tech was then able to provide large pieces of these packages. In its most successful projects, H-Tech provided all the technical support, training, product management, and other subsidiary services without which its hardware would have been useless. Ironically, many larger companies had stayed away from these projects, complaining that customers wanted them to continue supplying spare parts while they just wanted to sell hardware.

Products also sell services. Often, it is difficult for American companies to sell services in Pacific Rim countries because these countries think they can provide what they need by themselves. A way to make your service seem more valuable and substantial is to tie it to specialized products that local businesses cannot offer. One small U.S. company got a contract to sell rebuilt computers to China. The Chinese organization easily understood the cost of rebuilding the computers but balked at the separate subcontract for design services and management. It felt the U.S. company was charging too much for "just thinking." This glitch was resolved when the agreements were restructured so that the services were attached to the installation, troubleshooting, software testing, and training for each computer.

7. *Make the sale easier.* In developing nations, making the sale easier typically means offering financing concessions. For a government short on foreign exchange, you are more likely to make the deal when you are able to accept countertrade. For a private company, you are more likely to get the sale if you can offer a means of time payment. Both of these topics are discussed in Chapter 9.

8. *Handle your own promotion and advertising.* If advertising and promotion are important to sales in your domestic markets, it's likely that they will be even more important in Pacific Rim markets where customers are unfamiliar with your products or services. If it is worthwhile for you to do some advertising in overseas publications, work through an advertising agency that is familiar with your target area, whether it is a geographic or industry market. Support the local agency the way you support your market partner.

When you work with public relations companies and advertising agencies that have experience in your market, listen to what they say. Do not scoff at a practice that would not work at home but is essential there. To double-check what you hear, talk with members of the U.S. business community in that country.

Contact the American chamber of commerce there. Its staff members can provide valuable advice for your marketing efforts.

Before deciding which forms of promotion and advertising to use, prepare thoroughly for your market. To help the agency you select do the best job, you need to prepare almost as if you were sending your own advertising director there to design and line up ads. To lay the groundwork for your promotion, advertising, and public relations efforts in a Pacific Rim country, you should have a local marketing professional give you a thorough briefing on:

- The country's culture, customs, language, and political environment; the distribution channels for your type of product or service; and how these factors affect the way you promote
- The role played by various media—newspapers, trade publications, magazines, radio, and TV—and the advertising channels that reach your customers
- The local competitive environment as it relates to marketing practices
- Ways to adopt your marketing and packaging to local conditions

Be open-minded about which media will actually provide the greatest impact for your product or service. Set aside preconceptions that are based on your U.S. experience. It's not necessarily the largest-circulation periodical or the TV station with the greatest coverage that will serve you best. A specialized trade journal may succeed better than a consumer publication. What works on TV in the United States may do just as well on radio in your market. Participating in local trade shows is one of the best ways to get to know the media in your market. Visit the booths of all the trade publications. Get copies, talk with the advertising staff, and find out what you have that they are interested in.

9. *Develop a global strategy, with local messages.* If you are entering several markets, do not assume you can use the same marketing approach in each. Until you find out differently, it is better to assume the opposite—that you need separate messages tailored to each market to carry out your global marketing strategy.

10. *Use on-the-spot promotion.* In some markets, you must take an entirely different approach to promoting your firm or products. In addition to the means of promotion just described, participating in a trade mission is particularly valuable when you want to reach a government organization in a developing nation. The value of this was demonstrated by a trip to China made by manufacturers of U.S. semiconductor equipment and materials. The trade mission included reps from a number of leading U.S. companies and their Asian subsidiaries, and was led by a top Commerce Department official. The U.S. reps met with high-level Chinese government and industry officials and visited a number of plants.

Members of the mission gave technical seminars to Chinese engineers and technicians in Beijing, Wuxi, and Shanghai. Topics included crystal growing, wafer cutting and polishing, mask making and cleaning, and assembly process testing. The seminars were enthusiastically received, and the mission members gained face-to-face exposure to the people who could make purchases from them.

American participants learned vital information they could not have gained otherwise. Many of the Chinese engineers said they preferred the American-manufactured equipment (1) because they felt that it was more reliable and that American companies responded faster to service requests and (2) because many of the engineers had been educated in American universities using American equipment.

Selling Guidelines for Market Entry

- Use an intermediary.
- Appear local.
- Become part of the problem-solving process.
- Remember that products sell services, and services sell products.
- Use local people for promotion and advertising.
- Adopt a global strategy, with local messages.
- Take advantage of unorthodox promotion opportunities.

Understanding Different Business Cultures

What would you think of a foreign executive in the United States who had never heard of Chicago, the Super Bowl, or Independence Day and was surprised to find women in top-level positions? To start off on the right foot, you must understand the business cultures of your Pacific Rim markets. It's easy for American companies to trip themselves up by failing to observe certain business or cultural proprieties. You must know how to meet the right people, communicate with them, initiate a lasting business relationship, and negotiate agreements.

To do so, you need to understand the business culture of the nation—the set of customs, protocols, musts, and taboos distinctive to that market. The business cultures of the Pacific Rim nations are quite different, but they do share certain characteristics. (At the end of this chapter, I examine distinct facets of the business culture of each Pacific Rim nation.)

"Make a Friend, Then Make a Deal"

From Korea to New Zealand, it is important to establish good personal relationships as a foundation for doing business. The personal factor regularly trips up many American executives, who have the "let's get right down to business" approach to selling. Even U.S. companies that understand this in principle often fail to factor in the time and resources needed to build successful relationships.

The Necessity of Face-to-Face Meetings.   The people you want to work with will want to size you up in person. Deals are cemented and disputes settled in this way. This is one of the reasons it is so important to travel there—not just once, but on a regular basis.

The Importance of Saving Face.   Asian cultures place high priority on harmonious relations and interactions. During discussions and negotiations, you should avoid aggressive behavior and angry outbursts. Don't let people lose face by making them appear ignorant or stupid. Avoid driving such a hard bargain that your counterparts feel pushed into the corner. In every Pacific Rim country, the abrupt, aggressive, direct American approach is grating.

Even in Australia and New Zealand, a smooth working style is important. These two nations have fairly small business communities—concentrated in Melbourne, Sydney, and Canberra in Australia and in Auckland and Wellington in New Zealand. Since most business and government officials know one another, they have to get along and work well together, and their working styles minimize abrasiveness.

The Role of Status.   You can't send a sales rep to negotiate with a top executive. However, after initial talks or negotiations between top-level executives, lower-level managers and technical people—those who will be involved in day-to-day working relationships—can continue the detailed discussions and negotiations.

The Need for Third-Party Introductions.   Get an introduction first from a respected third party. Cold calls seldom work. In domestic markets, you can often contact potential customers with little or no prior arrangement. This rarely pays off in Pacific Rim markets.

How do you find this third party or intermediary? There are several ways. Ask your bank to approach its correspondent bank in the nation you're going to. Approach the country's trade and investment agencies in the United States. Work through the U.S. Commerce Department reps in that country, the American chamber of commerce in that country, and organizations such as the ASEAN-U.S. Business Council. Also, your trade or professional association may have a parallel organization in the country.

Go slow. Be patient. Building relationships and negotiating can take time, and those with the patience to allow business matters to unfold at the proper pace are much more likely to succeed.

The Importance of Business Cards.   In the United States, business cards are often dealt across a meeting table like playing cards. In the Asian Pacific Rim countries, there is a ritual to exchanging business cards that is very important. In general, a business card should be presented every time you are introduced to someone, so it's very important to have a large supply with you on a trip. It is a real blunder to run out of cards.

Your business cards should be printed on both sides: one side in English and the other side translated into the language of your target country. Having your title printed on your business card is very important, since it bespeaks your position and status.

Do not present your card in an offhand manner; rather, offer it as if it were a small gift. Stand up and present it with your right hand to the person to whom you've just been introduced. Have that person's language side up, and turn the card so he can read it. Keep your business cards in a handsome container—say, brass, with your name or monogram—not just a plastic envelope.

At meetings, you'll notice that the other people will keep your card on the table in front of them. This is common practice; it helps them remember a name with unfamiliar pronunciation, and you should always feel free to do the same.

You should be able to have the local-language translation of your business enterprise printed on the back of your cards when you first get to the country. This is another detail to plan for ahead of time. Many large hotels handle this service. Also, many American cities have foreign language newspapers—Japanese, Chinese, Korean—where you can find someone to translate and typeset your card for a reasonable price. Remember to get a back translation (see Chapter 2) before having a thousand cards printed in Chinese. If you are traveling to several countries, obviously you will need several versions of your business card.

The Language Factor

How many times have you heard Americans bemoan the fact that every foreigner they do business with speaks English, but they never know how to speak the foreigner's language? How important is it to learn to speak the language of the country in which you are going to do business? Unless you are already fluent or love to learn languages, you need make only one trip to Japan or China to realize how long it would take you to learn enough of the language to carry on business discussions—if you ever could.

If you are going to be doing business in a nation for a long period of time, it is definitely to your benefit to learn the language as well as you can. Just think about someone from a foreign nation trying to conduct business in the United States for more than a short period of time without being able to speak English. It's quite a profound disadvantage.

In the short run, though, you will be able to get by. For one thing, people everywhere speak English. They have learned it not just so they can speak with Americans, but so they can speak with one another. When a Korean and a Malaysian get together, they probably speak English. English is becoming increasingly common in business and government and professional circles, as more and more companies engage in international trade and as a younger, English-speaking generation of managers and officials comes along, many of whom have studied or worked in the United States. Keep in mind, too, that when the people you will be doing business with do not speak English they will normally provide an interpreter.

In addition to Australia and New Zealand, you can count on working with people who speak English in Singapore, Hong Kong, Taiwan, Korea, and the Philippines. In Japan and elsewhere in ASEAN you can usually but not always count on working with people who speak English. In China, presume that you need an interpreter until you find out otherwise.

There are, of course, benefits to learning to speak the language. If you know some of the language, and have practiced it with someone else who speaks it, you will be able to understand much more than you can express. This is an advantage: People will talk in your presence thinking that you cannot understand them at all. Also, many foreign businesspeople speak only a little English. The more you can speak their language, the more you will be able to communicate effectively without an interpreter. Finally, the more you do business in a country, the more likely you are to encounter people who do not speak English—at times when no interpreter is handy. This is especially true when you get out of the main cities, when you go sight-seeing or shopping, and when you must deal with customs or lower-level government officials.

Any degree of mastery of the language is useful, even if you learn just a few key phrases—*thank you, please, you're welcome, I'm pleased to meet you.* Learn what to say instead of no and how to ask the way to your hotel. If you know some of the language and try to use it, people will be appreciative and will try to help you.

Total Communication

The language issue is misleading in a way. The larger issue is communication. Your success will depend less on how well you understand, say, Japanese than on how well you can communicate with the people in Japan. Language is only one aspect of communication; cultural understanding is more important. Even if you can speak some Japanese, you will miss a lot if you are not familiar with the culture. Here are a few rules of thumb to make overall communication easier.

Nonverbal Signals. Don't assume that people who speak English will understand you. Pay attention to how they are responding to you. They are not likely to say, "I do not understand you," but you will learn to spot the gestures or facial expressions that mean the same thing. If necessary, repeat what you have said in a different way, making sure you avoid all idioms or unclear phrases. Stay away from jokes, puns, or offhand comments that will confuse, bewilder, or upset. Often, they will be taken literally.

Don't assume that someone who is U.S.-educated and speaks English well is Westernized. Many of the people you encounter will seem quite Westernized, and they are to a certain extent. So you will think, "Here are people who think like me." But you must remember that you're dealing with members of another culture, despite their Westernized manner. You can hope, not that they will think as you do, but that their cross-cultural experience will make them more tolerant of your gaffes.

If you can, use your market partner as your intermediary and perhaps even your interpreter. Hire local professional people whenever you can for legal and financial matters, for advertising and promotion, and for correspondence and other written material. You may also wish to include them on your team for appropriate discussions or negotiations. When you work with an interpreter, look at the person you are dealing with, not at the interpreter.

Learn to become aware not just of what words mean, but also of how they are used. Nonverbal language conveys as much as verbal language. Learn to understand gestures and facial expressions, actions and reactions. Find out what it means when people smile and nod, sit in silence, look away, come into the room, or get up and walk out. Much communication is indirect and purposefully imprecise. People will avoid saying no to you directly, but you still need to recognize when they do not agree with you.

Americans tend to be explicit verbal communicators; many Pacific Rim cultures rely much more on indirect and nonverbal communication. This can put you at a disadvantage. But if you are briefed on what to look for and if you are sensitive to the issue, you will learn to pick up important nonverbal messages. As you do so, you will become aware of any negative nonverbal messages you may be sending (such as signs of impatience).

Social Interaction.   Learn what conversational topics are safe or taboo. For example, in the Chinese cultures, it is taboo to talk about family, whereas in the Philippines it is one of the best topics of discussion. Politics is always dangerous unless you know a person quite well.

As a rule, it's better to talk about your host's country than about the United States, but there are exceptions. Many people will have U.S. work or educational experience that they will be delighted to talk about. You can talk about Michigan State or UCLA or Harvard—they may have difficulty finding the football scores of their alma mater in their local paper. If you went to the same school or lived in the same city, this gives you an instant rapport.

Accept social invitations even if you and your host cannot speak each other's language at all. This is often an essential part of learning about each other and building a business relationship.

Perhaps the best advice is, don't take all this advice as gospel. Watch out for stereotyping. The Japanese or Chinese you encounter will be as diverse as the Americans you meet as you travel across the United States. If you're new to Pacific Rim trade, paying attention to the business culture of your new market is very important. No doubt, the lists of musts and taboos will seem extremely complex and perplexing. What if you do in Japan what you're supposed to do in Korea or China? Don't take it all too seriously. You cannot master a new culture or language in a short period of time, if ever. The key is having a certain cultural sensitivity—an understanding of what is required to communicate across cultures.

The Pretrip Rehearsal. Before traveling to your new market, you need to prepare in several different ways. Read up on the country you are going to: its history, geography, and culture. Learn enough about it so that you can understand what your host is talking about and ask intelligent questions. People are flattered when you know enough to ask them about things they are proud of. Find out about the business culture: the protocols for making contacts, selling, negotiating, and conducting business; those for building business relationships; and those for social interactions and giving gifts. Learn the musts and the taboos.

Several organizations provide training and orientation for Americans traveling to the Pacific Rim, and numerous books are available on business cultures and doing business abroad (see the Appendixes).

The only way to learn appropriate behaviors is to practice them. Before you travel, find a rehearsal partner—someone who can help you practice bowing, presenting business cards, making introductions, offering greetings and toasts, pronouncing and understanding key phrases, presenting a gift, and thanking your host. You will know ahead of time who your meeting partners are, so learn how to pronounce their names. You should rehearse these behaviors physically and verbally before you depart. Knowing them in your head is no substitute.

You must also learn to recognize the likely responses to what you are saying. On my first trip to Japan, I carefully rehearsed telephone greetings so that I could say "Hello, may I speak to Mr. _____ ?" in Japanese. But the person on the other end of the line would respond in rapid Japanese, which I couldn't understand at all.

Arrange to have a local ally (perhaps your intermediary) join your team when you arrive. This "cultural translator" is just as important as your language translator, and can do everything from explaining the protocols of business meetings and the intricacies of negotiation to giving the taxi driver the correct instructions. Your ally can also give you invaluable feedback on the outcome of meetings and help you determine the best course of action to take.

Negotiating

One of the most important forms of communication you will engage in is negotiating. You will be involved in negotiations with different types of people in different countries—government officials, customers, agents, distributors, and partners. Each Pacific Rim nation has its own negotiating style, and you need to learn the pertinent points before conducting negotiations in any one. You should also be aware of the following general points for any negotiating session.

Preliminaries. Prepare thoroughly. The team across the table from you will surprise you with its knowledge of your industry. Many negotiations have been shot down because American negotiators did not know their industry, U.S. export regulations, financial information, or even their own product's technical specifications.

Make sure you are meeting and talking with the right people. Find out what should be sent beforehand, if anything, and send the right material in the correct form. Determine whether translated versions will be needed. Make your appointments and arrangements far in advance, confirm them before you leave the United States, and reconfirm them when you arrive in the country.

Discuss your negotiation beforehand with another American executive who has been through a similar session. The tips you garner can prove invaluable during the negotiation. Remember that negotiators must have authority to make decisions on the items being negotiated. This authority should be based on technical expertise, negotiating experience, or experience in the affected market or region.

Go into the negotiating session well rested. Don't fly halfway around the world and then begin a crucial negotiation at what is 2:00 A.M. for your body clock. After a long flight, leave time for you and your negotiating team to rest.

For business situations, rely on an interpreter—not on your limited understanding of the language. Usually your host will provide an interpreter. Do not use one provided by a "helpful" competitor. Make sure to brief the interpreter beforehand on the background of the meeting, what your goals and intentions are, and any technical issues that will be discussed.

Get there on time—not very early, not late. Punctuality is important, even if the person you are meeting with is late. Observe the customs and protocols of the local business culture. Remember the appropriate behaviors for the nation you are in. Treat your hosts with respect—as friends, not as adversaries.

The Negotiating Session.   Negotiate along with at least one other person. Never negotiate alone. Your team needs one person to talk and one to listen. Write up your notes at the end of each day's negotiations. Key team members should compare notes and analyze what was said and what happened. In this way, you can spot any disparities between today's statements and yesterday's.

Have your minimum position—or "walkaway" points—well established before entering the negotiations. Negotiate hard, then make a concession. If you yield ground on one point, have a clear idea of what you will require in return. If you reach an impasse, remember that knotty issues can sometimes be resolved much more effectively during informal evening conversations than across the negotiating table.

Do not get caught in the "ratchet effect." Many inexperienced negotiators sometimes yield on a series of small items one after the other—items that combined amount to a major concession. When going over your bid, for example, be careful not to allow small pieces to be whittled from each line item. Take all such demands under consideration, and look at the entire package at the end of the day. One common negotiating ploy is to wait until the deal appears to be negotiated, and then ask for just one more concession.

Have a prearranged delaying tactic to stave off an impasse or to gain time to come up with a counterposition. For example, even though you're using qualified negotiators, you can say you need to confer with the home office or with technical specialists. Don't force others to lose face. Allow them to save face. If they yield an important point to you, you need to make a minor, face-saving concession in return. Don't set a deadline. If you are in a hurry, you are at a disadvantage. The other party sees that you are under time pressure, and may adopt delaying tactics to pressure you into concessions. On the other hand, if you sense that discussions are being dragged out unnecessarily, it might help to whine a little. Say that you must return home soon and that if discussions aren't wrapped up, you may not be able to complete the deal. Often, your hosts will understand and speed things to a conclusion. The more time they spend with you, the more serious they are about doing business with you. They don't want to waste their time either.

Negotiate tough, but make sure everyone wins. The aim of negotiation should not be to get the absolute best deal for you, but to come up with the best deal that works for everybody. If you drive too hard a bargain, you may walk away feeling that you got a good deal—only to discover later that you have no deal at all, or that you have a deal your customers or market partner will not support. If you are satisfied with the deal you have negotiated, you may hold back one concession, perhaps even a symbolic one, to offer at this point.

The Final Agreement. If you reach a general agreement face to face, details can be handled later by fax, telex, or letter. But be wary of what you send through international communications. You have no guarantee that messages by common carrier will remain confidential, especially if you are negotiating with a government or other public agency.

The success of the agreement can be affected by the size of your negotiating team. In China, you will be sitting across the table from a team of half a dozen or more people, and you will be expected to bring a team of several people yourself. A large team suggests that you are someone important, someone worth negotiating with. If you come by yourself or with one other person, the Chinese will feel that you do not take the negotiation very seriously. This is also somewhat true in the other Chinese cultures: Taiwan, Hong Kong, and Singapore.

In Pacific Rim markets like Japan and Korea, team negotiating is becoming less common as these countries adopt the more hurried Western business style. Executives are busier and have to make decisions more rapidly. They are entrepreneurial and have more authority, so they can make decisions with less consultation.

To what extent should you insist that your final contract cover every point? In some Pacific Rim countries, it's important to have every detail covered, but in most countries it's expected that the contract will serve as a broad framework. Every detail need not be spelled out, and flexibility is important. Attorneys are rarely involved in hashing out all the contractual terms. It is assumed that vague or disputed items can be resolved out of a sound personal relationship and commitment to making the agreement work for both parties.

Business Cultures in the Pacific Rim

Now let's turn to some of the specific characteristics of business cultures in the Pacific Rim.

Japan

U.S. companies that do their homework find success in Japan. These companies emphasize that there are no real barriers to doing business there other than a company's own ignorance. You can succeed if you understand the way the Japanese think and learn to accommodate yourself to their consumer preferences. Japanese consumers are very quality-conscious, and Japanese manufacturers insist that you meet your delivery dates and provide aftersales service.

Examples of American ignorance include carpet makers whose rugs were too large for Japanese houses and bubble bath companies that did not understand how the Japanese bathe. Kentucky Fried Chicken almost failed until it learned to open its restaurants, not in suburban towns or along highways, but in downtown areas. Apple Computer initially sold its computers with manuals printed in English and software without kanji characters.

Companies that have succeeded in Japan have adapted to the peculiarities of the market. Levi-Strauss designed a special line of jeans for the shorter Japanese. Ore-Ida of Boise, Idaho, captured a third of the market for frozen fried potatoes by hiring Japanese workers in key sales positions. Japanese consumers are more demanding than Americans in certain areas. Packaging is extremely important. Cookies come individually wrapped, and ordinary bars of soap are purchased in stylish gift boxes.

Despite trade frictions, the common ground between Japanese and American markets points to greatly expanded trade in the future. Both countries share a political democracy, a capitalist economy, and consumers with high consumption patterns.

Face-to-face contact is essential in conducting business. It is more effective to initiate contact through a personal visit (set up by an introduction through an intermediary) than through correspondence. Initial contacts are usually formal meetings between top executives; more detailed negotiations may be carried out later by those who will be directly involved. During the first meeting, you get acquainted and communicate your broad interests; you size each other up and make a decision on whether ongoing discussions are worthwhile. At this point you should not spell out details or expect to do any negotiating.

Exchange business cards at the start of the meeting. The traditional greeting is the bow. Many Japanese executives who deal with foreign companies also use a handshake. If you bow, then you should bow as low and as long as the other person, to signify your humility. First names are not usually used in a business context. In Japan, the family name is given last, as in English. You should address

Yoshi Hinoda as "Mr. Hinoda," or "Hinoda-san." Expect to go through an interpreter unless you learn otherwise. Many Japanese speak some English, but you cannot count on its being adequate for undertaking a business negotiation.

Conservative dress is common for both men and women in public. Most Japanese professional men and women wear Western-style dress—European more than American, although during the hot summer months, men often do not wear suit jackets.

Concern about how others perceive you pervades business and social communication in Japan. Since saving and losing face are so important, you should avoid confrontation or embarrassing situations. A Japanese reporter who can't ask an intelligent question at a press conference will remain silent out of fear of losing face by asking a stupid question. A distributor that cannot follow up on a promise made to a customer loses face and may suffer damage to its reputation.

The Japanese tend to speak less precisely than Americans in business negotiations. Nonverbal communications—gestures, nuances, inferences—are very important in signaling intentions. "No" is seldom said directly, and rejection is always stated indirectly. Remember that the Japanese *hai* means "Yes, I understand you" rather than "Yes, I agree with you." The Japanese will sit in silence for some time. Americans are tempted to fill this void with words. But it is just a way to reflect on what has been said. Early business and social contacts are characterized by politeness and formality.

The Japanese like to launch new products or take other important initiatives on "lucky days." The luckiest day, called the *taian,* occurs about every six days. Your Japanese counterpart will probably want to delay a major announcement until the next *taian.*

The presentation of a new product is traditionally followed by a reception with the product on display; an *omiyage,* or gift, is given to each attendee. This adds to the overall cost of the event.

Japan epitomizes the rule "Make a friend, then make a sale." When selling to or negotiating with the Japanese, do not rush things. Whereas Americans are eager to get down to business and to put proposals on the table, the Japanese prefer a ritual of getting to know you, deciding whether they want to do business with you at all, and seeing whether agreement is possible within a broad framework.

American negotiators are direct and press for a negotiating agreement; the Japanese prefer to probe, to feel out the other party, and to reach some understanding of the other side's position before putting forth a proposal on which both sides can agree. Americans must learn to be patient with this process. You and your host should both strive to create an atmosphere of harmony in which both sides can achieve their main objectives. The Japanese prefer to close with a broad agreement and mutual understanding, preceded by thorough discussion of each side's expectations and goals. If they decide they want to do business, they will negotiate the details with you later.

A Japanese negotiator cannot give a prompt answer during an initial discussion. No commitment can be made until the group or groups he represents reach a consensus. Do not expect an immediate answer. Negotiations may take an extended period.

Japanese executives emphasize good faith over legal, contractual safeguards. They are not in the habit of negotiating detailed contracts that cover all contingencies. However, Japanese managers who are accustomed to Western business dealings are familiar with more structured contracts. In case of disputes, the Japanese prefer resolving issues out of court on the basis of the quality of the business relationship.

A Japanese partner or customer will usually prefer to develop a business relationship in stages, with a limited initial agreement that, if successful, is gradually extended into a broader, more binding agreement. The Japanese prefer a long-term, reliable, and exclusive business arrangement. So once you make a commitment, expect it to be for a long time. If you break it, it may be difficult for you to find a new Japanese business partner.

When you enter a traditional home, inn, or temple, remove your shoes on the enclosed porch and put on the slippers left there. Put your shoes on the shelf, toes pointing outward. Before entering a room with straw *tatami* mats, remove the slippers and enter in sock feet.

Modesty and humility permeate social interactions. If you are offered tea, bow slightly and hesitate momentarily before accepting. You may take a small gift such as fruit or candy to your host. Gifts are given and accepted with both hands and a slight bow. Compliments are usually denied graciously. If you offer effusive compliments to your host regarding a piece of art or decoration, he may feel obligated to give it to you.

When eating, chopsticks are usually used, but a fork and knife will be available for you. A bowl of rice, noodles, or soup may be held close to your mouth while eating.

During a meeting, sit up straight; don't slouch, and keep your feet on the floor. After the meeting, your host will probably accompany you outside to the elevator or to the front door.

China

China consists of many markets. You can no longer send a trade delegation to Beijing and assume that you have covered your bases and made contact with all the appropriate Chinese decision makers.

Success hinges on how well American companies understand Chinese protocol and etiquette. Again, the importance of face cannot be overstated. The Chinese dislike discourteous behavior and loss of self-control; visitors are expected to conduct themselves with restraint and to refrain from loud and boisterous actions. The Chinese are usually unwilling to give an explicit negative response, preferring a noncommittal answer when facing a difficult question. Remember that in China, contrary to how it's done in Japan, family names are given first. Chung Lin-Wu should be addressed as "Mr. Chung," not "Chung" or "Lin-Wu."

There are many cultural subtleties that must be appreciated and mastered. Who toasts whom and at what times? Who serves what, to whom first? Seating arrangements at meetings are carefully crafted. Be aware of sensitive political issues that could interfere with the delivery of your message. Avoid mixing politics and marketing. In your presentations, you can be tripped up by unexpected issues. For example, it is best to avoid using flags and maps, since international borders are controversial. Be careful how you refer to Hong Kong, and Taiwan—not as independent nations, but as part of a "greater China" that is not currently united.

At meetings, be careful of jargon, idioms, and humor that the Chinese do not understand. Expressions will be taken literally. Red is a festive color; white means death and mourning. Watch out for translations of names and idiomatic terms. One marketing reference to "an old friend" came out as "former friend."

Sex does not sell well in China; specifications do. Advertisements filled with specifications are much better received in China than they are in the United States. Sports images and sports events are also effective marketing vehicles in China. American companies have sponsored teams, provided uniforms and equipment, financed travel and coaching, and helped build training and competition facilities.

Industrial marketing programs should be aimed at technicians, trade officials, and business reps who are involved in purchasing decisions related to products and technology. Target the appropriate Chinese technical trade journals and business publications for both articles and advertisements. Participate in trade shows, exhibitions, product demonstrations, and technical seminars. Direct mail and newspaper announcements have been used effectively.

Negotiations can take months or even years, with repeated trips plus lengthy communications in between. This slow pace is due to the nature of the Chinese system: layers of government agencies with poor communication among them, goals and instructions that are often contradictory and sometimes in competition with one another, and constantly changing rules. You will be negotiating with a vast bureaucracy. The most common type of business arrangement is a licensing agreement or a joint venture, negotiated with a state company. The Chinese negotiate as a team, and decisions are made by consensus. On the other side of the negotiating table, they prefer to deal with a team of experts rather than one headstrong American entrepreneur.

Since the Chinese will provide you with an interpreter, it's not necessary to bring your own or to understand Chinese. However, if a member of your team speaks Chinese, negotiations and explanations of technical matters can be greatly speeded up. In China, more so than in any other Pacific Rim nation, it is important to have someone who can advise you on business practices and customs, although many companies have negotiated successfully in China without such a cultural interpreter. A major reason so many companies enter China through Hong Kong is that there are so many businesspeople there who are experienced in both Chinese and Western business practices.

The Chinese emphasize technical detail. During negotiations, they will try to get as much technical and commercial information from you as possible, but if you're unwilling to discuss proprietary technical information, the Chinese will understand. Chinese negotiators will use competition among Western businesses as a lever to get you to improve your offer. It's important that your negotiating team include highly qualified and tactful people to demonstrate your company's serious intentions, technical competence, and ability to resolve technical problems. Negotiations often include extensive discussion on relatively minor details. Careful preparation is essential, since the Chinese bargaining team will be very astute and extremely well prepared. It will have studied your company, your industry, and you beforehand.

The Chinese style of negotiating is to arrive at a decision fair to both sides in a smooth, nonconfrontational way. Negotiations are often interrupted while the Chinese team considers a presentation. Decisions are made by a group in coordination with various Chinese entities, including the relevant ministries and the end users.

The traditional Chinese negotiating approach has been tested in recent years as China has opened up to foreign business. The Chinese have demanded so much in return for access to their markets that many foreign companies have either accepted bad deals or been driven away. The Chinese have learned from this, and as they gain proficiency in business, they are becoming easier to negotiate with. They are tough negotiators, but a fair deal can be arrived at.

Standardized contracts are typically short and vague. Your negotiating partners will prefer to make oral understandings outside the written contract and will give you assurances that your concerns about unwritten terms are unfounded. Nevertheless, you should press for inclusion of all essential terms.

The Chinese emphasize mutual understanding in the development of good long-term relationships, both business and personal. They prefer to resolve disputes through "friendly discussion" or "friendly negotiations" between two parties rather than going to outsiders. They feel that such disputes can be resolved if the long-term relationship is sound. Only in cases of impasse will disputes go to arbitration.

If you are invited to dinner, arrive on time or a little early. There may be many dishes, and it is polite, but not mandatory, to sample each one. Place your chopsticks together on the table when finished eating. When eating rice or soup, you may hold the bowl close to your mouth.

The host will probably toast you, and after a short time you should reciprocate by toasting the host. At a banquet, you may be expected to rise and make a brief speech responding to what your host says. People will leave shortly after the meal is over, and the guest should make the first move to depart. Gifts to officials are forbidden or frowned upon, yet tokens of nominal value can be presented to the host's group. "Intangible" items such as banquets or trips to the United States are often given—and expected.

The business communities of Taiwan, Hong Kong, and Singapore share many aspects of their Chinese cultural heritage. There are also significant overseas Chinese communities in Malaysia, Indonesia, and the Philippines. Although ethnic Chinese are a minority in these countries, they are prominent in the business sectors, so you are quite likely to encounter Chinese cultural patterns in these nations as well. However, there are a number of important differences, because business in these nations is more entrepreneurial, less bureaucratic, and much more influenced by Western business practices. These differences are examined below.

Taiwan

Like all Chinese, the Taiwanese value education very highly. A very large proportion of Taiwan's professional and business students attend college in the United States. In contrast to Korea and Japan, business in Taiwan is dominated by smaller, family-run companies. You should initiate contact by a third-party introduction, very often through the Far East Trade Service, which has offices in the United States.

During visits and meetings, punctuality is important—even if you are kept waiting. When visiting a large organization, you will be greeted by a secretary and led to the office of an executive. Wait at the door until invited in, and remain standing until invited to sit. The normal greeting is a handshake, but a person of higher status than you may only nod.

In Taiwan (and Hong Kong), many men and women have an English given name as well as Chinese, e.g., "Fred Chang" and "Chang Lin-Shen." Remember, in the Chinese version, the family name comes first, and Chang Lin-Shen would be called Mr. Chang.

Again, bilingual business cards are essential. Since titles are important and indicate status, your title should be included on your card. Hand the card Chinese side up to your host with your right hand.

The official language is Mandarin Chinese, but the Taiwanese dialect is spoken locally. Most business representatives can speak English; most businesses correspond in English, and many in Japanese as well. Catalogs, promotional literature, and instructions are acceptable in English. Politeness and etiquette are important in all business exchanges. Since many Taiwanese are U.S.-educated, most of the people you contact will speak English. However, you cannot take this for granted, and for the first meeting, it's often advisable to be accompanied by a local associate who can serve as interpreter.

Personal relationships are very important. Your first priority should be to establish good personal rapport in all meetings. It is essential to cultivate a relationship before beginning serious negotiations. The Taiwanese want to do business with people they know and trust. These relationships are built through preliminary meetings, dinners, conversations, entertainment, and social events.

The Taiwanese, like the Japanese, will avoid saying no directly; rather, they will suggest a possible difficulty. A nod of the head means your point was understood, not necessarily agreed to. Personal contact other than a handshake should be avoided. Do not point with a finger; use your entire hand.

Rank is very important, especially in family-owned companies. Status and authority come with age, and the patriarch of the organization has the final say. In family-owned businesses, the oldest male typically has the greatest power, with his oldest son being second in command. However, Taiwan is undergoing a major generational power shift. Many of the people who came over from mainland China during the 1949 Communist takeover are being replaced by a younger generation of U.S.-trained managers.

As in mainland China, the size of the negotiating team indicates the seriousness of the negotiation. Having a team of specialists accompany you enhances your status. Taiwanese are master business people and bargainers. Negotiations will include very hard bargaining within an atmosphere of harmony and cooperation. Price and terms are very important.

Your contract will be flexible, with many terms left out. You must push to have all required terms included without insisting on a degree of detail that suggests you do not trust your counterparts.

Attorneys are rarely included in business dealings. Conflicts that do arise are normally settled out of court through arbitrators. Successful business grows out of a relationship of mutual respect.

Foreign guests are often honored by a dinner banquet. Unlike its U.S. counterpart, this banquet is not primarily a business meeting, although some business may be discussed. It often takes place right after your meeting, so allow for this in your scheduling. If it is scheduled for a later time, be sure to arrive on time. As a guest, you are expected to be served first from each new dish. A rice wine is served, but it is sipped only when making toasts. When the dinner is over, the guest should make the first move to leave; no tipping is expected. It is customary to give gifts—small, "practical" presents such as pens or items that represent your corporation.

If you are invited to your host's house, you should remove your shoes and don slippers in the outer hall. Always greet the oldest person first, and allow youngsters to show you respect. You may bring a small gift such as fruit. Use both hands when offering or accepting a gift, but the gift is not usually opened until later. Sincere compliments and thanks are appreciated, and they will be politely denied.

Hong Kong

Hong Kong is a bastion of free trade and entrepreneurship. As a longtime British colony, it has many British-style institutions and habits; yet its culture is Chinese. Family loyalty, politeness, modesty, and saving face are fundamental. The Hong Kong culture grows out of a mix of Taoism, Buddhism, Hinduism, and Christianity. Education is highly valued, and many Hong Kong executives and professionals have been to school in the United States, Canada, or England.

It is best to initiate contact through a third party. For example, your bank may be able to set up contact with a Hong Kong correspondent or establish contact through AMCHAM Hong Kong or the Hong Kong Trade Development Council, which has offices in several U.S. cities.

Business hours are 9:00 A.M. to 5:00 P.M. or later on weekdays and 9:00 A.M. to 1:00 P.M. on Saturday. Meetings will be held at your host's office. Your host's secretary will take you to the meeting room and you will be offered the most favorable seat, often with a view of the harbor. You will be introduced to each person and should shake hands and greet each one by name. Remember that the family name comes first. Exchange business cards with everyone there. Present cards with your right hand, Chinese side up, and turn them towards the recipient.

English is the official language of business and government. The local Chinese dialect is more likely to be Cantonese than Mandarin. Any executive you contact will probably speak English, so there is little need for an interpreter.

After introductions and a bit of small talk, your host will get down to business. The initial meeting will most likely be short. Its purpose is to establish contact and exchange information.

Hong Kong executives are more direct and will reach agreement more rapidly than executives elsewhere in the Pacific Rim. Even so, Hong Kong is traditional in its high emphasis on polite, respectful, and modest behavior. Loud language, angry outbursts, and other strong displays of emotion are avoided. Face saving is important. People will avoid saying no directly; thus disagreement may be expressed in a way that is confusing to you. You may think that you have come to terms when in effect you have not, so you need to test apparent agreements.

In contrast to China and Taiwan, Hong Kong rarely uses large negotiating parties. You can make a first visit on your own if you wish. It is important for you to learn who will be making the final decision and how that decision will be made. Bring in an attorney only after an agreement is reached and is being drawn up. You will probably need to make more than one trip to conclude a deal. It is still important to allow time to establish a relationship.

Your host may give a banquet in your honor during your visit. As the guest of honor, you will sit with your back to the wall, facing the kitchen. The person sitting next to you will serve you throughout the meal. Toasting is important, and you should offer toasts to friendship, success, health, and cooperation. If you use chopsticks, lay them on the chopstick rest when you are finished, not on the plate or in food. Your host will usually pay for such things as the restaurant tab and taxi fares.

It is considered poor taste to talk about your family or ask questions about your host's family. Discussing political issues is touchy unless you know your host quite well. Many conversations inevitably turn to 1997 and emigration from Hong Kong. It's better first to solicit your host's opinion before offering your own. Since calling attention to oneself is bad manners, your host may demur when you offer a compliment, and you should do the same. Self-effacing comments and humility are typical when describing your accomplishments.

Gift giving is not expected but is appreciated. Hong Kong is a free port and common gift items such as imported liquors are not special, so it is better to give something representative of your corporation or characteristic of where you live. Government agencies and larger corporations often frown upon gifts; providing business entertainment is more acceptable.

Singapore

Singapore is predominantly an overseas Chinese culture. Although Singapore is consciously cultivating an international, Westernized business approach, it retains many elements of the traditional Chinese style. Yet it is also a mix of several other cultures, especially Malay and Indian, so the customs you encounter will depend on the background of the person you are with. As in Taiwan, many businesses are still family-controlled. Third-party introductions are important. They can be arranged through U.S. banks or U.S. companies already located in Singapore. Make an initial approach through the Singapore Economic Development Board, which has offices in several U.S. cities.

Singapore business hours are from 9:00 A.M. to 5:00 P.M. or later on weekdays and from 9:00 A.M. to 1:00 P.M. on Saturdays. Meetings are usually held in your host's office. Punctuality is important. Since the climate is tropical year round, lightweight, conservative suits are the norm.

Shaking hands is a common greeting, along with eye contact and a smile. Forms of address are "Mr.," "Mrs.," and "Miss." Business cards are very important and are exchanged with all meeting participants after introductions have been made. Even though English is prevalent, bilingual cards should be used. English is even more widely spoken in Singapore than in Hong Kong.

Business gets under way rather rapidly after introductions and a short exchange of pleasantries. The senior representative from the Singapore company will start things off. Conversations (and correspondence) can be conducted in English. Business conversations and negotiations can be direct; at the same time, subtle nonverbal communications and saving face are important. Even though the conversation is in English, do not take it for granted that everything you say is understood perfectly. A nod of the head means that what you said is understood, not necessarily that it is agreed to.

Personal appearance and proper conduct are very important. Be friendly, show respect and courtesy, and take care in building proper business relationships. In general, questions about family should be avoided. However, for Singaporeans who are quite Westernized, virtually any topic can be discussed. Follow the lead of your host. Singaporeans are very proud of their country, so this is always a good topic of conversation.

Team negotiating is not the norm. Generally, one or two people from each side will take part. Many Singaporean managers, executives, and professionals have negotiated with people from many countries and are interested in moving quickly to the main points of the negotiation.

Many local companies, even high-tech entrepreneurial ones, are closely held, with the key executive or board positions filled by members of one family. Status within an organization may be based on entrepreneurial success; but in a closely held company the family patriarch has the highest status, and often the final word.

It is proper, but not mandatory, for you to arrange a dinner or reception for your host. Although you may discuss business over lunch, do not do so over dinner. At a formal dinner, the guest of honor serves himself first, and chopsticks are used. Gift giving is not as ritualized as it is in other Pacific Rim countries. At the end of your first trip, you may give something that represents your company, reserving more personal gifts for subsequent trips.

Korea

It has been said that the Koreans are the only people in the world who can make the Japanese look lazy. Korea has a very strong work ethic, and business is basically conservative. The country is going through some major transitions that will have an impact on the way business is done there. The society is moving from an authoritarian to a more democratic form. Many of the older generation of business leaders are retiring and being replaced by younger, more business-oriented professionals, many of whom have been educated in the United States.

Koreans were dominated by the Japanese until the end of World War II, and there is still some bad feeling between the countries. South Korea does not have formal relations with China, a position that goes back to the Korean War, when China was an ally of North Korea. However, China and South Korea are building many informal links for doing business with each other.

You should initiate contact through an influential third party. The Korean international community is not large, so many executives know one another. There is a handful of schools that most government and business leaders have attended. Affiliations with classmates from college, and even high school, can be a very important factor in getting doors opened.

Be on time for meetings—neither early nor late. The exchange of business cards is an important ritual. As in other Asian nations, the cards should be printed with the host country's language on the reverse, and handed with your right hand to each person during introductions. Business cards provide insight into your position and status and suggest the potential for negotiations. The traditional Korean greeting is a bow at the waist with palms on the hips, but a nod of the head or a handshake is often used. For a Westerner, perhaps the best greeting is a handshake with a slight bow. Gifts may be presented but are not required.

Most Korean professionals speak English, and most meetings can be conducted in English without an interpreter. Generally speaking, catalogs, promotional literature, and instructional material are acceptable in English. But don't take it for granted that those who speak English will understand everything you say. If a statement is met with silence, it may mean that you were not understood. Say the same thing in different words, perhaps with a clarifying example.

Koreans have been called the Irish of Asia because compared with the Japanese or Chinese, they tend to be direct and open. They love telling jokes and teasing, singing and storytelling, eating and drinking, yet this conviviality is carried off without raucousness or noisy laughter. Avoid argument and adversarial exchanges. When controversy occurs, Koreans will often seem to acquiesce, but this is primarily to allow the air to clear. Questions about your host's family are improper, but you can ask about personal interests or hobbies. Don't talk about politics; it's fine to talk about philosophical beliefs. Except for shaking hands, you should avoid touching.

Rank and status among the people in a group are important. Treat people of higher status and older people with respect. Otherwise, they may withdraw from further association with you. Allow your host to set the pace of the meeting. Initial inquiries into your background may be made to determine your relative position and status as well as to establish a personal basis for the business relationship.

In businesses managed by younger, more Westernized executives, negotiations are normally handled by a couple of people rather than by a team. You can get down to business fairly rapidly. Make a strong but not aggressive presentation. Use data and graphics. The Koreans are very open about what they are and are not interested in. It will not take as long to reach an agreement as it will in Japan or China, but approval will often be needed by higher-ups or by a technical staff. The managerial and negotiating approach emphasizes harmony and structure over innovation and experimentation. During negotiations, discussions normally start with broader topics and move to details and specifics, so it is a mistake to adopt a set position too early, before all the possibilities are explored.

The Koreans view a contract as a general statement of consensus, one that broadly defines the agreement yet leaves room for flexibility and later adjustment. However, with increasing exposure to international business, Korean businesses are developing more detailed contracts, especially technology licensing agreements.

Your hosts will want to show you a good time. They will appreciate hearing what you would like to do or see in their country. Informal and nonbusiness discussions during a luncheon or dinner are often important for building personal relationships. If you want to try local food, let your hosts know; otherwise, they will take you to an American or a French restaurant. Local meals typically consist of many small dishes brought in at one time. Don't wait to be served; sample as many dishes as you wish. Some dishes will be highly spiced and it is acceptable to ask about them. You'll have your choice of several drinks, including beer and a rice wine similar to Japanese sake.

Koreans often entertain in a *kisaeng* house, or nightclub. At the *kisaeng* house, you will be served more drinks by a hostess. Often everyone, including you, will take turns singing songs. Your glass will be refilled only if it is empty. If you are pouring, do not refill a glass that has anything left in it. If you are entertained in this way, you should reciprocate with a banquet at your hotel.

Remember to remove your shoes upon entering a Korean house or temple. If you are invited to your host's house, take a small gift—fruit, for example. If *you* receive a gift, wait until later to open it.

Australia and New Zealand

In Australia and New Zealand, your biggest risk is that you will feel so much at home, you will not be sensitive to the cultural differences that do exist. Both of these nations have traditionally been more laid back than the United States. However, like many others, they are finding that they have to fight for their position in competitive world markets.

Business is conducted much as it is in the United States. Appointments are made well in advance, and meetings start on time—so be punctual. Respond to correspondence quickly. When addressing executives or officials, use their personal titles. Dress is fairly relaxed in Australia, but wear conservative business attire on appointments. New Zealanders are a bit more formal in speech and dress—in some areas you might think you were in England.

There is an old-boy network in many industries, so it helps to have an introduction from someone within the network. Even so, your proposal will be evaluated on its merits, not just on the basis of your connections. You may be able to get the needed connection through your banker or through the American chamber of commerce there.

In Australia, U.S. companies seeking to trade with the entire nation typically work through local agents or distributors that handle other lines, since the market outside Sydney and Melbourne is so diffuse. An important criterion for selecting a market partner is its ability to provide you entrée into financial, government, and other important circles. There is a good bit of interchange between Australia and New Zealand, and an agent or intermediary in one nation may be able to assist you in the other as well.

Aussies and Kiwis (as New Zealanders are called) are much less rigorous about business cards than are other peoples of the Pacific Rim, but you should always present a business card at the beginning of the meeting. Because of the difference in accents, this will make it easier for people to get your name right.

Many top business executives and professionals in the two nations know one another, since they have worked together regularly. They have developed an open, easygoing style of interaction. Kidding and good-natured ribbing are very common; join in if you feel at ease doing so. Also, many executives and professionals have lived or worked in the United States and are familiar with American customs.

The business style is direct but not aggressive. Like Americans, Australians and Kiwis get down to business rapidly, so preliminary conversations may be short. Meetings are frequently informal: First names are used and suit jackets removed. Follow the lead of your host. Gifts are not normally presented in a business context. A handshake is the normal greeting, but a man should wait for a woman to extend her hand first. More effusive greetings, such as hugging, are frowned upon in public.

Present your whole proposal at one meeting without holding back items for later discussion. Be open about both the good points and the disadvantages. Don't beat around the bush or push too hard. The aggressiveness of Americans can be resented. Generally seek to avoid strong disagreement. Present a fair asking price, not one inflated with the expectation of bargaining.

Regardless of whether you are negotiating with top executives or top public officials, technical experts will probably have to be consulted before a final decision is reached. It does little good to push for a hurried response. Lawyers and bankers are usually not brought in until near the end, when final details are being ironed out. A written contract will specify all the issues and details.

Socializing after hours is a part of the business scene. Be wary of mixing business and pleasure. Talking business at business luncheons is one thing; avoid it during social events or recreational outings unless you know it is acceptable with members of your host's party.

The hospitality of Aussies and Kiwis seems unbounded. Often you will be invited to their homes. (Giving a simple gift then is acceptable.) If your host invites you to stay at his vacation cabin by the lake for a couple of weeks, it is not just a polite gesture—he means it.

The Philippines

There are many superficial similarities that can make you feel at home in the Philippines but that can also give you a false sense of security. Many Filipinos, especially the ones with whom you will be doing business, speak English. English is used in business circles and the government, even though the official language is Filipino, based on Tagalog (pronounced "ta GOLL ug").

Many local professionals have attended American universities, and the Filipino educational system is based on the American model. So too are many of the political, economic, and legal institutions. It seems as if everybody in the Philippines either has been to the United States or has relatives there. Yet beneath the surface, the differences are very important.

Friendship, camaraderie, and smooth interpersonal relationships have a very high priority. Your host will go to great lengths to make you feel at ease. Competitive behavior, aggressive bargaining, and open disagreement are avoided at all costs. Raising your voice in anger or reproach is a very serious breach of etiquette. Intermediaries are often used to convey information, especially unpleasant information. Indirect, nonverbal messages are a major part of communication.

The family is the center of life. Business and making money can never interfere with it. Family connections are very important in business, and you may feel as if everyone is related. Unlike many other Asian peoples, the Filipinos find questions about family very acceptable. There are unwritten rules of propriety enforced by a sense of shame, or *hiya*. If you violate these unwritten rules of behavior, whether consciously or unconsciously, your relationships and ability to conduct business there can be seriously damaged.

You will encounter a strong sense of fatalism, the belief that one must accept things the way they are and not expect to change them. For this reason, many Filipinos seem to lack the drive and initiative that Americans expect. Economic incentives mean less there than in many other Asian nations.

Because of the Filipinos' aversion to anger and conflict, negotiations must proceed smoothly if they are to proceed at all. A show of anger will force your Filipino partner to retreat behind superficial friendliness. Long discussion, gentle persuasion, and compromise are the means to reaching agreement.

Initial greetings are friendly and informal. Use handshakes for both men and women. Standard English greetings are typical. Pay special respect to older people, and allow young people to show respect to you. Because of the hot, humid climate, Philippine dress is less formal than in other countries, even for business. Men wear loose-fitting white or light-colored shirts without ties or jackets.

Thailand

Thailand is sometimes called the land of smiles. Thais are friendly and reserved, and they place great value on laughter, a happy attitude, and a sense of humor. It is considered poor taste to criticize others, and speaking loudly or showing anger in public is offensive.

Thailand means "land of the free," and Thai people are proud of the fact that their land is the only one in Southeast Asia never to be ruled by a colonial power. Thailand is a constitutional monarchy, headed by a prime minister. The Thai people are very proud of their king and queen, and it is rude, even illegal, to show disrespect for the royal family.

Unlike the Chinese, Thais are addressed by their first names except in writing and in formal situations: In business, the Western "Mr.," "Mrs.," and "Miss" are used with the last name. Although Thai people greet Westerners with a handshake, the traditional Thai greeting is the *wai* (pronounced "why"), made by placing both hands together near the chest as if praying and bowing slightly. The *wai* is used to say "hello," "I'm sorry," or "thank you." Failure to return a *wai* greeting is comparable to refusing to shake someone's hand.

Because Thailand is a Buddhist society, Buddhist attitudes deeply affect all aspects of Thai life. All Thai men are expected to live as Buddhist monks for at least three months at some time of their lives; some men do this several times during their lives, especially before major life transitions. In decision making, consensus is valued very highly; for some Westerners, this means that the pace for reaching a decision can be maddeningly slow. However, the Thais are very meticulous at arriving at a decision that meets the interests of everybody involved. Thai merchants are fierce competitors; at the same time, business is something that is not to be taken too seriously.

If your host invites you to his house, remove your shoes before entering. Also remove them before entering a temple. You should step *over* the doorsill, because tradition says that the home spirit resides there. It is not necessary to bring a gift, but you should show interest in the host's family. Thai people eat with a spoon and fork, with the spoon held in the right hand, and the fork used to push food onto it. Food dishes are placed in the middle of the table. The host will serve you. When you are finished, put the fork and spoon on the plate and leave a small amount of food to show that you have had enough.

There are several behaviors you must avoid. For one thing, men and women rarely show affection in public. Also, avoid touching another person's head. Feet can have negative meanings too; avoid stamping them, using them to move objects, or pointing them in the direction of another person.

Malaysia

Since Malaysia is a multiethnic society, you may well encounter several different cultural styles. The Chinese and Indians are most common in business, the Malays in government. Chinese culture greatly influences the style of doing business. The official language is Malay (Bahasa Malaysia) and is required for all citizens, but English is widely spoken, especially in government and professional communities. Many Malaysians have attended American and Australian universities.

Common Western greetings—"Mr.," "Mrs.," and "Miss"—are used. Only men shake hands. Bow or nod your head when greeting a woman or an older person. Men often use both hands to clasp the hand of a close friend. The exchange of business cards is common, but not as rigorous as in many Asian countries.

Informal dress is common even in business (the climate is too hot for coat and tie). Punctuality is less important than elsewhere, and Malaysians may be late for appointments with you; their attitude is that individuals are more important than schedules. There is also an attitude that success and opportunities are the result of fate.

Remove your shoes when entering someone's house or when visiting a temple. If you are offered tea or coffee, accept the cup with both hands. Eating habits vary according to your host's background: The Chinese use chopsticks; Malays and Indians eat with spoons and their fingers; Muslims do not eat pork; and Hindus and many Buddhists do not eat beef. The official religion of Malaysia is Islam, but there is quite a mix of religions, which coexist easily: Buddhism, Confucianism, Taoism, Hinduism, and Christianity.

Indonesia

The culture of Indonesia is based on honor and respect for the individual. Letters commonly begin with the greeting *dengan hormat,* which means "with respect."

Loyalty to family and friends is paramount, and open disagreement is distasteful. When first introduced, both men and women shake hands and bow their heads slightly. People seldom shake hands for subsequent greetings, but they do so more commonly for good-byes. Always show special respect for older people, greeting them with a slight bow, and always use a person's title in conversation and greeting.

Typical business attire is shirt and tie for men and a conservative dress for women. Suit jackets are worn for more formal meetings. Punctuality at meetings is not stressed, as schedules are thought to be less important than individuals. The tone of meetings is formal and respectful. Conduct your discussions in a quiet, unassuming voice, and avoid loud arguments and open criticism. You will find that an Indonesian will avoid saying no directly, saying *belum* instead, which means "not yet." Great importance is placed on reaching decisions by consensus. Westerners are often exasperated at the pace of business, but Indonesians in turn see Westerners as being too hurried, too serious, and too quick to anger.

Customs in the home can vary quite a bit, depending on whether the family is more traditional or somewhat Westernized. If you are invited to a private home, follow your host's lead. Shoes are often removed in the hallway. Gifts are not expected, but thank-you notes are appreciated. If you are offered a gift, it is impolite to refuse, but wait until later to open it. Also wait until your host invites you to sit down, to take a drink, or to begin eating. Westernized Indonesians usually eat with fork and spoon; traditional families use the fingers.

Public displays of affection are frowned upon. You should avoid several other behaviors as well: gesturing for someone to come to you or touching another person's head; using your left hand to eat, touch others, or give and receive things; crossing your legs while seated or standing with your hands in your pockets; and yawning without covering your mouth.

9 | Financing Pacific Rim Trade

- *Getting paid*
- *Financing your exports*
- *Using government finance programs*
- *Financing direct investment*

This chapter introduces the key financial considerations you will face in doing business in the Pacific Rim: getting paid for the business you do abroad and obtaining financing for trade or overseas investments. Compared with domestic business, international trade has several characteristics that require special approaches to finance.

• *Remote customers.* Even in an era of instant communication, lags occur, and it takes time to ship goods to remote locations. It is more difficult to judge customers' creditworthiness. It is much more difficult to spot trouble before it arises and harder to handle it when it does. All these difficulties arise because of the greater distances involved, the differences in language, and the differences in business and banking practices.

• *Different legal and political systems.* Rules and regulations differ from country to country and are often applied inconsistently within a country. Legal recourse is more difficult. Difficulties arise simply from the fact of doing business across international boundaries. Political factors are more likely to affect your ability to complete business.

• *Fluctuating currencies.* Variations in exchange rates, if not anticipated and compensated for, can be very costly.

U.S. banks and financial institutions are often unfamiliar with these differences, leaving many companies on their own to cope with the effects of the globalization of financial markets.

Getting Paid for Exports

As in any domestic business, the seller wants to get paid and the buyer wants to get what it has paid for. But in the Pacific Rim, several special problems arise:

218

- How can both seller and buyer ensure that they get what they agreed to when legal recourse in the case of disputes is very difficult?
- How can both seller and buyer know the actual figures involved when currency exchange rates fluctuate?
- How can the difficulty in obtaining credit in international transactions be overcome?
- How can the hindrances and regulations imposed by disparate governments be handled?

A specialized system has grown up to structure international payments in order to minimize these problems. In actuality, the greatest proportion of international sales come off without a hitch, particularly with Pacific Rim clients. You agree on a price, you agree on the terms, the contract is signed, both sides stick to the agreement, and you get your money. This section is designed to help you with the small percentage of transactions in which a problem may occur.

There are several basic methods of payment for goods and services in international trade. Even if you do not use all of them, you should understand the distinctions among them. Starting with the one that entails the least risk to the seller, I describe each method, when and how to use it, the risks involved for the seller and the buyer, and how to manage those risks.

Common Methods of Payment

- Payment in advance or upon order when the order is placed
- Letters of credit, through which the buyer's credit is guaranteed by its bank (and in turn the buyer's bank may be guaranteed by your bank)
- Documentary draft—similar to a promissory note
- Open account—similar to domestic sales on unsecured credit
- Consignment (rarely used in the Pacific Rim)

Table 9–1 distinguishes the different types of risks you will hear mentioned during negotiations over payment methods or types of export insurance coverage available. Companies seek export or investment credit insurance to reduce their commercial and political risks, and use financial risk management techniques such as hedging to reduce their foreign exchange and economic risks.

Payment in Advance

As desirable as it seems to the seller, getting payment in advance for an order is a "hard sell." The drawbacks to the buyer are obvious: Money is tied up before the transaction is completed; the buyer is dependent on the seller's honesty,

Table 9-1. Risks in international transactions.

Commercial risks	The normal risks of doing business with another company. For the seller, protracted default by buyer, buyer insolvency, or buyer's inability to pay as a result of natural disaster. For the buyer, receiving poor-quality or untimely goods from the seller.
Political risks	Any losses caused by actions of the government beyond the control of the buyer or seller: delays in foreign exchange transfer; not getting paid or losses of property because of political unrest, war, insurrection, revolution, expropriation, confiscation, or government interference in the business; unforeseen cancellation of an import or export license; extra charges arising from diversion of a shipment.
Foreign exchange risks	Any losses caused by events in the financial environment: devaluation or shifts in exchange rates; currencies no longer convertible into dollars; changes in government rules on foreign exchange.
Economic risks	Decreases in the relative book value of overseas assets resulting from shifts in currency values.

promptness, and solvency; and the buyer may resent the implication that it is not creditworthy. Companies that insist on advance payment find that unless they have unique products in high demand, they lose out to more flexible competitors.

Risks of Prepayment

Risk to seller	None
Risk to buyer	• Goods are not shipped.
	• They are the wrong goods.
	• There are delays.
	• Correct documents are not forwarded.

Despite the drawbacks for the buyer, there are five situations in which the seller may reasonably expect Pacific Rim customers to be willing to pay in advance:

1. The buyer places a special order to design a new product or modify an existing product for a special purpose.
2. The buyer is in a hurry, and there is no time to get a letter of credit. For example, a prospective customer asks you to send product samples.

3. The buyer's credit is weak, and the risk of losing the sale is less important than the risk of possible collection problems later.
4. There are restrictions to foreign exchange leaving the country, or there are hints that foreign exchange controls may tighten.
5. The seller is financially weak, and a strong customer is prepaying in order to provide working capital.

Common variants of prepayment include requiring a deposit—perhaps 25 percent of the total—along with the order, and obtaining partial prepayments as parts of the order are shipped.

Letters of Credit

Next to prepayment, a letter of credit entails the least risk to the seller. A letter of credit (often abbreviated "lc" or "LC") is a financial instrument obtained by the buyer through its local bank. It is a promise by the buyer's bank to pay for the shipment when the bank (or its correspondent bank in the customer's market) receives the proper shipping documents proving that the shipment has been made according to the agreed-on terms. In essence, the bank substitutes *its* credit for that of the buyer, thereby virtually guaranteeing that the seller will get paid—if all conditions are met.

A letter of credit is commonly used when you cannot ascertain the credit-worthiness of your customer. It ensures that you will get paid because the buyer has already obtained the necessary credit or guarantee from its bank and, further-more, your bank has obtained a guarantee that it will be paid by your customer's bank.

How Letters of Credit Are Set Up. After buyer and seller have agreed on all terms, the buyer initiates a letter of credit for the amount of the sale with its local bank, naming the seller as beneficiary—that is, as the one that gets paid. The buyer must pledge its credit, and may have to deposit some or all of the amount requested in the local bank. Typical terms of a letter of credit include:

- Product specifications—the description and quantity of the merchandise to be shipped
- The purchase price agreed on by buyer and seller
- Shipping instructions
- Insurance coverage for the merchandise during shipment
- The time period that the terms remain in force
- The latest acceptable delivery date
- A list of the documents that must be received by the banks as evidence that the merchandise has been shipped to the buyer as specified (typically, a negotiable bill of lading, U.S. export license and buyer's declarations, any required customs and inspection certificates, commercial invoice, and packing list)

The letter of credit instructs the buyer's bank to transmit payment to the seller's bank when all the stated conditions have been met. All these terms should be agreed upon in writing before your customer obtains a letter of credit from a bank. If you spot a problem after the letter is granted, you must negotiate an amendment with the buyer.

The Credit Request.   When you first contact your buyer and request a letter of credit, use wording such as this, and state all the terms to be included:

> Please request your bank to issue an irrevocable sight draft letter of credit in favor of X-Tech Company in the amount of [_____ dollars U.S. or foreign currency] to be advised via telex and payable and confirmed at a bank in [*your city*], preferably [*your bank*].

Confirmed and *irrevocable* are key words in this request. From the seller's perspective, the confirmed irrevocable letter of credit is the most desirable "standard method" of financing international trade. A confirmed letter of credit means that a U.S. bank (or a specialized confirming house) guarantees payment by the foreign bank: Your bank vouches for the foreign bank and assumes the country risk and the risk of currency problems. An irrevocable letter of credit is one that cannot be altered or canceled by the buyer without the seller's consent (a revocable letter of credit gives the bank or the buyer the right to cancel or alter the obligation any time prior to payment). Both terms are important: "Confirmed" does not imply "irrevocable." A confirmed irrevocable letter of credit means that your bank will pay you even if the customer's bank doesn't and that your customer and its bank cannot change terms without your agreement. Note that the letter of credit shown in Figure 9–1 is irrevocable but is not yet confirmed by the seller's bank.

There are other key terms in the request. *Sight draft* means you will be paid as soon as the customer's bank receives all the documents. Alternatively, you may agree on a *time draft,* which specifies a time period (usually in increments of thirty days) after the receipt of documents. In that case, you may request interest to be paid if the documents are not presented within the specified time. *To be advised* means that you must be advised through your local bank of any developments or problems. Your banker is in a much better position than you are to deal with problems and to ensure the authenticity of the letter of credit issued by a foreign bank.

Your bank will not confirm the letter of credit unless it is certain of the reputation and strength of your customer's bank, so it is important to discuss your proposed arrangements with a new buyer and its bank. When you receive the letter of credit through your bank, you must check to make sure that you can fulfill all the conditions stated within the time allotted. Again, if you cannot, you must obtain an amendment, because if you agree to certain terms and then fail to fulfill them, you jeopardize the sale.

When the seller meets all the terms and conditions, and presents the prescribed documents within the specified time, the buyer's bank ensures payment to the seller. Figure 9–2 summarizes the steps in obtaining a letter of credit.

Figure 9-1. A sample letter of credit.

Bank of China

ZHUJIANG BRANCH
P.O. BOX 211, GUANGZHOU
CABLE ADDRESS: ZHUJIANG

Date: 14th Dec. 19x8

To Beneficiary: M/S: Integrated Circuit Corp., 234 Silicon Street, Cupertino, CA 95014 U.S.A.	*IRREVOCABLE DOCUMENTARY CREDIT NO.* LC 123456. *valid for negotiation in* U.S.A. *until* Apr. 15, 19x9
	Amount: USDI, 1,800,000.—(U.S. DOLLARS ONE MILLION EIGHT HUNDRED THOUSAND ONLY.)
Transmitting Bank: Bank of China, New York Br., 410 Madison Ave., New York, N.Y. 10017, U.S.A.	*Applicant:* China Electronics Import & Export Corp., Guangzhou Br., Guangzhou, China.

Dear Sir(s):
   We hereby issue in your favour this documentary credit which is available by your draft(s) at ~~time~~/sight for 100% invoice value on us marked as drawn under this credit and accompanied by the following documents marked with numbers:
   (1) *Signed commercial invoice in*   6   *copies indicating contract No. and L/C No.* LC 123456
   (2) *Full set of clean on board ocean bills of lading made out to order and blank endorsed marked* Freight to collect *notifying* xmxmxmxmxmxmxmxmxmxmxmxmxmxmxmxmxmxmx applicant.
   (3) *Packing list/weight memo in*   3   *copies showing quantity/gross and net weight for each package*
   (4) *Certificate of quantity in*   3   *copies issued by* the seller.
   (5) Your certified copy of cable advising buyers of shipment.
   (6) Preliminary acceptance certificate signed by the seller and applicant in 2 copies.

evidencing shipment of:
   EQUIPMENT FOR MANUFACTURING INTEGRATED CIRCUITS.
   FOB San Francisco/Oakland, packing charges included.
   Goods under contract No. 4321
   Packing: Standard export packing in wooden boxes.
   Shipping Marks: —————————————
                   GUANGZHOU, CHINA.

> *BANK OF CHINA*
> *NEW YORK BRANCH*
>
> *Our Ref. # 6*
> *DEC 27 19x8*

Shipment from SAN FRANCISCO/OAKLAND, U.S.A., TO GUANGZHOU, CHINA. *not later than* Mar. 31 19x9	*Partial shipments allowed*	*Transshipment allowed*
Special Instructions:	*We hereby undertake that all drafts drawn under and in compliance with the terms of this credit will be duly honored on presentation at this office.* *for BANK OF CHINA* *Authorised Signature*	

Figure 9-2. Sequence of events in obtaining and using a letter of credit.

1 The buyer and the seller negotiate the terms of the sale.
2 The buyer applies for a letter of credit for the terms of the sale with its bank. The bank examines the application and the financial documentation of the buyer, and also considers the types of goods to be covered and other features of the sale. The bank may refuse to issue the letter of credit because the creditworthiness of the buyer is inadequate or because the government has placed limitations on the amount of credit the bank can issue.
3 The bank issues the letter of credit, sending it to the seller's bank.
4 The seller's bank and the seller check for inconsistencies in the terms and conditions.
5 The seller's bank transfers the letter of credit to the seller, who is called the beneficiary.
6 After the goods are produced, the seller checks the terms and conditions against the terms of sale negotiated with the buyer. Help is often obtained from the freight forwarder at this stage.
7 If the terms are in order, the seller ships the goods and receives shipping documents from the freight forwarder.
8 The seller presents the documents and drafts to its bank. Such documents should be submitted as soon as possible: If a problem arises, it may be correctable.
9 If the documents are in order, the seller's bank pays the seller (if it is a sight letter of credit) or accepts the draft (if it is a time letter of credit).
10 The seller's bank sends the documents to the buyer's bank.
11 The buyer's bank pays the seller's bank.
12 The buyer's bank releases the documents to the buyer.
13 The buyer takes the documents to customs to claim the goods.

Pros and Cons of Letters of Credit. A letter of credit protects both buyer and seller from loss. For the buyer, it eliminates the risk associated with making advance payment; for the seller, it eliminates the risk of selling on open account. And because letters of credit have expiration dates, buyers have greater assurance that shipments will be on time.

A letter of credit is disadvantageous to the buyer in three ways. First, it ties up the buyer's credit. The buyer must commit funds to a transaction long before merchandise or documents giving title to it are actually received. Second, the buyer, rather than the seller, usually assumes the cost of the letter of credit. Third, since the letter of credit deals only with whether all the documents are in order, it does not protect the buyer from receiving poor-quality goods.

There is an important pitfall for the seller as well. The buyer's bank is not obligated to honor the letter of credit if all the terms are not met precisely. If any term is not satisfied, or if there is the slightest discrepancy in the letter of credit—even a misspelled word—the buyer can say, "No, we won't pay." In this case, the letter of credit won't be honored by the buyer's bank, and the seller must collect payment directly from the buyer. So if you are not certain you can meet a certain condition, don't enter it into the letter of credit. And if a problem does arise—for example, if the shipping date becomes unrealistic—renegotiate with the buyer immediately and amend the letter of credit.

Risks of Letters of Credit

"Minimal risk for both buyer and seller—if done carefully."

Risk to seller • Commercial risks
• Country political risks
• Foreign exchange risks

Risk to buyer Quality of goods

Since letters of credit must be exactly right, it is important in the beginning to get help on your letters of credit from people who know how to spot and avoid the problems. An experienced banker can explain all the terms, variations, pitfalls, delays, and causes for extra fees. The Commerce Department, state export programs, banks, and other organizations often sponsor one-day seminars on handling letters of credit.

Variations. There are several variations on the "standard" letter of credit that provide more flexibility in certain situations.

• A *revolving* letter of credit—like a revolving line of credit. When you are shipping goods to an established customer over a period of time, the customer's bank pays only for those goods actually received; then the customer repays the bank. This instrument is useful if you have repetitive shipments to the same party, if you have partial shipments, or if partial payments are going to be made.

• An *assignable* letter of credit—allows you to assign the letter of credit to your supplier to pay for materials, thus taking yourself out of the finance loop.

• A *time draft* letter of credit—gives the seller a choice: The seller may hold it to maturity or discount it. For example, the discount on a 180-day draft might be 4 percent. The buyer may have agreed to pay interest or discounts—or the price of the goods may have been raised—to compensate the seller for this cost.

• An *evergreen*—a standing letter of credit that kicks in after a specified period of time—typically thirty or sixty days—if you are not paid the amount due on a time draft. This letter of credit must be for an amount large enough to cover your sales for ninety days.

• A *standby* letter of credit—used by a seller to back up a required performance bond. Some governments require that any company involved in construction, service, or sales contracts in their country post a letter of credit as a bond or guarantee, and the company must obtain a letter of credit from its bank to secure the bond.

With all letters of credit, there is a technical difference between goods shipped by sea and those shipped by air. If goods are shipped by sea, the bank still holds the bill of lading during shipment; if they are sent by air, the bank relinquishes title to the goods before shipment.

When Letters of Credit Are Not Used.   U.S. exporters used to rely fairly heavily on prepayments and letters of credit from their customers. In the "good old days" of a few years ago, U.S. exporters could demand that customers obtain a confirmed irrevocable letter of credit. This is no longer the case. Several things have happened.

Many companies can't qualify for letters of credit from their banks. Perhaps they are new companies, or their creditworthiness has declined. Conversely, in many countries, especially in the Pacific Rim, companies are mature and credit-worthy enough that the added complication of a letter of credit is no longer nec-essary or worth their while to obtain. Competing companies, especially from other countries, have been able to offer alternative types of financing to these customers, thus getting the sale. The U.S. company loses out.

Sometimes a government will restrict the outflow of foreign exchange. When this happens, insisting on a letter of credit can jeopardize a sale, especially when competitors are able to arrange alternative forms of financing.

However, there are other ways to provide financing and get many sales you would otherwise lose—while holding your financial risk to a manageable level. Let's examine several options that can be used in different circumstances.

Documentary Drafts

A documentary draft* is a request to your customer for his bank to pay a stated sum of money to you upon delivery of shipping documents or at some stated future time. It is a formal request for payment made by your bank on your behalf. It is called a documentary draft because, after shipment, the buyer receives the documents needed to claim the goods upon accepting the draft. We will use this term, or just "draft." A draft is used when you have greater confidence in the buyer's ability and intention to pay or when you have received credit insurance for the transaction.

You initiate the documentary draft through your bank, which has standard forms for it. You and your customer agree beforehand whether the draft will be prepared on a sight or time basis. As with letters of credit, a sight draft requires your customer to pay immediately to obtain the shipping documents from the bank; the buyer then uses the documents to claim the merchandise from customs.

* Also called sight or time draft, bill of exchange, or international collection.

With a time draft, the customer can claim the documents and the merchandise and then pay after a specified time period, usually stated in increments of thirty days. (A date draft is a variation of a time draft, and states that the customer must pay by a specified date.)

The documents accompanying the draft are the same as those accompanying a letter of credit: invoices, bills of lading, customs and inspection certificates, and so on. The instructions sent with the draft must state:

- How the draft will be presented for payment
- Whether it is payable on sight, or within what time period
- What fees are to be paid and by whom
- Who your agent is, if any
- How you shall be kept advised of payment status
- How payment will be transferred to you
- What action is to be taken in case of nonpayment

When you are ready to ship your merchandise, you send your bank all the shipping documents, plus your draft drawn on the importer. The bank then forwards all the documents to its correspondent bank in your customer's market. The overseas bank notifies your customer of the arrival of the documents. The customer must accept your draft in order to receive the shipping documents; that acceptance then makes the draft a legal obligation, like a promissory note. Figure 9–3 summarizes the steps.

Bank vs. Direct Collection. Collection of drafts can be handled through your bank or directly by you. If the bank acts as your agent in the trade collection process, you as seller deliver collection instructions, a draft, and the accompanying documentation to the bank, which then carries out your collection instructions. In this way, your bank becomes an essential agent in helping you retain control of the sales transaction until the buyer has paid or arranged to pay for the goods. To minimize your risk, you should use a bank that is part of an international network of correspondents, so that it can handle international collections for you. The bank assumes responsibility for transmitting the documents among its affiliates and correspondents.

If you handle the draft and collection process yourself, you transmit collection instructions directly to the buyer's bank. In this case, your instructions provide for the remittance of funds by the buyer's bank directly to your account. Direct collection can save you some time and paperwork, but even then you should work under the auspices of your bank. If there are problems in receiving payment, the bank can assist you in taking appropriate action.

Pros and Cons of a Documentary Draft. A draft is much simpler than a letter of credit. Buyers are much more willing to accept the terms of a draft, so you can make sales you might otherwise lose to a competitor.

On the downside, the seller loses control of the goods before payment is received, so if the buyer does not pay the draft—whether because of financial

Figure 9-3. Sequence of events in obtaining and using sight and time documentary drafts.

Sight Draft

1 The buyer and the seller negotiate the terms of sale and agree to the terms of the draft. The buyer makes arrangements with its bank.
2 The seller ships the goods and receives the shipping documents.
3 The seller presents the sight draft to its bank.
4 The seller's bank sends the documents to the buyer's bank.
5 The buyer examines, accepts, and pays the draft, then receives the documents needed to claim the goods.
6 The buyer presents the documents to customs and claims the goods.
7 The buyer's bank pays the seller's bank.
8 The seller's bank pays the seller and credits the seller's account.

Time Draft

1–4 Same as for a sight draft.
5 The buyer is notified by its bank that the draft has arrived. The buyer accepts the draft, obtains the documents, and promises to pay within the specified time.
6 The buyer presents the documents to customs and claims the goods.
7 At the maturity of the draft, the buyer pays its bank, which forwards payment to the seller's bank.
8 The seller claims payment from its bank.

---

problems or because it has decided against the order—the seller may find itself with merchandise in a foreign port that has no ready means of disposal and be stuck for return transportation costs.

A time draft is actually an extension of credit to a customer. If your buyer doesn't pay when the draft is mature, you may have trouble collecting. In principle, you can reclaim your goods from the buyer, but your recourse for collecting unpaid goods quickly diminishes as time passes.

The disadvantage to the buyer is the same as that associated with a letter of credit: The buyer is accepting the draft on the basis of its examination of documents, not of the merchandise itself.

The risk of a documentary draft stands midway between that of a letter of credit and an open account sale (discussed below). With a letter of credit, your bank and the buyer's bank jointly guarantee you payment as long as you fulfill the conditions of the agreement—because the buyer has previously satisfied the credit requirements of its bank. With a documentary draft, the banks are acting only as your agent: asking for payment, but not guaranteeing it. If a customer refuses to accept your bill of exchange, the customer cannot take possession of the shipment—but you don't get paid either! On the other hand, a draft is less risky than selling on open account. An accepted draft is comparable to a promissory note: It's a legal obligation to pay, and it provides a basis for legal recourse or for moral suasion.

Risks of Documentary Drafts

Risk to seller   • Commercial risks
                   • Country political risks
                   • Foreign exchange risks
Risk to buyer   Quality of goods

Sales of Services

If a company is selling services overseas, a letter of credit or a documentary draft can be used even if there are no tangible goods that are shipped. Instead of receiving shipping documents, the seller must receive a document on which the buyer has signed off, stating that the services have been performed as specified in the contract. The seller presents the document to the bank to receive payment.

A draft or a letter of credit may cover a combination of services and goods. For example, a letter of credit for $800,000 may cover the purchase of $500,000 worth of equipment, plus $300,000 for installation, testing, and operator training. The first $500,000 is to be paid against the letter of credit upon shipment of the equipment, with the remainder paid in increments as the required services are completed.

Open Account Sales

Open account financing is often used in domestic business. Your customer is not required to provide a letter of credit or to accept a draft. Instead, the buyer agrees to pay the balance on its account with you within a specified period of time. In international transactions, open account financing is common when you have confidence in a customer's ability *and* willingness to pay. It is commonly used with customers with whom you have an ongoing business relationship—or well-established and reputable customers—that are located in a nation with a stable, reliable business climate.

Open account payments are made in one of three ways: (1) foreign drafts (for small dollar amounts), (2) remittance orders (funds transferred by cable or by airmail), or (3) international checks. A major problem with overseas payment by check is the time it takes for your account to be credited. The check has to be sent back for collection, and there can be a delay even with a cashier's check.

Pros and Cons of Open Account Sales.   The ease of use and convenience of open account sales speak for themselves. However, with open account financing, the seller assumes all the risks:

- Even with good customers of long standing, problems can arise when, for example, political problems crop up in a country or when a normally creditworthy customer faces financial problems and is unable to pay a supplier.
- Foreign exchange problems can arise if sales prices are quoted in a foreign currency.
- Collection can be difficult if the buyer refuses to pay the bill, because there is no negotiable instrument to document the sale.
- The seller bears the burden of financing the shipment until payment is received; a customer may wait until the merchandise is sold before paying. Thus open account sales require the greatest amount of working capital.
- Some nations prohibit open accounts in international trade in an effort to restrict the outflow of foreign exchange, i.e., dollars.

Despite these disadvantages, competitive pressure may force you to use open account sales even in risky situations.

Since you are more likely to use open account sales with a strong customer in a stable country, you can manage your risk in the same ways you do in your domestic markets. In the most developed Pacific Rim nations—Japan, Australia, New Zealand, Singapore, and Hong Kong—you have effective legal recourse for legitimate disputes. Even so, the distance, unfamiliarity, time, and expense make legal action an unappealing prospect. A legitimate company won't risk its reputation by unfairly withholding payment, but it may reasonably question specific terms or the quality of goods. You protect yourself best by making sure that you have a clear understanding and agreement beforehand, and that you produce up to it.

Risks of Open Account Sales

Risk to seller • Commercial risks
             • Country political risks
             • Foreign exchange risks
Risk to buyer   None

Checking a Customer's Credit

When you must extend credit, there are several ways to obtain information on your customers.

- Banks prepare credit reports on the basis of information received from their overseas branches or from correspondent banks in your customer's market. These reports are made available to clients.

• The Department of Commerce publishes the *World Trader's Data Report,* a series of newsletters that contain credit profiles of companies around the world. Each profile describes the type of organization, when it was established, its size and reputation, the territory it covers, the product lines it handles, and the principal owners. The report also gives financial and trade references, plus a general comment by the investigating commercial officer on the company's reliability. Reports are prepared upon request at a nominal cost.

• Many industry or professional organizations keep tabs on the experience of their members with particular companies. You may be able to obtain a report from an organization even if your company is not in its industry.

• Other exporters who have dealt with a target company can often be identified through industry or trade organizations, or through the American chamber of commerce in the nation of the customer.

• Dun & Bradstreet has offices all over the world that collect data on foreign companies (as with domestic companies) and then prepare credit reports for sale to the business community.

• The Foreign Credit Interchange Bureau is part of the National Association of Credit Management. Members furnish the bureau with information on their dealings with foreign customers. Credit reports are compiled from this information and are made available to all members.

• The Overseas Private Investment Corporation insures the direct overseas investments of U.S. companies. To this end, OPIC gathers and analyzes detailed credit risk information on overseas countries and buyers. Because of OPIC's mission, it is a good source of information on the creditworthiness of your customers and their countries.

Addresses and phone numbers for these organizations are given in the Appendixes.

Export Financing

Depending on the form of your export operation, you may have to obtain several kinds of financing. For example:

• *Pre-export financing*—may be needed to expand your staff or facilities, to take on the commitment of international operations, or to conduct feasibility or market studies.
• *Working capital*—for inventory, labor, and materials needed to manufacture a product you have sold or intend to sell in international markets, or to finance the cost of completing an overseas project for which you have a contract.

- *Sales financing*—working capital needed to finance the purchases of your international customers.
- *Investment capital*—needed to establish a distribution or manufacturing operation in an international market, whether wholly owned or a joint venture.

For any of these, you must make sure you can obtain the financing you need before you make a commitment.

Sources of Export Financing

If your company needs a loan to obtain working capital or to finance sales for export, you will probably turn first to your bank. Obtaining bank financing for international trade has been a real stopper for many smaller businesses. Even bank executives agree that "financing is a trade barrier." Bankers are reluctant to finance the trade of smaller companies, especially those without a track record in international trade.

There is a big difference in what your bank *can* do for you and what it *will* do for you. Many U.S. banks—especially smaller ones, but also some fairly large ones—have very little to do with international trade. Even some larger banks that in the past had overextended themselves making loans to foreign countries have become very conservative in financing U.S. companies engaged in foreign trade. And many other banks have decided that domestic business is good enough for them.

Banks that are unfamiliar with the special characteristics of overseas transactions impose unrealistic requirements to perform certain services. For example, currency hedging is a common financial management technique that companies use to protect themselves against fluctuations in exchange rates. Yet many banks view hedging as currency speculation and impose very high margin requirements on customers.

Even larger banks that regularly engage in international transactions are often reluctant or unwilling to finance transactions by smaller companies or those new to international business. They prefer the larger, experienced multinationals that have a solid track record and major assets to back up their loan requests. This is another reason export and foreign investment has been a game for the big boys.

Even government loan guarantee programs have been slanted toward large companies. Many key federal agencies have offices only in Washington, so most businesses must deal with them at a great distance. In the past, the U.S. Export–Import Bank's loans have gone mainly to enormous multinationals like Boeing.

However, the picture isn't totally gloomy. New government programs (described later in this chapter) are structured to be more accessible to smaller businesses. Many states are beginning to set up loan guarantee and credit insurance programs with officials who are more accessible; they are willing to help small businesses put together packages and interface with banks or with federal programs located in Washington. As local banks participate in these state loan guarantee programs, they gain familiarity with financing overseas transactions and so become more willing to consider export loan requests on their merits. Finally, a number of Pacific Rim banks, especially Japanese banks, are entering U.S. domestic markets, and one of their major purposes is to finance trade.

Finding the Right Bank

Since your bank is going to put you through a rigorous qualifying process to grant a loan, you must start by qualifying your bank to make sure it is the right one for your international business. The dilemma for many smaller businesses is whether to deal with (1) a local or regional bank that is familiar with their business but has limited experience in international transactions or (2) a money center bank that is expert in international transactions but is remote, unfamiliar with their operations, and possibly biased toward larger companies. Many banks that are not directly involved with international transactions have correspondent relationships with experienced domestic or foreign banks. So you may be able to work with your local bank, yet obtain the services essential for international business through its correspondent bank.

A general rule is, deal with the smallest bank that can handle your needs. In this way, you will be regarded as an important customer and will not get lost in the shuffle. If you have more than $100 million in sales and are experienced in international transactions, you will probably end up dealing with the corporate division of a large international bank. Local banks are more accustomed to working with the middle market—companies with sales from $5 to $100 million.

When you are qualifying your bank to see if it is the one to use for your Pacific Rim trade, you need answers to several questions. For example:

- Is the bank willing to provide the types of services and financing you need? What is its track record in providing such financing to companies that are similar in size and circumstances to yours?
- Has the bank participated in any federal or state loan guarantee programs? Is it willing to do so?
- How experienced is the bank in the administrative aspects of international business: checking credit, handling transactions, collecting payments, dealing with overseas banks, and so on?
- How familiar is the bank with financial risk management strategies?
- What correspondent banks does it work with in your target market? If the bank lacks some crucial capability, what money center bank in the United States would it work with to make sure that service gets adequately provided to you?
- What would the bank's services cost?

- In view of the bank's track record with similar companies, what does it take to qualify for financing and how long does it take?

You come off looking better to your prospective banker when you ask these tough questions and understand the issues. A professional presentation and incisive questions can help you convince the banker that you are a good source of business. Needless to say, bankers will vary greatly in their answers to your questions, so it will be well worth your while to talk with several. If your current bank does not provide international trade services and does not have a correspondent bank through which it can work on your behalf, then you'd better find another bank.

Banks that are well connected in international trade can also perform valuable nonfinancial services for their clients. They can help locate potential interested customers, agents, and reps in your target market through either an international branch or a correspondent bank. For a good customer, a bank may provide a list of possible contacts for exports, and even write a letter of introduction. A bank may also give general information on the reputation and creditworthiness of a potential customer or partner.

As with many financial services, a bank's willingness to assist you relates to the length of your business relationship with the bank and the size of your account.

Banking Services Required for International Transactions

Does your bank

- Provide short-term financing for export sales?
- Offer longer-term financing, in cooperation with public agencies that guarantee credit?
- Obtain information on the creditworthiness of potential overseas customers?
- Issue commercial letters of credit?
- Handle export drafts for collection or for discount?
- Accept drafts for its customers' accounts?
- Handle foreign transactions for you?
- Handle futures contracts to assist you in hedging?

To get referrals to appropriate banks, or to get second opinions on a bank's reputation, talk to trade representatives from a Department of Commerce or Small Business Administration office in your area, your state's export promotion organization, or perhaps your city's chamber of commerce. Since many of these agencies are wary of giving specific endorsements, you will need to phrase your questions carefully. If your present bank agrees that it is inadequate for your export finance needs, it may give you some insight into the potential merits of other banks.

Obtaining Export Finance From a Bank

When you have selected the bank that you feel is best, here are some tips on creating a productive working relationship.

1. *Take your banker to lunch.* Approach the bank in the proper way. You've got to make the bank a partner or adviser in your business. Get to know your banker and get your banker to know you. Qualify your banker as well as the bank.

2. *Master the language barrier.* You must learn some banking terms to work with a banker, just as you must learn some Japanese terms to work in Japan.

3. *Be prepared.* When you make your presentation to a bank, project an image of capability. Make sure that you're prepared when you go to the bank—that you've put together all the information you need. Be armed with lots of numbers and show that you have a definite plan. Demonstrate your track record, your financial statements, and knowledge of your Pacific Rim market and customers. Furnish yourself with a lot of information on:

- The cost of everything involved
- How you will handle either better- or worse-than-expected results
- How payments will be made
- The kind of financing needed—trade finance (e.g., financing for export transactions) or project finance (i.e., an investment of over $50 million)
- How funds will be transferred

4. *Allow plenty of time.* Leave adequate time for all the financial arrangements that need to be made. Don't wait until the deal is closed. Talk to your banker first to explore the financial issues in whatever business you are enjoying. Discuss the realities of financing before you agree on price and terms.

Make sure that you can actually line up the financing before you close the deal. Too many engineering- or marketing-oriented companies go out and sell something, make promises, and then come to the bank needing something done in a hurry. When it takes longer than they think, these companies blame the bank for not responding quickly enough.

Qualifying for Bank Financing—When You Can Get It. We've already seen that obtaining bank financing is much tougher for foreign trade than for domestic trade. Not only must *you* qualify for the loan; your *customer* and the customer's *country* must qualify as well. And, of course, the bank must be interested in making this type of loan.

Terms of Export Financing

Short-term	Up to 180 days
Medium-term	From 181 days to five years
Long-term	Over five years

To qualify you for a line of credit to initiate international trade—as with credit for domestic trade—the bank will look at the "three C's": your character, your capital, and your capacity. The character or reputation of your company is very important, e.g., your past credit history, your record of fulfilling obligations, the quality and stability of your top management.

The bank will look at your capital and your financial statements to determine the overall financial strength of your company and the degree to which it can withstand loss. A small company that undertakes a large overseas transaction could be severely damaged by a major financial problem in that market.

In examining your capacity, the bank will consider your ability to repay the loan in case the buyer defaults on the merchandise, leaving you stuck with it in a foreign port and unable to dispose of it profitably. The bank will examine your experience as an exporter or foreign investor. And if you are new to this game, it will look at your track record in domestic markets. The bank will also look at the payment terms for the goods: Are you selling them on open account, under international collections, or through a letter of credit? The bank will be more wary of financing a sale on open account than on a letter of credit. Finally, the bank will examine the strength of your buyer and the situation in the overseas country, both economic and political, and will look at the foreign exchange climate.

You will often want a revolving loan to finance inventory or accounts receivable. Since banks don't like to finance inventory, you will most likely have to pledge something else, such as your company's assets or your personal assets. Even so, a bank may not finance overseas accounts receivable unless they are insured.

Federal Export Assistance Programs

The task of financing the export of goods or services becomes much easier if you take advantage of federal export assistance programs. Granting credit to your customers is less risky with credit insurance and loan guarantees. Banks love to have a secondary source of repayment. If you have a performance guarantee or credit insurance, banks will be much more willing to grant your request for financing through time drafts or open accounts. Thus these guarantees are invaluable to smaller companies and to those new to international trade. Export assistance programs are offered by the federal government, by some states, and by a few private organizations working in partnership with the government. Three main kinds of financial assistance are offered:

- Loans, perhaps as matching funds
- Loan guarantees, protecting a bank loan against your default
- Credit insurance, protecting you (and your bank) against commercial problems with your customer and political risks in the customer's country

Insurance for international transactions covers two types of risks: commercial risks and political risks. Commercial risks include buyer insolvency, protracted default, and inability to pay as a result of natural disaster. Political risks include nonconvertibility of currency, war, expropriation, and cancellation of an import license.

The main programs are described below. Addresses and phone numbers are listed in the Appendixes. You can also get more information from the Commerce Department.

Federal Programs

The U.S. Export–Import Bank. An independent, self-financing government agency set up to finance U.S. exports, the U.S. Export–Import Bank (Eximbank) promotes the export of American products and services through its various financing programs. These include direct loans, loan guarantees, and discount loan programs for the short, medium, or long term. Eximbank also offers insurance against both commercial and political risks on loans made by commercial banks to U.S. exporters. With this protection, the exporters can obtain lower interest rates from their banks to finance export sales.

Eximbank's Working Capital Loan Guarantee Program is specifically designed to help small businesses obtain crucial working capital to fund their export activities. The program guarantees 90 percent of the principal and some of the interest on working capital loans made by banks to eligible U.S. exporters. A loan may be used for pre-export activities such as the purchase of inventory or raw materials, the manufacture of a product, and marketing. Eximbank requires that the working capital loan be secured with inventory of exportable goods, accounts receivable, or other appropriate collateral.

Eximbank provides two types of loans—direct loans to foreign buyers of U.S. exports, and intermediary loans to responsible parties that extend loans to foreign buyers of U.S. capital goods and related services. These cover up to 85 percent of the U.S. export value and have repayment terms of one year or more.

Medium-term intermediary loans (less than $10 million with seven-year repayment terms) are structured as "standby" loan commitments. The intermediary may borrow against the remaining undispersed loan at any time during the course of the underlying debt obligation.

In this way, Eximbank can underwrite a transaction by arranging financing for the overseas purchaser. The purpose of the program is to promote the export of particular U.S. products (such as capital equipment). Under this program, an overseas buyer can get direct credits or financial guarantees to help line up financing in its own capital market. These two types of assistance are often combined, allowing both the foreign importer and the U.S. exporter to obtain loans at lower interest rates and for longer maturities than might otherwise be available. Assistance has typically been offered to large companies and large projects. Boeing Corporation, for example, has received billions of dollars in credits and loan guarantees. But recently Eximbank has teamed with the Small Business Administration to make the program accessible to smaller businesses.

Other Eximbank programs include:

- Loans or guarantees to U.S. companies to conduct feasibility studies overseas.
- The Commercial Bank Guarantee Program, a medium-term program often used by consulting, engineering, or technical services companies that are planning to bid on overseas contracts. You must apply through your bank.
- The Contractors Guarantee Program, which insures U.S. contractors against political and foreign exchange risks (including property damage or confiscation and currency inconvertibility) and against the failure of the client to honor an arbitration award or dispute resolution.

Eximbank-supported financing uses the repayment terms customary in international trade. For capital goods:

Contract Value	Maximum Term
Up to $50,000	Two years
$50,000 to $100,000	Three years
$100,000 to $200,000	Four years
$200,000 and over	Five to ten years

OPIC. OPIC is the federal government's principal catalyst to stimulate direct investment by U.S. companies in over a hundred developing nations around the world. The following Pacific Rim nations are eligible for OPIC programs: China, Indonesia, Korea, Malaysia, Taiwan, the Philippines, Thailand, and (to a limited extent) Singapore. The developed Pacific Rim nations—Japan, Hong Kong, Australia, and New Zealand—are not eligible.

OPIC's primary duty is to insure the direct investments of U.S. companies against political risks such as war damage and expropriation. It also has loan, loan guarantee, and insurance programs accessible to smaller U.S. exporters.

- Direct loans from OPIC help finance start-up projects or expansion of existing projects for U.S. companies. Direct loans of $100,000 to $4 million are available for projects sponsored by or involving U.S. "small businesses"—those having annual revenues of less than $22 million a year or a net worth of less than $44 million. OPIC can also finance preinvestment activities such as feasibility studies and missions to prospective markets.

- OPIC will guarantee loans of up to $50 million made by U.S. commercial banks.
- Insurance is provided against political and commercial risks—such as expropriation and inconvertibility of currency—for U.S. companies with overseas assets.
- To encourage exports of U.S. equipment, financial assistance is offered to established foreign leasing companies that purchase American products.
- OPIC's distributorship program provides financing for the sale and service of U.S. equipment in developing countries.

OPIC loans are available to American companies of any size. To be eligible for OPIC assistance, you must demonstrate that your investment has significant U.S. involvement and will generate advantages to both the host country and the United States. To be eligible for OPIC insurance, you must obtain a registration notice from OPIC before committing the investment to the project.

Small Business Administration. To be eligible for Small Business Administration (SBA) programs, a company must be defined as a small business (again, up to $22 million in sales or $44 million in net worth), must first attempt to secure private bank financing, and must apply to the SBA through its bank.

The SBA's Export Loan Guarantee Program guarantees up to $500,000 of commercial financing (to a maximum of 90 percent of the loan) for companies that want to establish or expand their export operations. You would negotiate the interest rate with the bank within a maximum established by the SBA. (It might be prime plus 2.25 percentage points.)

The SBA's Export Revolving Line of Credit (ERLC) can be used to finance the production and marketing costs required for export sales. It guarantees up to 90 percent of a bank's revolving line of credit of up to $500,000, with a term of up to eighteen months. You may use ERLC funds to pay for labor costs, to buy supplies and materials, to build inventories, and to provide working capital needed to fill a specific export contract. You can also pay for market development expenses, including overseas business travel, participation in trade shows abroad, and consulting fees for professional export marketing assistance.

Eximbank has teamed up with the SBA to co-guarantee the SBA's Export Revolving Line of Credit. By participating on an equal basis with the SBA, Eximbank has increased the maximum guarantee from $500,000 to $1 million.

The SBA continues to consider amounts of less than $200,000 solely for its ERLC program. For more information, contact the international trade loan specialist in your SBA district office.

Private Agencies

Private Export Funding Corporation. The Private Export Funding Corporation (PEFCO) is a private corporation owned by a group of commercial banks and industrial companies. It works through Eximbank and uses private capital to finance U.S. exports, primarily by making medium- to long-term loans to private and public borrowers overseas. A U.S. exporter can obtain financing for its overseas customers. PEFCO makes loans of $1 million or more, and its loans must be covered by Eximbank's unconditional guarantee.

Foreign Credit Insurance Association. The Foreign Credit Insurance Association (FCIA) is an association of private insurance companies, operating in partnership with Eximbank, that provides insurance against commercial and political risk to U.S. exporters. The private insurers cover the normal commercial credit risks, while Eximbank assumes liability for the political risks. The insurance enables a company to obtain a working capital loan (from a bank or other source) for an overseas transaction at a lower rate than would otherwise be possible. This lower interest rate may offset the premium on the export credit insurance. A typical policy covers up to 90 percent of commercial risks and 100 percent of the financed amount of political risks. FCIA insures against the buyer's becoming insolvent. The policy also insures against political risks, such as delays in foreign exchange transfer, cancellation of the import or export license, war, political unrest, and other unforeseen events.

FCIA's "master policy" covers most or all of a company's exports with short- or medium-term credit. Thus the exporter need not submit detailed credit and financial information for each transaction. Used with a deductible, this policy minimizes the cost and paperwork of export credit insurance. With FCIA insurance, you can better evaluate the quality of the payment terms you can offer (or allow)—that is, you can determine whether the transaction has enough solidity to sell on draft or open account instead of letter of credit.

Foreign credit insurance is sold through commercial insurance brokers, some of which specialize in export insurance. For information on FCIA, contact the regional Department of Commerce, your bank or insurance broker, or FCIA branch offices located in Atlanta, Chicago, Houston, Los Angeles, New York, and Washington, D.C. The main office is in New York.

State Export Finance Programs

Traditionally, U.S. states have done little to help smaller companies finance export and overseas investment. Since the mid-1980s, however, several states have initiated trade finance programs. If these live up to their early promise and catalyze similar programs in other states, they could prove to be a real boon to small and medium-size companies seeking entry to overseas trade. Two of the first ones, dating from 1986, were in California and Illinois. Let's take a look at what they provide and how they supplement the federal programs just described.

California Export Finance Program. In 1986, the California World Trade Commission, which has actively promoted California exports, initiated the

California Export Finance Program (CEFP) to provide small and medium-size companies with working capital to purchase inventory for export orders. CEFP guarantees up to 85 percent of the amount loaned by a bank. The guarantee is issued on behalf of the exporter, with the bank as beneficiary. CEFP evaluates the exporter just as the bank does, looking at the financial strength of the company and the soundness of the deal; it may specify that additional personal guarantees be offered. The maximum loan guarantee is $350,000, which means a company can borrow $411,000 from the bank. The loan guarantee fee is 1 percent. The products have to be primarily of California content.

CEFP takes more of a hands-on approach than do federal agencies. To start with, it has offices in cities throughout the state. If your company is small or new to exporting, or if your export sale is small, you may get caught in a "Catch-22": To a large bank, you are too small to bother with, and to a smaller bank your loan is too risky to handle. CEFP will go to bat for you, talk to your commercial bank, and get it to agree to make a loan through CEFP's loan guarantee. If one bank won't do it, CEFP will find you a bank that will. It will even help you put together the financial statements and other documentation needed to qualify for the loan. CEFP can put you in touch with the consultants you need to develop the required background information and can help you conduct market research.

CEFP helps an inexperienced exporter get a financeable contract. It does this, not out of altruism, but because CEFP is guaranteeing the exporter's performance, and if the exporter does not or cannot perform, CEFP is responsible for making good to the bank. CEFP also helps the exporter evaluate the viability of the deal: For example, are the margins high enough to sustain the company, and is the contract adequate?

How does CEFP assistance differ from SBA programs or Eximbank programs? To approach the SBA or Eximbank, you must put the transaction together and have your banker submit it to the agency. Many bankers do not want to be burdened with this task, which they feel should be done by the exporter. CEFP, on the other hand, helps you put the package together and gives you the commitment you need so that when you approach your banker, you already have the complete package.

In addition to CEFP, the California government has initiated programs tailored to the needs of specific California industries. The California Energy Commission, for example, assists in the export of varied energy technologies—everything from solar and wind power to small-scale hydroelectric dams.

Illinois Export Development Authority. The Illinois Export Development Authority (IEDA), established in 1986, has a $15 million fund to make loans to Illinois exporters. The purpose of IEDA is to provide low-risk, competitive rate financing for smaller companies. The maximum loan guarantee is $500,000 for up to 90 percent coverage, so a transaction of up to $555,000 can be handled. A loan can be processed in one or two days.

IEDA's staff helps an exporter prepare the applications and process the documentation, thereby saving time for both the exporter and the bank. This makes export financing similar to funding a commercial loan—in both complexity and risk. Since IEDA signs up local banks to participate in the program, a by-product is that for the first time a number of smaller banks are becoming involved in financing international transactions.

Companies must qualify as Illinois exporters in two ways. First, 25 percent of the final value added to the product must take place in Illinois, and the export must create or maintain employment in the state. Second, the exporter must qualify with Eximbank and FCIA for commercial and political risk insurance.

The overseas buyer must also qualify. Information on the buyer is submitted to Eximbank and FCIA, which investigate the creditworthiness of the buyer. FCIA must issue a Special Buyer Credit Limitation (SBCL), which establishes an insured credit line and the terms of sale. For a new exporter, it can take three or four weeks to receive approval from Eximbank and FCIA. IEDA helps exporters in the negotiations. Interestingly, a letter of credit backing IEDA was provided by the Bank of Tokyo.

Types of exports handled so far include breeder cattle, hardwood lumber, computer software, video movies, industrial floor scrubbers, high-tech electronics, and agricultural goods. Figure 9-4, which shows the steps for obtaining financing through IEDA, is illustrative of state programs.

Other states are beginning to initiate export assistance programs. Often, the state lieutenant governor coordinates export development activities. To see what your state has to offer, you might contact the lieutenant governor's office.

Because of the difficulty in obtaining financing, smaller exporters have sold internationally on two kinds of terms—cash in advance and irrevocable letter of credit. Both of these are often noncompetitive in today's global marketplace. With the emergence of government loan and insurance programs, smaller exporters can become competitive on terms of payment as well as price and quality.

Pros and Cons of Government Finance Programs

Federal Programs. The federal government finally seems to recognize the importance of stimulating overseas trade and investment by smaller companies, including service businesses. Programs from the SBA, Eximbank, and FCIA are aimed at these businesses. But it remains to be seen how well the programs meet the needs of smaller companies. There are several problems.

Government agencies say, "We are here to help you," but you must find the one that can meet your needs, and then structure your deal to meet all its criteria. Federal programs work best for strong, self-supporting companies with proven ability to implement an international operation. Eximbank and OPIC have main offices only in Washington, D.C., so it is difficult for smaller companies new to export—and their banks—to work with them and to obtain the needed "hand holding." Eximbank has opened a few local offices, but they are mainly for marketing. You must still work with the Washington office to put a deal together.

Figure 9-4. Sequence of events in obtaining state-assisted export financing (through the Illinois Export Development Authority).

1 Exporter receives purchase order for $100,000 in widgets from a Pacific Rim company.
2 Exporter applies for export loan at local bank.
3 Bank applies to IEDA for participation in financing program.
   a Exporter is approved by Eximbank and FCIA (required only for a first-time applicant).
   b Bank is approved by IEDA (required only for a first-time applicant).
   c Foreign buyer is approved by Eximbank and FCIA (approval needed for each foreign buyer but not for each transaction with buyer).
4 Upon approval, exporter is eligible to receive 90 percent financing of the export sale ($90,000 in this example). IEDA informs exporter and bank of interest rate on financing and documents required to draw down on line of credit for specific transaction. Bank provides 10 percent of financing at its interest rate. IEDA provides remaining 90 percent of financing at fixed rate. Maximum term for financing is 180 days.

$ 9,000	bank's portion (10 percent)
$81,000	IEDA's portion (90 percent)
$90,000	total amount financed

5 Exporter ships goods; bank delivers documentation to IEDA and requests it to draw down loan.
6 Participating bank collects from foreign buyer on exports receivable. Upon receipt of payment by the bank from the foreign buyer on the exports receivable, IEDA is repaid, and the bank retains its portion of the financing and remits the remainder to the exporter.
7 Entire transaction is insured by Eximbank and FCIA; coverage is 90 percent for commercial risk loss and 100 percent for political risk loss. Under a special hold-harmless and assignment agreement, the bank and IEDA are 100 percent insured at all times for all risks.
8 If there is a default in payment from the buyer, a claim is made to FCIA under the umbrella insurance policy. While the claim is pending, a moratorium on repayment of the loan is granted to the bank and exporter. Upon receipt of payment from FCIA, IEDA retains its portion of the loan and remits the bank's portion to the bank.
9 Cost to exporter includes:
   a Interest on bank's 10 percent financing
   b Interest on IEDA's 90 percent financing (fixed rate)
   c Equivalent of 1 percent per annum loan origination fee charged by the bank on the term of the total loan (for example, 180-day loan, 0.5 percent fee)
   d Loan commitment fee of 0.1 percent paid by bank, passed on to exporter
   e Premium for Eximbank and FCIA insurance (varies depending on amount, term, and ultimate obligor)
10 Total cost of financing (less insurance premium) averages 1 to 1.5 percent above the prime rate.

Companies must approach a federal organization through their banks, and banks are not excited about helping a new-to-export business put together and submit packages for what they consider to be small deals. Despite the guarantees available, banks and other financial institutions are reluctant to provide trade finance for smaller companies, even ones that are very strong in domestic markets.

The programs tailored to smaller, new-to-export businesses are not well publicized. Export assistance agencies, which after all seek to maximize U.S. exports and which are always understaffed, still place higher priority on putting together packages for larger companies and do not work as hard to attract smaller ones. Also, OPIC works only with 100 percent U.S.-owned banks. (Eximbank can work with any bank.) Unless OPIC changes this regulation, as more U.S. banks are bought by overseas banks, it will become harder to find a bank to work through for OPIC programs.

State Programs.   How well do the export promotion programs in the states fill the gap and meet the needs of small and medium-size companies? State programs seek to offer information through published material, seminars, and office assistance; they provide marketing assistance by introducing foreign buyers to local companies and in some instances by sponsoring foreign trade missions for industries in their states. But except in a handful of states, they do not offer financial assistance.

The state programs that do offer financial assistance are very promising. Besides offering loan guarantees, they take a more active approach, helping a company put its package together before taking it to the bank, and actively soliciting the participation of reluctant banks. Hopefully, these programs will stimulate other states to follow suit. Even with the existing programs, it remains too early to evaluate their effectiveness.

There are many little-used government programs whose outreach is sorely lacking, especially for small and medium-size businesses. So it is up to you to seek out the appropriate program. When you find the right one, be patient with the bureaucracy, fill out all the forms, and allow plenty of time.

Trade Financing From Pacific Rim Organizations

You may be able to obtain the financing you need from Pacific Rim banks in Asia or in the United States. Japanese banks in the United States initially focused on financing Japanese business here, but increasingly they are helping American companies to trade with Japan.

Also investigate government-run financial institutions in your target market. For example, Taiwan's Export-Import Bank offers medium- and long-term low-interest loans to U.S. exporters of certain goods and technology. This USA Exporter Financing Program lets American exporters extend favorable credit terms to Taiwanese importers of American products. It is a bank-to-bank arrangement between Taiwan's Eximbank and commercial banks in the United States or other countries for relending at a fixed rate to clients.

The types of products eligible for this program are being expanded. They range from machine tools and industrial machines to computer products, minerals and industrial chemicals, office machines and medical instruments, scientific instruments and technical services. Repayment terms are up to two years for loans of less than $100,000 and up to five years for maximum loans of $2 million.

Taiwan's Eximbank has already set up arrangements with a number of banks all over the United States. To obtain financing, contact your bank. If it doesn't have an arrangement, contact the Taiwan Eximbank in Taipei. (See the Appendixes.)

Other Sources of Trade Financing

Obtaining Export Working Capital

Despite all these great programs, there will be times when you find it very difficult to obtain bank financing for working capital. Several approaches have been successfully used by companies in such situations.

• If a customer is very strong, it may be able to obtain a letter of credit for an amount large enough to finance its business with you, and use the letter to collateralize your loan request.

• Your bank will view the letter of credit as if it were a strong purchase order and thus will want to examine your ability to produce the goods. If you have a time draft letter of credit, as soon as you ship the goods you can discount the letter of credit and receive cash right away.

• On a commercial investment project, e.g., a hotel—for which you have a contract, your customer may well have money put away, perhaps in Hong Kong banks, and be able to finance the transaction.

• If your joint venture partner, distributor, or agent is a strong company, it may be able to assist you with financing by obtaining a letter of credit, by co-signing a loan for you, or by loaning you the money itself.

• If you are working through an export management company, it may agree to carry the financing for export sales of your products. In this way, you obtain prompt payment and have no foreign credit risk.

• Factoring houses may purchase your inventory or accounts receivable, often without recourse. As with domestic factoring, they will discount the value of your receivables, most likely at a higher rate than the cost of bank financing—perhaps 35 to 40 percent per year. Against inventory, you might be able to receive 50 percent of the value; against receivables, probably 75 or 80 percent depending on what they are. Since factoring is a costly method of financing, it makes sense only in high-margin transactions. It's essential to work with a factoring house that is familiar with your area of business.

• You may be able to obtain an advance against your customer's letter of credit.

• You may have to offer personal guarantees. Anyone in a self-owned business is familiar with the pressure to mortgage a house or boat to provide collateral for a business loan; trade finance is just another source of such pressure.

Financing Export Sales

There are several methods of financing trade, in addition to those described above, that can enable a company to close sales that would otherwise be lost. Although these methods are generally more risky than sales specified in U.S. dollars, there are ways to manage the risk. The methods are also more costly, but normally the additional cost is borne by the buyer, not the seller. Because of the added costs and uncertainties involved, these approaches are often more appropriate for high-margin sales.

Use of these methods requires experience and knowledge of current conditions in capital markets. Inexperienced companies can get burned. Smaller companies that lack the expertise in house should work with a money center bank skilled in such transactions. If you are considering using any of these methods, it is essential to talk with your banker before you get too far along in your negotiations. Make sure that you can obtain the financing you need before making a commitment to a buyer. Each of these payment methods must be planned for in advance so that the additional cost can be taken into consideration in the price agreement.

Foreign Hard-Currency Pricing. Sometimes an export price may be quoted in a foreign hard currency rather than in U.S. dollars. Hard currencies are those—such as the dollar, yen, deutschemark, or pound sterling—which are widely traded in global financial markets. If payment in U.S. dollars is a major inconvenience for your buyer, you may become more competitive by pricing the goods and receiving payment in the buyer's currency. In some countries, it is illegal for the buyer to hedge dollars or to make forward cash agreements for exchanging dollars; or the buyer may not be able to obtain the dollars until it receives the bill of lading. The buyer must then accept the risk of fluctuation in currency values during this period. The U.S. company has a greater ability to hedge against the foreign currency in order to minimize the risk in currency exchange fluctuations.

Foreign Soft-Currency Pricing. Soft-currency pricing is similar in concept to hard-currency pricing, and is useful for larger transactions that cannot be

---

Alternative Methods of Trade Finance

- Foreign hard-currency pricing
- Foreign soft-currency pricing
- Foreign currency loans
- Confirming
- Forfaiting
- Countertrade
- Consolidation as export trading company
- Factoring
- Customer-financed sale or contract
- Joint venture partner, agent, or distributor financing or guarantee
- Export management company financed sales
- Advance against customer's letter of credit
- Discount time letter of credit
- Personal guarantees

---

handled in any other way. Soft currencies, while generally convertible, are less widely traded on global markets. The exchange rate may be less certain and more volatile. Since there is a lack of futures or options services to accommodate soft-currency pricing, you may have to use a large money center bank. Because of the degree of difficulty of such transactions, they are usually limited to sales of over $5 million. The price premium paid by the buyer can be quite large—50 percent or more. For example, if an Indonesian company wishes to buy equipment from Taiwan and pay in Indonesian rupiah instead of in U.S. dollars, it may have to pay a substantially higher price.

Foreign Currency Loans.   The exporter may borrow money to cover pre-export and trade finance from a bank in the buyer's market, collateralized by the buyer's obligation and using the same foreign currency that is used in the sale. If the foreign interest rate is lower, the seller is at an advantage. Sometimes, in order to protect its profit margin, the seller may hedge or take out an option on the amount of the profit, or require a payment from the buyer in dollars equal to the profit percentage.

Confirming Services.   The exporter may agree to pay a fee for the assurance of receiving payment on open account sales. Because of the competitiveness of many Pacific Rim markets, buyers often refuse to tie up funds through a letter of credit, and competing suppliers are willing to sell on open account. For a fee—which the seller passes on to the buyer—the confirming service takes responsibility for collecting payment from the buyer. The confirming service will pay the exporter at the agreed-on payment time, whether or not the buyer has paid. The confirming service is thus acting as insurer and collection agent. Confirming houses specialize in particular industries and regions and monitor foreign buyers closely to make sure the payments are made.

Forfaiting Services. Forfait services are provided by specialized banking organizations in major financial centers such as New York, London, and Frankfurt. These services accept a commitment from a bank to pay at a future date. The commitment is in the form of a certificate of deposit, arranged by the buyer, which is used to pay the seller at the time of sale, even though the buyer can't pay at that time.

Countertrade. Countertrade is an international transaction in which you accept other products as payment for your products or services. The simplest form of countertrade is a barter of one commodity for another, but there are many variations, several of which are described below.

Countertrade is included as a method of export financing because so many nations require that at least part of their international dealings be by countertrade. As much as 40 percent of Pacific Rim exporting involves countertrade. This practice is prevalent in China, and is encountered in Korea, Taiwan, Indonesia, Malaysia, Thailand, and the Philippines. It is particularly common with agricultural goods. U.S. companies that are unfamiliar with countertrade lose some deals to foreign companies that are adept at this type of transaction.

To engage in countertrade successfully and profitably, you must work with experienced professionals. The large Japanese trading companies are expert at this method, and most large U.S. multinationals have in-house units to handle countertrade. But many smaller companies are unfamiliar with countertrade, and few U.S. banks involved in financing international trade have people qualified to help structure countertrade deals. However, there are organizations that help exporters dispose of items acquired in countertrade transactions. Specialists in countertrade and compensation services will negotiate and manage the arrangement for a commission or a fee. Several are headquartered in Vienna, Frankfurt, and London, and some American banks in New York, Los Angeles, and San Francisco offer countertrade advice and brokerage.

There are three major variations of countertrade.

1. *Counterpurchase.* In this type of countertrade service, payment to the seller is in the form of a good unrelated to the seller's products. Suppose an aircraft manufacturer completes a sale in Indonesia that requires counterpurchase of plywood or latex. The exporter hires a counterpurchase service, which, for a fee of from one to 3 percent, accepts the payment in Indonesia in the form of goods, sells them elsewhere for dollars, and pays the exporter.

2. *Compensation.* Here, payment for a product is delayed until the product is used to manufacture another value-added product, which is then re-exported to obtain foreign exchange. For example, a raw material such as copper wire sold to China must be used in a product manufactured there. The product is then re-exported, and the seller of the copper wire is paid from the proceeds. Or a company that contracts to build and manage a factory in China may be paid in goods produced by the factory, which it then sells on international markets. So the ex-

porter is forced to wait a while in order to collect payment. This working capital cost is included in the agreed-on price.

3. *Clearing management. Clearing* refers to the accounts kept on the books of national barter authorities that administer international countertrade. Often, the goods taken for barter are not of the same value as the purchase, so the balance kept on the books must periodically be reconciled. Companies selling to countries using countertrade need to rely on a clearing management service to track this process and handle the reconciliations with the buyer's government. This is rarely encountered in the Pacific Rim.

Consolidation.   Trade finance can sometimes be facilitated through a technique called consolidation. A group of exporters combines into a single export trading entity that bargains for price with overseas customers. This approach is useful when several small sellers are dealing with a large buyer (such as a national government) that seeks to bid one exporter against another to drive the price down. Consolidation was made legal in the United States by the Export Trading Company Act of 1982. Although the initial flurry of ETCs was not very successful, consolidation has proved valuable for such structures as agricultural cooperatives. It is often used in conjunction with countertrade. The ETC finds it easier to dispose of countertraded goods.

Financing Pacific Rim Investment

Whether your company needs capital to establish a sales office, a distribution network, or a manufacturing facility, or to complete a project on contract, you will need to obtain investment capital. How does a small to medium-size company obtain financing for investment in Pacific Rim operations? Large multinationals have the clout to obtain the financing they need, but smaller companies have found financing to be a major barrier to direct overseas investment.

The U.S. government has shown very little support for overseas investment by smaller businesses. Because the government is so concerned with the trade deficit, federal programs emphasize exports over foreign investment, which, of course, is a major disservice if you are one of the many smaller companies that increasingly needs to establish overseas operations to retain your cost competitiveness or to enter many Pacific Rim markets. Starting in the mid-1980s, the federal government did begin to support overseas investment, but that policy has not yet been consistently translated into effective assistance.

Complaints aside, you have several options for obtaining investment capital for Pacific Rim operations, both in equity and in long-term debt, such as:

- Commercial banks, whether U.S. or Pacific Rim, that operate in your target market
- Venture capital firms that finance Pacific Rim enterprises

- A Pacific Rim joint venture partner or distributor
- Pacific Rim equities markets
- Development banks or agencies, including the Asian Development Bank (ADB), that fund development projects in Pacific Rim nations

Bank Financing for Pacific Rim Investment

Suppose your $5 million Los Angeles company, Med-Eq, is well established in domestic markets and has sold through reps in the Pacific Rim. To be more responsive to the emerging needs of health care facilities, which are your major customers there, you want to establish a subsidiary in Hong Kong, called Med-Eq Asia, to exportize and manufacture your products and distribute them throughout Southeast Asia. How do you get the financing needed to establish your facilities?

Your first stop will be your banker, but you will soon discover that you have other options as well—in particular, a Pacific Rim bank or venture capital firm. Here are several scenarios:

1. Your Los Angeles bank makes business and corporate loans from its subsidiary in Hong Kong. Your banker, with whom you have a solid, long-standing relationship, introduces you to the manager of the Hong Kong branch and suggests that you talk directly with that person.

2. The Hong Kong branch of your Los Angeles bank does not make the type of loan you need in Hong Kong. Like many U.S. commercial banks, your bank has drawn back from retail banking services in the Pacific Rim. It still handles major financial transactions of large companies that are established customers, including mergers, acquisitions, and stock market and currency market transactions, but its Pacific Rim branches do not offer investment finance to smaller American companies new to the market. Nor does it provide all the related banking services needed by a business like yours.

Your banker gladly introduces you to the manager of a correspondent bank. For example, if you bank with Union Bank, you may be introduced to officers at Standard-Chartered of Hong Kong, a British-owned bank with which Union has a close working relationship. Many Standard-Chartered and Union executives know each other personally, so a letter of introduction and recommendation mean a lot.

3. Your Los Angeles bank is not involved in international banking and financial transactions. Nevertheless, it has local and overseas correspondent banks and can identify particular banks suitable to your needs and write a letter of introduction to whatever bank you choose. When you establish an overseas banking relationship, your home bank will be able to assist you by endorsing your company and supplying requested financial information.

Yet this is a relationship that is one step removed, and you may find it more difficult to gain the initial ear, or confidence, of the best Pacific Rim banker. You may find yourself presenting your case to a banker in a market with which you have little experience and track record, but if you are successful, you may well establish your banking relationship with a bank headquartered in Hong Kong.

A couple of lessons can be drawn from these scenarios. First, regardless of whom you bank with now, you are most likely to receive investment finance from a bank in your target market. It matters little whether you seek financing from an American bank or a Pacific Rim bank. (In many instances the difference has become blurred, as domestic banks buy banks in Pacific Rim nations and vice versa.) Who owns the bank matters less than where it is located. Even if you continue working with the same bank, the local bank branch that handles your domestic business is unlikely to make the loan you need. Banks want local collateral, and they want to be able to check out the proposed investment personally.

Second, you may need a guarantee from your local bank in order to obtain the needed financing in the Pacific Rim. This is precisely where smaller, rapidly growing, highly leveraged companies run into difficulties. Despite the attractiveness of your technology and products in its market, the Pacific Rim bank may be unwilling to finance you directly because you lack a track record there. (If you plan to purchase land or buildings, they can collateralize part of the loan, but many Pacific Rim nations limit your ability to buy real estate, and initially you may prefer to lease facilities.) However, your U.S. banker may be less than enthusiastic about providing the Pacific Rim bank with the required financial guarantee for such a remote operation, despite the quality of your relationship and collateral. If your banker does not refuse, he or she may impose requirements so stringent that you cannot accept them without crippling your ability to raise further working capital.

In such a situation, you may be strongly pressured to accept a local joint venture partner with a track record in the market. Many companies seek out joint venture partners who can either obtain or supply the needed capital for the Pacific Rim operation.

This discussion presumes that you are new to the Pacific Rim market in which you seek financing. However, like many companies, you may have previously established a local presence through a rep, distributor, or other market partner, so you already have the local contacts and experience that make it much easier for you to establish the needed banking relationship.

Having a strong Asian partner can make it easier to obtain financing in the United States. For example, SpectraPhysics obtained start-up capital for its R&D operations after completing an agreement to manufacture and distribute its products in Japan with established Japanese companies.

Venture Capital in the Pacific Rim

Some companies that find it difficult to obtain needed investment financing from commercial banks have better luck attracting venture capital. Organized venture capital is new to the Pacific Rim, and many American companies are still unaware of its availability. Until the mid-1980s, Pacific Rim venture capital was limited to obtaining a private placement of a financial offering—usually through a banker who was informally linked to institutions and wealthy individuals with money to invest.

Venture capital in the Pacific Rim has been slow to emerge for several reasons. In Japan and Korea the degree of financial risk entailed by backing entrepreneurs touting new technologies has been incompatible with traditional methods of financing, so large corporations and banks—often having interlocking directorates—have provided capital to subsidiaries to commercialize new technologies. In the overseas Chinese cultures, most companies are family-owned and -controlled and have had no desire to open themselves up to the outside "meddling" that necessarily comes with venture capital infusion. Thus they get a bank loan or private placement from a money manager representing a corporation or wealthy individual who wants a good return but remains in the background. This type of venture capital is still prevalent—probably predominant—but it is not organized or institutionalized.

Other factors have also hindered the emergence of institutionalized venture capital. Good market research on changing consumer tastes and life-styles has been scarce, especially across borders. Many local financiers have lacked experience in conducting the due diligence studies required for venture capital, and have been reluctant to apply strict standards to screen local management. Government policies have restricted investments by foreigners and have obstructed domestic entrepreneurs by overregulation. Finally, stock markets for new issues have been poorly developed.

These situations are all rapidly changing. Closely held family companies are diversifying with their need to grow larger. A younger generation of men and women with American MBAs is coming along. To meet competitive pressures, companies need an infusion of capital. Stock exchanges are growing in importance as an increasing number of companies go public, and the number of mergers and acquisitions is increasing. Thus venture capitalists have outlets for realizing their investment.

Consequently, since the mid-1980s, venture capital institutions have been emerging throughout Asia. Initially the markets were separate and uncoordinated, but by 1988, loose regional venture capital associations began to appear. Most American venture capital firms have so far stayed away from Pacific Rim ventures, but some, especially Advent International (Boston) and Hambricht & Quist (San Francisco), have been major players.

Who Can Get Venture Capital?   In several Pacific Rim nations, including Taiwan and Korea, venture capital is closely intertwined with government policies of attracting desired technologies, so it is much easier for a high-tech company to obtain funding. Hong Kong venture capitalists lead in backing other types of enterprises, including service or distribution companies and medium-tech manufacturing. Some countries, such as Singapore and Australia, have both independent and government-affiliated venture capitalists. Companies in many different types of industries have received venture capital—for example, a company processing edible oils in Malaysia and a manufacturer of chocolate candy in the Philippines.

Hong Kong and Japan lead in regional venture capital. One Japanese fund specializes in packaging American ideas and entrepreneurship and uses Japanese money to establish manufacturing operations in ASEAN. A leading Hong Kong company searches out American businesses that are ignoring opportunities in lucrative Asian markets. Certain Taiwanese and Korean companies are trying to set up joint ventures to transfer technology or operational skills.

The investment criteria of Pacific Rim venture capitalists are similar to those of their American counterparts. Those firms will rigorously appraise the technology, concept, market, competitive edge, management personnel, and financial needs of your proposed investment. You must have a good current record, be well managed, and have good future prospects, and your Pacific Rim operation must make sound sense compared to other options. Pacific Rim venture capitalists want a company that is headed by an entrepreneur with a technical rather than a financial or marketing background, since they can help provide people with skills in the latter two areas, but not in the former.

U.S. and European venture capitalists typically want to back projects that will allow them to recoup their investment, plus earn a sizable capital gain, within a fairly short period—perhaps three to seven years. The same is true of many Pacific Rim venture capitalists, but others have a longer horizon of up to ten years or more.

Besides capital, venture capitalists provide other services for their clients: They can help you to find a top-quality general manager and to build a good local management team. They will give guidance as needed, especially in nonoperational areas where you are weak. Also, they can introduce your company to customers and suppliers. Since many venture capital groups prefer a debt-equity package over an all-equity arrangement, they will help line up bank loans from local banks and will often bring in outside private investors to provide either debt or equity capital.

If you want to set up a Pacific Rim subsidiary but have no operational track record in the local market, it will be hard for you to get venture capital initially. Before a venture capital firm will support you, it will usually require that you work with it for a while on a service contract and allow it to consult for you on financial or other management services. Often, a firm such as H&Q Taiwan will do a feasibility study of your manufacturing and marketing plans, including the viability and strength of your international management. It may recommend that you hire a Taiwanese manager or form a joint venture with a local company. After it has confidence in you, you can arrange venture capital financing.

It is common for American and Pacific Rim venture capitalists to back a company jointly. For example, Advent International provided start-up capital for a $5 million American company that produced specialized industrial software. Advent and its affiliate, Technoventures Hong Kong, helped the company identify an untapped niche among Asian manufacturers; they then jointly financed the establishment of the company's subsidiary in Hong Kong, a joint venture with a local business.

If you ask what types of investments cannot be financed, the answers will be similar to those you hear in the United States: investments involving unproven technologies, poorly established customer bases, and overly strong competition. However, the desire to avoid unproven technologies poses a dilemma, since unproven technology is the latest technology, and that is what Pacific Rim governments are avidly seeking. If it cannot be financed, then the latest technology cannot be transferred.

It is often difficult to obtain funding for a straight licensing agreement, because the capital sources prefer joint ventures in which both partners have a significant stake in the venture's success. It is essential to note that many U.S. companies have obtained financing and investment for two-way trade. Part of the financing deal was their willingness to re-export products from the Asian Pacific Rim to the United States and other countries.

How to Make a Venture Capital Investment in China. Until China allows issues of stock for new companies and private mergers and acquisitions, it will have no domestic venture capital industry. An even larger problem is the difficulty in getting foreign exchange out of China. Yet even now, it is possible to obtain venture capital for a manufacturing facility in China. For example: Hong Kong Venture Capital, Ltd. (HKVC), sets up a joint venture with US-Tech, Inc., called HK Holding Co. HK Holding Co. then identifies a suitable enterprise in Shanghai: Chung Enterprises. Together, HK Holding Co. and Chung Enterprises set up a joint venture in Shenzhen to assemble products for sale by US-Tech throughout the world. After a few years, the joint venture becomes very productive and profitable, but there is no way to sell its shares.

However, HK Holding Co. goes public on the Hong Kong stock market, allowing HKVC to sell its shares in HK Holding Co. and realize its investment. That leaves US-Tech as the principal stockholder in a Hong Kong company engaged in a joint venture with a Chinese organization in China.

The Appendixes list American and Pacific Rim organizations that provide venture capital to American companies for Asian operations. They include both private and government-affiliated sources. However, the list is not complete, as new sources appear every year. *Asia Venture Capital*, a magazine published in Hong Kong, will help you to keep up with this emerging field. In addition, become familiar with the ADB, headquartered in Manila, which coordinates and sponsors several regional venture capital activities.

Pacific Rim Equities Markets

The securities markets in several Pacific Rim nations have deregulated and opened up to international capital flows. Some are listing foreign companies as well. Until recently, listings have been limited to markets in Australia, Japan, and Hong Kong. However, Singapore is making a major bid to establish a regional securities market for established and start-up companies. Some companies have raised capital on the Bangkok and Manila markets. Taiwan and Korea are also in the process of liberalizing. Thus it is becoming increasingly possible for companies to raise second-tier (or "mezzanine") financing through these markets.

Pacific Rim equities markets are a very new phenomenon, and on the surface they do not seem like a good source of capital for smaller companies. There are both financial and political constraints. Some countries have limits on how much equity a foreigner can have. An equities market makes it harder to track who owns what companies, a problem that can restrict access by foreign businesses to such a market. However, conditions are developing so rapidly that it may be worthwhile for you to investigate this source.

Pacific Rim Development Banks

All of the developing Pacific Rim nations, including the NICs, have development banks that seek to attract foreign investment in specified industries or sectors. In addition, there are international and regional institutions, such as the World Bank and the ADB.

Pacific Rim nations are actively seeking investment from the United States, yet they have trouble interesting U.S. companies. For example, the Thailand Board of Investments recently solicited applications for a variety of projects in Thailand, but all the applications returned were from Japan, Europe, and Taiwan. There was not a single application from a U.S. company. The Indonesian Board of Investments gave a series of seminars to potential investors in the United States in 1987, but the Board found it difficult to attract companies that weren't already involved in Indonesia. To some degree, this lack of interest is due to the barriers these nations erect, but lack of awareness by American businesses seems to be a much greater factor. A call to the consulate of any nation will quickly bring you a thick packet of information on investment opportunities, including capital sources, in that country.

OPIC

Government programs administered by OPIC and Eximbank are described in the previous section. The OPIC programs in particular are aimed at financing overseas investment by U.S. companies in developing nations. All the Pacific Rim nations except Japan, Australia, New Zealand, and Hong Kong are eligible for OPIC programs.

Differences Within the Pacific Rim

In order to obtain investment capital, you must provide what the market wants and what the development agencies will allow. To illustrate, look again at the different types of Pacific Rim investment climates (also described in Chapter 6):

- *Open (relatively unrestricted):* Japan, Hong Kong, Singapore, Australia, New Zealand
- *Restricted:* Taiwan, Korea, Thailand, the Philippines
- *Controlled:* Indonesia, Malaysia, China

You can see that these classifications depend not only on the nation's level of development but also on its economic philosophy. Among the NICs, Singapore and Hong Kong are more open than Taiwan and Korea, and within ASEAN, Thailand and the Philippines are less restrictive than Malaysia and Indonesia.

This grouping correlates closely the ease of making investment decisions with the requirements for obtaining investment capital. To invest successfully in an open investment climate, you must meet the demands of the market. To obtain investment financing in a controlled or restricted market, you will have to heed the priorities of the development agencies. These agencies seek investment that increases the skill levels of their workers and managers, uses their raw materials and other resources, and increases their exports and level of technological sophistication. Often, a new venture cannot compete with existing local concerns.

Pacific Rim Government Incentives

An essential part of your investment finance package will be any investment incentives, such as tax holidays, provided by the government of a Pacific Rim country. Many nonfinancial incentives have a financial impact: access to particular resources or facilities, or construction of infrastructure, for example. These types of incentives must obviously be taken into account in your calculations, because they affect the amount of capital you must raise initially, the payback period, and the rate of return.

Questions for Pacific Rim Capital Sources

If you are seeking capital from any of the sources described above, you need facts about the specific group or agency long before making a presentation to it. Not all of your questions may be answered to your satisfaction by talking directly with the agencies, so you will also want to check with other sources. Here are some of the questions you should ask about whatever source you choose for financing:

- Is it a private business or an arm of the government? To what extent are its investments limited by government priorities?
- What is the range of investment it will consider? In which industries?

- Will it fund operations that are wholly owned by U.S. companies, or must there be a local joint venture partner?
- Does it arrange debt-equity combinations? What percentage of equity does it want, and what level of control?
- What is the time horizon for its investment planning? Will it arrange or provide second-stage financing when you need it?
- What does it take to apply for and obtain financing? How long does it take, and what are the fees involved?
- What is its track record?
- What is the source of its funds?
- How well connected is it to the government and to local financial communities? Will working with it improve your access to government investment incentives?
- Does it finance investments only in its own country, or does it fund operations in other Pacific Rim countries as well?

You can contact the institutions mentioned directly or enlist your banker's help. Remember this about financing Pacific Rim investment: Money is not the problem. A sentiment often expressed in the Pacific Rim is: "Liquidity is available; good projects, with people who believe in them strongly, are financeable."

10 | Pacific Rim Business Planner

Questionnaires to help you determine
- *If your company should enter Pacific Rim trade*
- *If your product or service is right for Pacific Rim trade*
- *Which market to target initially*
- *Your potential profitability*

This chapter presents a set of guidelines and questionnaires to help you decide whether your company should be involved in Pacific Rim trade and, if so, where and how. It offers a simplified, generalized approach to planning Pacific Rim operations. Many important distinctions have been fuzzed over so that the guidelines can be used for different kinds of businesses. Sophisticated businesspeople may feel the structure is too simplistic; others may feel intimidated just by the number of questions asked. I suggest you first skim the planner briefly to see which parts are of most benefit to you. Figure 10-1 shows the general sequence of topics covered. The planner starts with basic questions and moves into more complex financial and investment issues.

Even complete answers to all these questions will not tell you whether you should be in export or which market you should go into. At best, they show you the factors you must consider to make an informed decision for your company. Some companies that have used the planner have concluded that it just did not make sense to enter an international market at the present time. My point of view is that no single item need stop you, but together, the factors do influence the way you choose to operate.

You cannot answer all the questions right now. You will need a good bit of outside input that may take some time to assemble. The planner guides you in obtaining the input you need.

Evaluating Your Organization: Should Your Company Be in Pacific Rim Trade?

To assess the readiness of your company to take on Pacific Rim trade, rate yourself, your key people, and your operation on the factors listed in the following questionnaire (and also discussed in Chapter 2). In some areas, you are probably

Figure 10-1. Flow chart for predicting your success in trading in the Pacific Rim.

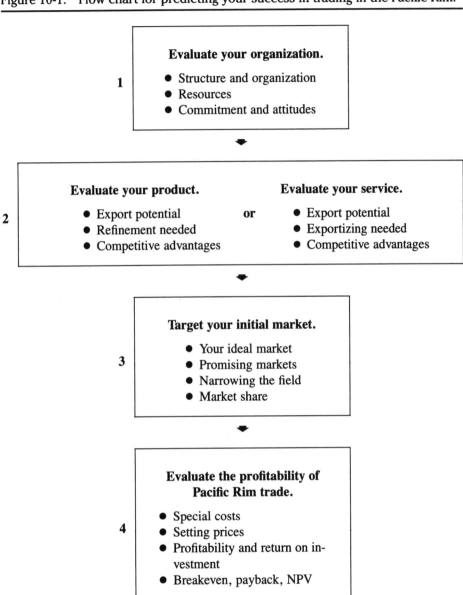

1

Evaluate your organization.

- Structure and organization
- Resources
- Commitment and attitudes

2

Evaluate your product.

- Export potential
- Refinement needed
- Competitive advantages

or

Evaluate your service.

- Export potential
- Exportizing needed
- Competitive advantages

3

Target your initial market.

- Your ideal market
- Promising markets
- Narrowing the field
- Market share

4

Evaluate the profitability of Pacific Rim trade.

- Special costs
- Setting prices
- Profitability and return on investment
- Breakeven, payback, NPV

strong, and in others weak; or you may have both strengths and weaknesses in the same area—for example, you may have little unused productive capacity yet be able to subcontract easily for additional production over the short run.

The purpose of the following exercise is not to get a yes or no answer but to identify strengths you can build upon and weaknesses you need to take into consideration when planning how you will operate.

A. Organizational Qualities

Factor	Strengths	Weak-nesses	Rating*

Management Depth

1. Does your management team have the experience and sophistication required to expand into Pacific Rim markets? ____ ____ ☐

2. Can your management team handle added strains introduced by undertaking an overseas operation? ____ ____ ☐

3. Are your accounting and administrative systems flexible enough to handle an overseas operation? Will you be able to compare it to domestic operations? ____ ____ ☐☐

4. How would you handle the increased level of administrative complexity? ____ ____ ☐☐

Management Commitment

1. Can you make a commitment to enter Pacific Rim trade for the long haul? ____ ____ ☐

2. Will Pacific Rim trade be important in its own right, or simply be a weak "stepchild" to your domestic operations? ____ ____ ☐

Facilities

1. Can you expand production in your current facility, or will you require additional space? ____ ____ ☐

2. Will Pacific Rim trade be complementary to your current mode of production? (You may not know this until you have assessed product needs in likely markets.) ____ ____ ☐

*10 = strong; 1 = weak

Factor	Strengths	Weak-nesses	Rating*
3. If you sell services, are your current facilities large and adequate enough to run an expanded Pacific Rim operation?	___	___	☐
4. To what extent will your current level of administrative overhead be adequate for an extended operation?	___	___	☐
Financial Strength			
1. Can you commit needed levels of working and investment capital?	___	___	☐
2. Do you have sufficient retained earnings to initiate operations without outside financing?	___	___	☐ ☐
3. Can your company raise needed funds for working or investment capital?			
4. Do you have access to financial institutions that provide the type of financing you will need (see Chapter 9)?	___	___	☐
Complementarity			
How complementary is your current business to the type of opportunity you will encounter in the Pacific Rim? (You may want to reassess your answer to this question after investigating market opportunities more fully.)	___	___	☐
Personnel			
1. Do you have the personnel available to commit to:			
• Investigating opportunities for Pacific Rim trade?	___	___	☐ ☐
• Organizing a Pacific Rim operation?			

*10 = strong; 1 = weak

A. Organizational Qualities (*continued*).

Factor	Strengths	Weak-nesses	Rating*
• Producing additional products and services?	___	___	☐
• Managing a new overseas venture?	___	___	☐
2. Do you have people in the following areas:			
• Technical and engineering staff?	___	___	☐
• Marketing and sales?	___	___	☐
• Administrative personnel?	___	___	☐
• Start-up specialists?	___	___	☐

Time

	Strengths	Weak-nesses	Rating*
1. How much time can you allow for a new operation to take off and become successful?	___	___	☐
2. How long is your company's planning horizon? Can it be lengthened if needed?	___	___	☐
3. Do you have the patience to stick with an operation that takes a longer time to pay off than you are accustomed to?	___	___	☐

Timing

	Strengths	Weak-nesses	Rating*
How do various factors impact the timing of your company's entering Pacific Rim trade (e.g., recent, ongoing, or planned expansion in domestic or other markets)?	___	___	☐

*10 = strong; 1 = weak

Factor	Strengths	Weak-nesses	Rating*
1. What resources will this draw upon, at what time, and for how long?	————	————	☐☐
2. What are the returns, risks, and timing of these?	————	————	☐
3. What is the impact of the business cycle on your markets and profitability—in both domestic and targeted markets?			
4. Are there changes in the competitive environment, such as:			
• Merger of competitors?	————	————	☐☐☐
• Emergence of new competition?	————	————	
• Emergence of new competing products or services?	————	————	
5. Are there emerging changes in the trade environment, such as:			
• Trade restrictions dropped against your product or service in a target market?	————	————	☐☐
• Emerging political or economic factors?	————	————	

*10 = strong; 1 = weak

B. Attitudes and Personal Qualities of Key People

1. Who within your organization would have overall responsibility for success of all phases of Pacific Rim operations? _____

2. Who has the personal qualities needed for Pacific Rim operations?

    Name(s) of key person(s): _____

    If you do not have such a key person, how will you recruit one? _____

Now assess the personal qualities and attitudes important for success in international trade.

Factor	Strengths	Weak-nesses	Rating*
1. Commitment; stick-to-itiveness; ability to devote adequate attention and energy to the new enterprise	_____	_____	☐
2. Mastery of the business; the thoroughness essential for successful negotiation	_____	_____	☐
3. Integrity; trustworthiness; ability to follow through and keep word	_____	_____	☐
4. Authority of the person handling the Pacific Rim operation to make independent decisions within policy guidelines	_____	_____	☐
5. Interest in international business and affairs	_____	_____	☐
6. Adaptability, flexibility in new and unfamiliar situations	_____	_____	☐
7. Ability to handle an international operation without undue stress	_____	_____	☐
8. Patience to deal with the delays and frustrations inherent in international business	_____	_____	☐
9. Awareness of and interest in different cultures	_____	_____	☐
10. Sensitivity to people of different cultural backgrounds	_____	_____	☐
11. Ability to read, speak, and understand the language of potential markets	_____	_____	☐

*10 = strong; 1 = weak

Table 10-1. Sample chart for bridging deficiencies.

Characteristic Needed for Success	Specific Deficiency	How to Bridge the Deficiency	Cost of Bridging Deficiency
Management depth and strength	Lack of experience in export operation	Find an export management firm that will work closely with our management team	
Production flexibility	Operating at near capacity	Subcontract production in short run	
Financial strength	Insufficient working capital to carry risk sales	Obtain OPIC loan guarantee for bank trade financing	

Bridging Your Organizational Deficiencies

In this section, first list the weaknesses or deficiencies that you identified on the questionnaire (see Table 10.1). Where you have a weakness, specify what you lack. Next, list how you can bridge or overcome each of these deficiencies.

If your product or service has good export potential, deficiencies in your company's organization and resources can usually be compensated for by the type of operation you select. For example, if you cannot make a major commitment to Pacific Rim trade yet want to test the waters, you might try such strategies as:

- *Sticking to indirect exporting.* Sell through a trading or management company that doesn't require you to have a continuing interest in servicing or maintaining your products.
- *Promoting your products through Commerce Department announcements.*
- *Participating in a trade mission.* These are sponsored by the Commerce Department or your industry trade association.

• *Getting special assistance from governments or organizations.* This could include working closely with the Department of Commerce, a trade or investment rep from a Pacific Rim nation, your state trade development agency, or your industry trade association.

Your Company's Strengths	How You Can Exploit Your Strengths	The Advantage This Gives You
(Only a few examples are shown.)		
• Strong engineering and design capabilities	• Form joint venture with company having latest production processes.	• Greater productive capacity than you could develop on your own initially
• Many small producers in similar and complementary lines of business	• Form a cooperative for joint export marketing	• Greater clout in obtaining financing, conducting market research, and promoting products in new markets
• Access to hardwood forest and skilled furniture craftspeople	• Participate in trade missions and overseas trade shows for fine furniture.	• Gain exposure in markets that seek unusual luxury American goods to import

It is often useful to talk with an outside consultant who can help you evaluate your strengths and weaknesses and identify ways to correct or work around them. Many companies allow themselves to be stymied by a deficiency that could be easily overcome by someone with more experience.

After you have identified ways to overcome a deficiency, prepare a rough estimate of the cost of overcoming it, since cost is an important selection criterion. Table 10-1 shows how you might go about this. You may discover that the cost of overcoming a deficiency is prohibitively high in terms of money, time, or attention; again, an outside consultant may be able to spot less expensive ways (see also Chapter 2).

Next, summarize from the foregoing to answer these questions:

1. What are the strains that would be created in your organization if you undertook Pacific Rim trade? How can they be resolved? _____

2. What critical resources are most likely to limit your expansion into the Pacific Rim?

3. If management limitations are holding you back from going after the type of operation that would be best for your product or service, how can you begin operations to most quickly develop the type of experience and resources you need?

_____

_____

Taking Advantage of Your Strengths in Organization and Management

The other side to bridging your deficiencies is taking advantage of your strengths. As you did with weaknesses, list each of your major strengths in each of the categories. Then identify ways to exploit them in Pacific Rim trade (see Table 10-2). Think about what advantage they can give you in entering markets and beating competitors.

Table 10-2. Sample chart for taking advantage of strengths in organization and management.

Strength or Competitive Advantage	How to Exploit the Strength	Advantage This Gives You
Strong engineering and design capabilities	Form joint venture with company having latest production process	Greater productive capacity than could be developed on own initially
Many small producers in similar and complementary lines of business	Form cooperative for joint export marketing	Greater clout in obtaining financing, conducting market research, and promoting products in new markets
Access to hardwood forest and skilled furniture craftspeople	Participate in trade missions and overseas trade shows for fine furniture	Exposure to markets that seek unusual luxury American goods to import

Now list the existing and only partially employed resources in your company that can be tapped to enter Pacific Rim trade without a large additional outlay of time and capital. For example, (1) *better utilization of your technical and executive manpower*; (2) *unique skills and experience your company can bring to Pacific Rim operations*; (3) *experience in dealing with distant and different markets and in reaching markets through different channels such as distributors and agents*; or (4) *an ability to provide technical services, maintenence, parts, and service to your Pacific Rim customers.*

1. _____
2. _____
3. _____
4. _____
5. _____
6. _____

Evaluating Your Product/Service

You next need to determine the suitability of your product or service for Pacific Rim trade. Use the questionnaire on the following pages to evaluate products and services. Use Parts A and B if your company sells a combination of products and services, such as engineering services and instruments or industrial components with follow-up service. You should do this type of evaluation for each product or class of products and perhaps for different potential markets as well, since the product you plan to sell in Japan may well be different from the one you want to sell in China.

For each factor listed, evaluate how your product rates. In the third column, specify what the product needs in order to make it suitable for its intended markets and uses. This is a first cut; you may need to refine after you have identified your intended market. In the final column, estimate the cost of exportizing or refining your product. These figures will be used in the financial analysis later on.

Examples.   Suppose your product is packaged spiced nuts to be sold from a vending machine. Market tests suggest it might gain substantial acceptance if the nuts were vacuum-packed in a can. However, your cans will not fit the vending machines in your most likely markets of Japan, Hong Kong, and Australia. To make your product suitable, you must find a source for cans of correct sizes, have production equipment that would handle these cans, and redesign your labels and packaging for the new can sizes.

If what your product needs for Pacific Rim success is adaptability for a variety of emerging opportunities, but it is designed to be a standardized component in the domestic market, you may have to re-engineer it for modularity and flexibility. Or, if what is needed for success is a price 20 percent below competing products to attract attention, you may have to cut the costs of your production process to reduce unit cost.

A. Is Your Product Suitable for Pacific Rim Trade?

Product _____

Factors Affecting Exportability	*How Your Product Measures Up*	*What You Need to Do*	*Cost of Exportizing*
1. Are there any U.S. limitations to its export?	_____	_____	$_____
2. Are there any Pacific Rim nation restrictions to its import?	_____	_____	_____
3. In what kinds of markets would your product be suitable as is?	_____	_____	_____
4. What refinements would adapt it to different markets?	_____	_____	_____
5. What market restrictions might your product encounter?	_____	_____	_____
6. How could it be modified to meet these restrictions (e.g., product standards)?	_____	_____	_____
7. What related products, services, technologies, or other factors must also be available in the market in order for your product to be in demand?	_____	_____	_____
8. How well can you protect key technologies, trade secrets in your product?	_____	_____	_____
9. How quickly can your product be refined to adapt to emerging opportunities?	_____	_____	_____
10. How transportable is your product?	_____	_____	_____
11. Is repackaging required for surface or air shipment?	_____	_____	_____
12. What factors, such as rough handling, temperature and humidity, resistance to pilferage and pests, duration of			

shipment, and distribution,
affect repackaging for each
stage of distribution to the
end user? _____ _____ _____

After you have completed Part A of the questionnaire, assess the impact on your domestic operation of refining your product for Pacific Rim markets. For example, under "Benefits," you might list (1) *new products for domestic markets as well;* (2) *new manufacturing processes available for domestic products;* or (3) *increased flexibility and rationality in product design, engineering, and production.* And under "Negatives," you might list (1) *conflicting noncomplementary production processes;* or (2) *struggle of two poorly integrated operations for scarce corporate resources.*

Benefits	*Negatives*
1. _____	1. _____
2. _____	2. _____
3. _____	3. _____
4. _____	4. _____
5. _____	5. _____
6. _____	6. _____

B. Is Your Service Suitable for Pacific Rim Trade?

Service _____

Factors Affecting Exportability	How Your Service Measures Up	What You Need to Do	Cost of Exportizing
1. Are there any Pacific Rim nation restrictions to its import?	_____	_____	$_____
2. Can it be adapted to trade restrictions?	_____	_____	_____
3. Are your systems to control quality of delivery and cost-effectiveness adequate?	_____	_____	_____
4. How can you adapt to local needs and tastes?	_____	_____	_____
5. How can you adapt to local inputs, e.g.:			
• Management.	_____	_____	_____
• Labor and personnel.	_____	_____	_____
• Ingredients and materials.	_____	_____	_____

- Facilities, special processes, other intellectual property. _____ _____ _____
- Means of promotion. _____ _____ _____

6. How can you protect trade secrets from competitors? _____ _____ _____

7. Can continuity of service be provided? _____ _____ _____

8. Can needed products and equipment be provided? _____ _____ _____

After you have completed Part B of the questionnaire, assess the impact on your domestic operation of refining your service for Pacific Rim markets. For example, under "Benefits," you might list (1) *new services for domestic markets*; or (2) *increased flexibility to adapt to different markets yet maintain quality standards*. And under "Negatives," you might list *noncompatible administrative and control systems*.

Benefits	*Negatives*
1. _____	1. _____
2. _____	2. _____
3. _____	3. _____
4. _____	4. _____
5. _____	5. _____
6. _____	6. _____

Which Markets to Target Initially

Defining the *Ideal* Market for Your Product or Service

The first step in selecting the best market to target initially is to define the *ideal* market for your product or service. To do this, you must know what you sell, who buys it, and why. This is a step many companies do not take for their domestic markets, let alone their international ones. You are not likely to find the ideal market, but defining what it is provides a baseline against which to evaluate and rank available markets. Some of the factors you need to consider are included in the questions below:

1. Who are your ideal customers?
   - If government agencies, which ministries, and at what level is the buying decision made? _____
   _____

   - If business or industry, what kinds of businesses or companies? Who makes the buying decision? _____
   _____

- If consumers, how do you reach them? Do you sell directly to them, or through distributors? What kind of distributors? _____

    _____

2. What are your buyers' demographics (e.g., for a consumer product: their affluence, culture, age, and sophistication; where they live, what other products they use; and their knowledge or experience)? _____

    _____

3. What related products, services, technologies, or other factors must also be available in the market in order for yours to be in demand? _____

    _____

4. What are the best means of distribution and promotion for your product or service?

    _____

    _____

5. What size market do you need? _____

    _____

6. What kind of competition are you best equipped to meet in your markets? _____

    _____

Basic Needs Met by Your Product or Service

Identify your customers' needs and then list how your product or service fulfills those needs. Some needs are suggested.

Need	*How Your Product/Service Meets Need*

For consumers

Basic food, shelter, and security	_____
Convenience	_____
Stylishness	_____
Efficiency	_____
Other	_____

For commercial or industrial customers

Producing products at low cost	_____
High quality	_____
Other	_____

For government

Providing energy to citizens _____
Providing education or
    health care _____
Other _____

Identifying Potential Markets

After you have defined the ideal market for your product or service, you must find the Pacific Rim market that best approximates it. Using the approach described in Chapter 3, answer the following questions for potential markets for your product or service, using information locally available to you. Your goal is to list the Pacific Rim nations in which there is a current or emerging market for your product or service.

1. In which nations or markets is your product or service used currently? _____
_____

2. In which nations or markets are conditions ripe for its introduction? Where is there an emerging readiness for it? _____
_____

3. Where are related products or services used, even though yours is not yet used?
_____
_____

Now list and prioritize the nations or markets, and select the most desirable or promising. You may begin by listing the ones you are eliminating from further consideration.

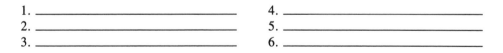

1. _____   4. _____
2. _____   5. _____
3. _____   6. _____

Analysis of Promising Markets

For your selected promising existing markets—or markets that you can create—answer the following questions:

1. *What are the demographics of the market?* Who buys what you sell? What characteristics apply to the customers for your products or services? Take into consideration the refinements you may introduce to your products or services so that they better fit the demands of the market.

• *For a consumer product or service*:
—Number of potential buyers _____
—Where and how they live _____
—Their affluence, disposable income _____
—Culture _____
—Other products they use _____
—Taste, style, quality preferences _____
—How concentrated or diffuse _____
—Age distribution _____
—Sophistication _____
—Knowledge or experience _____
—Customs and religious preferences _____
[*List other pertinent characteristics.*] _____
_____
_____

• *For a commercial or industrial product or service*:
—Nature and quality of buyers' products _____
—Manufacturing processes used _____
—Quality and performance of components _____
—Level of technology _____
—Cost structure _____
—Market strategy (e.g., low cost vs. high quality) _____
—Labor intensive vs. capital intensive _____
[*Add other pertinent factors.*] _____
_____

2. *What customer needs does your product or service meet? How do customers currently meet those needs?* _____
_____

3. *How close is the fit between your product or service and the needs of that marketplace?* _____
_____

4. *In what alternative ways can your product or service be used to satisfy these needs?*
_____
_____

5. *How would your product or service need to be refined, reengineered, repackaged, or refocused?* _____
_____

6. *What does a consumer need in order to purchase, operate, maintain, and repair your product or service?* Consider related products, services, technologies, or other factors that must be available in the market in order for yours to succeed. _____
_____

7. *How can you compensate for any needed demographic or market factors that are not available?* _____

_____

8. *How easy or difficult would it be to reach targeted customers?* _____

_____

9. *What means of distribution and promotion are available, and how appropriate are they for your product or service?* _____

_____

10. *How might you refine your product or service in order to make it more suitable for a target Pacific Rim market?* Examples might be: (1) *re-engineering and lowering cost to make the price more competitive*; (2) *changing the range of sizes*; (3) *changing the options available*; (4) *simplifying it so that less skill is required for its use or maintenance*; (5) *making it part of a more complete package*; (6) *changing the quality or considering making a higher- or lower-quality product with lower price*; (7) *using different raw materials*; or (8) *adapting it to the tastes, customs, styles, or religious preferences of your customers.* _____

_____
_____
_____
_____
_____

A. Market Factors

1. What is the size of the target market?
   - Total market size
     - At present _____
     - Potential for growth _____
   - Proportion of the market you can expect to capture, considering the competition

   _____

2. How many units can you expect to sell? _____

3. What market-entry restrictions will you encounter in the market?
   - U.S. export licensing requirements _____
   - Quotas, tariffs, and import licenses _____
   - Prohibitions, limitations, and delays _____
   - Lack of protection _____
   - Exchange permits _____
   - Barriers to competing with existing competitors _____

4. How will you be able to sufficiently protect your intellectual property (patents, trade secrets, copyrights)? _____

5. What incentives are available from the government for your type of business? ___
_____

6. What special factors might increase the potential market size (is the market a regional distribution center, as Singapore is for ASEAN)? _____

7. Are needed resources available? _____
   - Are sources of trade or investment finance accessible to you? _____
   - Do needed distribution channels exist, or must they be created? _____
   - Are suitable market partners available (a distributor, representative, licensee, joint venture partner)? _____
   - How easy or difficult is it to start up operations there? What are the unusual cost factors? How long can it take? _____
   - Can you find qualified and affordable personnel (sales, management, technical, production)? _____

8. How long should it take to commence operations, to become profitable, and to recover costs? _____

B. Political Stability

1. What positive and negative factors may affect your ability to carry on business successfully? _____
   - What are local attitudes toward business, foreign investment and ownership, imports, American goods? _____
   - How much flexibility exists in types of permissible operation? _____

C. Economic Stability

1. How secure would your payments be? _____

2. What is the risk of not being able to get your profits or capital out? _____

3. Can you obtain credit insurance or guarantees? _____

4. How stable is the currency? Is it pegged to the dollar? _____

D. Political Factors Favoring Your Competitor

- Government protection _____

- Local company, old-boy network _____

• Established traditional supplier _____

• Size and clout _____

Comparisons With Competitors in Your Intended Markets

Determine how competitive world markets are for your product or service. Who provides it now? What is the customer's current alternative to your product or service? What does it cost him? Where is he getting it? What competitive advantages do you have and what disadvantages would you face? At what price would it have to leave plant or headquarters to meet the competitive market price? What is the best strategy to beat the competition?

Identify each of the likely competitors for your product or service in your potential Pacific Rim markets, as shown below. These may include American or multinational companies or local companies in your intended market. List your competitors, their product or service that competes with yours, and their strong selling points. You should consider not just similar products manufactured by competitors but also any other products that fill the same need for the end user.

Your Competitive Advantages and Weaknesses

Ideally, this type of evaluation needs to be done for each product, for each market, and against each competitor. The more thorough you are, the more likely it is that

Chief Competitors	*Competitive Product/Service*	*Its Strong Selling Points*
Other U.S. companies		
1. _____	_____	_____
2. _____	_____	_____
3. _____	_____	_____
International competitors		
1. _____	_____	_____
2. _____	_____	_____
3. _____	_____	_____
Local businesses in that market		
1. _____	_____	_____
2. _____	_____	_____
3. _____	_____	_____

you will identify competitive advantages that reveal lucrative opportunities for you. Identifying competitive weaknesses is equally important. They may signal that you should avoid that market or may point out needed refinements in your products or distribution. You may also be able to emphasize your competitive strengths in a way that compensates for your competitive weaknesses.

The following list of qualities is not intended to be exhaustive. Add other features desired by distributors and end users of your product or service.

	Your Competitive Advantages	*Your Competitive Weaknesses*
Low-price provider	_____	_____
Low-cost producer	_____	_____
Unique product, service, or features	_____	_____
Complete, turnkey package of products and services	_____	_____
Availability		
To distributors	_____	_____
To end users	_____	_____
Prestige ("Made in USA")	_____	_____
Quality, reliability	_____	_____
Special technological capability	_____	_____
Special production capability	_____	_____
Special design, engineering, or R&D	_____	_____
Flexibility of design or application	_____	_____
Financing available to customer	_____	_____
Responsiveness to changing customer needs, to competitive pressures	_____	_____
Easily sold by local market partners	_____	_____
Postsale service and maintenance, spare parts	_____	_____
Assistance to distributors		
Promotion and advertising	_____	_____
Training and sales assistance	_____	_____
Postsale technical support	_____	_____
Rapid response	_____	_____
Product/service that is part of complete line	_____	_____
Other	_____	_____
	_____	_____
	_____	_____

Now summarize the features of your current products or services that provide a competitive edge for entering Pacific Rim markets.

1. _____
2. _____
3. _____
4. _____

Sales Volume

To determine sales volume, begin by attaching some numbers to the rough estimates of market size you have made. For each product or service you intend to sell, ask yourself: If I am able to sell at a competitive price in the market, how many *units* am I likely to sell? Make high and low estimates. Ignore price for now; just assume you can sell profitably at a competitive price.

1. What is the total size of the market? _____

2. How much of it can you hope to capture, considering the existing competitors, how entrenched they are, other products or services that meet the same needs for your customers, your strengths, and the difficulties in penetrating the market? _____
   _____

3. What will your strategy be? _____
   • How much market share can you capture? _____
   • How big a market can you create? _____

4. What will be the upper constraint on how much you can sell in the short run? _____
   • Size of the market? _____
   • Competitive pressure? _____
   • How much you can produce? _____

5. Is your initial probable demand high enough for you to consider investing in additional facilities, or will you be able to produce enough in your existing facilities? _____

6. Will refinements on exportizing—or the development of new products—require substantial investment in engineering or new facilities? _____
   _____

7. Your sales volume will, of course, vary with different prices. You must decide, based on market characteristics, whether you will adopt a strategy of (1) low price, low profit, high volume—market penetration; or (2) high price, high profit, low volume—skimming the cream. What is your likely marketing and pricing strategy? _____
   _____

You can estimate market share only in an existing market with established competitors. If you are supplying a product or service new to the market (or a unique version of existing products or services), then you must analyze the customer needs that your product or service satisfies and estimate how many potential customers you can induce to switch from the way they are presently fulfilling those needs (including neglecting them). You should use that figure as your estimated market share in item 3 of the preceding list and in item 2 of the following table.

Your goal is to make an initial rough estimate of market size and your potential sales volume, since production volume is an essential factor in determining cost and setting your price.

1. Size of the market   _____ units
   Share of the market you can reasonably expect to
   capture   _____ %
   Resulting sales volume, at the "market price"   _____ units
2. Discounted expected market size by uncertainty   discount by _____ %
   about how secure and stable the market would be
   for you   _____ units

Is the Market Big Enough?

Market size is often very hard to determine, especially for smaller companies with new products or services. An alternative way to evaluate the promise of an undefined market is to work backward. First determine how much you need to sell initially in the market to meet your goals. Then research the market and evaluate the chances of your selling that much.

If your likely market size or share is very uncertain, then, to compensate, you need a very low overhead export operation so that a lower than expected level of sales is not disastrous (you may set prices using a marginal contribution approach described later); or else you must be well capitalized and willing to operate at a loss while you build market share.

Evaluating Profitability of Pacific Rim Trade

Setting Your Price

What will determine your price? Is there an existing market price for the same or very similar products or services? Are related products or services similar enough to allow you to guesstimate a workable initial price for yours, or will your product or service be unique enough for you to price it by full cost? There are two basic approaches to setting your price: (1) You can set your price to cover your costs plus profit or (2) you can set your costs to sell profitably at the market price. Often prices are set by a combination of the two approaches, and initially you should cost things out both ways. The approach you adopt depends on how unique your product or service is and the price sensitivity of the market.

How Price Sensitive Is Your Market?

To gauge the sensitivity of sales to price level in a potential market, look at such factors as:

- *The availability of substitutes.* If competing products are not readily available, then yours are less price sensitive.
- *How often customers purchase your product.* If infrequently, then your products are less price sensitive.
- *The impact of the purchase on the buyer's budget.* If little, then there is less price sensitivity.

If the market is small and diffuse with few competitors, then prices and margins are typically higher, to compensate for greater risk and uncertainty. In many cases, companies decide that a concentrated market with more competition and slimmer margins may be more attractive than a diffuse market with higher margins—one reason why more companies establish operations in Japan than in Australia.

A. Set Your Price to Cover Costs Plus Profit

Make this calculation first, even if you strongly suspect your price will be largely controlled by market forces. There are several different kinds of costs to consider, depending on the form of your Pacific Rim operation.

Incremental costs of production or delivering a service	$ _____
Special costs of exporting	_____
Start-up and marketing costs	_____
New facilities and product development	_____

Incremental Costs of Production or Delivering a Service. If you will be selling essentially the same product or service with little need for additional inventory or working capital, your price must cover direct costs of whatever you produce for export—plus allocations to overhead and profit. Find the unit price for the following:

Direct cost of producing the goods for export, such as labor and
materials (cost of goods sold) $ _____
Manufacturing overhead,* related to the production facility, such as
rent, maintenance, and depreciation of equipment   _____
Nonmanufacturing overhead;* selling and administrative expenses:
  Cost of selling, such as travel, sales salaries, packaging, com-
    missions, or discounts   _____
  Costs of exporting   _____

*Based on estimated sales volume

Cost of working capital needed to finance this expansion $ _____
Standard profit margin based on estimated annual sales volume   _____

You are most likely to use this approach to setting prices if (1) you have extra capacity or other unused resources (e.g., production labor) you can apply to produce goods for export (otherwise, the investment in expanded facilities or resources must be factored in); (2) you will sell currently available products or services in the new markets (otherwise the cost of development or re-engineering must be factored in); or (3) you have a unique product or service that competitors cannot match, so that you can get full price.

You can use your unit price as the basis for making initial quotations if you have trouble getting information on competitive prices. If your quotation is rejected, then you can begin negotiating, and thus discover the real market price.

Using Incremental Costs to Price Your Services. To price a service using the approach just described, replace "cost of goods sold" with "cost of services delivered." Your direct costs will emphasize labor, communication, and travel, plus management and quality control costs. Do not ignore costs associated with shipping fixtures, equipment, supplies and materials, literature, and sending people into the new market.

You may be bidding for jobs by making a price quotation in competition with similar businesses. Too many service businesses fail to include all cost factors in bids and price estimates, so they are actually losing money on each sale; they are subsidizing their customers. Your costs for a service include:

Direct materials, parts, and supplies used on specific jobs $ _____
Direct labor   _____
Direct transportation (shipping and travel) and communication—usu-
   ally a major factor in Pacific Rim services   _____
Overhead   _____
Profit margin   _____
Setup costs   _____

Special Costs of Exporting. Make sure you do not neglect the special costs of exporting either a product or a service as compared with producing for a new domestic market. If you hold title until your goods reach the final user, then you must identify every cost element through distribution. You should do this even for a service business, such as a franchise, for which you must ship equipment, supplies, or some components. If you sell through a market partner, it is still important for you to know all these costs. These include:

Extra inventory (to build up enough to fill a shipping container or to
   meet greater variability in your shipping schedule) $ _____
Packing for overseas shipment. Cost of containers are based on volume,
   not weight. Companies redesign packages to reduce volume of packing material.   _____

Paperwork $ _____
Inland transportation charges and loading fees   _____
Freight forwarder fees   _____
Insurance at each stage   _____
Transportation by sea or air   _____
Cost of capital for time of shipment and storage   _____
Hiring customs brokers   _____
Storage fees while awaiting customs   _____
Customs clearance charges   _____
Import duties and related fees   _____
Repackaging for distribution and sale in your destination   _____
Replacing lost or damaged goods   _____
Financial management strategies (e.g., exchange rate hedging)   _____

B. Set Your Costs to Meet the Market Price.

Can you sell profitably at the market price? To find out, work backward from the prevailing price to determine the price at which the product must leave your facility in order for it to be competitive in your intended market. You must first find out current market prices of comparable products or services, including others used in its place.

To induce potential customers to switch, you must overcome their cost of establishing new arrangements with a different supplier. This takes time for the buyer, and there is a social cost as well. This factor is particularly important in the Pacific Rim, where relationships are of crucial importance in doing business.

If you are developing products to create a new niche in an otherwise established market, then you can get a good idea of a competitive price by analyzing other related products or substitutes. You may then work backward to find out if you can design a product or service and profitably supply it to the market at that price.

Then progressively deduct all costs from that price until you reach your front door, and compare that market-based cost with your actual unit cost (including overhead burden and profit margin).

From End User.   If you will be selling to end users, start from the retail price.

Prevailing market price of comparable products or services (converted
    to $US) $ _____
Deduct a discount from market price that you must offer in order to
    induce customers to switch from their current product to yours   – _____
Then deduct:
    Selling costs (salaries, commissions, discounts) $ _____
    Distribution costs   _____
    Promotion and advertising costs   _____

Export costs (shipping, insurance, documentation, fees, repackaging)	$ _____
Import fees, costs, and duties	_____
Cost of sales financing	_____
Allowances for returns, breakage, loss	_____
Export overhead burden	_____
Total	− _____

Market-based cost $ _____

From Market Partner. If you will be selling through a market partner, work from the wholesale price at which you would supply the product to him.

Discounted price to market partner (converted to $US)	$ _____
Deduct:	
Any export costs borne by you (most, but perhaps not all, will be paid by the market partner)	$ _____
Any selling costs borne by you (e.g., travel to the market)	_____
Ongoing costs associated with sales (technical support)	_____
Warranty, service, and maintenance	_____
Total	− _____

Price you can get FOB your U.S. port $ _____

Can You Sell at That Cost? The market-based cost that you have determined is the price at which it must leave the United States for it to be competitive in your intended market. Can you profitably supply it FOB at a U.S. port at that price?

If NO, Then . . . If the market-based cost is lower than your current "out the door" cost, you still have several options:

1. *Don't enter that market now.*

2. *Don't recover all your costs.* Enter the market if the market price still covers direct costs and selling costs and makes some contribution to profit and to overhead. You must pay those costs even if you are not producing anything. This is called marginal contribution pricing.

You would normally use this approach only where you have excess productive capacity that cannot be used in domestic markets and if—because of competitive pressures—you cannot export at a price high enough to cover all costs. If that is the case, it may be better to sell at a lower price and obtain some contribution to overhead and profit than to leave resources idle.

If you price on this basis for too long, you reduce your overall profitability.

However, companies choose to do this in order to gain a foothold in a new market. You may decide you can live with thinner profit margins initially until you can develop new products that can be produced more cheaply.

3. *Push features that justify higher price.* Differentiate your product or service in the minds of your buyers. Promote features so that it can command a higher price than competing ones. Too many companies pay lip service to this but neglect to follow up on a regular basis. What features can you promote to justify a higher market price?

4. *Cut your costs to meet the price.* Redesign the product or production process so that your product can be produced more cheaply and still fit the needs of the market, and thus can be sold profitably at the prevailing market price. How can you supply equal quality at lower cost? Can you create acceptance for a lower-quality, lower-priced product? As essential as cost cutting is, it is often only a temporary tactic to market success. In the longer run, you must invest in the R&D to turn out innovative products.

5. *Redesign your product or service to obtain market share.* The market-share philosophy, used so effectively by the Japanese, rejects the "cost + profit = price" approach. Instead, start with a price that will best develop a desired market share, and then design a product and a production method for a cost that will leave your company with a profit. The price should include not just direct costs but also the cost of R&D, design, production processes, and facilities.

Needed Investment and Cost of Capital

Including the Cost of New Investment in Your Price. Unless you can enter your new market using existing products and resources, you will have to make an additional investment, and the cost of capital for this investment is a factor that must be covered in your price. You need initial ballpark estimates of additional capital needed so that you can obtain sufficient capitalization and estimate its cost. Make sure you take into consideration all the different kinds of investment costs. To determine the initial investment required, enter all the costs incurred before production or selling commences on the following chart.

Cost Factor	*Cost*	*Time Required*
1. Identify markets, market partners.		
Market research	$ _____	_____
Travel to the markets	_____	_____
Outside consultants and information	_____	_____
Establishing relationships	_____	_____
Finding and selecting a market partner *or*		
setting up distribution network	_____	_____

Investigating and selecting
    Facilities $ _____   _____
    Personnel   _____   _____
2. Expand production in your current facility.
    New equipment   _____   _____
    New production processes   _____   _____
    Administrative facilities   _____   _____
    Distribution facilities   _____   _____
3. Expand working capital and inventory.
    Domestic raw materials   _____   _____
    Finished goods at Pacific Rim distributor   _____   _____
4. Redesign or exportize your product,
   service, and packaging.
    Re-engineering or redesign   _____   _____
    Repackaging   _____   _____
    Translating packaging; selling, marketing,
       and technical materials   _____   _____
5. Research and develop new product or service for
   the market.
6. Initial marketing and promotion.
    Public relations, advertising   _____   _____
    Participating in trade missions   _____   _____
7. Determine start-up costs for entering the
   market.   _____   _____
8. Establish Pacific Rim operation.
    Sales and distribution facilities   _____   _____
    Production facilities   _____   _____
9. Develop new financial and administrative systems.
    Legal groundwork   _____   _____
    Contractual preparation   _____   _____
    Obtaining licenses and permissions   _____   _____
    Hiring and training new people   _____   _____
       Sending your people to the new market   _____   _____
       Bringing Pacific Rim people to your facil-
          ities   _____   _____
10. *Enter cost of capital*   (_____)   _____
    Total $ _____   _____

Now list sources and costs of capital. Sources might include internal, short-term loan, long-term loan, or equity.

Use of Capital	When Needed	Source	Amount Needed	Cost of Obtaining	Annual Percentage Rate	Annual $ Cost
Working capital	_____	_____	$ _____	$ _____	_____ %	$ _____
Financing sales	_____	_____	_____	_____	_____	_____

Long-term
  investment_____   _____ $ ____ $ _____   _____ % $ _____
Other   _____   _____   _____   _____   _____   _____

    Total (average) $ ____ $ _____   _____ % $ _____

Total Investment Capital Needed

From these estimates you can get a rough idea of how much capital you will need. Remember two rules (the first one offered is only partially tongue in cheek):

1. Since everything costs more than you expect, double whatever totals you come up with.
2. Even if you are well-capitalized and do not need new outside capital, figure your cost of capital.

Total capital needed (from above totals) $ _____
Fudge factor   × _____
Capital really needed $ _____

Cost of Capital in Your Price. The purpose of doing all this is to determine costs so you can set a price that will give you a profitable operation. The following equation

Annual cost of investment = amount of investment needed × interest rate for capital

will give you an estimated dollar cost of capital that must be allocated to yearly volume of sales in the same way as anticipated overhead and profit margin. You can easily include your cost of investment in any of the approaches described: cost-based pricing, market-based costing, or marginal contribution estimates.

Investment Amortization in Your Price. To set prices that recover your cost of additional investment, you must write off some portion of the investment each year as a cost of doing business. This write-off (or amortization) period can be related to your cost of capital, the useful life of your investment, or a targeted payback period. If you made a onetime investment of $1 million in your new Pacific Rim operation and wanted to recover your investment in ten years, then you would have to set your prices to recover and write off $100,000 each year.

Initial investment $ _____
Desired payback period (in years)   ÷ _____
Investment to be amortized each year
    (and included in your projections $ _____
    as a cost of business)

Need for Ongoing Investment. Outside of your operational expenses, you must allow for an additional annual investment in these same categories. It is the "recurring nature of nonrecurring expenses." These are very difficult to estimate, since they are by definition unknown and unanticipated. However, you should at least guesstimate a percentage of the initial investment for each item, for example:

Further additions to your administrative or production facilities   _____ %
Further refinement of your product, service, and packaging   _____ %
Ongoing hiring and training of new people   _____ %
Increases in working capital as sales increase   _____ %

A schedule of these figures on a year-by-year basis should be included in your calculations of payback period or net present value (NPV).

Pro Forma Financial Statements

If you have several different options, then financial return is an important criterion for selecting among them. You should have enough data now—for each of your most promising options—to put all the information together into a financial statement. Use a format similar to the one on the following pages to do a pro forma profit and loss (P&L) statement for each option—as it will look after it is under way—using the price, sales volume, and cost figures that you have previously calculated for each option. You can see whether an option "pencils out," and can also begin to compare the return of different options. The profit figures can be used to compare investments (as discussed in the next section).

You may want to use the following approaches to compare the many different types of options. For example:

- Low-cost, high-volume provider versus high-price, lower-volume, top-of-the-line provider
- Investing in Singapore versus Taiwan
- Establishing your own operation in Australia versus selling through an established distributor
- Building your own factory versus joint venturing with an existing plant owner
- Selling through an export management company versus finding a representative in the target market

For figures on which to base meaningful estimates, you may want to obtain industry averages. You could also rely on your own company's past performance. Those approaches are extremely dangerous, however, when going into new markets that are very different from what you are used to.

Pro Forma Revenue and Profitability Estimate

Project _____
Year _____

	Amount	*Percentage of Gross Revenue*
GROSS REVENUE	$ _____	

Units sold _____ × price @$ _____ − direct selling costs

Less cost of goods sold (or cost of services delivered)

	Amount	*Percentage of Gross Revenue*
Labor, materials, equipment leasing	_____	_____ %
Subcontracted services	_____	_____
Shipping and other export costs	_____	_____
Sales finance	_____	_____
GROSS PROFIT	$ _____	
GROSS MARGIN		_____ %

ONGOING COSTS OF OPERATION
Manufacturing Overhead

	Amount	*Percentage of Gross Revenue*
Facilities cost and depreciation	$ _____	_____%

Administrative Overhead

Facilities cost and depreciation	_____	_____
Communication	_____	_____
Professional services	_____	_____

Selling and Marketing Costs

Sales salaries	_____	_____
Advertising and promotion	_____	_____
Field servicing and technical support	_____	_____
Inventory carrying cost	_____	_____
Travel	_____	_____
Cost of capital	_____	_____
Total	$ _____	_____

	Amount	*Percentage of Gross Revenue*
NET PROFIT	$ _____	_____ %
Less taxes	_____	_____
Plus value of tax incentives		
U.S. incentives	_____	_____
Target country incentives	_____	_____

NET PROFIT AFTER TAXES $ _____

RETURN ON SALES   _____ %

Return on Investment

For return on investment (ROI) use the following equation:

$$\text{Rate of ROI} = \frac{\text{net profit after taxes}}{\text{total investment for operation}} \times 100$$

Rank the net income figures and ROI for each option. Estimate how soon you will begin getting revenue. If you sell through an export management company, you may begin generating revenue quicker than if you set up your own distributor, even though profit rate may be lower.

Option	Net Income	ROI	Rank
1. _____	_____	_____	☐
2. _____	_____	_____	☐
3. _____	_____	_____	☐
4. _____	_____	_____	☐
5. _____	_____	_____	☐
6. _____	_____	_____	☐

Comparing Profitability of Your Investment Alternatives

To compare the attractiveness of alternative operations, consider how long it takes to begin getting a return, since revenue sooner is better than revenue later.

Payback Period. The easiest tool to use for comparing investments is the payback period—the number of years it will take for profits from the operations to repay your investment. Use the figures from above to calculate your payback period. Make sure you include not just your initial investment but your ongoing investment.

a. Initial and ongoing investment $ _____
b. Years until operation becomes profitable   _____
c. Estimated annual profit thereafter $ _____
d. Payback period $= b + (a \div c)$ _____

The drawback to using the payback period is that it ignores the time value of money (that is, it assumes a 0 percent cost of capital). Even so, it is useful for a first-pass evaluation of situations in which other sources of uncertainty overwhelm the cost of capital. It also assumes that there is no residual value to your investment—that it is completely written off by the end of your payback period. That may well be the case, especially if the bulk of your investment is for items other than plant and equipment. Another drawback is that comparing payback periods biases you toward favoring short-term payoffs, which is just the opposite of the thinking needed for many Pacific Rim markets. Yet Pacific Rim investors use payback period as an essential tool to judge investments with long-term uncertainty. In Hong Kong, for example, many companies insist that their investment be recouped by 1997, when China resumes sovereignty.

Breakeven Level of Sales for Pacific Rim Operation. It is often useful to estimate how many units you need to sell, given a particular price, in order to break even. You break even when the gross profits left after direct costs just cover the fixed costs, which include overhead, cost of capital, and amortization of initial and ongoing investment. In other words, breakeven occurs when:

The number of units sold × (unit price − incremental cost of goods sold CGS)
= incremental fixed costs
(= overhead + cost of capital + investment amortization)

Reshuffling these terms gives you:

$$\text{Breakeven level of unit sales} = \frac{\text{incremental fixed costs}}{\text{unit price} - \text{incremental CGS per unit}}$$

If you can get needed data about your intended market, project your market share and sales for different prices at which you might sell, and then do a breakeven calculation for the price that maximizes your revenue.

NPV. The value of cash flows to be received in the future must be discounted, since getting a dollar next year is less valuable than getting a dollar today. To find the NPV of an investment you may make, calculate the present value of the expected future returns from the investment, discounted by the cost of capital, and subtract from this the initial cost of the project. The net return for each year is defined as the net profit after taxes, plus depreciation. It is calculated by using this formula:

$$\text{NPV} = \left[\frac{R_1}{(1 + k)^1} + \frac{R_2}{(1 + k)^2} + \cdots + \frac{R_N}{(1 + k)^N}\right] - C$$
$$= \sum_{t=1}^{N} \frac{R_t}{(1 + k)^t} - C$$

where:

C = initial investment for the project

R = net cash inflow for each year of the project's useful life (R_1 is the inflow from year 1, R_2 from year 2, and so on)

N = number of years in the project's expected useful life

t = any particular year

k = cost of capital expressed as a decimal

To see how you can use NPV to compare investment alternatives, look at the example shown in Table 10-3. Two projects have an initial cost (C) of $9 million and $12 million respectively, and have different lifetimes and different net cash flows. Capital cost (k) is 10 percent for both. First set up a table of inflows and outflows as shown in the table. For a simple example, this can be done by hand. For more complex jobs, use a calculator with this function built in, or a simple personal computer program that can guide you through these calculations. If you are not familiar with such calculations, turn the task over to someone who knows what he or she is doing.

The result, as shown in Table 10-3, is a pair of figures that rank the present values of the future ROI for each option. Since both projects have positive NPVs at a capital cost of 10 percent, both could be profitably undertaken. If an NPV is negative, then the project will lose money. If you could undertake only one project or the other as shown in the table, you would select Project B, with the higher NPV, even though it would cost more initially and take longer to begin yielding returns.

Table 10-3. NPVs of two investments.

Year	Project A ($000)			Project B ($000)		
	Net Cash Inflows	$\frac{1}{(1+k)^t}$	Present Value	Net Cash Inflows	$\frac{1}{(1+k)^t}$	Present Value
1	$4,000	.91	$ 3,640	$ 0	.91	$ 0
2	5,000	.83	4,150	2,000	.83	1,660
3	3,000	.75	2,250	4,000	.75	3,000
4	1,500	.68	1,020	5,000	.68	3,400
5				5,000	.62	3,100
6				6,000	.56	3,360
Present value of inflows:			$11,060			$14,520
Less project's initial cost:			9,000			12,000
NPV:			$ 2,060			$ 2,520

You can elaborate quite a bit on NPV analyses. For example, you can take into account ongoing investments that are spread over several years, such as market research and product refinement in year 0, new product development in year 1, and upgrading production facilities in year 2. Each of these can be treated as part of the initial investment (*C*) by calculating its present value for year 0. Remember, however, that you are using this calculation as a tool to compare the viability of several different alternative investment options, so don't get too complicated.

The NPV figures for two investments with greatly different initial cash outlays are hard to compare, since they are dollar figures. To neutralize this factor to better compare two different-size projects, convert them into a ratio by dividing the NPV of each project by the amount of its initial cost.

Drawbacks to NPV. NPV is biased toward short-term projects. The method was developed to evaluate a new machine that wears out and has a known useful lifetime. Pacific Rim investments often take several years to begin paying off, and may pay off more in the longer run. Relying too much on NPV can bias you against the long-term outlook that is often so essential for a successful Pacific Rim operation.

The opposing viewpoint is that since the degree of uncertainty increases rapidly as you expand your horizon, it is appropriate to greatly discount returns in more distant years. Thus, many companies select a certain period or a number of years during which a new project must justify itself.

I am suggesting that you use the NPV method to help make a strategic decision: not just whether to buy Machine A or Machine B but whether to expand your Silicon Valley plant or instead form a joint venture with a Japanese manu-

---

Investments Having a Definite Useful Lifetime

- Plant and equipment
- Knowledge, technology, patents, designs, trade secrets that will eventually be eclipsed or be supplanted or become common knowledge

Investments That Can Last Indefinitely
(IF you continue to nurture them)

- Working relationships, customer relationships
- General expertise or knowledge of an operation or a market
- Good location
- Reputation; brand or name recognition
- Human capital; trained and dedicated people
- "Corporate habits," e.g., of product and market R&D and production quality and productivity

facturer in Osaka. To use NPV as a strategic tool, you must think about the true useful lifetime of the items in which you may invest.

Internal Rate of Return.   We should mention the internal rate of return (IRR) method, which is also used by many businesses and is closely related to NPV. The IRR (or *r* in the following formula) is defined as the interest rate that equates the present value of the expected future net returns to the initial investment.

$$\frac{R_1}{(1 + r)^1} + \frac{R_2}{(1 + r)^2} + \ldots + \frac{R_N}{(1 + r)^N} - C = 0$$

As you can see, IRR and NPV both use the same basic equation. The IRR formula is the NPV formula solved for the value of *k* (the cost of capital) that makes the NPV equal zero. *r* must be solved by trial and error or by plugging figures into a computer program. In many situations, NPV and IRR will rank projects in the same order, and in those where the ranking is different, most financial officers feel that the NPV provides a better guideline.

"Wild Card" Factors

In selecting your market, you cannot rely solely on a quantitative analysis. The danger of relying on numbers is "garbage in, gospel out"—especially when numbers appear on a nice computer printout. The tools just described tend to put too much emphasis on numerical comparison, even though the underlying numbers may conceal a lot of uncertainty. You also need to consider other hard-to-quantify factors such as the following, which may turn out to be at least as important as how the numbers stack up. To what extent is each of these true for your situation?

- ☐ A unique opportunity fell into your lap.
- ☐ You have a special connection to a certain country or market.
- ☐ There are easy existing channels that you could take advantage of.
- ☐ Your domestic or other international markets will soon be saturated or are already shrinking.
- ☐ You have too much production capacity for current domestic markets.
- ☐ You see new opportunities for profit in related product lines or markets, and expanding overseas is the best way to gain access.
- ☐ You can compete better in international than in domestic markets. There is too much domestic competition, and you have greater competitive advantage in Pacific Rim markets. Your company may find it easier to penetrate Pacific Rim markets than to increase its share of the domestic market.
- ☐ You need to keep pace with competitors, domestic or foreign. You need to go international to protect trade secrets in international markets and market share in domestic markets.

☐ You need to counter incursions by overseas companies into your domestic markets.

☐ You have been exporting to other nations or regions such as Latin America or Europe and are having problems with some of these markets. You need to replace them.

☐ You need to improve your company's performance by upgrading or broadening your production or marketing skills.

These quantitative tools are decision aids, not decision makers. They are no substitute for traveling to the markets and checking things out on your own.

11 | Pacific Rim Profiles

* *Current economic situation*
* *Trade and investment opportunities*
* *Developments to watch for*

This chapter sketches each Pacific Rim nation we have discussed, describing the current economic situation, trade and investment opportunities, some of the problems of doing business there, and developments to watch for.

JAPAN

Despite the intense competition in Japanese markets, on the whole, they have never been more open to American goods, services, or investment. Japan is busy importing American popular culture. Many of the U.S. companies that do best there are those that sell consumer items: fast food, ice cream, pop music and movies, and fashion. Competition in these areas comes largely from the NICs, which, after all, are major suppliers of consumer products to the United States.

Japanese consumers have a growing appetite for foreign goods, and there is a large growth of imports to Japan substituting for Japanese-made goods. Although many of these are supplied by the NICs, which have labor-cost advantages over the United States, there are clearly opportunities in this area for aggressive American companies that seek market opportunities. So far, the Europeans have been much more aggressive than the Americans in grabbing Japanese markets.

In the commercial and industrial sectors, the greatest opportunities for American companies lie in electronics components (often sold in conjunction with a Japanese partner), telecommunications equipment (often sold through Nippon Telephone and Telegraph), computer hardware and software (custom-designed software accounts for 93 percent of this market), and medical and dental equipment (recent changes have eased the certification process). Other promising markets for U.S. exporters include CAD/CAM (computer-aided design and manufacturing), agricultural chemicals, and graphic arts equipment. In the consumer products sector, opportunities include apparel, jewelry, housewares, household electrical appliances, sporting goods, recreational equipment, automobile parts and accessories, health foods, and pet foods. U.S. service companies are making inroads in product design, marketing, advertising, R&D, management services, health care services, consumer financial services, insurance, banking, and data communications. Japanese financial markets have been liberalized, allowing foreign companies to enter Japanese banking and finance.

Japan

Exchange rate (US $1 =)	135 yen
Population	120 million
GDP or GNP	$2.8 trillion
Growth rate of GNP	4%
Per capita income	$23,000
Inflation rate	1.7%
Budget deficit	
Labor force	60 million
Unemployment	2.6%
Trade balance	$101 billion
U.S. exports to	$27 billion
U.S. imports from	$88 billion
Trade balance with United States	+$48 billion
U.S. share of imports	22%
Percentage total U.S. direct investment	%
Language	Japanese
Ethnic makeup	Japanese
Religion	Buddhist, Shinto
Government leader	Prime Minister Noboru Takeshita
Government	Prime minister decided by brokering within leading party
Relative size	California

Distribution

Japan has four times as many wholesalers and retailers per capita as the United States. Smaller companies seeking to enter Japanese markets often start out by working through a Japanese trading company. The nine largest trading companies, called the *sogoshosha,* handle about half of all Japanese imports and exports, but if your company handles more specialized products, you should investigate the specialized trading company, *senmosha,* that handles your type of product. A specialized trading company can handle most phases of your products' journey through customs to end user. The right one will have access to the various special distribution channels and provide the aftersales service required. You might also look into "captive" trading companies owned by Japanese manufacturers or merchandisers. Many of these are essentially foreign buying agents for their parent companies.

A number of American trading companies are located in Japan as well, but your selection of a trading company should not be based on nationality but on whether it has access to the needed distribution channels and can provide the aftersales service required by your product.

New, independent distributors are springing up to circumvent established middlemen and meet the skyrocketing demand for lower-priced, high-quality, and imported consumer products. Discount stores are challenging the big department store chains. Many of these are eagerly seeking foreign suppliers.

U.S. and European companies in Japan are profitable and, according to a 1987 report by the consulting firm of Booz, Allen, and Hamilton, Inc., are increasing their investments. The earnings of foreign companies in Japan are as high as they are in other countries. These companies are not hampered by high operating costs or government barriers. According to the 400 American and European companies surveyed, their major problems include the complexity of doing business in Japan, the difficulty of finding professional staff, winning customers from competitors, and mastering the distribution system.

These companies agree that in order to compete globally, it is essential to have a presence in Japan. Thus the trend is to increase investment, particularly in R&D, manufacturing, and financial services. The importance of having a presence in Japan is to keep a finger on the pulse of your markets there. Many more companies are exporting to Japan from American factories as the dollar drops and Japan's import barriers diminish.

The Booz, Allen, and Hamilton report shows that new subsidiaries take on the average four years to break even—seven years to reach corporate profit levels. It also suggests that joint ventures are not a faster route to profitability. The trend is for foreign companies to set up their own subsidiaries in Japan rather than to establish joint ventures with Japanese partners.

Contracting

American companies now have the opportunity to participate in major Japanese construction projects. Under strong pressure from the United States and other countries, Japan is allowing foreign businesses to compete fairly in the bidding process for planned projects of more than $60 billion. These projects include airports, bridges, port facilities, roads, and tunnels. There will be opportunities for American companies in all phases of the projects, from design through construction to equipment.

Smaller Companies

Multinationals are not the only companies setting up operations in Japan. According to the Japan office of the U.S. Electronics Industry, dozens of smaller electronics companies have been setting up Japanese offices each year since the mid-

1980s, despite the very high costs. Many executives of these companies say that despite the high cost of keeping American personnel in these offices, the rewards make it well worth it.

These smaller companies have succeeded in the United States by an entrepreneurial responsiveness to what customers want, especially quality, reliability, and quick response. The same factors allow them to succeed in the tough Japanese markets against Japanese companies.

R&D Labs

Major multinationals in the chemical and pharmaceutical industries such as Kodak, Dupont, Upjohn, and W. R. Grace & Company are building research laboratories in Japan. These pioneers have opened the door for smaller companies.

These multinationals have set up Japanese subsidiaries for several reasons: Even though it is very expensive to begin operations in Japan, they see it as a vital link in the research triad that also includes the United States and Europe. The only way to compete with Japanese companies is to become part of the system. Genya Chiba, a director of Japan's Research Development Corporation, says that the new foreign laboratories are treated just like any other Japanese laboratory. The companies themselves are recognized in Japanese society. The recognition factor helps to attract customers in Japan who won't deal with suppliers that don't have technical support people nearby. Since one of Japan's greatest production strengths has been its just-in-time supply system, components must be delivered just before they are assembled. In these industries, American companies with plants in Japan are having much greater success than those exporting their products from plants in the United States.

Because the Americans have been accepted into Japan's research community, they have access to Japan's latest technologies, a fact that greatly benefits companies dependent on having the latest technology in their industry. In turn, the Americans' contributions to Japanese developments have increased their acceptance in that country. Having a physical presence has also helped. Thomas F. Jordan, the head of Dupont's Japanese subsidiaries, says, "We've had new customers coming to us out of the blue just because they toured the facilities."

Although many of these labs are concentrating on tailoring existing products to Japanese users, a few are now also doing basic research to develop new technologies. American and European companies are discovering that they can attract the growing pool of bright young science graduates, who traditionally have preferred working for Japanese companies, because of the freedom and responsibility offered.

Many businesses operating in Japan find it essential to have a Tokyo address. Unfortunately, it is very expensive to operate and live there; it takes a lot of cash to lease an office or residence. Companies may have to put up a deposit equal to three years' rent, and the rents are very high. Having an expatriate in Tokyo may cost from $10,000 to $20,000 per month! Skyrocketing costs are forcing Japanese and foreign companies to reevaluate this decision and to establish headquarters in Japan's other cities.

Opportunities

Sales prospects for U.S. exporters are improving in the areas of electronic components, computer hardware, peripherals and software, analytical and scientific instruments, automotive parts and accessories, medical instruments and equipment, and many kinds of consumer products and services.

Watch for the progress of the Market Oriented Sector-Selective (MOSS) discussions on telecommunications, electronics, forest products, medical devices, pharmaceuticals, transportation machinery, and automobile parts.

AUSTRALIA AND NEW ZEALAND

Australia

If you spin your desktop globe, you are likely to greatly underestimate the size of Australia, which is as large as the United States. It is hard to realize that its westernmost electoral district, which covers most of the western third of Australia, is almost the size of Western Europe yet contains only about 100,000 people.

Eighty-seven percent of its population is concentrated on a narrow coastal strip. The states of Victoria and New South Wales, which include the cities of Melbourne and Sydney, account for two thirds of the population. The climate of this populated southeast coast, where most business is conducted, is temperate to tropical, similar to California, with Melbourne being like San Francisco and Brisbane more like San Diego.

American companies have quite a task keeping abreast of the laws that affect market conditions. Three tiers of government, which employs almost a quarter of the population, exist: federal, state, and local. Also, Australian states are much more autonomous than are U.S. states.

Regionalism matters in Australia. In addition to the national newspapers, there are four national TV networks, but the many local TV and radio stations, newspapers, and weeklies, together with the 500 trade and specialized publications, may offer Americans the best means of promotion. Competition between Sydney and Melbourne is friendly, but you should beware of doing the same type of promotion in both cities.

The economy, which at the beginning of this century was much more affluent than that of the United States, has tremendous potential, but to realize it, Australia needs to act more like Hong Kong and less like Argentina or Western Europe. Business has been overregulated and overprotected, and has only recently been forced by competitive pressures throughout

Australia and New Zealand

	Australia	*New Zealand*
Exchange rate (U.S. $1 =)	A$1.28	NZ$1.60
Population	16.2 million	3.3 million
GDP or GNP	US$193 billion	US$28 billion
Growth rate of GNP	5%	2.4%
Per capita income	$12,000	$8,400
Inflation rate	5.3% (declining)	4%
Budget deficit	0	3.7%
Labor force	8 million	1.6 million
Unemployment	7.3% (declining)	10%
Trade balance	$1.7 billion	$1.8 billion
U.S. exports to	$5.3 billion	$800 million
U.S. imports from	$2.5 billion	$1 billion
Trade balance with United States	− $2.7 billion	− 220 million
U.S. share of imports	17%	10%
Language	English	English
Ethnic makeup	European 97%	European, Maori
Religion	Protestant 33% Catholic 33%	Protestant Catholic
Government leader	Prime Minister Bob Hawke	President David Lange
Government	Democracy fed/state	Democracy
Relative size	Continental United States	Colorado

Asia to open up to international competition and begin trusting open markets.

Australia has reversed its isolationist tendencies of the early 1980s, both militarily and economically. It has cut its corporate tax rate from 49 percent to 39 percent, and reduced import tariffs for a number of industries, starting in 1988, to a maximum of 15 percent. As a result of the increased openness, Australia's 1987 GDP rose by over 5 percent.

Australia is becoming more efficient, flexible, and outward-looking in the world marketplace. It has cut public-sector spending, reduced inflation, introduced sweeping tax reforms to improve competitiveness of Australian exporters, abolished exchange control regulations and interest rate controls, and opened its banking system to foreign competition. It is encouraging the growth of industries that produce high-value-added items in both manufacturing and services, especially in information processing, communications, and biotechnology.

Since the deregulation of financial markets in 1983, Australia has been seeking to develop into a global financial center and to compete against regional rivals Hong Kong and Singapore. In fact, four leading Australian and New Zealand banks are among the top twenty foreign exchange dealers in the world.

Australia wants to shift its economic and political attention away from Europe to the Pacific Rim, but a cultural gap remains. However, the feeling on the part of many Asians that Australia has treated them as second-class citizens is rapidly changing. Many students in the Pacific Rim are migrating to Australia. In fact, it has been one of the favorite destinations for Hong Kong emigrés in anticipation of the 1997 Chinese takeover. Australia and Japan have been discussing coordinating their efforts to aid Southeast Asia's developing economies.

Good Opportunities for U.S. Exporters

The best opportunities for U.S. exporters include advanced ceramics, avionics, agricultural equipment, building supplies, computer hardware and peripherals, software (especially for data base management and desktop publishing), construction equipment, electric power machinery, food processing, franchising, genetic engineering, hospitality services, industrial process controls, manufacturing automation, medical instruments, oil and gas field machinery, printing and graphic parts, and telecommunications equipment.

Australia's 30 percent offset requirements on many government and military contracts can be met in ways such as technology transfers, R&D, and purchase of Australian components and services.

Investment Opportunities

The foreign investment environment has liberalized substantially, making Australia much more attractive than before. Its Foreign Investment Review Board (FIRB) no longer poses a barrier to foreign investments except in cases involving national security. Compared to other Pacific Rim nations, Australia's tax levels, inflation, and transport and labor costs are still high.

Total U.S. investment in Australia declined to only about $12 billion in 1987. Even so, as many as 25 percent of Australian nonfarm exports come from U.S. subsidiaries, and U.S. companies have over 10,000 agency agreements and over 2,000 licensing agreements there. Other promising sectors for investment include textiles, basic metal products, chemicals, petroleum, and coal.

Critical Factors

Watch for the strength of Australia's recovery from its recent recession, the movement of its exchange rate, and how well it brings down the inflation rate.

New Zealand

In 1950, New Zealand had the third-highest per capita income in the world. By the early 1980s—as a result of high taxes, high state subsidies, high import barriers, and government policies that kept resources in the wrong industries and stifled innovation—it had the slowest rate of growth of the developed nations and a greater per capita debt than Brazil!

David Lange's Labour government was elected in 1984. His finance minister, Roger Douglas, instituted "Rogernomics" to cut the government budget deficit and free the markets. Wage and price controls, interest ceilings, credit controls, and foreign exchange restrictions were eliminated, and the corporate tax rate was cut from 48 percent to 28 percent. Foreign banks were allowed in, trade barriers lowered, and subsidies eliminated. Businesses that depended on subsidies and protection are now forced to use resources efficiently and compete on international markets.

New Zealand is selling off state assets, including Air New Zealand, Development Finance Corporation, and Petrocorp of New Zealand. The government's free-market specialists have requested the remaining state-run enterprises to justify their continued existence and to draw timetables for their own privatization. Some of these enterprises are being sold to foreign bidders. Should all these organizations be sold, New Zealand will have the lowest level of state involvement in the developed world.

Several problems remain: Tariffs on some manufactured goods are still too high, the labor market remains rigid, and some business tax loopholes remain; and New Zealand needs to make further cuts in social welfare, yet spend more on education.

New Zealanders have heartily embraced the more competitive environment. Despite some disruption, this medicine has been surprisingly effective, and New Zealand's slow decline has been dramatically reversed. The new policies have attracted a large influx of foreign capital, and that country is now competing with Australia for regional banking business.

Export Opportunities

Although New Zealand's market is small, it provides a number of interesting opportunities for U.S. business, both in high tech and in consumer goods and services. American companies can sell technologically sophisticated products in New Zealand, such as microcomputers, software, food processing systems, office systems, security systems, and industrial machinery. Government-owned enterprises, newly forced to operate by market principles, provide opportunities for suppliers of telecommunications and airport ground support equipment.

Australia and New Zealand have a free-trade agreement, so products or services sold in one market have equal access to the other. New Zealand, the regional superpower for the South Pacific, is a major market center and distribution point for the many small island nations of the Pacific.

Investment Opportunities

Deregulation of the business and financial sectors has provided new opportunities for investment. Foreign investment opportunities, especially in tourism, manufacturing, forestry, and agriculture, are actively encouraged, and there are no problems with repatriation of capital or profits. New Zealand's financial sector has been deregulated, creating opportunities for financial institutions, and areas formerly closed to foreign investment, such as agriculture and air transportation, are now open.

If you are a smaller company seeking to enter the New Zealand market, contact the American Business Centers in Auckland and Wellington, recently established by the U.S. Foreign Commercial Service.

Critical Factors

Economic reform has led to a short-term decline in buying power and to a cut in customary social services. This has hit the poorer sector hardest—especially the Maori minority. If economic growth does not soon reverse these declines, a political backlash could set in, threatening the progress made.

CHINA

When an elephant wakes up and starts running, everyone pays attention, and everyone is paying attention to China now as it charges erratically but pell-mell from a tightly controlled to a free-market economy.

China's transformation since the late 1970s is so major that visitors returning after only a few years are dumbfounded by its extent and rapidity. The words *openness, democracy,* and *capitalism* seem to describe the social environment much more accurately than *socialism, central planning,* and *suspicion of foreigners.* China is Communist in name only. Both the Chinese people and foreigners are holding their breath and keeping their fingers crossed that this is not just another periodic mood swing but is in fact a basic transformation of the Chinese economy and culture. Political reversal is still possible, although it would carry a tremendous cost for China. A few of the recent changes demonstrate the breadth of this transformation and may help you recalibrate your attitude toward potential opportunities there.

In 1988, Federal Express launched full-scale operations in thirty-six Chinese cities. American banks are receiving permission to establish branches in China, and foreign insurance companies can now sell life insurance policies to Chinese citizens. Since the introduction of foreign TV commercials in 1982, advertising and public relations have become so pervasive that foreign advertisers must compete for media space with local Chinese concerns. Securities exchanges are emerging—a belated attempt by the Chinese government, forced by economic growth and the insatiable need for capital, to lead the economy in the direction it is already going.

Price controls are being freed up, and markets are now allowed to set prices. Enterprises sink or swim according to their financial performance—a new law even allows companies to go bankrupt! In an effort to privatize state-run enterprises, China is auctioning them to the highest bidder. Anyone can run a business, Chinese citizen or foreigner. The government is also auctioning ninety-year leases to vacant land in special economic zones.

China

Exchange rate (US$1 =)	Rmb 3.7 (official)
	Rmb 7 (unofficial)
	(not convertible)
Population	1.1 billion
GDP or GNP	$368 billion
Growth rate of GNP	11.2%
Per capita income	$356
Inflation rate	10–20%
Labor force	510 million (official)
Unemployment	widespread underemployment
Trade balance	-9%
U.S. exports to	$5.3 billion
U.S. imports from	$8.3 billion
Trade balance with United States	$3.3 billion
U.S. share of imports	11%
Percentage total U.S. direct investment	14%
	$3.2 billion
Language	Chinese dialects
Ethnic makeup	Han Chinese, 94%
Religion	Confucian, Buddhist, Muslim, Christian
Government leader	Zhao Ziyang
Government	Communist Party-led
Relative size	United States

Chinese industrial output is increasing very rapidly, by over 10 percent a year. That has led to overheating of the economy and inflation, sometimes running 20 percent in some sectors. Peasant incomes are rising faster than those of urban workers, although they are only one third as high. In urban areas, 80 percent of the homes have TV sets (yet making a long-distance phone call is nearly impossible, and the mail is highly unreliable).

China's policy is to have its coastal provinces establish new links with foreign investors and seek to enter world markets. China seeks to attract foreign expertise to help manage the nation's low-cost labor. Top leaders such as Zhao Ziyang say China should not begrudge foreign businesspeople their profits if those people also work for the benefit of China by increasing exports. Such statements make it easier for foreign businesses because they reduce the foot dragging by Chinese bureaucracy.

If you stand back and look at some of China's recent policies, you will notice that they are surprisingly similar to those that transformed Korea and Taiwan and allowed Japan to catch up with the United States. These changes are now taking place in a nation with a billion people, a strong cultural emphasis on education, and a tradition of entrepreneurial drive.

Difficulties

Despite the hopeful signs, the obstacles to trade with China, or even direct investment, are formidable. Sales to China are complicated by the severe shortage of foreign exchange, making it difficult to arrange payment. Foreign exchange shortages cause the Chinese government to continually shift policy on foreign investment. That makes it harder for companies to obtain foreign exchange to upgrade even such essentials as energy supply, transport, and telecommunications and to spread out the terms to pay for imports. As a result, 1986 foreign investment in China fell by 40 percent.

This means that a key element in your ability to sell in China will be how well you can arrange export credit finance or government grants and how willing you are to accept countertrade. China has recently established a ministry of foreign economic relations and trade (MOFERT) to coordinate large countertrade deals.

China's leaders often overreact to its economic problems by clamping down, canceling projects, controlling prices and wages, and/or restricting credit and foreign exchange. Such moves exacerbate the very problems they are meant to ease, especially since they further restrict the availability of raw materials and essential imported components.

Another thing that has kept small businesses out of China has been the time and money needed to stay with an enterprise until contracts are finalized, production is started, and profits are made and allowed to be taken out of the country.

Export Opportunities

Despite these difficulties, the potential for business with China—even for smaller companies—is undeniable. Your best prospects for exporting to China include scientific and control instruments, commercial aircraft, plastics and resins, synthetic rubber, computers, timber, telecommunications equipment, chemicals, machinery, rail equipment, air navigation, road- and bridge-building equipment, satellite transmission, and electronic analysis instruments. If you deal in computers, focus on mainframes and their peripherals and software components. COCOM restrictions on high-tech exports to China are being relaxed, which will affect China's access to electronics, machine tools, computers, and telecommunications equipment.

American financial institutions and Commerce Department officials have been negotiating with Chinese representatives to lay the groundwork for the leasing of equipment by Chinese enterprises. This provides an opportunity for U.S. financial institutions and for vendors of leasable equipment. The potential U.S. market for leasing equipment in China is already $1 billion a year.

China's expanding tourist industry is creating a need for many services that Western tourists are used to but which the Chinese are unable to provide. For example, China is importing not only Chinese chefs from Hong Kong but chefs who can prepare the kinds of meals that Western tourists are used to. Many of these chefs are busy teaching Chinese cooks the tricks of the tourist hospitality trade.

Smaller Companies Selling to China

Since China has one of the most difficult markets for small to medium-size companies to tackle, here are several suggestions:

• The best place for a smaller company new to the Chinese market to enter is through Hong Kong, where visas can be easily obtained. Twenty percent of China's world trade flows through Hong Kong, and 80 percent of China's foreign investment is arranged there. Most Chinese provinces, cities, and organizations have representative offices in Hong Kong, and most Chinese foreign trade organizations have subsidiaries, joint ventures, and agents there. Transportation and communication links between Hong Kong and China are extensive. Chinese banks are located there, and Hong Kong's capital markets are increasingly used to raise capital for Chinese ventures.

You may want to enter the Chinese market using a joint venture partner or agent experienced in the Chinese market. Again, Hong Kong is a good source for these agents (other sources include Singapore, the Philippines, and California).

An immense amount of data are available for market research in China, much of which is most easily obtained in Hong Kong—especially the English versions. Major banks, such as the Hong Kong and Shanghai Banking Corporation or the Bank of China, maintain up-to-date computerized data bases on Chinese markets. Note:

• The commercial office of the Chinese embassy or consulate can arrange for a commercial counselor to visit your plant to see your product being manufactured. The office may be able to give you feedback on the potential applications and markets for your products or technology in China, and perhaps even link you up with potential end users.

• There is probably a Chinese foreign trade commission that specializes in your product. Many of the commissions have representatives in the commercial offices of the embassies and consulates. Prepare a proposal that is succinct but has enough technical information to allow the potential end user to properly evaluate your products. It should be translated into Chinese and be accompanied by technical literature. Include your company's background and credentials. You will need many copies of this proposal, as the commission may ask you to send as many as twenty to its head office as well as twenty to branch corporations. You will hear from the commission in between one and three months, and if there is interest, you will then be invited to visit China.

• Experienced companies send proposals and literature directly to end users, advertise in one of the many Chinese-language publications, including technical journals, and offer technical seminars in China.

Visiting China as a member of an exhibition or mission is described in Chapter 4.

Opportunities for Direct Investment

The Chinese government eagerly seeks foreign investment, especially in advanced technology and products to be re-exported, and there are a number of ways of investing in China. Investors receive many tax incentives and other preferential treatment. Even so, the fact that the Chinese currency is not convertible makes it difficult to repatriate your profits. Thus, the first rule is: Get expert help before contemplating direct investment in China.

You can form a joint venture or have a wholly owned operation, or you can contract to build and operate a processing and assembly plant, where a Chinese partner provides the factory, labor, raw materials, and utilities while you supply components, fixtures, and equipment. You will pay a fee to your partner as if it were a subcontractor, and then re-export some or all of the goods produced to sell in other markets.

Three kinds of businesses do well:

1. *Transfer of technology.* The Chinese will bend over backward for you in this area. Examples include telephone communications, medical equipment and supplies, and chemical processing.
2. *A venture that provides a strategic raw material that the Chinese lack.* Examples are copper needed in wiring for electricity and raw materials for chemical processes.
3. *Industries that develop foreign exchange for China, such as tourism, hotels, airlines, restaurants, or tour buses.* Many of these are handled by large multinational companies, yet opportunities—such as for management training—have opened up in these areas for smaller companies as well. *A caveat:* Some of these industries are such popular investments that they are overdone. Hotels, for example, have been overbuilt. Many existing ones are unprofitable, and half-built hotels have had their financing suspended.

American companies sometimes forget that China is a developing country. It needs highways (but not cloverleafs). It needs technology. It needs advanced machinery to cut fabrics for clothing, but the machinery must include training for the people who will use it. The slogan for success in China is "Bring materials, use labor." Here are some areas of investment opportunity:

- Oil exploration and exploitation
- Electrical power generation
- Rail and air transportation, commercial aircraft, diesel locomotives
- Telecommunications
- Electronics, computers, office equipment
- Technological upgrade for large industries
- Scientific equipment
- Natural gas pipeline

Preferred types of foreign investment will enjoy several privileges:

- *Tax incentives*. Investors are exempt from the profit remittance tax.
- *The corporation income tax holiday*. Industrial and commercial taxes are exempted, and land fees are often reduced or exempted.
- *Priority in the supply of water, electricity, transportation, and communication facilities*.
- *Access to capital such as short-term revolving funds*.
- *Autonomy of management and operational decisions*. You can provide for your own planning, wage levels, personnel, and firing.

China's Special Economic Zones

Shenzhen, Xiamen, Zhuhai, and Shantou have been created along China's southeastern coast: Xiamen is opposite Taiwan; Shenzhen borders Hong Kong; Zhuhai is opposite Macao; and Shantou is in the lace-making city once called Swatow. These towns are all new, each one built near an existing capitalist enclave that offers natural markets plus access to investment money and managerial talent. China's strategy is to attract foreign money, technology, and expertise to rebuild and expand this existing industrial base. However, so far, most of the investment has not been high-tech but low- to medium-tech, and most of it has come from Hong Kong, not from the United States or Japan.

The Shanghai Economic Zone consists of Shanghai, China's oldest and largest industrial city, and the surrounding provinces. With 12 million people, Shanghai is one of the largest cities in the world, producing over 10 percent of China's industrial output, one sixth of its revenues, and one sixth of its exports. Shanghai also handles over one third of China's port tonnage.

Hainan Island, a few hundred miles southwest of Hong Kong, is being designated the latest special economic zone and will become a separate province. Extra incentives will be provided to foreign investors, with a conscious effort being made to bring in American technology and Hong Kong capital. Foreign investors will need no visas and will be able to lease land for seventy years, manage businesses without Communist Party interference, and have the right to hire and fire workers. The government is already being flooded with letters from citizens wanting to move to Hainan. However, developing the island's resources will require an infrastructure investment of $20 billion in roads, water, and electricity, which no one knows how long it will take to develop.

Foreign investment has been restricted to these special economic zones (shown on the map), which were seen as laboratories for economic reform where the risk of experiments could be controlled and the contamination of other Chinese enterprises could be limited. But now the government wishes to extend the privileges of these zones to the entire Chinese seaboard. The new policy represents a profound change of attitude—a recognition that China's economic development depends on the development of the entire coastline, not just special enclaves.

Difficulties of Investing in China

U.S. companies have discovered that initial investment costs are very high, the risks are very real, and the payoff takes years to obtain. You may become frustrated by high costs, price gouging, tight foreign exchange controls, limited access to the Chinese market, bureaucratic foot dragging, lack of qualified local personnel, and unpredictability. You can also be crippled by corruption, endless quibbling, delays, and infighting between competing ministries.

China was initially spoiled by a parade of businesses willing to undergo any difficulty to gain the vague promise of future business; the companies became giddy about the prospects and ignorant of the realities. The Chinese phrase for the resulting misperceptions translates to "same bed, different dreams."

Because of events beyond their control, foreign companies encounter a continual ebb and flow of the business and investment environment. Changes in the political winds have the highest impact on imports and investments of marginal importance to the Chinese. In the recent foreign exchange crunch, foreign companies already established in China were not hurt at all, whereas those still in the negotiation phase were virtually shut out for a while.

The various provinces and cities in China have additional plans and regulations, and limited autonomy to attract their investments. If you intend to invest in a particular province or city, you must become familiar with its laws and regulations as well.

Markets are blocked by a myriad of laws, tariffs, and currency restrictions. Chinese officials spring unpublicized internal rules called *neibu gui-ding* on foreign companies.

China's legal system is unprepared to deal with modern business relations. In some areas, the laws drafted are inadequate; in others, e.g., joint ventures, laws are promulgated in a flurry, too fast for foreign companies to keep up with them. But the drafting of new laws is not adequate to produce a fair legal system.

MONGOLIA

LIAONING

NORTH
KOREA

Qinhuangdao

Beijing

Dalian

LIAODONG
PENINSULA

Tianjin

SOUTH
KOREA

Yantai

Qingdao

SHANDONG

SHANDONG
PENINSULA

Lianyungang

Nantong

Shanghai

YANGTZE DELTA

Ningbo

Wenzhou

Fuzhou

FUJIAN

GUANGDONG

MINNAN DELTA

Xiamen

TAIWAN

Guangzhou
(Canton)

GUANGXI

Shantou

Zhuhai

Shenzhen

Beihai

HONG KONG

VIETNAM

PEARL RIVER DELTA

Zhanjiang

HAINAN

LAOS

Key:

⊡ Special economic zones

⠿ Special open areas

● The 14 coastal open cities

Judges are still trained to make decisions according to traditional legal principles rather than new regulations. Too often one is presumed guilty until one admits he's guilty.

To help remedy this, in 1986, China invited a thousand lawyers and businesspeople from the United States to a conference to help develop China's rudimentary laws on foreign trade and investment. As a result, it becomes increasingly possible to use a lawyer and turn to the courts for redress of grievances.

Workers for joint ventures are not required to be provided by state enterprises, but even your Chinese partner will have difficulty attracting skilled workers. Even if candidates are eager to work for the foreign joint venture, their former employers may not release them, since employers still have the legal right to deny an employee's request to resign and work elsewhere.

A major problem for U.S. businesses, particularly small and medium-size companies, has been the inexperience of Chinese officials in talking shop with them. Chinese managers and technicians have few skills in applying the technology that has been transferred. Nor are they skilled in management and strategic planning.

Companies must deal with disputes on how to price products for domestic and foreign markets and on the valuation of land and U.S.-made equipment. The taxes and profits a joint venture will accumulate during its operation are based primarily on the contract, so it is critical for you to have a thorough understanding of what has been agreed to.

A final difficulty is that the country's transportation and energy systems have serious bottlenecks.

How to Pronounce Chinese Names

Pinyin, a system of romanization invented by the Chinese, has now replaced the familiar conventional spellings in China's English-language publications.

Complex Initial Sounds		*Final Sounds*	
c	like the *ts* in "its"	e	like the *oo* in "book"
q	like the *ch* in "cheap"	eng	like the *ung* in "lung"
x	between the *s* in "see"	ai	as in "aisle"
	and the *sh* in "she"	ui	like the *ay* in "way"
z	like the *ds* in "lids"	uai	like the *wi* in "wide"
zh	like the *j* in "just"	i	like the *i* in "skin"*

*When *zh, ch, sh* are followed by an *i*, the *i* is pronounced like *r*.

This still causes confusion among many English speakers, as they see familiar names rendered in ways difficult for them to pronounce. For example:

Familiar	*Pinyin*
Peking	Beijing
Canton	Guangzhou
Mao Tse-tung	Mao Zedong

Rules for Doing Business in China

Because many companies are interested in China—even though, of the Pacific Rim nations, its system is by far the least familiar to Americans—it is worthwhile listing a few rules of thumb for doing business there. Of primary importance is that as you build a business relationship in China, remain cautious and realistic at all times. "Lower your expectations every time you hear good news," advises experienced trader Jimin Ma of Silk Road Enterprises in San Francisco. Also:

1. *Minimize risk.* It is often better to take only a minority ownership share and contribute your technology than to contribute *both* know-how and capital to the joint venture. Since situations will develop that neither you nor your Chinese partner can control, limit your financial exposure in that way.

2. *Use common sense.* When confronted with promises, check everything out. For example, AMC was told that most parts needed for building the Jeep Cherokee could be manufactured in China, but it turned out that most components had to be brought in from the United States at disastrously high costs.

3. *Understand China's needs and build a business plan to accommodate them.* China's economic needs are laid out in its five-year plan, but very few American businesspeople check the plan out.

4. *Keep abreast of China's changes in policy.*

5. *Match your technical expertise with China's industrial base.* Find a way to enhance an existing Chinese industry.

6. *View China as a site for overseas manufacturing, not as a huge market to penetrate.*

7. *Use local capital.* The Chinese government will pay to build a production line if you contribute know-how and management expertise.

8. *Manage very closely.* Constantly monitor your operations, worker productivity, and product quality.

9. *Try to find a qualified Chinese manager.* The Chinese will insist that you staff your venture with Chinese citizens, a requirement that may be impossible to fulfill. Many companies have successfully brought Chinese managers from Hong Kong or Singapore, acceptable to the Chinese government because, in its eyes, an ethnic Chinese living anywhere is a Chinese citizen. However, many ethnic Chinese from the United States may have become too Americanized to work well in China. Language ability is only one requirement. Management ability is also crucial, as is the ability to manage a Chinese work force and to deal with the Chinese bureaucracy.

THE NICs

Newly Industrialized Countries: Hong Kong, Taiwan, Korea, Singapore
Also called "The Four Tigers" and "The Four Dragons"

If you return to the NICs after an absence of a few years, you are in for a shock. "NIC" originally meant "newly industrializing country," but there is no question that this now means "newly industrial*ized* country." NICs are developed countries, ready to take their place among the world's economic leaders. Some people have replaced the term NIC with NIE (pronounced *knee*), which means "newly industrialized economy." This change is urged by China, which holds that Hong Kong and Taiwan are indeed separate economies but are not separate countries.

The new affluence was brought home to me in a brief conversation I had with a street vendor, a middle-aged Chinese woman who had just dished me out a variety of steaming vegetables over noodles from her sidewalk cart. I assumed she was just eking out a living. Then she asked me, "Where are you from?" "California," I responded. "Ah, California. Nice place. My son goes to Stanford. Next year I go to his graduation."

These four nations may offer the best new opportunities for American companies, at least through the mid-1990s. (See Table 11–1 for a comparison of the four countries.) Taiwan and Korea are both opening up rapidly to imported consumer products and services, and Hong Kong and Singapore are probably the easiest locations for American companies to first establish Pacific Rim operations.

Hong Kong

"There's almost nothing that can't be exported to Hong Kong, and there's a great demand for American products," says a spokesman at the New York office of the Hong Kong and Shanghai Banking Corporation.

Walking down a street in Hong Kong gives one a visceral experience of free-market capitalism. Commerce is everywhere, from the thousands upon thousands of street vendors to the high-rise bank buildings sporting some of the most audacious architecture in the world.

Two and one half million people—most of whom are refugees from China—are crowded onto a strip of landfill at the base of mountains. There are six different forms of public transportation, and every one of them is jammed. The crowding and noise and pollution are overwhelming to some, but the energy and vitality are undeniable.

It is a city of skyscrapers—as if Manhattan were relocated to the hills of San Francisco. Even the factories are in high-rise buildings. An electronics company may have a factory on the fourteenth floor of a building that is across the street from a plant that renders carcasses. When the electronics company expands,

Table 11-1. Comparison of the four NICs.

	Hong Kong	Singapore	Korea	Taiwan
Exchange rate (US$1=)	HK$7.82	S$2.05	792 won	NT$28.55
Population	5.6 million	2.65 million	44 million	20 million
GDP or GNP	$43 billion	$19 billion	$164 billion	$120 billion
Growth rate of GNP	8%	5%	12%	8%
Per capita income	$9,400	$7,300	37%	$6,700
Inflation rate	7.8%	2.1%	8%	6.5%
Budget deficit	+0	+.1%	+7%	-1%
Labor force	2.8 million	1.3 million	17 million	2 million
Unemployment	2%	.4%	3.5%	2%
Trade balance	-$1 billion	-$2.1 billion	$7.2 billion	+$19 billion
U.S. exports	$4.0 billion	$4.0 billion	$8 billion	$13 billion
U.S. imports	$10.5 billion	$6.4 billion	$23 billion	$26.4 billion
Trade balance with United States	$6.5 billion	$2.8 billion	$6 billion	$10 billion
U.S. share of imports	8%	15%	23%	21%
Language	English, Cantonese	English, Chinese	Korean	Taiwan Chinese
Ethnic makeup	Han Chinese: 98%	Malay, Chinese	Korean	Taiwanese
Religion	Confucian, Buddhist, Christian	Confucian, Buddhist, Muslim	Buddhist	Confucian, Christian
Government leader	Colony of United Kingdom	Lee Kwan Yew	Roh Tae Woo	Lee Teng-hui
Government	Self-governing colony	President selected by ruling party	Democracy	President selected by ruling party
Relative size	San Francisco	San Francisco	Indiana	Massachusetts + Connecticut + Rhode Island

it will be lucky to get needed additional space on the eighth floor of the same building; its second expansion might be to the fifth and sixth floors of a building a block away. This is one reason why such companies are moving assembly operations into China, where there are brand-new spacious plants and the latest equipment.

The British administration epitomizes laissez-faire, and that is just the way Hong Kong merchants want it. There is less government interference with business here than in any other Asian economy. There are also fewer government incentives, but the commercial freedom is its own incentive, along with the unexcelled financial services, communication links, air and sea transportation, and skilled, highly motivated work force.

Hong Kong is a free port and has no important tariffs or quotas. The corporate tax rate of 18 percent is low, and the investment climate for foreign companies is favorable. Hong Kong's propensity to consume makes it an ideal destination for U.S. companies. Surprisingly, U.S. exports of textiles to Hong Kong have been booming.

Opportunities for American Business

Hong Kong's growth should be between 5 and 10 percent over the next few years. There are major opportunities for American companies to export or to set up operations in the consumer, commercial, and industrial sectors.

For example:

• *Commercial and industrial products.* American companies are discovering they may be the low-cost provider of materials and components needed by computers, peripherals, and software, food processing and packaging equipment, medical instruments and equipment, telecommunications equipment, textiles, and security and safety equipment. The service industries provide many opportunities for exporters of equipment, materials, supplies, and services.

• *High-value-added agricultural products.* Many purchases of fruits and vegetables, poultry, meat, tobacco, grains, textiles, and furs are for re-export, but Hong Kong itself has a sizable affluent market. The main competition for many of these goods supplied by American companies comes from China, since freight costs from the United States are much higher than from China.

• *Service industries.* American companies are already heavily involved in Hong Kong's service sector, but new opportunities are emerging all the time, both for operating service businesses and for supplying them with needed products and services. Current hot areas include hotels and medical services. Franchises are growing rapidly in fast food, convenience stores, and many consumer services. Another booming field is professional service franchising: computer training, corporate health care, management training, and travel. In the telecommunications field, cellular phones and cable television are expanding (not just in Hong Kong, but also into China).

• *Setting up operations.* Over 1,000 American companies operate in Hong Kong, and many thousands more are represented by local agents. Many U.S. companies use Hong Kong as an entrée to China. As one of the most competitive and commercial markets in the world, Hong Kong is very attractive for regional financial and marketing firms, as well as for manufacturing companies.

American companies are the largest (a total of $6 billion) investors in Hong Kong, followed by China and Japan. Investment in manufacturing includes electronics and electronic components, telecommunications equipment, appliances and other consumer products, textiles, and toys. Investment in services includes banking and accounting, legal services and insurance, electronic data processing, restaurants, and many consumer franchises.

Advantages of Doing Business in Hong Kong

Hong Kong offers many advantages to companies new to overseas operations: an extensive American business community, an established code of commercial law based on the British legal system, and ease in setting up a business. Hong Kong has a strategic location on the Pacific Rim, and is the gateway to China. It has a stable, dependable government that believes in free enterprise and minimum interference with market forces. There are no exchange controls or restrictions, and intellectual property is strongly protected.

Banking and other commercial services are of the highest international quality. Transport and communications facilities are highly developed, including an excellent harbor and a nearby airport. (Hong Kong, Singapore, and Rotterdam are the three busiest container ports in the world.) Hong Kong is the main deepwater port for China, and about a third of its business is transshipment to China.

The work force is skilled, well educated, highly disciplined, and backed up by a strong educational system. Despite the shortage of space, there is a wide choice of industrial sites. Manufacturers find a wide range of supporting industries and services, and it is very easy for them to import and export. Hong Kong is cutting its already low corporate tax rate to counter incentives offered by other Southeast Asian governments to foreign investors.

Disadvantages of Doing Business in Hong Kong

Some companies are deterred by the high cost of office and residential space, overcrowding, overuse of infrastructure facilities (especially transport), and a labor shortage. However, many manufacturers cope with this by subcontracting with facilities in nearby parts of China.

1997

What will be the impact of China's takeover on Hong Kong? Those with a stake there fear that it is already facing a major "brain drain" and financial exodus in anticipation of 1997. Many professionals and middle-class people are moving to Canada, Australia, and the United States, where they obtain residency permits and set up a safe haven for their money. Some then return to Hong Kong. If after 1997 China allows Hong Kong to continue as it has, these people, and probably a vast proportion of their capital, will return to Hong Kong; but if China meddles and interferes, they will then move permanently to their new nations.

Hong Kong residents suspect that de facto hegemony may be assumed by China long before the agreed transfer date of June 30, 1997 (Britain's Royal Navy departs in 1989). Since the common rule of thumb is that it takes five years to recoup a Hong Kong investment, the attitude of local residents and investors can be gauged by the degree of capital flight after 1992—five years before the takeover.

To counter the fears of its citizens, Hong Kong is increasing its efforts to attract investment from the United States, Japan, and Europe in order to reassure many Hong Kong financiers and professionals that stability will remain after 1997. Their thinking is that the more foreign investment there is by Hong Kong's major trading partners, the less China is likely to stir things up.

In some ways, the takeover will be a mere formality. Most of the substantial changes have already taken place in anticipation: Hong Kong's affairs are increasingly dominated by Beijing-run enterprises—the Bank of China, the China Resources Group, and the Xinhua News Agency (which has long been China's unofficial consulate)—while the British colonial administration is beginning to act like a lame duck.

The intense discussions between Chinese and Hong Kong officials demonstrate the commitment to making the Chinese takeover a smooth one, and to avoiding any disruption of Hong Kong's economy. Despite the understandable fears and uncertainty, it is hard to believe that the Chinese government would intentionally perturb this smoothly spinning dynamo, which is the source of 30 percent of its foreign exchange. More worrisome is what the Chinese might do unintentionally to this goose that lays its golden eggs—out of unfamiliarity with the kind of social and political climate necessary to sustain Hong Kong's economic vitality.

A Hong Kong entrepreneur is building a $1 billion superhighway linking Hong Kong to Canton and Macao. This toll road, complete with restaurants, gas stations, and tollbooths, will open up China's Pearl River Delta to trade and investment. Hong Kong's economic influence already extends beyond Canton and up and down China's coastline. To me, these developments suggest that it may be more likely that Hong Kong will end up taking over China.

Singapore

A sign of the times for Singapore is that the new subway cars have cellular telephones for businesspeople to use as they ride. What's more, the phones are being made part of an integrated network, which will allow the high-quality digital transmission of not just voice but also pictures, computer data, and text.

Singapore has been described as the Switzerland of Southeast Asia. The country is clean, efficient, and free of corruption. It has the best-educated population of Asia outside Japan, and most of the population speaks English. Over half a million students are in school. In this city-state of 2.6 million, 75,000 people work in Singapore's electronics industries, mostly for American or Japanese companies. It is almost up to Japan's standard of living. There are a million

Comparison of Hong Kong and Singapore

Both

- English-speaking
- Regional centers for finance, information, transshipping
- Have small but affluent internal markets
- Easy first step for companies new to overseas operations
- No-strings-attached investment environment
- Have many investment incentives
- Provide varied support for businesses of all sizes and types
- Very expensive to live and operate a business in

Hong Kong	*Singapore*
• Gateway to selling to China	• Gateway to selling to ASEAN
• Can provide low-cost labor from China	• Can provide low-cost labor from Malaysia
• Fearful of 1997 takeover	• Fearful of political disruption
• Vulnerable to Chinese political winds	• Vulnerable to ASEAN economic swings

telephones and half a million motor vehicles. The issues of race, language, religion, and culture have been largely defused. An entire generation believes strongly in an egalitarian, multiracial society.

Singapore is trying to overtake Hong Kong as the most important Asian financial center outside of Tokyo. It would like to become Southeast Asia's center for technology as well as for trade and finance, and hopes to challenge Taiwan, Korea, and Japan. This is why it offers generous incentives to entice companies that bring in sophisticated skills and technologies.

One symbol of Singapore's evolution is that it recently destroyed a quarter of a million pirated cassette tapes to demonstrate enforcement of its 1987 copyright law. Intellectual property is its new bread and butter, and Singapore now intends to develop high-tech, high-capital industries and move away from assembling circuit boards and computers for U.S. companies. It is also beginning to assemble genes and biotech clones—for example: Diagnostic Biotechnology, which cultures the AIDS virus for diagnostic kits; Plantek, which clones plant tissues; and Singapore Biotech, which manufactures vaccines for hepatitis B. In 1987, Singapore opened the Institute of Molecular and Cell Biology.

Singapore represents a small but very affluent market, and also serves the rest of the ASEAN and Southeast Asian markets. Communication links and international sea and air transportation facilities are excellent. It has built up high-quality manufacturing infrastructure and a stable, efficient government dedicated to promoting business and investment. Singapore is one of the world's busiest ports, right up there with Rotterdam, Hong Kong, and Taiwan's Kaohsiung. The efficiency of shipping facilities is unexcelled, both inbound and outbound: Goods are containerized and documentation is computerized.

Trade and Investment Opportunities

Many smaller U.S. companies are being attracted to Singapore to service their larger customers. There is a rapidly growing market—for either export or local manufacture—for such products as:

- Electronic industry production and test equipment. Singapore is trying to become a Silicon Valley of the Far East.
- Aviation and avionics support equipment.
- Computers, peripherals, and office systems and equipment.
- Machine tools and metalworking.
- Medical and health care equipment and instruments. Singapore is the health care center of Southeast Asia and has the best facilities. It is usually the first country to acquire new medical equipment and facilities.
- Biotechnology, officially targeted as a growth industry for the future.
- Tourism.
- Consumer products, including clothing, cosmetics, toys, electrical appliances, furniture, jewelry, gifts, and cooking utensils.
- Food. Singapore imports most food for increasingly sophisticated, affluent, and health-conscious consumers seeking quality food products from the United States and other countries.

Because so many American hard-disk-drive manufacturers are located in Singapore, it has earned the name "Winchester Island" (after the Winchester model hard-disk drive). No restrictions are placed on the movement of capital to or from Singapore, including repatriation of profits or capital. Singapore tries to make its investment environment as attractive as possible for businesses engaging in activities it considers suitable. Although few industries are excluded, the government is highly selective in offering investment incentives; it seeks to promote those industries it feels are best for its overall development. Companies wishing to invest in Singapore must negotiate their incentives with the Economic Development Board, which administers investment incentives.

Design and engineering support is available to U.S. companies. Singapore has actively attracted service companies, from a 4-person management consultancy to a 500-bed hospital. Opportunities exist in the following areas: medical services; transportation and distribution; computers, telecommunications, and information; leisure and entertainment; education and training; agritechnology services; technical and engineering consulting, management consulting, legal and accounting, laboratory and testing, advertising and public relations, and exhibition services; and services to regional headquarters.

Service companies will find special incentives tailored especially to them, e.g., a tax holiday if the service activity is the first of its kind in Singapore. There are also investment allowance and operational headquarters incentives, and financial assistance programs for service companies investing there, including direct loans, training and consultatory support, and product development assistance.

Three dozen American companies have been attracted to Singapore's Science Park, including leading-edge companies such as Tata-Elxsi, which designs and manufactures esoteric supercomputers.

Advantages of Doing Business in Singapore

Of the Pacific Rim nations, Singapore has the fewest restrictions on American business and American expatriates: Its government is among the easiest to work with; investment processes are very easy; companies encounter no problems with customs clearances, shipping, or airfreight.

There are few labor problems. Engineers are educated overseas, and the local technical schools are good. American companies in Singapore that just a few years ago had to hire expatriates for their advanced research now find they can hire very good local engineers, many of whom have been trained at the best American schools.

The Chinese culture is compatible with the way Americans like to do business. Singapore speaks our language in two senses: First, English is the language of education and business; second, the languages of high technology and Western-style management are dominant in business.

For expatriates, Singapore is a good place to do business. Secretaries efficiently arrange appointments, speaking the lilting Singapore-style English that is learned well because English is a language of instruction in most schools here. A colonial house with a swimming pool is half the price of an executive-style apartment in Tokyo.

Singapore—with the most modern airport in the world, with its rapid transit and freeway systems, with its focus on environmentalism and helpful living—makes Silicon Valley look underdeveloped! It is the center of Southeast Asian shipping, air travel, telecommunications, and information processing.

Disadvantages

However, Singapore is expensive: Except for Japan, it has the highest labor cost. The cost for engineering labor is the highest in Asia. There are not enough technical people to meet industry needs. Wages are being bid up rapidly, and some workers display an I-don't-have-to-work-for-you attitude.

Compared with Hong Kong, information flows more sluggishly in Singapore, and despite the openness of the Singaporean government, some businesses feel it is suspicious of them.

The contrast between Singapore and Taipei is striking. Unlike Taipei, Singapore is a place where a motorbike without a muffler gets impounded, where garbage thrown from a car can cost a week's pay. Smoking is discouraged—the latest in a long series of government campaigns toward sanitation, efficiency, and productivity.

Because of continuing labor shortages, guest workers from Malaysia—and even China—are common. While larger companies are able to attract the skilled people they need, the expansion of smaller companies is often slowed by a tight labor market. Circuit board companies that initially went to Singapore for cheap labor are now looking to China's special economic zones.

While Singapore has come far in one generation through efficiency, a hard-working labor force, and low labor costs, it must now make the transition to creativity, entrepreneurism, and professionalism if it is to continue its advance. Like Korea, Taiwan, and other Asian nations, Singapore faces the challenge of political maturation, the challenge of how to grow into a society where freedom and prosperity nurture each other.

Korea

The tallest building in Asia is Seoul's Daihan Life Insurance Building. It is meant to deliver the same message that the Empire State Building did for the United States in the 1930s—the country's coming of age as an economic power.

Korea's economy is one of the fastest growing in the world because of declining oil prices, low interest rates, the depreciation of the won against the yen, and the hard work of the Korean people—it's often said that Koreans make the Japanese look lazy! The 1987 current account surplus was $9.8 billion, up from $4.8 billion in 1986.

A rapid middle-class revolution is occurring, and Koreans are demanding a steadily increasing voice in the political affairs of their nation to match their economic clout. Indications of middle-class growth are the number of refrigerators, telephones, and TVs: In the 1970s, 2 percent of the households had refrigerators, 4 percent had phones, and 6 percent had TVs; now 75 percent have refrigerators, 50 percent have phones, and almost all have TVs. In addition, half the adult population are university students or graduates.

At the end of the Korean War, South Korea was a land of peasant farmers; it did not overtake North Korea until the 1960s. Now 65 percent of South Koreans consider themselves middle-class according to Lee Hong Koo, a political scientist at Seoul National University. South Korean consumers are increasingly affluent; in some important measures, such as commuter time and house size, a Korean white-collar worker's standard of living is already higher than his Japanese counterpart's.

Economic change has been astounding. Per capita income has increased tenfold in sixteen years. Exports have increased by a factor of 46. Things get done fast. A tailor offers overnight service for "Saville Row suits"; a hotel laundry only requires a 2:00 P.M. delivery for same-day service.

The rapid growth has come from tourism and exports of cars, electronics, machinery, and textiles, but even as Korea captures manufacturing markets previously dominated by the Japanese, it finds itself challenged by Thailand and

Malaysia—both of which are now exporting inexpensive cars—and even China, which is now producing low-end TV sets.

Korea is trying to position itself as a medium-tech economy for the next generation. It is switching from large-scale manufacturing to smaller-scale medium-tech applications and services. However, it is not reinventing all the technology developed by Japan and the United States but is applying it to products appropriate for markets in developing nations, especially China. Korea has a lot of catching up to do to rival the infrastructure and living standards of the Organization for Economic Cooperation and Development (OECD) countries.

Korea once relied on adapting outdated technologies from Japan and the United States to reduce the price of low-cost goods and offer low-end consumer goods to Japanese and American markets, a strategy that has been phenomenally successful. Now it is also seeking to develop high-end, high-profit products—those that currently make up Japan's prime market.

Not having been able to get the technology it wants from Japan, Korea has been developing the needed technology itself. In a crash effort to invade upscale consumer markets now dominated by the United States and Japan, it is producing better video recorders, more luxurious cars, and more powerful computers. Korea is also conducting R&D on industrial robots. Although most of the robots have so far been supplied to companies such as Hyundai, some are now being exported to the United States. On the horizon for Korea's industry are biotechnology, superconductivity, artificial intelligence, organ transplants, and space launches.

Long scientist-poor, Korea is now sending thousands of students to top U.S. universities. In 1988, about a hundred young Koreans were enrolled in masters and Ph.D. programs at MIT.

Labor costs are rising faster than in almost any other country in the world. The long quiescent labor force has been brought to life by the new political democracy, and unions have sprung up in most major businesses. Thus, employers will have to deal with the new reality of labor unrest. Korean laborers have worked the longest hours for the lowest wages of the NICs. Even though labor productivity has increased by 10 percent during the 1980s, wages have not kept up with the cost of living. This has caused workers to strike, asking for pay increases to make up for lost purchasing power.

Korea's goal is to join OECD by 1993 and have a per capita income of $5,000. But for Korea to make the transition from NIC to industrialized nation, its controls on credit, foreign borrowing, the stock exchange, prices, and market access will have to diminish drastically. Korea needs to graduate from export-led, mercantilist growth—as Japan is now doing—in order to avoid Korea bashing by American and European politicians.

Opportunities for U.S. Exporters

Because of the concern about reducing its trade surplus with the United States, the government is encouraging Korean companies to buy U.S. products, and U.S.

exports have been increasing to Korea. Much of the current growth in Korean imports is in components for assembly and re-export. Strong sales potential for U.S. exporters exists in industrial raw materials, heavy machinery, electronics, scientific products with a high technology content, advanced production equipment, medical equipment and supplies, telecommunications equipment, analytical and scientific instruments, electronic industry production and test equipment, electronic components, food processing and packaging equipment, industrial controls, special machine tools, special-purpose computers and peripherals, and agricultural and industrial commodities. With the fall of the U.S. dollar, American companies are currently selling even steel and textiles to Korea.

Demand for electronic components is especially strong, as computers are spreading rapidly throughout all sectors of Korean business and government. The United States dominates the market for computer hardware, but Japan still dominates the market for peripherals.

The Korean government has established a $2 billion fund to provide easy credit to importers of goods from countries other than Japan. In 1987, Korea sent five buying missions to the United States, and also arranged for 3,000 buyers to attend an exhibit of U.S. products at a trade show in Seoul. In 1987, Korea's Trade and Industry Ministry led executives of forty-seven companies on a U.S. shopping spree to buy $2 billion worth of raw materials and industrial goods, the purpose of which was to dampen desire for protectionist measures in the U.S. Congress.

Tariffs have been cut on many manufactured and agricultural products, including cars, TVs, communications equipment, home appliances, beer, lemons, plums, newsprint, timber, and plywood.

Despite the recent liberalization, restrictive administrative regulations and high tariffs make it difficult or impractical to sell in many markets, but in some instances, buying American isn't easy for the Koreans. Japanese suppliers are closer and often provide better service. Also, some U.S. steelmakers are unwilling to fill small-lot orders, and U.S. machinery is often more expensive than Japanese. Aggressive marketing and strong aftersales service will be essential in a market that lies only a few hundred miles from Japan.

Investment

More and more U.S. companies are successfully investing in Korea, and licensing and technical assistance agreements are increasing rapidly in the electronics, electrical machinery, and petrochemical sectors. Despite improvements, however, poor patent protection is a major impediment to foreign investment and licensing. American pharmaceutical companies have filed for patents in Korea, only to see leading Korean companies obtain government subsidies to develop products similar to theirs.

Foreign investment is surging as confidence in Korea's continued political stability and economic growth increases. Businesses should watch for opening access to additional service industries, including advertising, insurance, and transportation.

Korea faces several major challenges: It must maintain its newly won democracy, keep the economy growing fast enough to accommodate the population boom and increase the standard of living, use some of its burgeoning GNP to invest in social development, and reduce the tension with North Korea. In 1988, a major step was taken when trade between North and South Korea was reopened with initial shipments of North Korean clams and coal.

Despite threats of political upheaval as Korea moves from an authoritarian to a democratic political system, there are several stabilizing influences, such as the desire of the middle class to continue its climb to prosperity and a strong core of trained, educated government bureaucrats. Perhaps most important, Koreans are very patriotic and do not want their demands for democratic reforms to harm their country.

Taiwan

Taiwan may have the most rapidly changing economy in Asia. Three events symbolize these changes and the new opportunities for American businesses. First, since the import of foreign cars was first legalized in the mid-1980s, American cars, led by Ford, have become the fastest-selling imports in Taiwan. Second, Avon, which had long produced cosmetics there for the domestic market, has ceased Taiwanese production and is now exporting cosmetics from its U.S. plants to Taiwan. The protective tariff of 150 percent was cut to 15 percent, exposing Avon to new competition; in addition, Avon discovered that production costs were lower in America. Third, Acer Computers, one of Taiwan's most prominent success stories, started out producing products on contract to Texas Instruments and putting TI's name on them. Acer computers are now selling very well in the United States, and TI now contracts to produce computer components for Acer.

Taiwan is a land of newfound affluence. City streets are choked with cars, all of them new. It seems as if every driver has traded up from a motorcycle within the past five years (and people drive as if they were still on motorcycles!). Many of the greatest changes have taken place just since 1986–87. Several factors came together, leading to a sudden, visible surge in prosperity and a changed economic climate for foreign business in Taiwan.

The Taiwanese government, facing a $70 billion trade surplus, saw the necessity of shifting from an export-led to a consumer growth economy. Government policies changed to encourage imports and consumer spending. The New Taiwan dollar, which had been pegged artificially low to the U.S. dollar, has appreciated 40 percent against the dollar. Tariffs, which were previously high to protect domestic industries and keep out many foreign products, have dropped precipitously, making it profitable to import many products. Many barriers to the operation of foreign companies have been eliminated, especially in consumer products and service industries. Laws to protect intellectual property of foreign companies have been passed and are being enforced, making it easier for Taiwan's industries to attract the innovative technologies it needs for continued economic advancement.

Even into the early 1980s, Taiwan was known as a low-cost labor market. Now labor is so expensive that even Taiwanese companies are going to the Philippines and Thailand for cheap labor. Taiwan's industries are rapidly being upgraded from labor-intensive to high-tech, engineering-intensive.

Taiwanese people have been gaining in affluence very rapidly, due to several factors besides the success of the export-led manufacturing sector. Because of the labor shortage and the upgrade of job skills, wages have shot up: For engineers and technicians, they rose at least 10 percent a year during the late 1980s; skyrocketing real estate values have made many farmers suddenly wealthy merely by selling a piece of land; and since many financial restrictions have been lifted, people have been able to make lucrative investments—including overseas investments—more openly.

An extensive underground financial economy throughout Taiwan had long provided financial services—loans, investment capital, and foreign transactions—which were either banned by the government or were not provided by commercial banks to small companies. As these restrictions were lifted, two things happened: First, many previously underground transactions were now made legally and openly, causing the official wealth of the Taiwanese people to take a sudden jump. Second, smaller companies that had long been starved for expansion capital found that capital easier to obtain, and began profitable expansion.

Opportunities for American Companies

The changes just described open many doors for American companies that wish to export to Taiwan or to open operations there.

Consumer Goods and Services.   There is a tremendous market for foreign goods and services, sometimes for reasons of status, but often because these goods are not produced locally. Many Taiwanese firms that are very skilled at manufacturing on contract for foreign marketers have been caught unprepared. They are inexperienced at marketing and promoting their own products, even in their domestic markets. Foreign companies are filling the gap, in franchising, home appliances, and tourism and travel services for both Taiwanese and foreign travelers.

Many items common in the United States are not available in Taiwan and would be well received. Every Taiwanese who has lived in the United States has a story about what he misses most, from copy shops to parking structures to shopping malls.

Commercial and Industrial Products.   The best prospects for U.S. exports include laboratory and scientific instruments, electronic components, telecommunications equipment; computers, peripherals, and software for business; industrial process controls; and organic chemicals. Taiwan's growing environmental concerns have created markets for pollution-control equipment and related services.

Many companies selling consumer and commercial products display their wares at Taipei's World Trade Center. In keeping with Taiwan's export orientation, the first six floors are dedicated to displaying the products Taiwanese manufacturers wish to sell to the world. On the seventh floor "Import Mart" are displays of merchandise for the rest of the world to sell to Taiwan. American companies have been slow to take advantage of this resource, but twenty-some states and several cities have set up representative offices to promote their products. Trade shows held here attract buyers from all over the world, not just from Taiwan.

Professional Services.   The Taiwan business community is undergoing very rapid changes and is becoming more sophisticated. Small, family-run businesses are growing larger; they need capital, professional management, and marketing services. American companies are well positioned to provide the needed business, technical, and professional services, since so many of the younger generation of Taiwanese managers and engineers are American-educated and have worked for American companies. Areas of opportunity include retail banking for small business, insurance, computerization and information services, accounting and financial management, expertise on mergers and acquisitions and going public, product design and marketing, management consulting and market research, education and training, research, legal services, and architecture. Many of these services are still restricted by the government, yet American firms are finding ways to provide them, often by forming a joint venture with a Taiwanese partner. An American architect or attorney may be designated a "trainee" for a local company yet still provide full professional services.

Construction Projects.   Taiwan is contracting with foreign companies to help build major projects, including a rapid transit system for Taipei, aircraft manufacturing capacity, several major hospitals, electric power generation and transmission, and an islandwide telecommunications network.

Manufacturing Infrastructure.   For a manufacturing economy to hum, it requires a myriad of small support companies: job shops to produce tools and components; suppliers of parts and materials; testing and calibration labs; and repair shops. Taiwan has many of these, but with its rapidly upgrading industry, there are many gaps, creating opportunities for smaller American companies to provide products and services needed by high-tech manufacturers, things taken for granted in Chicago or Cleveland—maddening if not available. The Taiwan government offers generous incentives to such companies.

High-Tech Manufacturing. Taiwan actively encourages both domestic and foreign investment and licensing in electronics, computers, telecommunications, and other high-tech products. Despite the escalation in wages, engineering costs are still half the level of those in the United States. The government seeks to attract companies that can use—and teach valuable skills to—Taiwan's technicians and engineers. You wouldn't go to Taiwan to design and manufacture clock radios, or even disk drives. Nor would you establish an R&D facility for artificial intelligence or superconductivity. The trick is to set up operations in industries that are just coming into commercial maturity. These best utilize Taiwan's technical resources, such as research institutes, and attract the most government incentives.

Science-Based Industrial Park

About an hour's drive from Taipei in Taiwan is the Science-Based Industrial Park (SIP) at Hsinchu. The Taiwanese government is trying to recreate Silicon Valley by attracting high-tech firms that will aid in the development and diversification of Taiwan's industrial base. Just as Silicon Valley grew up around Stanford University, Hsinchu is surrounded by three universities.

This industrial park has few requirements for entering businesses, so it is appropriate for smaller companies. It seeks high-tech firms, loosely defined as "whatever technology we are seeking to attract." The SIP emphasizes engineering and high-tech services over cheap labor. For a company to set up operations in the park, it must meet several criteria: It must agree to carry on R&D activities there, even if the company is purely a manufacturing one—this is to allow Taiwanese engineers and other skilled workers to gain experience in the technologies and techniques that are used. The technology must be current, not obsolete; the company must be nonpolluting; and if a company wishes to set up a plant that competes with an existing one, that fact will be taken into consideration.

A company can operate either as a wholly owned subsidiary or as a joint venture. There are over sixty companies from the United States, Japan, and Europe already located in this well-landscaped industrial and residential park. Government officials predict that by 1996 there will be 250 companies at the SIP employing 73,000 workers selling $6 billion worth of high-tech products. The Taiwanese government offers a variety of incentives: low-interest loans, tax holidays, exemptions from some tariffs, even venture capital. Buildings are available. CCNAA* can also help companies find top people to staff key positions—in particular, overseas Chinese. Industrial Technical Research Institute, a research development and testing laboratory serving companies in the park, has divisions

* CCNAA, the Co-ordination Council for North American Affairs, has been Taiwan's unofficial embassy in the United States since we derecognized Taiwan in favor of the People's Republic of China.

for materials, chemicals, and information processing. These incentives are available even to start-up companies.

U.S. companies already operating in SIP include WYse Technology, OEM-Tech, Mettel International, Qume Corporation—many from Silicon Valley. Companies of many sizes have located there, from AT&T down through start-ups. Not all of them are manufacturers. The SIP is seeking professional services needed by other companies in the park—such as accounting and financial services, engineering, and design.

To be accepted, apply through the Mountain View, California, branch of CCNAA, which specializes in SIP; for information, however, first approach the nearest CCNAA office. CCNAA can also help companies setting up in SIP find top people to staff key positions—in particular, overseas Chinese. This policy has apparently been very successful: Chinese managers jokingly say that SIP should be renamed the Chinese-American Industrial Park.

Skilled workers and technical personnel are much more available here than in Hong Kong or Singapore, but unskilled labor is scarce. Hong Kong draws from China, and Singapore from Malaysia and Indonesia; but Taiwan, which is also very crowded, has so far resisted allowing immigration from Southeast Asia, although there are many illegal "guest workers" from the Philippines and Indochina.

The Outlook for Taiwan

As Taiwan tries to make the leap into becoming a fully industrialized nation, several political and economic barriers remain to be overcome. Taiwan has chaotic small-scale industrial organizations. Japan and Korea have huge industrial and trading companies that market their goods worldwide, but in Taiwan, most industrial output comes from small, family-run companies, which may not be able to adapt to the rigors of global management and marketing. However, there is a pool of 50,000 highly educated Taiwanese now living and working in the United States, many of whom are now returning.

The government-controlled banks are still somewhat leery of lending money to smaller, entrepreneurial companies that need capital to upgrade their aging capital equipment. However, if that policy does not change, Taiwan could well begin to fall behind other competing nations, particularly Korea.

Taiwan is in the midst of a massive change in government. President Lee Teng-hui is the first Taiwan-born president. Many other government leaders, in power since they fled mainland China in 1949, are now being replaced by younger people, born in Taiwan but often educated in the United States. The change in leadership is sparking a reversal of the recent political and economic timidity, opening up many opportunities for U.S. business.

On the horizon lies an important benefit of trading in Taiwan. Many companies enter Chinese markets through Hong Kong, but Hong Kong is an expensive place to do business. Watch carefully for the opening door between China and Taiwan; regardless of politics, the two countries' economic links are likely to deepen, and American firms may soon be able to use Taiwan as an alternate base for entering Chinese markets.

ASEAN as a Region

The Association of South East Asian Nations (ASEAN—usually pronounced *AH-say-on*) (see Table 11–2 for a comparison of the countries) is an association of nations having mutual interests and a united international voice. It has not been an economic alliance, but it is working in that direction. ASEAN nations sit in a strategic location between the Indian and Pacific oceans, and make up one of the most dynamic and fastest-growing areas in the world. Since the late 1970s, U.S. exports to ASEAN have increased ninefold in a wide range of fields from agribusiness to highly sophisticated electronics and telecommunications. With its generous supply of natural resources, it is potentially very wealthy. ASEAN's total population of over 300 million is itself a promising market as affluence spreads and markets open up.

Gateways

- Singapore as strategic gateway for U.S. goods to ASEAN, especially to Malaysia and Indonesia
- Hong Kong as gateway to China for U.S. goods
- ASEAN as gateway to India, since there are many Indians living throughout ASEAN nations
- Thailand as gateway to Indochina (Vietnam, Cambodia, Burma, Laos) as these nations move from isolation and militarism toward development

---

ASEAN provides a laboratory for the United States in head-to-head competition with Japan. If U.S. companies can succeed in ASEAN markets and work out the service problems there against Japanese companies, it will bode well for U.S. chances in the other Pacific Rim markets.

Reasons for Investing in ASEAN

The traditional reasons for setting up operations in ASEAN have been (1) to take advantage of low-cost labor for low-skill assembly and (2) to exploit natural resources. There are other reasons as well:

Table 11-2. Comparison of the four ASEAN nations (except Singapore).

	Thailand	*Philippines*	*Malaysia*	*Indonesia*
Exchange rate (US$1 =)	Baht ~26	21 pesos	Ringgit ~2.5	Rupiah 1,650
Population	60 million	58 million	17 million	176 million
GDP or GNP	$40 billion	$34 billion	$22 billion	$54 billion
Growth rate of GNP	9%	6.5%	7.3%	4.3%
Per capita income	$763	$700	$1,500	$401
Inflation rate	3.4%	8%	3%	8%
Budget deficit	—	$1.1 billion	$3.2 billion	$3 billion
Labor force	28 million	23 million	6.25 million	—
Unemployment	7%	10%	9.5%	—
Trade balance	− $2.5 billion	− $741 million	− $238 million	− $2 billion
U.S. exports to	$1.3 billion	$1.7 billion	$1.25 billion	$427 million
U.S. imports from	$2.2 billion	$2.4 billion	$2.8 billion	$2 billion
Trade balance with United States	+ $200 million	+ $700 million	+ $550 million	+ $1.5 billion
U.S. share of imports	19%	36%	18%	7%
Language	Thai	English, Tagalog	Malay	Indonesian
Ethnic makeup	Thai, Chinese	Filipino, Chinese	Malay, Chinese, Indian	Irianese, Chinese, Malay
Religion	Buddhist	Catholic, Muslim	Muslim, Confucian	Muslim
Government leader	Premier Chatichi Choonhavan, King Bhumibol	President Aquino	Prime Minister Mahathir	President Suharto
Government	Constitutional monarchy; premier negotiated by leading parties	Democracy	President selected by ruling party	President selected by ruling party
Relative size	Colorado	Half of Texas	>Alaska 3,000 miles across	< Texas

- The availability of long-term capital financing, with excellent terms.
- Government incentives, including equity funds from some government agencies.
- Products and services needed for infrastructure and industrial development. Foreign management and technical expertise are eagerly sought to move these nations towards strong industrial economies.

If you are interested in this region, link up with ASEAN-U.S. Business Council, a bilateral, private-sector association of business executives.

*   *   *   *   *

Let's now look at each ASEAN nation individually (Singapore is grouped with the NICs).

Thailand

Thailand is being touted as the fifth NIC. It is rapidly changing from a traditional agrarian economy to a modern agroindustrial one. It is being transformed from a producer of primary products to a manufacturer of processed food and light industrial products. After recovering from the deep recession of 1985–1986, Thailand is now booming. Its serious foreign indebtedness has been brought under control, and, as a result, monetary and fiscal policies have been loosened to stimulate growth. In industry, agriculture, and foreign investment, diversification is the standard. (Even so, agriculture is still the biggest sector of the economy, and tourism the greatest source of foreign exchange.)

Led by large export-driven manufacturing industries, Thailand is expected to continue growing at the same rate throughout the 1990s to develop one of the most dynamic and promising economies in the region. Thailand is learning to be a sophisticated world marketeer, adapting quickly to changing international markets, and is a good place to invest, because of its demonstrated international competitiveness and wide range of new and promising industries.

Thailand has several major comparative advantages:

- *A very strong homegrown private sector, both in industry and in agriculture.* Thailand has a very dynamic entrepreneurial class that is adaptable and flexible and goes after emerging opportunities. Because of the Buddhist culture, education and getting ahead are important. The Thais understand the concept of making a profit, and believe they have some control over their destiny, unlike people in cultures where it is felt that one's fate is not in one's own hands.
- *Easily trained and relatively inexpensive labor.*
- *Traditionally limited government involvement.* This provides a framework in which private investment can flourish. The Thai government's direct involvement in private enterprise is much lower than in other ASEAN nations—even Singapore.

- *A growing number of Western-educated people who want to do business.* The government manages the economy enough to maintain stability and stimulate growth, but the allocation of both foreign and domestic investments is left mostly to market forces. The Thai government tries to direct foreign investment towards certain industries, but it lacks the control to be very successful because local competition against foreign-owned companies is so strong.
- *A welcoming of foreign private investment.* Thailand maintains a pro-business stance and conservative fiscal and monetary policies. Its abundant natural resources, skilled labor, and impressive infrastructure all help create a good investment climate.
- *Bangkok as an air traffic hub.* Shipments in and out of Bangkok are easy.
- *Link of Thailand's future with surrounding nations.* Unlike the NICs, Thailand does not rely primarily on U.S. or European markets. Over two fifths of its exports go to other Asian nations.

Trade and Investment Opportunities for U.S. Companies

As a result of its many advantages, industries are migrating from more advanced countries to Thailand. Although many U.S. companies have ignored opportunities in Thailand, leaving them for the Japanese, it is once more becoming a good place in which to invest and sell, with higher than average growth. The Japanese are investing so heavily that the Thais are getting nervous about having foreign investment dominated by one nation. The second echelon of Japanese companies that are now investing is precisely the level of American company that should now be reevaluating its chances in Thailand. With the dollar down against the yen, you should look again at the potentially lucrative opportunities in the following industries that provide opportunities for companies that both export from Thailand and manufacture there for the Thai market.

- *Construction projects.* U.S. businesses have shown too little interest in construction and are missing golden opportunities.
- *Food processing and packaging machinery.* There are no local manufacturers. An increasingly affluent population boosts domestic demand for quality food products, beverages, and household goods.
- *Computers and peripherals.* This industry has good prospects despite strong competition from Japan.
- *Medical equipment and supplies.*
- *Avionics and ground-support equipment.* Thailand has no local producers; the competition is from Japan and Italy.
- *Telecommunications equipment.*

One major opportunity lies just over the horizon. Recent hints that neighboring Indochinese nations are turning toward rational economic development policies have made Thai businesspeople ecstatic because, if Vietnam, Cambodia,

Burma, and Laos begin emphasizing economic development, foreign investment, and tourism, Thailand will benefit immensely. Bangkok would be the hub for tourist flights into Indochina and the natural channel for development dollars from the World Bank, the Asian Development Bank, and other agencies. The amount of infrastructure-related services and products funneled through Bangkok would be astronomical. Americans have a magnificent opportunity to take advantage of this.

Distribution

Companies wishing to sell in Thailand have a broad range of opportunities. For one thing, the government is the largest buyer in Thailand, since it controls or owns a major part of the country's economy. There are different types and qualities of trading companies; the difficulty comes in identifying the one that will provide the service you require. Also, while companies can sell directly into many Thai markets, their activities are covered by the Alien Business Act, and consumer goods must be retailed by Thai nationals.

Drawbacks

Despite the rosy picture, there are several drawbacks to doing business in Thailand:

- Much of the population does not speak or read English.

- Growth of foreign investment and tourism in Thailand is proceeding so rapidly that it is completely outstripping the ability of the infrastructure to hold it. Transport and communication bottlenecks are major barriers in Bangkok, through which everything flows.

- Thailand lacks supporting industries for manufacturing, such as precision tooling and laboratories. Thus a desperately needed part may have to be flown in from Hong Kong.

- Many Thai exports can easily be hurt by U.S. protectionist legislation. "When two elephants fight, the grass gets trampled" expresses the concern that protectionism spawned by the U.S.-Japanese trade imbalance will smother Thai economic growth.

- There is a great deal of inconsistency and ambiguity in the application of business laws and regulations. Sometimes policy changes are applied retroactively.

- Foreign currency exchanges are regulated. Foreign exchange transfers require permission from the Bank of Thailand. Although in practice there are few obstacles to funds transfer, it is very important that correct procedures be followed. The Thai government has the power to disapprove foreign currency investment, but hasn't used it much.

• There are still problems with intellectual property protection.

• Despite its long-term commitment to free enterprise, many government officials and civil servants seem to hold a deep distrust of the private sector. Some Thai officials as individuals maintain small personally controlled areas of enterprise.

• *Critical factor:* There is a split in affluence between urban and rural citizens and increased rural anger at this disparity.

Some companies that considered setting up a manufacturing facility in Thailand have chosen to go into China near Hong Kong instead, citing three reasons: First, they expect wages and labor costs to begin accelerating in Thailand; second, it is difficult to find skilled Thai managers, whereas managers from Hong Kong and Singapore can be brought in for Chinese plants; and third, it is often easier to obtain needed parts and components in China through Hong Kong.

There is some fear about changes in government policy, but such changes have generally had little effect on the business environment. The government of Thailand has long made investors nervous because it changes often. However, every emerging coalition has so far maintained an orientation towards free enterprise, which is deeply embedded in the Thai philosophy. The bureaucracy has maintained stability throughout the changes of governments. King Bhumibol has been on the throne since 1946, and in 1988, Mr. Chatichai became the first elected premier in many years. A succession of military coups that gave Thailand the reputation of political instability in truth never caused that instability, and now even the coups have tailed off.

The Philippines

If the government can keep the economic recovery on track, the Philippines could once again become an excellent nation for trade and investment by U.S. companies because of the American's traditionally close ties with the Philippine people. Now may be a very good time for new companies to get involved with the Philippines, although its negative aspects are still very strong: poverty, 3 percent population growth per year, unemployment, the Communist insurgency, the potentially restive military, and latent support for Marcos.

However, there are also many signs of economic improvement: Foreign exchange reserves are at an all-time high; inflation is down from 50 percent to less than 10 percent; the Philippine peso has stabilized against the U.S. dollar; and the rescheduling of nearly half of the Philippines' $28 billion of foreign debt at a lower interest rate has cut interest payments in half.

Former Colonial Rulers of Pacific Rim Nations

Japan	None except the United States immediately after World War II
Korea	Japan
China	None substantial
Hong Kong	Britain
Taiwan	None, except for brief Japanese occupation
Thailand	None, except for brief Japanese occupation
Malaysia	Britain
Singapore	Britain
Indonesia	Netherlands
Philippines	Spain, United States
Australia	Britain
New Zealand	Britain

The significance of this lies in the structure of the legal and accounting systems.

The economy has begun expanding again. Growth is up to over 5 percent a year, and that growth has been based largely on domestic capital, since foreign investment is still skittish. Many see a continuing economic upswing including a nationwide construction boom. Domestic manufacturing and service sectors are growing very rapidly. Foreign businesses already in the Philippines are expanding. The Philippine stock market is up, as measured by the Makati Index (equivalent to the Dow Jones Average). The top 1,000 Philippine companies boasted a 10.6 percent increase in gross revenues in 1986. Topping the profitability list were the San Miguel Corporation and the Philippine Long Distance Telephone Company.

Consumer confidence is high. Consumption is growing at 5 percent a year. Supermarkets are full, restaurants are crowded, and house prices are spurting upward. The rapid rise in imports and consumer spending has led to growth in the manufacturing and trade sectors. The affluent urban population is demanding better-quality goods and services, providing major markets for companies selling capital equipment to modernize domestic industries.

Much of the Philippine recovery is being fueled by internal growth rather than expansion of export-related industries, as has been the case with other members of ASEAN. Domestic factories are operating at full capacity, and the industrial base is crying out for foreign investment. Flight capital from the Philippines is returning—$1.7 billion in 1986—but there is much more to bring back. The biggest foreign investor is not the United States or Japan, but Taiwan.

Many outside investors have retained their wait-and-see attitude, but those that have already invested in the Philippines seem to be doing quite well. Despite the fact that the deep-seated social problems still worry investors, some new foreign investment is beginning to flow into pharmaceuticals, automobile assembly, shrimp raising, and tire manufacturing.

Concern about political stability is only one impediment to foreign investment. There are also the frustrating foreign investment laws. Although in principle, most foreign investment is acceptable, the approval process can move so slowly that potential investors go elsewhere—to Malaysia, Singapore, Indonesia, and Thailand. Imports may be delayed for weeks while companies comply with import regulations. Such delays may fuel the same kind of corruption that was rampant under Ferdinand Marcos.

The Philippine trade and investment climate is freer and less restricted than in Malaysia and Indonesia. The government is actively stimulating economic recovery and growth by running a controlled deficit and instituting policies to open up trade and investment. The Omnibus Investments Code was passed in 1987 to offer the same incentives to investors that other ASEAN nations use to encourage capital inflows (including the return of Philippine flight capital). Foreign investors were once limited to owning 40 percent of a Filipino company, but new regulations will allow companies to be 100 percent foreign-owned in certain areas where the projects expand export markets. Many import restrictions have been lifted.

Many of the most dominant and profitable corporations in the Philippines are partially or wholly owned by American businesses. In 1986, there were 862 foreign corporations there: Of these, 431 were American, 348 were joint ventures, and 83 were wholly owned American companies.

If the resurgence of foreign investment and export revenues continues, the Philippines will soon be well on its way to challenging Thailand as the next NIC. The Philippines used to be by far the poorest member of ASEAN, but if the government implements policies that maintain political stability and foster economic development, the Philippines could overtake Malaysia and Indonesia within a few years as an attractive market for American investors and exporters.

Trade and Investment Opportunities

For U.S. investors, the Philippines offers a good combination of a low-cost yet relatively well educated, highly skilled, English-speaking work force, as compared with Malaysia and Thailand. It has an abundant supply of technical and managerial people—many with U.S. college degrees. Other ASEAN nations are two or three times more expensive, which is why U.S. investment in the Philippines has increased rapidly in spite of continuing uncertainty about the political stability of the Aquino government.

U.S. companies are investing in data processing, agribusiness, aquaculture, and light manufacturing. They are also exporting a wide range of capital equipment, chemicals, telecommunications, computers (especially micros and minis), software, peripherals, safety and security equipment, and food processing and packaging equipment. Some are getting contracts for infrastructure construction projects.

If you have a smaller company that would like to establish operations in the Philippines, you can obtain assistance from the Philippine Department of Trade and Industry's Board of Investment, which provides "one stop shopping," and will process investment applications in two or three weeks.

Critical Factor

Watch for the outcome of talks on the Clark Air Force and Subic Bay naval bases. The United States has strong support and very strong interests in the Philippines, but that, in itself, stirs up a "big brother" image as well as resentment and protest that sometimes flare into violence. It is possible, but not likely, that this may threaten U.S. investment and business interests there.

Malaysia

Opportunities for U.S. Companies

Malaysia has meant two things for Americans: a leading source of many raw materials and a low-cost labor market for assembling medium-tech manufactured goods for re-export. It has long depended on commodity markets. Because of the wild price fluctuations in primary commodities such as oil and tin, Malaysia has been seeking to broaden its industrial base to upgrade its industrial sophistication. The government deficit may be eliminated by 1989. U.S. imports from Malaysia have been shifting from commodities to manufactured goods. Most U.S. products exported to Malaysia consist of electronic components for products re-exported to the United States or other markets.

Malaysia keeps flirting with NIC status, but despite its primarily open-market orientation, it has suffered from overmanagement of the economy and government intervention in business. There has been a behind-the-scenes struggle between those who favor a rational, unfettered private sector and those who wish to expand government-owned businesses and improve the political and economic interests of some groups and individuals. Overcontrol has drastically slowed a formerly booming economy. The guiding hand of the Malaysian government has led to interference in the commodities and financial markets. Arbitrary actions taken against the news media, opposition politicians, and ethnic minorities sow distrust in the minds of exactly those investors who are needed by Malaysia to rekindle its growth.

Prime Minister Mahathir's wish to create a heavy industrial base for Malaysia has led to some outstanding facilities: Penang Island—the original outpost of Britain's East India Company 200 years ago—is the home of a number of multinational electronics companies, which Malaysia hopes will propel its economy from plantations and mines into the technological age. Penang has become perhaps the most cosmopolitan city in Malaysia. But some of the projects have been costly and questionable, including the Proton Saga automobile, produced in Malaysia for domestic and export markets; each Saga sold in Malaysia costs the government over $1,000.

Culturally, Malaysia is split. Business is dominated by overseas Chinese who have lived there for several generations, but the Malay-dominated government has adopted policies aimed at giving native Malays (Bumiputras, or "sons of the soil") a greater stake in the economy. Thus, the government gets involved in whom you can hire, but there are not enough well-educated Malays to support the desired foreign investment.

Malaysia has recently liberalized imports and foreign investment. Its New Economic Policy (NEP) now allows foreign investors to have a wholly owned operation if they export 50 percent of their products or employ more than 350 Malaysians. Companies that export less than 50 percent still benefit from liberalized rules for expatriate management and technical people.

There are also growing opportunities for a broad range of operations in and exports to Malaysia.

Consumer Goods

Malaysia's growing affluent middle class likes Western foods and consumer products. Merchandisers for supermarkets and department stores are always looking for new products, and there is a tremendous growing demand for convenience foods and fresh fruit.

Industrial and Commercial Markets

American businesses should seek opportunities in several industries and markets:

- *Telecommunications*—being privatized, expanded, and made more flexible. A potential market exists for equipment and related services, data communications, and software.
- *Computers and peripherals*—growing market for minis and supermicros in business.
- *Software*—new copyright law will slowly improve the market.
- *Food processing and packaging*—especially for import substitution products.
- *Oil and gas equipment.*
- *Scientific instruments, medical instruments, and aircraft avionics parts.*
- *Infrastructure*—major investment in highways and railroads; power stations and transmission lines; gas pipelines; and gas and petrochemical processing.

Distribution

Companies selling to Malaysia normally sell through an established trading company that has its own branches and traveling salespeople. The larger trading companies provide a full range of marketing services, maintaining inventories and their own distribution networks and providing spare parts and maintenance, as well as financing. Many of these companies are British or are based in Singapore. Smaller American companies may find it easier initially to enter through Singapore—in the same way American companies may enter China through Hong Kong.

Local trading companies are usually owned either by Chinese or Indian Malaysians. Your difficulty will be in finding a qualified trading company that will give your product the attention it requires. Since there is a shortage of qualified distributors, many businesses find that they must assist their local distributor with marketing efforts. This, of course, takes a greater degree of commitment to and awareness of the market, including travel there to evaluate, select, and work with the distributor.

Investment

Your greatest opportunity in Malaysia may be through direct investment. Even though most foreign investment is still in the petroleum sector, over $1 billion has been invested by American-owned manufacturers. Some large American companies have also invested in Malaysian service industries, including life insurance and mutual funds.

Recent developments, such as the National Council for Scientific Research and Development's planned technology park, also make it easier for smaller companies to establish operations in Malaysia. The park will be located near government research institutes and universities in order to attract foreign investment; R&D and limited manufacturing will be performed. A government venture capital fund is expected to provide start-up capital, and may subsidize operating costs. Additional financing will be available from local banks.

Indonesia

Indonesia is a 3,000-mile-long archipelago of 13,700 islands called locally by the name *Nusantara*. Indonesia has unparalleled wealth and should be an Asian superpower. It has dozens of ethnic groups, and the 170 million Indonesians speak 300 different languages and dialects. One island, Java, with a population of 100 million, is the size of Greece—which has only 10 million people. Two fifths of the Indonesians are under age 15, so the population is among the fastest-growing in the world. Of the labor force, 60 percent work the land.

Agriculture—rubber, oil, palm, coffee, sugar, bananas—is still the biggest sector of the economy. Growing conditions are ideal for these crops. Even so, too many plantations are government-controlled, and are 40 percent less efficient than in neighboring Malaysia.

Indonesia has a strong core of Javanese culture, but still has a major challenge in maintaining harmony among the diverse ethnic groups such as Christian Bataks, Hindu Balinese, and Muslim Javanese. It has been much more successful in meeting that challenge than many other multiethnic nations; even intermarriage is accepted. The harmony is the result of planning and control, and the elements that threaten it—such as fundamentalist Islam or Communism—are ruthlessly suppressed. Despite its 90 percent Muslim population, Indonesia is no more fundamentalist Islamic than the United States is fundamentalist Christian.

Despite the explosive population growth among Indonesian peasants, especially on Java, Indonesia has an expanding, affluent middle class. Nevertheless, a growing exodus from rural areas to the cities has created a pool of urban poor that, while providing low-cost labor, is a source of political unrest.

President Suharto has ruled Indonesia since 1965 and is likely to continue well into the 1990s. Although he is viewed by some as a military dictator, his popularity is very widespread within the country. However, the government is still inward-looking, nationalist, protectionist, and bureaucratic. It prefers self-sufficiency and has a we-can-do-it-ourselves attitude. Its feeling about foreign investment and goods seems to be, "We'll take you on our terms."

Even though Indonesia has long recognized the importance of foreign investment, it has acted ambivalently, posing many barriers to imports and investment. Many items are prohibited, and you must usually sell through an established Indonesian distributor. Its very high taxes, tariffs, surcharges, excess profits levies, and fees have all slowed foreign trade. Rules and regulations are applied inconsistently and arbitrarily, and it is hard to get reliable, pertinent marketing information.

Many of these barriers have virtually kept smaller companies from doing business there. The Investment Coordinating Board must approve each technology licensing agreement, and there are stringent guidelines for investment. Software, copyrights, pharmaceuticals, and chemicals have been poorly protected, and foreign companies have been pressured to dilute their equity.

Besides the official policies, corruption is also a major impediment. Payoffs to gain approval and to obtain operating licenses and building permits or work permits are standard. Payments are expected to speed things up.

The cost of entry into Indonesia is quite high. It is important to work with local partners, but there are few qualified organizations and people to fulfill that role. As a result, most American businesses operating in Indonesia have been large multinationals involved in oil extraction or other primary products.

Debt has risen dramatically since world oil prices began to fall in the late 1970s. The falling oil prices have decreased Indonesia's ability to repay its debt, and the country has sought debt relief from Japan—its main trading partner and foreign investor—and from the World Bank. About two fifths of its debt (like that of other Asian nations) is denominated in the yen, which has doubled in value over the last several years.

The current debt squeeze is pushing Indonesia towards a more open market. It is trying to free itself from overdependence on oil exports and to diversify its industrial base by attracting foreign investment. Indonesia's economic technocrats—an American-educated group called the Berkeley Mafia—have unveiled a new package of economic reforms relaxing many rules on foreign investment.

Recent Measures to Revitalize the Economy

Indonesia has recently taken several steps towards economic liberalization.

1. *Foreign investment rules have been relaxed.* Foreign investors have been allowed into almost 300 sectors from which they had previously been banned. Licenses for manufactured goods used to require product-by-product permits. These have been replaced by blanket categories so that companies can produce varied products in an overall category without requiring a new permit each time. Any company that 'now holds a general business license may export any product except those that are governed by export quotas, such as textiles and coffee. Output ceilings have also been relaxed.

The period during which foreign investors must transfer 51 percent of a joint venture to domestic shareholders has been increased from ten to fifteen years. A recently enacted tax treaty makes taxation practices more consistent with those of other nations.

2. *Indonesia has enacted copyright legislation and patent protection.* As the government again seeks foreign investors, it is finally cracking down on pirated music cassettes—a major industry in Indonesia. Fines and jail terms are imposed for copyright infringement. Thus does the government try to reassure potential investors about the safety of their intellectual property rights.

3. *Import regulations have been relaxed.* Foreign companies now have the right to distribute their own products. Indonesian companies can buy materials and components abroad. Local sourcing is no longer mandatory if imported components and materials are cheaper. Tariffs have been reduced, and some duties and quotas have been abolished. Some import monopolies have also been abolished. A Swiss company is now in charge of assessing customs duties; this has reduced import and export costs by more than 20 percent.

Tightly controlled or monopolized industries such as shipping have been deregulated, which greatly cuts transport costs. Controls on steel imports have been eliminated, and now foreign companies may form joint ventures for steel distribution. Importing of plastics is no longer a state monopoly.

4. *The nation's banking system and capital markets are undergoing major reforms.* The growth of private banks—including foreign banks—has been stim-

ulated by allowing state-run enterprises to put up to half their deposits in private banks. Foreign banks can open branches in Jakarta and elsewhere if they joint venture with an Indonesian bank having at least a 15 percent equity share.

5. *The stock exchange has been revived.* A new, over-the-counter exchange that is open to foreign participation will supplement the stock exchange. Foreign investors will have access to rupiah loans from state banks.

6. *Domestically, Indonesia has enforced World Bank-approved austerity programs.* It is pushing policies to develop efficient agribusiness and to deregulate industry. The rupiah has been devalued.

Since 1987, foreign investment in Indonesia has begun to increase, reversing a decline of several years. It is now seeking to stimulate nonoil exports, seeking investment in plywood, textiles, instant coffee, soap, candy, nails, steel coils, paper pulp, and chemicals.

The best prospects for American suppliers appear to be industrial machinery, telecommunications equipment, professional and scientific instruments, plastic materials and resins, inorganic chemicals, electrical machinery, and equipment for power generation, oil and gas, avionics, computers, and electronics. Indonesia is seeking help to build its agroindustry, highways, and electrical power generation and electric grids.

However, Indonesia's rapid population growth, especially on Java, could well aggravate economic problems and political instability. Many government policies will be aimed at providing jobs for the tremendous number of young people entering the labor force into the year 2000. This will generate both risks and opportunities. On the one hand, there will be a tremendous demand for services that the Indonesian government cannot provide, such as training and education. On the other hand, there will be pressure for import substitution in order to create manufacturing jobs for the growing population.

If you can take advantage of these opportunities, Indonesia holds numerous benefits. Margins are high, and there is a short-term horizon for recouping investments, but costs are low—especially for labor—and the attitude of the work force is positive. It is a place for the long term if you're able to take the risks.

Malaysia and Indonesia Through American Eyes

Americans who feel frustrated with the policies of Malaysia and Indonesia should reflect on their own history. In many ways, these two nations seem similar to the United States of the early 1800s: wealthy, with tremendous resources waiting to be developed; very friendly, outgoing, generous people, but with a culture a bit hard to understand by the leading nations; a people determined to develop, but in their own way; a bit suspicious of foreign capital; and willing to accept investment from leading nations, but on their own terms.

Other similarities to the early United States are that they are inward-looking and isolationist politically; feel insulated from major world struggles; are absorbed in their own efforts to mold a nation out of diverse cultures and former colonial status; are trying to make their democracies work but at the same time are determined to hold their nations together at whatever cost; and consist of affluent, cosmopolitan areas mixed with frontiers remote from central control.

It is no accident that the Pacific Rim nations that have advanced most rapidly in the global economy have been those with the fewest internal resources. Japan and the NICs are small, crowded, resource-poor nations that have been forced to look outward to survive. The same pressures are increasingly exerting themselves on the remaining Pacific Rim nations—ASEAN, China, Australia, and New Zealand—whose greater land area or resources have allowed them more respite from the pressures of becoming global marketeers.

Until recently, that is.

Now, the same social and economic imperatives are forcing them to open up to the world economy, and that will create openings for companies that can perceive their needs and supply them competitively.

CRITICAL FACTORS TO WATCH

Virtually every Pacific Rim nation is in the midst of a major economic transition. Japan is trying on the mantle of leading global economic power. The NICs are moving from developing nations to mature economies—ready to enter the Organization for Economic Cooperation and Development (OECD). Several ASEAN members are approaching NIC status. Australia and New Zealand are shifting from being the protected larders of Great Britain to high-tech, high-service Pacific Rim partners. China is perhaps changing the most, since it is undergoing a complete transformation of its economic system.

As each nation comes up against its particular transition, there's a bit of resistance—especially from government policy makers, but also from some sectors of society—to adopting policies in keeping with the new, more mature economy. We're seeing the effects of that now in the form of continuing emphasis on export-driven and mercantilistic economies, particularly in Japan, Korea, and Taiwan. However, there will be increasing pressure both internal and external for these countries to change their policies, open up their markets, and encourage consumer spending. *Internal* pressure will come from a populace that wants to reap more of the rewards of the nation's growing affluence, while *external* pressure will come from nations such as the United States and those of Western Europe that feel the effects of the trade imbalances. As a result, more opportunities should open up to sell consumer goods and other types of products and services to these economies.

Some of the factors listed in the remainder of this chapter pertain mainly to a particular group of nations, but most relate in some degree to every Pacific Rim nation.

Table 11-3.   Pacific Rim nations as investment targets.

Japan	Has to remain the major target.
Hong Kong	Great for now; very strong financially.
Singapore	Good human resources; improved financial sector and engineering.
Australia	Easy to invest in. In some sectors, Australian businesses still have a big economic advantage.
New Zealand	Easy to invest in. Companies here also have access to Australia. Gateway to South Pacific nations.
Taiwan	Very good for the types of industries they want.
Thailand	Good, although an experienced hand is needed. Many opportunities for smaller American companies.
Korea	Domestic market just beginning to open up. Good for manufacturing products for re-export.
Indonesia, Malaysia, and the Philippines	Many say, "Stay out unless you have to be there," but this is changing, liberalizing rapidly. Keep your eye on these nations. Gain a foothold through Singapore.
China	Requires a long-term commitment. Gain a foothold through Hong Kong.

For the Early 1990s

Let's finish these profiles by summarizing a few critical factors for the Pacific Rim region as a whole (see also Table 11–3). You should monitor these trends in order to keep a finger on the future course of events in your markets. Many of these factors point either to problems or to opportunities, so it is important for you to get in the habit of watching these trends.

1. Developing nations are improving their technological capabilities. Japan is moving into basic research; Singapore and Hong Kong, into applied research and increased R&D; and China and ASEAN, into effectively applying more advanced technologies.

2. The ASEAN nations' attitude toward trade and investment is changing. They are still concerned both about overdependence on their trading partners and sources of technology and about cultural domination, especially by the United States.

3. Watch for the trend towards privatization of formerly government-run enterprises. See if they will be turned back to the private sector in such a way that they can operate efficiently according to market forces, or whether they will still be hamstrung by regulation.

4. A key leading indicator is the percentage of public-sector employment. If the proportion of people on a nation's government payroll actually begins to decline, it is a sign of serious commitment to increasing economic efficiency.

5. Watch the development of financial structures. Financial institutions in several Pacific Rim nations have been controlled and closed off. This is changing in Korea and Taiwan. These nations want to deal with their huge reserves. The incentive for financial liberalization is not just economic but also political. A closed financial system tends to lead to corruption, whereas a liberalized one leads to political stability.

6. Several countries have suffered debilitating capital flight for years, much of it going to the United States. If conditions stabilize politically, and if economic policy becomes more favorable to private investment, watch for the repatriation of this capital. It could provide a large source of investment capital for direct investment. Also watch for increasing importance of private funds and local banks for trade and for nontrade development and for lending and underwriting development. But these forms of development will require participation of the local sector—in joint ventures, for example.

7. Similarly, several nations have suffered a brain drain, since many of their best students have received higher educations in the United States and then stayed there. When conditions improve, many of these young men and women will return home. Look at the number of people who came back to the Philippines when Marcos was overthrown, bringing not only their money but also the education and business skills gained in the United States. Returning nationals may provide a very important source of managerial skills for U.S. companies. To the extent that that happens, expect to find growing number of policy makers who understand the United States and are friendly to it.

8. A growing pool of skilled managers educated in American management styles is becoming available. These English-speaking men and women have spent time in the United States, are familiar with American management methods, and may have worked for American companies. Thus, if you want to go to Indonesia and hire a local person for a management position, it is easier to do so than it was in the past.

Many graduates from Pacific Rim countries are hired by American companies right out of MBA programs, then given further training in the United States, and sent back to their home countries to work in local offices. Initially, many of these graduates go into large companies, either American- or large Pacific Rim-owned, but this does have the secondary effect of increasing the region's pool of skilled managers who are available for other companies as well. On the other hand, of course, much of the returned capital and brains will go into locally owned companies, signaling increased competition for U.S. companies.

9. NIC currencies have been pegged to the U.S. dollar. This has spurred rapid growth because the currencies have been overvalued compared to the dollar;

with easy access to American markets, the NICs have thus run up a large trade surplus with the United States. Pressure is strong for the NICs to raise their exchange rates, and Taiwan and Korea are doing so.

These pegged currencies may create a liability for these nations because of their artificially low values. Companies may not have been stimulated to achieve the levels of efficiency and productivity that will permit them to compete in international markets. Many Korean companies, in particular, have received financial support from the government on extremely preferential terms. The large conglomerates, like those in the United States during the 1960s, may have developed critical flaws in organization, strategy, and staffing.

10. Look to the growth of regionalization. One purpose of ASEAN, for example, is to foster trade among member nations. But also watch for links between ASEAN and the NICs or Australia. Since so many of these countries have relied on primary resources, their markets have not been complementary to each other. But as their industries become more sophisticated and diverse, more complementary markets will appear within the region. Already, items that are assembled and manufactured—in, for example, Taiwan for re-export to the United States or Japan—are finding an important secondary market selling to other ASEAN nations. Taiwan has become the largest investor in the Philippines. It will be increasingly important for companies locating in one country, e.g., Singapore, to look at the regional market potential.

11. The pattern of foreign investment is important. Influence follows money, and the extent to which Japan, Taiwan, Korea, and Australia make "altruistic," no-strings-attached development loans and grants is one way in which U.S. influence will be seriously challenged.

12. Also, take into account the China factor: China as an opportunity for investment, especially for Korea and Taiwan; China as a goad, a competitor, driving the others up the value-added curve; China as a source of political stability, keeping a lid on North Korea and Cambodia. Although China may never provide a huge import market, it provides a solid center, and can perhaps help actualize a concept of a Pacific Basin more so than even Japan.

Keep an eye on the "Greater China" phenomenon: Taiwan's engineering, Hong Kong's finance and managerial skill, and China's market and resources. Economic integration will far precede political integration. All three agree that there is only one China.

13. The population of the Pacific Rim nations is growing rapidly. Many young men and women are entering the work force, becoming very hard to absorb given current policies. Despite efforts to develop secondary and rural areas as viable economic sectors, many people are moving toward urban areas. Unemployment is growing in Indonesia, China, Japan, and even Korea. Guest workers in the Philippines may be sent home.

14. Keep an eye on patterns of political transition and succession. So far so good in Korea; looks smooth in Taiwan, Thailand, and China; and in Indonesia, Malaysia, and Singapore, the current leaders still appear to be very much in charge.

Regarding the impact of leadership change on the United States, watch for possible anti-Americanism in some opposition quarters. The business climate may become less favorable. Political stability has always been a key factor to the success of Pacific Rim nations. If new leaders provide less stability, the business climate could change, especially given other critical factors.

The U.S. Factor

It is essential to look at current and proposed U.S. policies and evaluate their impact on Pacific Rim markets in general and your markets in particular. Two major thrusts of U.S. policy are to open up Pacific Rim markets to American services and to improve the protection of intellectual property. To help in your evaluation, consider the following:

- U.S. trade policy may be moving toward protectionism. Watch the multilateral versus bilateral orientation. Watch the outcome and implementation of the Uruguay round of GATT talks.
- There is evidence of a renewed willingness of U.S. banks to finance international development.
- The U.S. government has only recently begun to take notice of the need to promote small and medium-size businesses and, secondly, to promote overseas investment rather than just trade.
- The strength of the U.S. dollar will be a major factor to consider. Watch how it relates to other Pacific Rim currencies, particularly those that have been pegged to the dollar. For example, currencies in Taiwan and Korea were both pegged to the dollar at an artificially low rate. As those currencies float up, opportunities for U.S. investors increase.

On the Horizon

The antieconomic leaders are passing from the scene in Vietnam, Burma, Cambodia, and Laos. If these nations turn from self-destruction to economic development, the entire atmosphere of the Pacific Rim will change. There will be a tremendous opportunity for U.S. businesses as development efforts are funneled into these nations, which are all as well endowed as Thailand. Also, American companies will be able to offer many of the skills and resources most needed. But such development signals not just opportunity but a challenge as well, because the settling of differences in Indochina will only follow if the superpower tensions among the United States, the USSR, and China ease. As superpower tensions ease, the upcoming economic powers of the world will become much more independent—and competitive. U.S. competitiveness will be determined on strictly economic terms. American products will no longer be given an edge just because the United States is the bulwark of freedom in the region.

Pacific Rim Currencies and Exchange Rates (as of Mid-1988)

Even though these exchange rates shift over time, this chart will still give you a general idea of their relationship to the dollar and to each other. These rates may conflict with those shown elsewhere in this book.

Country	Currency	Exchange Rate
Australia	Dollar	1.40
China	Renminbi yuan	3.72
Hong Kong	Dollar	7.77
Indonesia	Rupiah	1,650.00
Japan	Yen	123.60
Korea	Won	792.20
Malaysia	Ringgit	2.49
New Zealand	Dollar	1.55
Philippines	Peso	20.73
Singapore	Dollar	1.99
Taiwan	Dollar	28.55
Thailand	Baht	25.05

U.S. Government Services

Department of Commerce (DOC)

For help and information, contact your local International Trade Administration office (on pp. 354–357), or:

The Department of Commerce Exporter Assistance Staff
Room 1099D
U.S. Department of Commerce
Washington, D.C. 20230
(202) 377-4811

Also at the Department of Commerce in Washington, D.C., are country desk officers for each nation. The desk officers for each Pacific Rim nation are listed in Appendix IV.

Many of the DOC services entail a nominal charge. Current fees are listed here, but check for any changes.

Licensing

You can get a preliminary written advisory opinion on what kind of license you need from the Commerce Department by calling (202) 377-4845.

Applications for Validated Export Licenses should be sent to:

Office of Export Licensing
Box 273
Ben Franklin Station
Washington, D.C. 20044

Publicity

New Product Information Service (NPIS). The NPIS provides worldwide publicity for new U.S. products available for immediate export. NPIS information is distributed via the monthly publication *Commercial News USA,* which contains brief promotion

351

descriptions of products and information on how to contact your company. This magazine is sent to over 240 U.S. embassies and consulates and fifty American Chambers of Commerce abroad, reaching approximately 200,000 key business and governmental leaders worldwide. The charge for the service is currently $150 per product listing.

International Market Search (IMS).   Products that do not qualify as new producuts for the NPIS may be eligible for publication under the IMS program. The IMS issue of *Commercial News USA* is limited to a specific product and/or industry grouping, such as security and safety equipment. For a listing of products and/or industries scheduled for promotion, check with the Commerce Department. The charge for the IMS is $150 per product.

Worldwide Service Program (WSP).   WSP helps U.S. companies to (1) publicize the availability of their services overseas and (2) test market interest. WSP is designed to encourage foreign companies to contact U.S. service companies interested in doing business overseas so that the U.S. companies explore foreign market interest, find representation, and make sales. A fee of $150 is charged for this service.

Market and Distribution Information

Libraries.   Many Commerce Department offices have libraries, or International Marketing Centers, that contain DOC trade statistics and publications, such as *Overseas Business Reports, Foreign Economic Trends,* and pertinent regulations.

Exporting Mailing List Service (EMLS).   A computerized mailing list, the EMLS provides data about foreign companies that have traded with the United States. Specific information is given about the product(s) you are interested in selling, the markets you wish to sell in, and the kinds of companies you want to sell to. Such a tailored EMLS list provides information, such as the name and address of the business, name and title of the chief executive, year established, type of business (e.g., manufacturer, wholesaler, distributor), and other information. The cost for this service is $25 (computer access charge) plus twenty-five cents per name appearing on your list.

Agent/Distributor Service (ADS).   The ADS will help your company locate interested and qualified overseas agents or distributors for your products or services. Through commercial offices abroad, the ADS provides you with information on up to six qualified contacts that have expressed interest in your company's sales proposal. The charge for this service is currently $125 per country. The ADS is available for most countries and usually takes approximately sixty days for processing.

Comparison Shopping Service.   The U.S. and Foreign Commercial Service (US&FCS) of the Commerce Department offers market research service custom tailored to individual U.S. companies. This will provide you with key marketing and foreign representation facts about your specific product. All responses are based on on-the-spot personal interviews conducted by US&FCS personnel. The service is offered in fourteen countries, including Indonesia, South Korea, the Philippines, and Singapore.

Requests are confined to standard, off-the-shelf products, rather than specialty or custom-built products. Standard products are easier to describe in catalogs, have clear-cut prices associated with them, are influenced by routine competitive factors, have relatively straightforward distribution channels, and have a number of suppliers and potential agents that can serve as contact points. The fee for the service is $500 to survey a specific market for a single product in one country. To order, contact your local US & FCS office (listed in this Appendix).

Promotion

Overseas Shows.   Overseas promotions organized and recruited by the U.S. Department of Commerce are scheduled worldwide. Costs vary according to the specific event. The type of events held include:

- Solo exhibits—trade shows that are initiated and staged by the U.S. Department of Commerce and that feature only U.S. exhibitors and their products.
- International trade fairs—shows in which the U.S. Department of Commerce establishes a U.S. section or pavilion featuring U.S. products and exhibitors. The objective is to create a separate U.S. identity at an event that is usually multi-product and multicountry in nature.
- Catalog shows—overseas promotion utilizing product catalogs and literature. These worldwide exhibitions feature displays of a large number of U.S. product catalogs, sales brochures, and other graphic sales aids at U.S. embassies and consulates or in conjuction with trade shows. Such shows offer an excellent and inexpensive way for U.S. companies to test product interest in foreign markkets, develop sales leads, and locate agents and distributors.
- MATCHMAKER—an important trade fair event. In this program, foreign commercial officers match U.S. companies to potential business partners in the host country. U.S. companies conduct pre-scheduled, one-on-one meetings with foreign company representatives. They meet key business and financial officers, learn market requirements, and establish important contacts. Nine MATCHMAKERS were held in 1988.

Trade Missions.   Overseas sales promotion missions are sponsored, arranged, and recruited by the U.S. Department of Commerce. A trade mission visits one or more countries in a geographic region. The missions are industry specific (e.g., computers, process control instruments), and are normally limited to representatives from eight to twelve U.S. companies. Mission members are responsible for their own expenses, and must make a contribution to defray general mission expenses.

See also Appendix III at Credit Checking.

Intellectual Property Protection

Several U.S. government offices can answer questions about intellectual property protection overseas. Many issue publications on the subject. A number of publications also are available through intellectual property law and trade associations. Two offices of the Commerce Department are listed below, along with three other government offices:

Patent and Trademark Office (DOC)
Washington, D.C. 20231
(703) 557-3341, Public Affairs Office
(703) 557-3080, Patent Information
(703) 557-3497, Trademark Information

International Trade Administration (DOC)
International Economic Policy
Washington, D.C. 20230
(202) 377-4501

U.S. Customs Service (Treasury Department)
Entry Licensing and Restricted Merchandise Branch
Washington, D.C. 20229
(202) 566-5765

Copyright Office
Library of Congress
Washington, D.C. 20559
(202) 287-8700

U.S. Trade Representative
Trade Policy Staff Committee Subcommittee on Intellectual Property
Washington, D.C. 20506
(202) 395-6161

International Trade Administration/US&FCS District Offices

Alabama

2015 2nd Ave. N.
Berry Building
*Birmingham, Ala. 35203
(205) 731-1331

Alaska

701 C St.
P.O. Box 32
Anchorage, Alaska 99513
(907) 271-5041

Arizona

Federal Bldg. & U.S.
  Courthouse
230 North 1st Ave., Rm.
  3412
Phoenix, Ariz. 85025
(602) 261-3285

Arkansas

Savers Fed. Bldg., Suite
  811
320 W. Capitol Ave.
Little Rock, Ark. 72201
(501) 378-5794

California

11777 San Vicente Blvd.,
  Rm. 800
Los Angeles, Calif.
  90049
(213) 209-6707

116-A W. 4th St., Suite 1
†Santa Ana, Calif. 92701
(714) 836-2461

6363 Greenwich Dr.
San Diego, Calif. 92122
(619) 293-5395

Fed. Bldg.
Box 36013
450 Golden Gate Avenue
*San Francisco, Calif.
  94102
(415) 556-5860

Colorado

U.S. Customhouse, Rm.
  119
721 19th St.
*Denver, Colo. 80202
(303) 844-3246

Connecticut

Fed. Office Bldg., Rm.
  610-B
450 Main St.
*Hartford, Conn. 06103
(203) 240-3530

*Denotes regional office with supervisory regional responsibilities
†Denotes trade specialist at branch office

Delaware

Serviced by Philadelphia
    District Office

District of Columbia

(Baltimore District)
Department of Commerce
Rm. 1066 HCHB
14th St. & Constitution
    Ave., N.W.
†Washington, D.C. 20230
(202) 377-3181

Florida

Fed. Bldg., Suite 224
51 S.W. First Ave.
Miami, Fla. 33130
(305) 536-5267

128 North Osceola Ave.
†Clearwater, Fla. 33515
(813) 461-0011

1200 Gulf Life Dr., Suite
    #104
†Jacksonville, Fla. 32207
(904) 791-2796

75 East Ivanhoe Blvd.
†Orlando, Fla. 32804
(305) 425-1234

Collins Bld., Rm. 401
107 W. Gaines St.
†Tallahassee, Fla. 32304
(904) 488-6469

Georgia

1365 Peachtree St., N.E.,
    Suite 504
Atlanta, Ga. 30309
(404) 347-4872

120 Barnard St., A-107
Savannah, Ga. 31402
(912) 944-4204

Hawaii

4106 Fed. Bldg.
P.O. Box 50026

300 Ala Moana Blvd.
Honolulu, Hawaii 96850
(808) 541-1782

Idaho

(Denver, Colorado Dis-
    trict)
Statehouse, Rm 113
Boise, Idaho 83720
(202) 334-9254

Illinois

1406 Mid Continental
    Plaza Bldg.
55 East Monroe St.
Chicago, Ill. 60603
(312) 353-4450

W. R. Harper College
Algonquin & Roselle Rd.
†Palatine, Ill. 60067
(312) 397-3000, ext. 532

515 North Court St.
P.O. Box 1747
†Rockford, Ill. 61110-0247
(815) 987-8100

Indiana

357 U.S. Courthouse &
    Fed. Office Bldg.
46 East Ohio St.
Indianapolis, Ind. 46204
(317) 269-6214

Iowa

817 Fed. Bldg.
210 Walnut St.
Des Moines, Iowa 50309
(515) 284-4222

Kansas

(Kansas City, Missouri
    District)
River Park Pl., Suite 565
727 North Waco,
†Wichita, Kans. 67203
(316) 269-6160

Kentucky

U.S. Post Office and
    Courthouse Bldg., Rm.
    636B
Louisville, Ky. 40202
(502) 582-5066

Louisiana

432 World Trade Center,
    No. 2
Canal St.
New Orleans, La. 70130
(504) 589-6546

Maine

(Boston, Massachusetts
    District)
1 Memorial Circle
Casco Bank Bldg.
*Augusta, Maine 04330
(207) 622-8249

Maryland

415 U.S. Customhouse
Gay and Lombard Sts.
Baltimore, Md. 21202
(301) 962-3560

Massachusetts

World Trade Center, Suite
    307
Commonwealth Pier Area
Boston, Mass. 02210
(617) 565-8563

Michigan

1140 McNamara Bldg.
477 Michigan Ave.
Detroit, Mich. 48226
(313) 226-3650

300 Monroe N.W., Rm.
    409
†Grand Rapids, Mich.
    49503
(616) 456-2411

---

*Denotes regional office with supervisory regional responsibilities
†Denotes trade specialist at branch office

Minnesota
108 Fed. Bldg.
110 S. 4th St.
Minneapolis, Minn.
  55401
(612) 348-1638

Mississippi
328 Jackson Mall Office
  Center
300 Woodrow Wilson
  Blvd.
Jackson, Miss. 39213
(609) 965-4388

Missouri
7911 Forsyth Blvd., Suite
  610
*St. Louis, Mo. 63105
(314) 425-3302
601 East 12th St., Rm.
  635
Kansas City, Mo. 64106
(816) 374-3141

Montana
Serviced by Denver District Office

Nebraska
11133 "O" St.
Omaha, Nebr. 68137
(402) 221-3664

Nevada
1755 E. Plumb Ln., #152
Reno, Nev. 89502
(702) 784-5203

New Hampshire
Serviced by Boston District Office

New Jersey
3131 Princeton Pike Bldg.
  4D, Suite 211

*Trenton, N.J. 08648
(609) 989-2100

New Mexico
517 Gold, S.W., Suite
  4303
Albuquerque, N. Mex.
  87102
(505) 766-2386

New York
1312 Fed. Bldg.
111 West Huron St.
Buffalo, N.Y. 14202
(716) 846-4191
121 East Ave.
†Rochester, N.Y. 14604
(716) 263-6480
Fed. Office Bldg.
26 Fed. Plaza
Foley Square
New York, N.Y. 10278
(212) 264-0634

North Carolina
324 W. Market St.
P.O. Box 1950
*Greensboro, N.C. 27402
(919) 333-5345

North Dakota
Serviced by Omaha District Office

Ohio
9504 Fed. Office Bldg.
550 Main St.
*Cincinnati, Ohio 45202
(513) 684-2944
666 Euclid Ave., Rm.
  600
Cleveland, Ohio 44114
(216) 522-4750

Oklahoma
5 Broadway Executive
  Park, Suite 200

6601 Broadway Extension
Oklahoma City, Okla.
  73116
(405) 231-5302
440 S. Houston St.
†Tulsa, Okla. 74126
(918) 581-7650

Oregon
1220 S.W. 3rd Ave., Rm.
  618
Portland, Oreg. 97204
(503) 221-3001

Pennsylvania
9448 Fed. Bldg.
600 Arch St.
Philadelphia, Pa. 19106
(215) 597-2866
2002 Fed. Bldg.
1000 Liberty Ave.
Pittsburgh, Pa. 15222
(412) 644-2850

Puerto Rico
Fed. Bldg., Rm. 659
Hato Rey, P.R. 00918
(809) 753-4555

Rhode Island
(Boston, Massachusetts
  District)
7 Jackson Walkway
†Providence, R.I. 02903
(401) 528-5104, ext. 22

South Carolina
Strom Thurmond Fed.
  Bldg., Suite 172
1835 Assembly St.
Columbia, S.C. 29201
(803) 765-5345
17 Lockwood Dr.
†Charleston, S.C. 29401
(803) 724-4361

*Denotes regional office with supervisory regional responsibilities
†Denotes trade specialist at branch office

South Dakota

Serviced by Omaha District Office

Tennessee

Parkway Towers, Suite 114
404 James Robertson Parkway
Nashville, Tenn. 37210-1505
(615) 736-5161

555 Beale St.
†Memphis, Tenn. 38103
(901) 521-4237

Texas

1100 Commerce St., Rm. 7A5
*Dallas, Tex. 75242
(214) 767-0542

P.O. Box 12728
Capitol Station

†Austin, Tex. 78711
(512) 472-5059

2625 Fed. Courthouse
515 Rusk St.
Houston, Tex. 77002
(713) 229-2578

Utah

U.S. Courthouse, Rm. 340
350 S. Main St.
Salt Lake City, Utah 84101
(801) 524-5116

Vermont

Serviced by Boston District Office

Virginia

8010 Fed. Bldg.
400 North 8th St.
Richmond, Va. 23240
(804) 771-2246

Washington

3131 Elliott Ave., Suite 290
Seattle, Wash. 98121
(206) 442-5616

P.O. Box 2170
†Spokane, Wash. 99210
(509) 456-4557

West Virginia

3309 New Fed. Bldg.
500 Quarrier St.
Charleston, W. Va. 25301
(304) 347-5123

Wisconsin

Fed. Bldg.
U.S. Courthouse
517 E. Wisconsin Ave.
Milwaukee, Wis. 53202
(414) 291-3473

Wyoming

Serviced by Denver District Office

Other U.S. Government Services for Export and International Operations

State Department.   The State Department handles locations too small to have full-time business or commercial offices. *State Department Cable Grams* update business climate pertinent to specific countries.

Small Business Administration (SBA).   Two divisions of the SBA are of interest:

Office of International Trade
1129 Twentieth Street, N.W.
Suite 412
Washington, D.C. 20416
(202) 653-7794

Service Corps of Retired Executives (SCORE)
211 Main Street
San Francisco, Calif. 94105
(415) 974-0599

*Denotes regional office with supervisory regional responsibilities
†Denotes trade specialist at branch office

Export-Import Bank of the United States (Eximbank). The Eximbank Office of Export Counseling offers advisory services to help promote small and growing businesses to sell overseas. You can obtain information and materials on the availability and use of export financing from:

Office of Export Counseling
(202) 566-8860 or (800) 424-5201

Office of Exporter Credits and Guarantees
Export-Import Bank of the United States
811 Vermont Avenue, N.W.
Washington, D.C. 20571
(800) 424-5201 or (202) 566-8990
Cable: EXIMBANK
Telex: 89- 461

United States Agency for International Development (USAID or AID). Call the Office of Public Affairs at (202) 632-1850 or the Office of Asian and Near East Affairs at (202) 647-3853 to find the phone number of the desk officer for the country you are interested in. Country-specific information on developing nations is available. If you are interested in bidding on AID procurement requirements, contact:

Office of Small Business
AID/SDB/SB
Washington, D.C. 20523
(703) 235-1822

U.S. Department of Agriculture, Foreign Agricultural Service (FAS). Contact FAS at (202) 447-6363.

U.S. Department of Transportation. For information, contact:

U.S. Department of Transportation
400 7th St., S.W.
Washington, D.C. 20590

Federal Highway Administration, Chief
Foreign Projects Division
(202) 426-0380

Federal Aviation Administration, Chief
International Liaison and Policy Division
(202) 366-4000

Army Corps of Engineers. For information, contact:

U.S. Army Corps of Engineers
Construction Division
(202) 272-0649

Department of Housing and Urban Development (HUD) Office of International Affairs. Request their pamphlet "Selected Publications Checklist, Department of Housing and Urban Development" by calling (202) 755-5770.

U.S. Government Publications

Basic Guide to Exporting. Describes how smaller businesses can either enter the export market or expand their export trade. Order from:

> Superintendent of Documents
> U.S. Government Printing Office
> Washington, D.C. 20402
> *Stock order no.:* 003-009-00349-1

A Guide to Selling Your Service Overseas. This 84-page book is designed to help potential service-industry exporters enter new markets and assist experienced exporters in expanding business abroad. This guide is a "one-stop" tool for any service company which seeks to increase its company's profit through overseas business. Cost is $17. Order from:

> NORCALDEC
> 450 Golden Gate Avenue
> P.O. Box 36013
> San Francisco, Calif. 94102

Business America. The principal U.S. Commerce Department publication for presenting international business news and exporting leads. Twice monthly. Annual subscription is $57; $14.25 extra for foreign mailing; single copy, $2.50. Order from:

> Superintendent of Documents
> U.S. Government Printing Office
> Washington, D.C. 20402
> (212) 783-3238

Commerce Business Daily. This daily publication of U.S. government procurement opportunities also publishes some foreign trade leads, including foreign governments' needs. Annual subscription is $160 for first-class postage and $81 for second-class. Order from:

> Superintendent of Documents
> U.S. Government Printing Office

Washington, D.C. 20402
(202) 783-3238

The Commerce Department District Office library maintains recent back issues of this publication.

How to Get the Most From Overseas Exhibitions. Details the steps a company should take to participate in an overseas exhibition. Contains helpful hints in planning participation. Free.

Export Promotion Calendar. Designed to help U.S. businesses take advantage of sales opportunities in overseas markets. Contains an eighteen-month schedule of U.S. Export Development Office exhibitions, international trade fairs in which U.S. participation is planned, and a number of other overseas promotional activities planned and organized by the U.S. Department of Commerce. Revised quarterly. Free. Order the two above from:

> Office of Event Management and Support Services
> Export Awareness Division, Room 2106
> International Trade Administration
> U.S. Department of Commerce
> Washington, D.C. 20230

Export Administration Regulations. The Office of Export Administration's "bible" is available from:

> Superintendent of Documents
> U.S. Government Printing Office
> Washington, D.C. 20402
> (202) 783-3238.

A reference copy of these regulations is available in libraries.

Foreign Business Practices. Provides basic information about some of the laws and practices governing exporting, licensing, and investment abroad. $4.75. Order from:

> Superintendent of Documents
> U.S. Government Printing Office
> Washington, D.C. 20402

Three publications available from the Copyright Office are *International Copyright, Copyright Basics,* and *International Copyright Regulations of the United States. Customs Regulations* can be obtained from the U.S. Customs Service. Available from the U.S. Government Printing Office are *General Information Concerning Patents, General Information Concerning Trademarks,* and *Q&A's About Trademarks,* published by the Patent and Trademark Office.

Background Notes. A series of brochures prepared by the U.S. State Department. These reports on individual countries describe their history, government, political conditions, economy, and foreign relations. Annual subscription is $34, $42.50 for foreign mailing. Single copies domestic, $2.

Foreign Economic Trends (FET). Country-specific reports that provide in-depth reviews of business conditions and current prospects. Contain data about such items as the gross national product, foreign trade, wage and price indexes, and unemployment rates. These reports pinpoint the economic and financial conditions of the various countries and how they can affect U.S. business there. Prepared on the scene by U.S. Foreign Service and Foreign Commercial Service experts. Annual subscription is $70.

Overseas Business Reports (OBR). Detailed information about overseas trade and investment conditions and opportunities, as well as the latest marketing information on countries offering good potential as sales outlets for U.S. goods. Information about trade, trade patterns, industry trends, distribution channels, natural resources, populations, and transportation. Approximately sixty reports per year. Annual subscription $14 per year; $17.50 for foreign mailing. Order current reports from:

> Superintendent of Documents
> U.S. Government Printing Office
> Washington, D.C. 20402

For reports from other years, order from Publication Sales.

Foreign Trade Report (FT 410) U.S. Exports—Commodity by Country. Published by the Bureau of the Census. Provides a statistical record of shipments of all merchandise from the United States to foreign countries, including the quantity and dollar value of exports to each country. A review of the reports for the past three to four years reveals the countries that are the largest, most consistent markets for specific U.S. products. FT 410 reports are available at Commerce Department district office libraries for reference on a walk-in basis. Annual subscription is $100; single copies, $9.50.

Market Share Reports. Basic data needed by exporters to evaluate overall trends in the size of markets for manufacturers. These reports measure changes in the import demand for specific products; compare the competitive position of U.S. and foreign exporters; select distribution centers for U.S. products abroad; and identify existing and potential markets for U.S. components, parts, and accessories. There are reports for over eighty-eight countries at $9 each. There are also 1,672 commodity reports at $6.50 each. For a free catalog, write to:

> National Technical Information Service
> 5285 Port Royal Road
> Springfield, Va. 22161

International Market Research Surveys. Comprehensive studies covering a variety of industry and country subjects. The studies are generally performed in-country by private contractors. Provide detailed information on market prospects and range up to 400 pages in length. These reports also list key potential buyers, government purchasing agencies, and similar relevant organizations. Generally range in price from $50 to $100.

Country Market Surveys. Summaries of the more detailed *International Market Research Surveys.* They are available for various product categories, including agricultural machinery/equipment, communications equipment, computers and peripherals, electric power systems, electronic components, equipment and materials for electronic components production, food processing and packaging equipment, graphics industries equipment, industrial process controls, laboratory instruments, machine tools, medical equipment, sporting goods, and recreational equipment. The charge for these reports is $10. The market research surveys can be ordered from:

> Superintendent of Documents
> U.S. Government Printing Office
> Washington, D.C. 20402
> (202) 783-3238

Single copies may be purchased from:

> U.S. Department of Commerce, Room 1617-D
> Washington, D.C. 20230

Reference libraries also have copies of these reports.

Global and Country Market Surveys (GMS). These provide detailed information about fifteen to thirty of the best foreign markets for the products of a single U.S. industry or a group of related industries. Prices vary. Copies may be obtained from:

> International Market Research, Room 1320
> U.S. Department of Commerce
> Washington, D.C. 20230

Export Trading Company Guidebook. Order from:

> Office of Export Trading Company Affairs, Room 5618
> U.S. Department of Commerce
> Washington, D.C. 20230
> (202) 377-5131

The EMC—Your Export Department. Describes the services provided to exporters by export management companies (EMCs), as well as how to go about selecting a suitable EMC. Order from:

> Office of Event Management and Support Services
> Export Awareness Division, Room 2106
> International Trade Administration
> U.S. Department of Commerce
> Washington, D.C. 20230

U.S. Export Management Companies, Directory. U.S. Department of Commerce, 1981, $7.00.

Investment Climate in Foreign Countries, vol. 3: "Asia" (excluding Japan). Published by the U.S. Department of Commerce, International Trade Administration. Available from:

National Technical Information Service
5285 Port Royal Road
Springfield, Va. 22161

International Countertrade, U.S. Department of Commerce, $3.75.

East-West Countertrade Practices: An Introductory Guide for Business, 1978.

Overview of Export Administrative Program. Regulations, licensing, export. Clearance for certain products and nations.

Services for Exporters From U.S. Government, 1984, $4.25.

Agent/Distributor Service (ADS). Describes how businesspeople can find overseas representation through the U.S. Department of Commerce. Free. Order from:

Office of Event Management and Support Services
Export Awareness Division, Room 2106
International Trade Administration
U.S. Department of Commerce
Washington, D.C. 20230

EXIMBANK Programs Summary. Explains U.S. export financing programs. Free. Available from:

Export-Import Bank of the United States
811 Vermont Avenue, N.W.
Washington, D.C. 20571

Overseas Private Investment Corporation (OPIC). Reviews how OPIC can assist companies that are interested in investment in developing nations. Free. Available from:

Overseas Private Investment Corporation
1129 20th Street, N.W.
Washington, D.C. 20527

Helpful Private Organizations

Credit Checking

The Department of Commerce, although not a private organization, publishes the *World Trader's Data Report* series, which contains credit information on companies around the world. Information includes the type of organization, when it was established, its size and reputation, the territory it covers, the product lines handled, principal owners, financial and trade references, plus a general comment by the investigating commercial officer on the company's reliability. These reports are prepared upon request and cost $40 per search.

Dun & Bradstreet provides credit reports that focus on a company's financial standing rather than overall business background. These reports are based on unaudited responses to questionnaires. Check your local directory.

Foreign Credit Interchange Bureau (FCIB) is part of the National Association of Credit Management. Members furnish the bureau with information on their dealings with foreign customers, and credit reports are compiled from this information and are made available to all members.
   For information, contact:

   Foreign Credit Interchange Bureau
   475 Park Avenue South
   New York, N.Y. 10016

Export Management Companies

There are several associations of export management companies in the United States that you can contact for names and addresses of U.S. exporters and export management companies. Ask also for names and addresses of similar associations in major industrialized countries, particularly in Western Europe, since some of their members may be good outlets into specific Pacific Rim markets.

   National Association of Export Management Companies, Inc.
   65 Liberty Street

New York, N.Y. 10005
(212) 766-1343

Overseas Private Investment Corp. (OPIC) insures the overseas direct investments of U.S. companies. To do so, OPIC gathers and analyzes detailed credit risk information, so it is a potential source of information on the creditworthiness of your customers and the countries in which they are located.

The following Pacific Rim nations are eligible for some or all OPIC coverage: China, Taiwan, Thailand, Indonesia, South Korea, Malaysia, the Philippines, Singapore, Fiji, Papua New Guinea, Tonga, Western Samoa, and Kiribati. Contact:

OPIC
1615 M Street, N.W.
Washington, D.C. 20527
(202) 457-7200

Credit Insurance

Foreign Credit Insurance Association (FCIA). The main office is:

40 Rector Street
11th floor
New York, N.Y. 10006
(202) 306-5000

FICA branch offices are located in Atlanta, Chicago, Houston, Los Angeles, New York, and Washington, D.C.

Private Export Funding Corp (PEFCO). For information request the brochure *How to Work with PEFCO.*

280 Park Avenue
New York, N.Y. 10017
(212) 557-3100
Telex: 1-2250

Export Management Companies

There are several associations of export management companies in the United States that you can contact for names and addresses of U.S. exporters and export management companies. Ask also for names and addresses of similar associations in major industrialized countries, particularly in Western Europe, since some of their members may be good outlets into specific Pacific Rim markets.

1. National Association of Export Management
     Companies, Inc.
     65 Liberty Street
     New York, N.Y. 10005
     (212) 766-1343

2. Overseas Sales and Marketing Association of America, Inc.
   P.O. Box 45446
   Chicago, Ill. 60645
   (312) 583-6060
3. Pacific Northwest Association of Export Managers
   5316 S.W. Westpage Drive
   Portland, Oreg. 97211
   (503) 292-9219
4. Export Managers Associations of California
   24549 Victory Boulevard
   Van Nuys Calif. 91411
   (213) 479-3911

Franchising

Companies interested in franchising in the Pacific Rim should contact:

International Franchise Association
Attn: Peter Holt
1350 New York Avenue, N.W.
Suite 900
Washington, D.C. 20005
(202) 628-8000
Fax: 202-628-0812

Franchise Network International
Attn: J. J. Reyes
First Interstate Bank Building
1314 S. King Street, Suite 407
Honolulu, Hawaii 96814
(808) 524-5065
Fax: 808-524-5105

Pacific Rim Cultural Training Organizations

International Public Relations Group operates in major U.S. cities. It prepares American firms and individuals for entry into the unique business climate of Japan. Check your phone directory.

Monterey Language Institute, in Monterey, Calif. It provides language training, cultural training, translation services, and management training (including an MBA program) for U.S. managers going overseas.

Moran, Stahl, Boyer, in Boulder Colo. (303) 444- 8440. It provides cross-cultural training for companies.

The Asia Society was founded with the purpose of educating Americans about Asian culture, economics, and politics. It presents a wide array of lectures, films, seminars, short courses, performances, art tours, and information on Asian cuisines. The Society covers Asia broadly: from Iran to Japan, including China, India, Southeast Asia, and Australia. Meetings for corporate members provide opportunities to meet Asian and American business and government policy makers. It has sixteen country councils and publishes a monthly magazine entitled *ASIA*. The Society has headquarters in New York and other centers in Washington, Houston, and Los Angeles.

> The Asia Society
> 725 Park Avenue
> New York, N.Y. 10021
> (212) 288-6400

The Asia Foundation is a nonprofit, multipurpose organization concerned with the social development within Asian nations. The Foundation maintains a U.S. representative on twelve Asian countries. Sponsors exchange programs with the United States.

> The Asia Foundation/San Francisco
> 406 California Street
> San Francisco, Calif. 94104
> (415) 982-4640

Trade Organizations

U.S. Chamber of Commerce. Contact:

> U.S. Chamber of Commerce
> 1615 H. Street, N.W.
> Washington, D.C. 20062

United States Council for International Business can be reached at the following locations:

1212 Avenue of the Americas
New York, N.Y. 10036

353 Sacramento Avenue
San Francisco, Calif. 94111

1900 East Golf Road
Schaumburg, Ill. 60195

3345 Wilshire Blvd.
Los Angeles, Calif. 90010

Society to Promote International Relations and International Trade (SPIRIT) promotes California exports and reverse investment. The Society identifies ways to locate potential trade partners and acts as a catalyst between local companies to overseas importers. It creates visibility of reverse investment to other countries, publishes trade information, organizes trade missions, and sponsors trade shows.

> James Hume, President
> SPIRIT
> 257 Castro Street, Suite 110
> Mountain View, Calif. 94041
> (415) 967-0171

Countertrade

American Countertrade Association. Contact:

Dan West
Monsanto
P.O. Box 31432
St. Louis, Mo.
(314) 694-5703

American Indonesian Chamber of Commerce. See listing in Appendix IV at Indonesia,
Private Business Organizations.

Appendix IV | Pacific Rim Organizations

I have grouped together the various agencies and organizations you may wish to contact for each Pacific Rim nation. The Commerce Department desk officers for each country are in Washington, D.C. Letters should be addressed to the individual at the appropriate room number, U.S. Department of Commerce, Herbert C. Hoover Building, Washington, D.C. 20230.

Pacific Rim phone numbers include the country code and city code, if any. The fax numbers given are often shared by several offices, including Foreign Commercial Service and U.S. Information Service.

Association of South East Asian Nations (ASEAN)*

U.S. Commerce Department Desk Officer

George Paine,
(202) 377-3875, Room 2032.

The U.S. Export Development Office in Singapore (EDO)

The EDO has overseas responsibility for the Commerce Department's trade promotion in the ASEAN Region. It works closely with the Foreign Commercial Service at U.S. Embassies and consular posts in the region and helps firms identify markets for trade promotion.

The EDO offers U.S. business representatives visiting Singapore a temporary base of operations by providing office facilities, access to telephone and telex services, identification of prime business prospects, and assistance in hiring secretaries and interpreters to help with appointments.

Also available at the EDO in Singapore is a conference room that may be reserved by individual firms or small groups of firms for product displays. Electric power to op-

* In addition, look under each of the ASEAN member nations: Indonesia, Malaysia, Philippines, Singapore, and Thailand.

erate equipment is available, as are 8 mm and 16 mm projectors, overhead and opaque projectors, and carousel slide projectors. Convenient parking is available.

U.S. Export Development Office
111 N. Bridge Road,
#15-01
Peninsula Plaza
Singapore, Republic of Singapore 0617
Phone 65-336-3100
Telex: RS25079 (SINGTC)

Private Business Organizations in the United States

ASEAN-U.S. Business Council, U.S. Section.   Contact:

Chamber of Commerce of the U.S.
1615 H Street, N.W.
Washington, D.C. 20062
(202) 463-5460
Telex: (RCA) 248302 COCUSA
Mark Van Fleet, Executive Director

Pacific Basin Economic Council (PBEC).   The Pacific Basin Economic Council, an organization composed of private business representatives from five national committees—Australia, Canada, Japan, New Zealand, and the United States, assists in improving the business environment and stimulating trade and investment in the Pacific region. PBEC maintains close relations with the governments and business organizations of ASEAN.

Pacific Basin Economic Council
333 Ravenswood
Menlo Park, CA 94025
(415) 859-4455

American ASEAN Trade Council, Inc. (AATC).   The American ASEAN Trade Council is a trade organization originally founded by the Philippine-American Chamber of Commerce and the American-Indonesian Chamber of Commerce, both based in New York. Membership is now open to individuals and companies that conduct business in any of the ASEAN nations. The AATC acts as a clearing house of information for its 240 member banks and corporations. The Council maintains contact with the Asia-Pacific Council of the American Chamber of Commerce (APCAC) and various other ASEAN regional groups. It provides information and services to those interested in doing business in ASEAN and publishes a newsletter.

American ASEAN Trade Council, Inc.
40 East 49th Street
New York, N.Y. 10017
(212) 688-2755

Australia

U.S. Commerce Desk Officer

Gary Bouck and Barbara Korthals-Altes, (202) 377-3647, Room 2038

U.S. Embassy and Consulates

U.S. Embassy

Moonah Place
Canberra, ACT 2600
APO San Francisco 96405
Phone 61-6-273-3711

U.S. Consulates

24 Albert Road South
Melbourne, Victoria 3205
APO San Francisco 96405
Phone 61-3-699-2244
Fax 61-3-690-2585

246 St. George's Terrace
Perth WA 6000
Phone 61-9-322-4466

T & G Tower, 36th Floor
Hyde Park Square
Park and Elizabeth Streets
Sydney 2000, NSW
APO San Francisco 96209
Phone 61-4-264-7044
Fax 61-2-264-9908

383 Wickham Terrace
Brisbane, Queensland 400
Phone 61-7-229-8955

U.S. Export Development Office

4 Cliff Street
Missions Point
Sydney NSW 2611
Phone 61-2-929-0977

Official Representation in the U.S.

Embassy of Australia
1601 Massachusetts Avenue, N.W.
Washington, D.C. 20036
(202) 797-3000

Australia Consulate General
3550 Wilshire Blvd., Suite 912
Los Angeles, Calif. 90010
(213) 380-0980

Information Office of Australia
636 Fifth Avenue
New York, N.Y. 10111
(212) 245-4000

Australia Consulate General
1000 Bishop Street
Honolulu, Hawaii 96813
(808) 524-5050

Australia Consulate General
111 East Wacker Drive
Chicago, Ill. 60601
(312) 329-1740

Australia Consulate General
3 Post Oak Central, 8th Floor
1990 South Post Oak Road
Houston, Texas 77056
(713) 877-8100

Australia Consulate General
636 5th Avenue
New York, N.Y. 10020
(212) 245-4000

Graham Rice
Senior Trade Commissioner
360 Post Street
San Francisco, Calif. 94108
(415) 362-6160

Private U.S. Trade Organizations

American Chamber of Commerce in Australia

50 Pitt Street, Third Floor
Sydney, New South Wales 2000
Phone: 61-2-241-1907
Cable: AMCHAMSYDNEY
Telex: 729 ATTIAU
Kevin Bannon, Executive Director

66 Queens Street, 23rd Floor
Brisbane, Queensland 4000
Phone: 61-7-221-8542
Dianne Hopkins, Manager

80 Collins Street, Level 41
Melbourne, Victoria 3000
Phone: 61-3-654-5100
Randall G. Upton, Manager

Business Organizations in the Pacific Rim

The Melbourne Chamber of Commerce,
Commerce House, Level 1
World Trade Center
CNR Flinders and Spencer Streets
Melbourne 3005

China (People's Republic of China)

U.S. Commerce Desk Officer

Jeffrey Lee, (202) 377-3583, Room 2317.

U.S. Embassy and Consulates

U.S. Embassy
Guang Hua Lu, 17

Consulate General
Shanghai

Beijing, China
FPO San Francisco 96655
Phone: 86-1-52-2033

Consulate General
Guang Zhou (Canton)
Dong Fang Hotel
Box 100
FPO San Francisco 96659
Phone 769900 ext. 1000.

1469 Huai Hai Middle Road, Box 200
FPO San Francisco 96659
Phone 379-880.

Official Representation in the United States

Embassy of the People's Republic of
China
2300 Connecticut Ave. N.W.
Washington, D.C. 20008
(202) 328-2500

China Consulate General
3417 Montrose Blvd.
Houston, Texas 77006
(713) 524-0780

China Consulate General
520 12th Avenue
New York, N.Y. 10038
(212) 279-4275

The People's Republic of China
Consulate
Consulate General
1450 Laguna
San Francisco, Calif.
(415) 563-4885, 563-4857

Private Trade Organizations

American Chambers of Commerce in China

Michael Bickford, General Manager
c/o Weyerhaeuser Ching, Ltd.
Noble Tower No. 907
22 Jain Guo Menwki Dajie
Beijing, China
Phone: 86-1-512-2288, ext. 2907
Telex: 211111 WEV BJ

Business Organizations in the Pacific Rim

Bank of China
Trust and Consultancy Company
Xijiao Minxiang, 17
Beijing, China
Phones: 86-1-65.5681, 65.5586, 65.4413
Telex: 22254 BCHO CN

Hong Kong

U.S. Commerce Desk Officer

JeNelle Matheson, (202) 377-2462, Room 2317.

U.S. Consulate

Until 1997, Hong Kong is governed by Great Britain, so for embassy-level contacts, you must go through the British Ambassador.

U.S. Consulate General in Hong Kong
AMCONGEN
26 Garden Road, Box 30
FPO San Francisco 96659
Phone: 852-5-239011
Fax: 852-5-845-0943

Official Representation in the United States

Hong Kong Economic Affairs Office
126 East 56th Street, 14th Floor
New York, N.Y. 10022
(212) 355-4060

Hong Kong Economic Affairs
Industrial Promotion Office
180 Sutter Street
San Francisco, Calif. 94104
(415) 956-4560

Hong Kong Trade Development Council
World Trade Center
350 South Figueroa Street, Suite 520
Los Angeles, Calif. 90071
(213) 622-3194

Hong Kong Tourist Association
421 Powell
San Francisco, Calif. 94104
(415) 781-4582

For industrial investment opportunities, contact the Hong Kong Government Industrial Promotion Offices

548 Fifth Avenue, New York, N.Y. 10036. (212) 730-0777.
333 North Michigan Avenue, Suite 2028, Chicago, Ill, 60601. (312) 726-4515.
P.O. Box 58329, Dallas, Texas 75258. (214) 748-8162.

Private Trade Organizations

American Chamber of Commerce in Hong Kong
1030 Swire House

Hong Kong
Cable: AMCHAM
Telex: 83664, AMCC HX

Business Organizations in the Pacific Rim

The Hong Kong General Chamber of Commerce
United Centre, 22nd Floor
95 Queensway
P.O. Box 852
Hong Kong

Indonesia

U.S. Commerce Desk Officer

Don Ryan and Linda Droker, (202) 377–3875, Room 2032.

U.S. Embassy and U.S. Consulates

Embassy of the United States of America
J1. Medan Merdeka Selatan 5
Jakarta, Indonesia
Phone: 62- 21–360360
Fax: 62-21-360644
Telex: 44218 AMEMBJKT
Mailing Address:
Box 1, APO San Francisco 96356

Consulate of the United States of
America–Surabaya
J1 Raya Dr. Sutomo 33
Surabaya, Indonesia
Phone: 62-21-69287/8
Telex: 031-334
Mailing Address:
Box 1, APO San Francisco 96356

Consulate of the United States of
America–Medan
J1. Iman Bonjol 13
Medan, Indonesia
Phones: 62-21-322200, 322060, 322463
Telex: 51764
Mailing Address:
Box 1, APO San Francisco 96356

Official Representation in the United States

Embassy of the Republic of Indonesia
2020 Massachusetts Avenue, N.W.

Consulate General of the Republic of
Indonesia

Washington, D.C. 20036
(202) 293-1745

Consulate General of the Republic of
  Indonesia
5 East 68th Street
New York, N.Y. 10021
(212) 879-0600

190 Post Oak Boulevard, #1900
Three Post Oak Central
Houston, Texas 77056
(713) 626-3291

2 Illinois Center, Suite 1422
233 N. Michigan
Chicago, Ill. 60601
(312) 938-0707

Consulate General of the Republic of
  Indonesia
645 South Mariposa Avenue
Los Angeles, Calif. 90005
(213) 383-5126

Consulate General of the Republic of
  Indonesia
111 Columbus Avenue
San Francisco, Calif. 94133
(415) 474-9571

Private Trade Organizations

American Chamber of Commerce in Indonesia

Acting Executive Director
Nick P. Petroff,
Citibank Building, 8th Floor
J1, M.H. Thamrin 55
Jakarta, Indonesia
Phone: 62-21-332602
Telex: 48116 CIBSEM IA

Indonesia Chamber of Commerce and Industry (Kadin)

Jalan Medan Merdeka Timur 11
Jakarta, Indonesia

Private Business Organizations in the United States

American Indonesian Chamber of Commerce, Inc.

711 Third Avenue, 17th Floor
New York, N.Y. 10017
Wayne Forest
(212) 687-4505

Japan

U.S. Commerce Desk Officer

Ed Leslie, (202) 377-4527, Room 2318.

U.S. Embassy and Consulates

U.S. Embassy Tokyo
10- 1, Akasaka 1-chome Minato-ku 107
APO San Francisco 96503
Phone: 87-3-583-7141
Fax: 81-3-589-4235

U.S. Export Development Office
World Import Mart, Seventh Floor
1–3 Higashi Ikebukuro, 3-chome
Toshima-ku
Tokyo 170
Phone: 81-3-987-2441
Fax: 81-3-987-2447

Consul General Osaka-Kobe
APO San Francisco 96503
San Kei Building 4-9, 9th Floor
Umeda 2-chome
Kita-ku, Osaka 530
Phone: 81-6-341-2754
Fax: 81-6-361-5978
(Building includes American merchandise display)

Official Representation in the United States

Embassy of Japan
2520 Massachusetts Avenue, N.W.
Washington, D.C. 20008
(212) 939-6700

Japan Information Service
845 North Michigan Avenue
Chicago, Ill. 60611

Japanese Consulate
50 Fremont Street
San Francisco, Calif. 94105
(415) 777-3533

Japan External Trade Organization (JE-
TRO)
Qantas Building, Suite 501
360 Post Street
San Francisco, Calif. 94108
(415) 392-1333

JETRO
McGraw-Hill Building, 44th Floor
1221 Avenue of the Americas
New York, N.Y. 10020-1060
(212) 997-0400

JETRO
401 North Michigan Avenue, Suite 660
Chicago, Ill. 60611
(312) 527-9000, 9177, 9119

JETRO
1221 McKinney
One Houston Center, Suite 1810
Houston, Texas 77010
(713) 759-9595, ext. 7

JETRO
229 Peachtree Street NE, Suite 2011
Atlanta, Ga. 30303
(404) 681-0600

JETRO
725 South Figueroa Street, Suite 1890
Los Angeles, Calif. 90071
(213) 624-8855

JETRO
1200 Seventeenth Street, Suite 1410
Denver, Colo. 80202
(303) 629-0404

Private Trade Organizations

American Chamber of Commerce in Japan
Fukide Building #2
4-1-21, Toranomon
Minato-ku, Tokyo 105
Phone: 81-3-433-5381
Cable: AMCHAM Tokyo
Fax: 81-3-436-1446

Private Business Organizations in the United States

Japanese Chamber of Commerce of
  Northern California
World Trade Center, Ferry Building
San Francisco, Calif. 94111
(415) 986-6140
Ms. Kinuko Kobayashi, Managing
  Secretary

Japan Business Association of
  Southern California
345 Southern Figueroa Street
Los Angeles, Calif. 90071
(213) 475-0160

Japanese Chamber of Commerce of
  Southern California
224 South San Pedro Street, Room 504
Los Angeles, Calif. 90012
(213) 626-3067

Japanese Chamber of Commerce and
  Industry of Chicago
401 North Michigan Avenue, Room
  2108
Chicago, Ill. 60611
(312) 332-6199

Japanese Chamber of Commerce of New
  York
145 West 57th Street
New York, N.Y. 10019
(212) 246-9774

Business Organizations in the Pacific Rim

The Japan Chamber of Commerce and Industry
2-2, 3-chome
Marunouchi, Chiyoda-ku
Tokyo 100

Korea

U.S. Commerce Desk Officer

Karen Chopra and Scott Goddin, (202) 377-4957, Room 2034.

U.S. Embassy and U.S. Consulates

U.S. Embassy
82 Sejong
Chongro-ku
Seoul ROK
APO San Francisco 96301
Phone: 82-2-732-2601
Fax: 82-2-739-1628 (Economic Development Office)

Official Representation in the United States

Embassy of Republic of Korea
2320 Massachusetts Avenue, N.W.
Washington, D.C. 20008
(202) 483-7383

Anchorage Consulate General
101 Benson Blvd., Suite 304
Anchorage, Alaska 99503
(907) 561-5488

Atlanta Consulate General
Cain Tower, Suite 500
229 Peachtree Street
Atlanta, Ga. 30303
(404) 522-1611, 1613

Chicago Consulate General
500 N. Michigan Avenue, Suite 600
Chicago, Ill. 60611
(312) 822-9485, 9487

Honolulu Consulate General
2756 Pali Highway
Honolulu, Hawaii 96817
(808) 595-6109, 6274

Houston Consulate General
1990 Post Oak Suite 745
Houston, Texas 77056
(713) 961-0186

Los Angeles Consulate General
5455 Wilshire Blvd., Suite 1101
Los Angeles, Calif. 90036
(213) 931-1331

New York Consulate General
460 Park Avenue at 57th St., 5th Floor
New York, N.Y. 10022
(212) 752-1700

San Francisco Consulate General
3500 Clay Street
San Francisco, Calif. 94118
(415) 921-2251

Seattle Consulate General
United Airlines Bldg., Suite 1125
2033 Sixth Avenue
Seattle, Wash. 98121
(206) 682-0132, 0133, 0294

Trade Organizations in Korea

American Chamber of Commerce in
  Korea
Chosun Hotel, Room 307
Seoul, ROK
James W. Booth, Executive Vice
  President
Phone: 82-2-753-6471
Cable: AMCHAMBER
Telex: 23745 28432 24256 Chosun

Foreign Investment Promotion Division
Ministry of Finance 1
Choongang-dong
Dwachon City, Dyonggido, 171–11
Seoul, Korea
Phone: 82-2-9277
Telex: K23243 MIOFFI.

Korea Foreign Trade Association &
  Korea World Trade Center
CPO Box 1117
Seoul, ROK
Telex: COTRASO K24265
Fax: 82-2-754-1337

Private Business Organizations in the United States

Korea Economic Institute of America
1030 15th Street NW, Suite 662
Washington, D.C. 20005
(202) 371-0690

U.S.-Korea Economic Council, Inc.
88 Morningside Drive, Suite 2-L
New York, N.Y. 10027
(212) 749-4200
Dr. William Henderson, Executive
Director

Korea Chamber of Commerce
981 South Western Avenue, Room 201
Los Angeles, Calif. 90006
(213) 733-4410

United States-Korea Society
725 Park Avenue
New York, N.Y. 10021
(212) 517-7730

Korean-American Midwest Association
  of Commerce and Industry
  (DAMACI)
c/o Swift Agricultural Chemicals Corp.
111 W. Jackson Blvd.
Chicago, Ill. 60604
(312) 431-2533
Edward R. Urablik, President

Business Organizations in the Pacific Rim

Korea Chamber of Commerce and Industry
45, 4-ka, Namdaemum
Chunku, KCCI Building,
P.O. Box 25
Seoul, ROK

Malaysia

U.S. Commerce Desk Officer

Gary Bouck and Joan Walsh, (202) 377–3875, Room 2308.

U.S. Embassy and U.S. Consulates

Embassy of the U.S.A.
A.I.A. Building, Jalan Ampang
Kuala Lumpur, Malaysia
Phone: 60-3-26321
Fax: 60-3-243-2450
Telex: MA-32956 FCSKL
Mailing Address:
P.O. Box 35
Kuala Lumpur, Malaysia.

Official Representation in the United States

Embassy of Malaysia
2401 Massachusetts Avenue, N.W.
Washington, D.C. 20008
(202) 328-2700

Consulate General
Commercial Section
350 South Figueroa, Suite 400
Los Angeles, Calif. 90071
(213) 617-1000

Consulate General
2 Embarcadero Center
San Francisco, Calif. 94111
(415) 421-6570

Malaysia Consulate General
140 East 45th Street, 43rd Floor
New York, N.Y. 10017
(212) 490-2722

Malaysian Trade Commission
630 Third Avenue, 11th Floor
New York, N.Y. 10016
(212) 682-0232

Malaysian Industrial Development
Authority (MIDA) Office
630 Third Avenue, 11th Floor
New York, N.Y. 10016
(212) 687-2491

MIDA
John Hancock Center, Suite 3350
875 N. Michigan Avenue
Chicago, Ill. 60611
(312) 787-4532

MIDA
350 South Figueroa, Suite 400
Los Angeles, Calif. 90071
(213) 626-2661

MIDA Headquarters:
Director-General
Malaysian Industrial Development
  Authority
3rd–6th Floor
Wisma Damansara, Jalan Semantan
P.O. Box 10618
50720 Kuala Lumpur, Malaysia

Malaysia Tourist Information Center
Ahamad Yusop, Director of Malaysian
  Tourism
818 W. Seventh Street, Suite 1000
Los Angeles, Calif. 90017

Private Trade Organizations

American Business Council of Malaysia
Erin Ariff, Executive Secretary
15.01, 15th Floor
Amoda, Jalan Imba
Kuala Lumpur, Malaysia 55100
Phones: 60-3-281-223, 60-3-281-224
Telex: MA 32388A1A

American Chambers of Commerce of
  Malaysia
905, 9th Floor
Wisma AIA, Jalan Ampang
Kuala Lumpur, Malaysia
Telex: 01-281223

National Chamber of Commerce & In-
  dustry of Malaysia
Bangunan UDA (Lama) (6th Floor)
Jalan Sultan Ismail
Kuala Lumpur, Malaysia.

Private Business Organizations in the United States

See ASEAN on pp. 369 ff.

New Zealand

U.S. Commerce Desk Officer

Gary Bouck and Barbara Kovthals-Altes, (202) 377-3647, Room 2308.

U.S. Embassy and Consulates

(U.S. Trade Center) US Embassy, Wellington
29 Fitzherbert Terrace, Thorndon
American Embassy Private Bag, Wellington
FPO San Francisco 96690
Phone: 64-4-722-068
Fax: 64-4-781-701

Consul General Auckland
Yorkshire General Bldg, 4th Floor
Shortland & O'Connell Streets
Private Bag, Auckland 1
FPO San Francisco 96690
Phone: 64-9-32-724.

Official Representation in the United States

Embassy of New Zealand
37 Observatory Circle, N.W.
Washington, D.C. 20008
(202) 328-4800.

New Zealand Consulate General
630 Fifth Avenue, Suite 530
New York, N.Y. 10111
(212) 586-0600

New Zealand Consulate General
Tishman Building, Suite 1530
10960 Wilshire Blvd.
Los Angeles, Calif. 90024
(213) 477-8241

Private Trade Organizations

American Chamber of Commerce in New Zealand
P.O. Box 3408
Wellington N.Z.
John L. Gordon, Executive Director
Phone: 64-4-767-081
Cable: AMCHAM
Telex: 3514 INBUSMACH NZ

Business Organizations in the Pacific Rim

The Wellington Chamber of Commerce
Commerce House
126 Wakefield Street
P.O. Box 1590
Wellington 1 N.Z.

The Philippines

U.S. Commerce Desk Officer

George Paine, (202) 377-3875, Room 2308.

U.S. Embassy and U.S. Consulates

U.S. Embassy
1201 Roxas Boulevard
Manila, Philippines
Phone: 63-2-521-71-16
Telex: 722-7366

Commercial Section
395 Buendia Avenue Extension Makati
Metro Manila, Philippines
Phone: 63-2-818-3738
Fax: 63-2-818-2684
Telex: 66887 COSEC PN

U.S. Consulate
Jones Avenue
Cebu, Philippines
Mailing Address:
Embassy of the United States of America
  (or American Consulate)
APO San Francisco 96528
Phone: 7-95-10

Official Representation in the United States

Philippine Embassy
Office of the Trade Representative
1617 Massachusetts Avenue, N.W.
Washington, D.C. 20036
(202) 462-6322

Trade Commissioner
Philippine Consulate
447 Sutter Street, Suite 514
San Francisco, Calif. 94108
(415) 981-3303

Trade Commissioner
Philippine Consulate
556 Fifth Avenue
New York, N.Y. 10036
(212) 575-7925

Trade Commissioner
Philippine Consulate
3460 Wilshire Boulevard,
Suite 1210
Los Angeles, Calif. 90010
(213) 383-9475

Trade Commissioner
Philippine Consulate
30 N. Michigan Avenue, Suite 1909
Chicago, Ill. 60602
(312) 236-3676

Philippine International Trade Mart
2 Canal Street
New Orleans, La. 70130
(504) 524-2755

Philippine International Trade Mart
2433 Pali Highway
Honolulu, Hawaii 96817
(808) 595-6316

Philippine International Trade Mart
810 Third Avenue
Seattle, Wash. 98104
(206) 624-7703

Philippine Ministry of Tourism
Tourism Attaché
447 Sutter Street, 6th Floor
San Francisco, Calif. 94108

Private Trade Organizations

American Chamber of Commerce of the Philippines
J. Marsh Thompson, Executive Vice President
P.O. Box 1578

MCC
Phone: 63-2-818-7911
Cable: AMCHAM COM
Telex: (ITT) 45181 AMCHAM PH
Fax: 63-2-471-267

Private Business Organizations in the United States

Philippine-American Chamber of Commerce, Inc.
565 Fifth Avenue
New York, N.Y. 10017
(212) 766-1348
Walter Vasquez, Executive Director

Philippine-American Chamber of Commerce
c/o Philippine Consulate
447 Sutter Street
San Francisco, Calif. 94108
(415) 433-6666

Singapore

U.S. Commerce Desk Officer

Don Ryan and Joan Walsh, (202) 377-3875, Room 2032.

U.S. Embassy and Consulates

Embassy of the United States of America
30 Hill Street
Singapore 0617
Phone: 65-30251
Mailing Address:
FPO San Francisco 96699

U.S. & Foreign Commercial Service
111 North Bridge Road., # 1505
Peninsula Plaza
Singapore
Phone: 65-338-9722
Fax: 65-338-5010
Telex: RS25079 SINGTC

Official Representation in the United States

Embassy of Singapore
1824 R Street, N.W., Washington, D.C. 20009
(202) 667-7555.

Singapore Economic Development Board (SEDB)

Head Office: 1 Maritime Square #10-40
World Trade Centre (Lobby D)
Singapore 0409
Phone: 65-2710844

SEDB
911 Wilshire Blvd.
Los Angeles, Calif. 90017
(213) 624-7647
Peck H. How, Regional Director of U.S.

SEDB
55 East 59th Street
New York, N.Y. 10022
(212) 421-2200

SEDB
5 Wheeler Street
Cambridge, Mass. 02138
(617) 497-9392.

SEDB
233 North Michigan Avenue
Chicago, Ill. 60601
(312) 644-3730

SEDB
Park Central VII
12750 Merit Drive
Dallas, Texas 75251
(214) 450-4540

Singapore Tourist Promotion Board
8484 Wilshire Blvd., Suite 510
Beverly Hills, Calif. 90211
(415) 956-7487
Nelli Yong

Private Trade Organizations

American Business Council of Singapore
Joyce Rasmussen, Executive Director
354 Orchard Road
10-12 Shaw House
Singapore 0923
Phone: 65-235-0077
Telex: 50296 ABC SIN

Singapore Manufacturers Association
118 World Trade Center
Telok Blangah Road
Singapore 0409
Phone: 65-275-1211

Private Business Organizations in the United States

See ASEAN on pp. 369 ff.

Business Organizations in the Pacific Rim

Singapore International Chamber of Commerce
6 Raffles Quay
05.00 Denmark House
Singapore 0104

Taiwan (Republic of China)

U.S. Commerce Desk Officer

Dan Duvall or Jeff Hardee (202) 377-4957, Room 2329

U.S. Embassy and Consulates

Since the U.S. has no official representation in Taiwan, a separate agency—The American Institute in Taiwan (AIT)—performs the same functions as an embassy and maintains commercial control and other relations. AIT works closely with the U.S. Commerce Department and performs the same functions. It has offices in Arlington, Virginia, Taipei, and Kaohsiung.

American Institute in Taiwan
7 Lane 134
Hsinyi Road, Sec. 3
Taipei, Taiwan ROC
Phone: 886-2-709-2000

Official Representation in the United States

Taiwan is represented in the United States by the Coordination Council for North American Affairs (CCNAA), whose offices provide information on trade, business, and investment opportunities.

Coordination Council for North American Affairs Office in the United States of America
5161, River Road
Bethesda, MD. 20816
(301) 657-2130
Telex: 248314 CEWH UR (RCA)
440022 CEWA UI (ITT)

Coordination Council for North American Affairs Office in Atlanta
Suite 2412
Peachtree Center, Cain Tower

229, Peachtree St., N.E.
Atlanta, Ga. 30303
(404) 522-0182
Telex: 54-2561

Coordination Council for North American Affairs Office in Boston
Two Center Plaza
Second Fl., Suite #221
Government Center
Boston, Mass. 02108
(617) 227-4663, 227-5523
Telex: 948023 SINOOFFI

Coordination Council for North American Affairs Office in Chicago
20 North Clark Street, 19 Fl.
Chicago, Ill. 60602
(312) 372-1213
Telex: 253320

Coordination Council for North American Affairs Office in Honolulu
2746, Pali Highway
Honolulu, Hawaii 96817
(808) 595-6347 ~8
Telex: 8600 CCNAA HR

Coordination Council for North American Affairs Office in Houston
Eleven Greenway Plaza
Suite 2006
Houston, Texas 77046
(713) 626-745 ~6
Telex: 790178 ISNOOFFI HOU

Coordination Council for North American Affairs Office in Kansas City, Missouri
Penntower Office Center
3100 Broadway, Suite 1001
Kansas City, Missouri 64111
(816) 531-1298
Telex: 4314025

Coordination Council for North American Affairs Office in Los Angeles
3731 Wilshire Boulevard, Suite 700
Los Angeles, California 90010
(213) 389-1215
Telex: 691130 (WUI)

Coordination Council for North American Affairs Office in New York
801, Second Avenue, 9th Fl.
New York, N.Y. 10017
(212) 697-1250
Telex: 224068 CGROC (RCA)
420124 CGROC (ITT)

Coordination Council for North American Affairs Office in San Francisco
555 Montgomery Street
Suite 501
San Francisco, Calif. 94111
(415) 362-7680
Telex: 67634 SINOOFFI (WUI)

Coordination Council for North American Affairs Office in Seattle
Suite 2410, Westin Building
2001 Sixth Ave.
Seattle, Wash. 98121
(206) 441-4586
Telex: 320335 "LYHTS SEA"

Import-Export

The Far East Trade Service, Inc. (FETS) is Taiwan's principal trade promotion organization in foreign countries, and provides information to businesses interested in marketing products in Taiwan.

FETS
41 Madison Avenue
New York, N.Y. 10010
Phone: (212) 532-7055

FETS
555 Montgomery Street, Suite 403
San Francisco, Calif. 94111-2564
(415) 788-4304, 788-4305

FETS
The Merchandise Mart, Suite 272
Chicago, Ill. 60654
(312) 321-9338

The China External Trade Development Council (CETDC) is the parent organization of FETS.

China External Trade Development
Council
201 Tun Hwa North Road, 9th & 10th
Fl.
Taipei 105
Taiwan, Republic of China
Cable: CETRA TAIPEI
Telex: 21676 CETRA
Fax: 02-7168783
Phone: 886-2-715-1515.

Taiwan Visitors Association
66 Geary
San Francisco, Calif. 94104
(415) 989-8677

Direct Investment

The Industrial Development and Investment Center (IDIC) promotes foreign direct investment in Taiwan and provides services and information to potential investors. These investment and trade offices are found in the CCNAA offices in Chicago, Los Angeles, and Houston.

Commercial Division
Coordination Council for North American Affairs
20 North Clark Street, 19th Fl.,
Chicago, Ill. 60602
(312) 332-2533, 332-2539

3660 Wilshire Boulevard, Suite 918
Los Angeles, Calif. 90010
(213) 380-3644, 3647

1360 Post Oak Blvd, Suite 2150
Houston, Texas 77056
(713) 961-9794

Main office: Industrial Development and
Investment Center (IDIC)
7 Roosevelt Road, 10th Floor
Sec. 1, Taipei
Taiwan, Republic of China
Phone: (02) 3947213
Telex: 10634 INVEST

The Science Division of CCNAA provides information on the Science-Based Industrial Park.

CCNAA, Science Division
555 Castro Street, Suite 1214
Mountain View, Calif. 94041
(415) 969-6688

CCNAA, Science Division
3731 Wilshire Blvd., Suite 760
Los Angeles, Calif. 90010
(213) 387-8091, 8095

CCNAA, Science Division
201 Wisconsin Avenue N.W. MB-09
Washington, D.C. 20016-2137
(202) 895-1930

CCNAA, Science Division
11 Greenway Plaza
Summit Tower, Suite 1412
Houston, Texas 77046
(713) 963-9433

Main office:
Science-Based Industrial Park Administration
2 Hsin An Rd.
Hsinchu
Taiwan, R.O.C.
Phone: 886-35-773311
Telex: 32188 NSCSIPA
Fax: 886-35-776222

Private Trade Organizations

American Chamber of Commerce in Taiwan
Herbert Gale Peabody, Executive Director
P.O. Box 17-277
Phone: 886-2-551-2515
Cable AMCHAM Taipei
Telex: 27841 AMCHAM

Private Business Organizations in the United States

The Chinese Chamber of Commerce of New York Inc.
Confucius Plaza, Room C203
33 Bowery Street
New York, N.Y. 10038
(212) 227-2795
Y. T. Huang, Chairman

Chinese Chamber of Commerce of San Francisco
730 Sacramento Street
San Francisco, Calif. 94108
(415) 982-3000
Harry S. Y. Leong, Executive Secretary

Thailand

U.S. Commerce Desk Officer

Donald Ryan and Linda Droker, (202) 377-3875, Room 2034.

U.S. Embassy and U.S. Consulates

Embassy of the United States of America
Commercial Office
"R" Floor, Shell Building
140 Wireless Road
Bangkok, Thailand
Phone: 66-2-251-0260/2
Fax: 66-2-253-4448 (Customs Attaché)
APO San Francisco, Calif. 96346

Official Representation in the United States

Royal Thai Embassy
2300 Kalorama Road NW
Washington, D.C. 20038
(202) 667-1446

Commercial Section:
1990 M Street NW
Suite 380
Washington, D.C. 20036
(202) 467-6790

Thailand Consulates General
801 North La Brea Boulevard
Los Angeles, Calif. 90038
(213) 937-1894

35 East Wacker Drive
Suite 1834
Chicago, Ill. 60601
(312) 236-2447

53 Park Place
Room 505
New York, N.Y. 10007
(212) 732-8166

Thai Trade Center
5 World Trade Center
Suites 2447 and 3443
New York, N.Y. 10048
(202) 466-1777

Thailand Board of Investment
5 World Trade Center
Suite 3443
New York, N.Y. 10048
(212) 466-1745
Deputy Secretary General, Staporn
  Kavitanon

Thai Trade Center
3440 Wilshire Boulevard
Suite 1101
Los Angeles, Calif. 90010
(213) 380-5934
Director, K. Kitiyakara

Private Trade Organizations

The American Chamber of Commerce in Thailand
Thomas A. Seale, Executive Director
P.O. Box 11-1095
140 Wireless Road
Kiangwan Building, 7th Floor
Bangkok, Thailand
Phone: 66-2-251-9266
Cable: AMERCHAM
Telex: 8287 KGCOM TH

Private Business Organizations in the United States

(*See* ASEAN on pp. 369 ff.)

Business Organizations in the Pacific Rim

The Association of Thai Industries
7th Floor, Suriyothai Building
260 Phaolyothin Road
Bangkok, Thailand

Pacific Rim Region

Private Trade Organizations

Association of Asian-American Chamber of Commerce
P.O. Box 2801
Washington, D.C. 20013
(202) 638-5593
Co-Executive Director, Bernard B. Blazes
Co-Director, K. Nakatsukasa

Private Business Organizations in the United States

Far East-American Council of Commerce and Industry, Inc.   This organization is composed of multinational enterprises with business interests in the Far East. Its objectives are to aid the development of two-way trade with, and investment in, the various countries in Asia, and to establish lasting ties of friendship and cooperation. The Council schedules meetings and seminars for visiting businesspeople and government officials to exchange information on Asian trade and investment climates.

> 475 Park Avenue South
> New York, N.Y. 10016
> (212) 683- 4677

The Asian American Manufacturers Association (AAMA)

> P.O. Box 525
> Mountain View, Calif. 94042

The Asia-Pacific Council of American Chambers of Commerce (APCAC). APCAC was formed in 1968 to represent the views and interests of American businesses in the Asia-Pacific region to the legislative and executive branches of the U.S. Government, as well as to U.S. domestic business, labor, and the American public. It also represents the views of American businesses to agencies and organizations within the respective host countries. APCAC formed an ASEAN committee in 1979 composed of U.S. business executives abroad in each of the ASEAN countries.

APCAC
c/o The Director, Asia-Pacific Affairs
International Division
Chamber of Commerce of the U.S.
1615 H Street NW, Washington, D.C. 20062
(202) 463-5460,
Telex: (RCA) 248302 COCUSA

APCAC
Pacific Asia Travel Association
1 Montgomery
West Tower, Suite 1750
San Francisco, Calif 94104
(415) 986-4646

Helpful Books, Periodicals, Audiovisual Materials, and Computer Data Bases

General Guides and Directories for Exporting and International Operations

Exporter's Encyclopedia

Dun & Bradstreet, Inc.
P.O. Box 3088
Grand Central Station, N.Y. 10017

Published annually with supplements.

Moody's International Manual

Official Export Guide

North American Publishing Company
401 North Broad Street
Philadelphia, Penn. 19108
(215) 238-5300
Price: $259
Over 1,200 pages

A major reference guide updated yearly. Survey of world ports, export regulations, how to use Schedule B, samples of required documents for export documentation, directories of custom's lawyers, freight forwarders, foreign trade ministers, international banks, air cargo, port authority officials; documentary requirements for 180 countries.

International Trade Reporter. Pacific Rim trade policy and government/business relations. Shifts in business policy by Pacific Rim governments with the impacts on companies doing business there. Export shipping manual for each country.

International Trade Reporter
Bureau of National Affairs (BNA)
Washington, D.C.

Foreign Commerce Handbook by International Division, Chamber of Commerce of the United States. Updated periodically. Order from:

Chamber of Commerce of the United States
1615 H Street NW
Washington, D.C. 20062
Price: $10
300 pages

A reference book which describes and gives addresses for a very broad range of government nonprofit and private organizations involved in foreign trade, including the United Nations, World Bank, and other development banks. Finally, it has brief encyclopedic entries on many of the terms and issues of foreign trade.

Directory of American Firms Operating in Foreign Countries, 11th edition, 1987. Three volumes. Published by:

Uniworld Business Publications, Inc.
500 East 42nd Street
New York, N.Y. 10017

Volume 1 lists in alphabetical order American firms that have operations overseas. Volumes 2 and 3 list the American firms operating in each country. Listings include foreign companies in which American firms have substantial direct capital investment.

Principal International Businesses—The World Marketing Directory, 1988 edition. Published by:

Dun & Bradstreet International
Three Century Drive
Parsippany, New Jersey 07054
(800) 526-0651

Contains detailed data on 55,000 leading firms in 133 countries. Arranged three ways: geographically, by industry classification, and alphabetically by company names.

Asia's Top 7500 Companies. Published by:

Dun's Marketing Services
Dun & Bradstreet Corporation
Three Century Drive
Parsippany, New Jersey 07054

Directory of Asia's leading private and public companies in the Asian and Pacific region.

World Development Report 1988. Published by The World Bank. Reviews how the developing countries have fared in the face of international economic trends and emphasizes the potential for increasing development performance through better resource management. The thirty-three statistical tables provide instant access to the most comprehensive and current data available on social and economic development in 128 countries. Available from:

World Bank Publications
Dept. 0552
Washington, D.C. 20073
(202) 473-2939
Price: $12.95

International Marketing Data and Statistics, 1986/87, 11th edition. Euromonitor Publications, LTD, London. Distributed in North America by:

Gale Research Company
Penobscot Building
Detroit, Michigan 48226
Price: $180
About 360 pages

An annual statistical handbook of market information on major trading companies. (Companion volume to *European Marketing Data and Statistics*.) Statistical information on all basic marketing parameters for 132 countries around the world including Pacific Rim countries. Major topics include population, employment, production, trade, economy, standard of living, consumption and market sizes, retailing, consumer expenditure, housing, health, education, communications, tourism, and travel.

Findex, the Directory of Market Research Reports, Studies, and Surveys. Published by:

Find/SVP
The Information Clearing House
500 Fifth Avenue
New York, N.Y. 10110
(212) 354-2424
Telex: 148358

Findex is a reference guide to published, commercially available market and business research. More than 9,000 reports from over 400 U.S. and non-U.S. research publishers are included. It contains descriptions of consumer and industrial studies and surveys, syndicated and multiclient studies, audits and subscription research services, as well as published reports on general management and business topics. *Findex* also lists reports produced by investment researchers covering individual companies and industries.

Individual reports may cover an entire industry, a specific segment of an industry, an individual product, or series of related products. Reports are arranged by twelve broad industry classifications and are further divided into subcategories to allow for quick scanning for a particular market or product area.

Updated annually. Price: around $200. Copies are available in Commerce Department and other business libraries, though not necessarily the latest edition.

You can use the Findex directory to locate a market research company suitable to your needs, since it lists the names and addresses of the hundreds of market research organizations worldwide whose reports are listed in *Findex*. *Findex* also contains a geographical index so you can identify all the reports on a particular country.

National Trade and Professional Associations of the United States and Canada

Columbia Books, Inc.
777 145th Street NW
Washington, D.C. 20005

Encyclopedia of Associations

Gale Research Company
Book Tower
Detroit, Michigan 48226
(313) 961-2242

The Directory of Leading U.S. Export Management Companies

Bergano Book Company
P.O. Box 190
Fairfield, Conn. 06430
Price: $45

The Rand McNally International Bankers Directory

Rand McNally and Company
P.O. Box 7600
Chicago, Ill. 60680
(313) 673-9100
Four volumes

Volume 4 is "international." Volumes 1 and 2 give data on every bank operating in the United States, listed by state and city, including overseas banks. Volume 4 lists all the offices of international banks that are involved in foreign exchange or foreign trade outside the U.S. It includes U.S. banks operating overseas.

Comparative Investment Incentives: Hong Kong, Indonesia, Korea, Macau, Malaysia, Philippines, Singapore, Taiwan, Thailand. Published by the SGV Group, 1984

SGV and Company
6760 Ayala Avenue
Makati, Metro Manilla 3117 Philippines
P.O. Box 589 Manilla 2800
P.O. Box 256 Makati 3117

The SGV Group periodically surveys current investment incentives in these nine Pacific Rim nations and summarizes the results in a brochure. Topics covered include investment policy of state, types of enterprises eligible for investment incentives, regulations regarding ownership, corporate tax structure, basic rights and guarantees to investors, protections, schemes, and priorities given to investors, exemptions from taxes and tariff duties, tax deductions and tax credits, special incentives, assistance to investors. Approximately 100 pages, this brief summary gives an easy to grasp overview of the variety of investment incentives.

Managing for Joint Venture Success and *Strategies for Joint Ventures*. Written by Katherine Rudie Harrigan. Lexington Books, Lexington, Massachusetts.

Although these books are written for domestic joint ventures, they pertain to international joint ventures as well.

Export Training Resource Guide. National Association of State Development Agencies

Hall of States, Suite 611
444 N. Capital Street NW
Washington, D.C. 20001
(202) 624-5411

Business Customs and Protocols

The Global Edge by Sondra Snowden. (Simon & Schuster.) Price: $19.95. Reports on the business protocols and customs of twenty-five leading trade nations, including most in the Pacific Rim.

Do's and Taboos Around the World: A Guide to International Behavior by Roger E. Axtell. (John Wiley & Sons, Inc., New York: 1986.) Price: $9.95. 183 pages. Gives advice on proper etiquette to business travelers, avoiding common blunders commited overseas, overcoming language barriers, and accepting cultural taboos. Includes after-hour etiquette for traveling businesswomen and advice on gift giving and receiving.

Doing Business Abroad by Gavin Kennedy. (Simon and Schuster, 1985.) Price: $18.95. 268 pages. The author, an economist, clearly shows some cultural differences between American entrepreneurs and their overseas counterparts. These differences can easily thwart a prospective deal. The key to successful business is to negotiate with an understanding of cultural influences.

The International Businesswoman by Marlene L. Rossman. (Greenwood Press.) This practical guide for women describes and realistically assesses career opportunities. It looks at international business operations, especially negotiations, to which, the author suggests, women may bring particularly valuable skills. Next, the world marketplace is discussed region by region, and capsule profiles of the countries and cultures that constitute the major areas of business opportunity are provided. Finally, specific issues and problems in key areas are examined: breaking down barriers women face in the international business world; effective self-presentation; managing the life of an international traveler; and balancing career, emotional, and family needs. Particularly valuable are five case studies of women who have made it in the international business world. Price: $12.95. 137 pages with a bibliography.

Managing Cultural Differences (Second Edition) by Philip R. Harris and Robert T. Moran. (Gulf.) This widely used and respected volume has been thoroughly revised and updated and substantially expanded. *Managing Cultural Differences* begins by analyzing the impact of culture on managers in the roles they play as communicators, negotiators, and organizational leaders. The authors then discuss how culture affects international business operations in five areas: managerial effectiveness, foreign deployment, business protocol and the transfer of technology, human resource management and training, and professional collaboration. In the last section of the book, they provide detailed guidelines on doing business and offering services in the principal world markets. Price: $29.95. 622 pages with appendixes, bibliography, and indexes. Hardbound.

Going International, How to Make Friends and Deal Effectively in the Global Marketplace by Lennie Copeland and Lewis Griggs. (New American Library.) What is the secret to success in international business? *Going International* answers that question and gives specific rules for developing the strategy, style, and sensitivity needed to succeed in any kind of business anywhere in the world. Authors Lennie Copeland and Lewis Griggs, producers of the award-winning *Going International* film series, have combined the wisdom, know-how, and experience of America's most savvy travelers into a practical guide for those involved in any kind of international business. Deals with getting started, marketing, negotiating, communicating, managing people, training, business and social etiquette, communicating with headquarters, and personal and family life. Price: $11.95. 302 pages with appendixes and index.

Introduction to Intercultural Communication by John C. Condon and Gathi Yousef. (Macmillan.) This comprehensive introduction to intercultural communication is written in a lively style, rich with illustrative incidents and anecdotes. Examines cultural behaviors and practices, explores the process of intercultural communication, and introduces the concepts of values and value orientations in an especially lucid and engaging manner. Price: $14.95. 325 pages with bibliography and index.

Business Practices and Customers of Pacific Rim Nations

Most of these books and tapes, plus others, are available from:

Intercultural Press, Inc.
P.O. Box 768
Yarmouth, Maine 04096

Doing Business With the Koreans, and *How to Do Business With Taiwan Chinese.* Two handbooks for executives by Paul Leppert. (Patton Pacific Press.) These concise, practical guides are for business executives, their families, and others setting out to do business with Koreans or Taiwanese. Price: $15.

Thais and North Americans by John Paul Fieg. (Intercultural Press.) Thais and North Americans share some ways of looking at the world—both are freedom-loving, pragmatic, and dislike pomposity and arrogance. However, they differ significantly in their approach to these commonalities and, of course, have sharply contrasting views on other issues. This book defines the differences and offers useful advice for dealing with them; explores social relations, attitudes toward work, interaction in the workplace; and closes with a look at the overall patterns that provide a basis for cooperation. Price: $10. 82 pages.

Australians and North Americans by George W. Renwick. (Intercultural Press.) Australians and North Americans have a common heritage, similar environments and backgrounds, and share some personal characteristics. They assume, therefore, that they understand and can agree with each other more readily than they do. In this exploration of their similarities and differences, points of potential conflict are clearly defined, followed by practical guidelines for developing more productive and enjoyable work and social relationships. Examines such things as attitudes toward equality, approaches to leadership, conversational styles, decision making and risk-taking. Price: $10. 60 pages.

In Search of What's Japanese About Japan by John Condon and Keisuke Kurata. (Tuttle.) Japanese culture has been the subject of so much discussion lately it is hard to conceive of a book having something different to say. But this one does. Condon and Kurata distill thirty-one central themes or distinctive characteristics from Japanese culture and, through the interplay of text and photographs, provide the reader with insights of striking breadth and depth. Here is a sampling of the themes: ritual exchange; symbolism of nature, form, color, and feeling; the group; silence; arrangement; the bath; space; knotting, typing, and linking. It is a small book (though it has over 300 photos, fifty-five in full color), but it captures the essence of Japanese culture. A good introduction to Japan and the perfect companion to Condon's more recent *With Respect to the Japanese*. Price: $11.95. 145 pages.

With Respect to the Japanese, A Guide for Americans by John C. Condon. (Intercultural Press.) This is a practical and indispensable handbook for Americans who must deal with Japanese in a business, work, or educational setting. It examines the critical values, attitudes, and behaviors that affect the way Japanese and Americans perceive and react to each other, and offers concrete guidelines for establishing effective relationships. Price: $10. 110 pages.

Communicating With China, Robert A. Kapp, Editor. (Intercultural Press.) A collection of essays, a tour of the country. A hard-nosed look at negotiating styles and practices, and the inadequacies of the communication process. Chapters on the Chinese language, the art of interpreting, and the use of interpreters. Published in association with the China Council of the Asia Society. Mr. Kapp is executive president of the Washington Council on International Trade. Price: $6.95. 80 pages with bibliography.

Korean Etiquette and Ethics in Business by Boye De Mente. (National Textbook.) This author has been writing about the Far East for more than three decades and is particularly well-known for his works on Japan. Now he has focused on Korea, describing the historical, social, economic, and cultural factors that have moved Korea into the international business spotlight. He places particular emphasis on the "Korean Way," the fundamental aspects of the culture that affect how Koreans perceive the world. He also discusses the role of government and examines major problem areas for foreign corporations and business executives. Includes a valuable chapter on adapting to the Korean business environment. Price: $14.95. 158 pages with glossary.

Japanese Etiquette and Ethics in Business (Fifth Edition) by Boye De Mente. (National Textbook.) New, revised edition of this classic guide to the cultural characteristics that epitomize the Japanese character and business mentality. Shows how the fundamental ideas on which Japanese values and behaviors are based extend to business dealings. The author, a long-standing expert and consultant on doing business in Japan, has honed this book to perfection through five editions over a period of twenty-five years. Price: $14.95. 191 pages, appendix (glossary of terms).

Culturegrams. Four-page cultural orientations covering customs, manners, lifestyles, and other specialized information. Also includes maps, socioeconomic statistics, and key addresses. Available for every Pacific Rim nation. Price: 50 cents each. Volume discounts are available. Request (by country) from:

David M. Kennedy Center for International Studies
280 Clark Building
Brigham Young University
Provo, Utah 84602
(801) 378-6528

Films and Videotapes on Business Customs and Protocols

Films and Videos by Going International.
Going International publishes a series of films/videotapes and training guides that help the traveler and expatriate develop the cross-cultural skills required for a successful, enjoyable international experience.

Going International
302 23rd Avenue
San Francisco, Calif. 94121
(415) 668-4200
Fax: 415-668-6004

1. *Bridging the Culture Gap* (on the significance of cultural differences and the need for cultural awareness when working abroad)
2. *Managing the Overseas Assignment* (on communication problems in the overseas situation)
3. *Beyond Culture Shock* (guidelines for effective cross-cultural adjustment for the family going overseas)
4. *Welcome Home Stranger* (how to deal with problems attendant upon reentering one's home environment)

China Business Negotiations (Executive Information Network). A videotape and book package designed to help American business executives more effectively approach the China market and negotiate with the Chinese. Weaves together on-site film, background narrative, and commentary of nine experts experienced in doing business in the Pacific Rim. Covers planning, preparations, negotiating strategies and tactics, and practical aspects of conducting the negotiations.

Taking Your Product Into the Japanese Market (marketed in the United States through Sietar International, 202-296-4710). A comprehensive videotape designed to help foreign businesspeople operate in Japan. Depicts an encounter between a fictional Yankee trader and his prospective Japanese customers. Shows how the Japanese react to inappropriate American sales approaches.

Publications From Banks and Other Financial Institutions

Asian Development Bank DACON 1600. Bidding registration form. Available from:

> William R. Thomson
> U.S. Alternate Executive Director
> Asian Development Bank
> P.O. Box 789
> Manila, Philippines 3800
> Telex: 23103 ADB PH
> Phone: 843444

Development Form Business Edition. Contains information on the World Bank and the Asian Development Bank. Helpful to companies wishing to sell products or services to the World Bank. Order from the United Nations Publications Sales Office:

> Development Form
> United Nations
> Room 1061
> New York, N.Y. 10017
> (212) 754-6858

The Chase Manhattan Foreign Trade Service

> Chase Manhattan Bank
> 1 Chase Manhattan Plaza
> New York, N.Y.

Contains an annual issue with periodic supplements. Available free on request.

Foreign Information Service. The First National City Bank of New York (Citibank).

Doing Business Abroad. Morgan Guaranty Trust Company of New York.

International Trade Information. Bank of America.

Accounting Firms. Major accounting firms publish a series of reports for countries in which their clients do business. Many of these reports are available to outside companies. Cost may be $100, but can be very worthwhile. For example: Price-Waterhouse and Ernst-Whinney.

Periodicals

Daily Commerce

> 210 S. Spring Street
> P.O. Box 54026
> Los Angeles, Calif. 90054
> (213) 624-3111

Asian Wall Street Journal Weekly. Provides an authoritative and comprehensive account of the key business, financial, economic, and political news important to those interested in Asian business. Focuses on the region as well as on individual Pacific Rim nations and markets. Published by:

Dow Jones and Company, Inc.
200 Burnett Road
Chicopee, Mass. 01020
Subscription rate: $214 per year.

The *Weekly* is sometimes confused with the *Asian Wall Street Journal*—the Asian version of the *Wall Street Journal*—which is printed daily in Hong Knog, Singapore, and Tokyo, and contains American news of interest to Asian business. Asian news from this paper is recapped in the *Weekly,* thus the *Weekly* is usually of greater interest to American business. If you are interested in the *Asian Wall Street Journal,* contact:

G.P.O. Box 9825
1 Stubbs Road
A1A Building
Hong Kong

Business Asia. Periodical published by Business International.

Asiaweek. Hong Kong.

Far Eastern Economic Review. Published weekly for $98 per year by Review Publishing Company Limited, Hong Kong. U.S. Mailing Agent:

Data Movers, Inc.
38 West 36th Street, New York, New York 10018

The Exporter: The Magazine for the Business of Exporting. Published twelve times a year by:

Trade Data Reports, Inc.
6 West 37th Street
New York, N.Y. 10018
(212) 563-2772
Subscription rate: $95.
   (*The Exporter* is also available online via Newsnet. Call (800) 345-1301.)

   Services and resources for every aspect of exporting for exporters of all sizes who need to understand and meet foreign import or U.S. export requirements.

The Economist

P.O. Box 966
Farmingdale, N.Y. 11737-9896
Weekly
Subscription: $98 a year

Excellent coverage of world economic and political news from a non-American (British) perspective. Has a section each issue on Asia. Each issue has an in-depth analysis of some nation or economic development.

World Press Review

Post Office Box 915
Farmingdale, N.Y. 11737-9615

Excerpts of current news stories from newspapers around the world. Varied non-American perspectives, essential for anyone entering international trade.

Global Executive. Published by:

North American Publishing Company
401 North Broad Street
Philadelphia, Penn. 19108
Monthly
$45 a year

Formerly *Global Trade Executive* (often found at Department of Commerce Library).

International Trade Forum. Published by:

International Trade Center
UNCTAD/GATT
Palais de Nations
1211 Geneva 10, Switzerland
Quarterly.
Subscription: $16 per year.

Publications on the Pacific Rim Region

The Pacific Guide. Published in 1987 by:

World of Information
21 Gold Street
Saffron Walden, Essex CB10 IEJ, England
Price: $17
192 pages

A guide to the economies to business in all the Pacific Rim nations plus many Pacific island nations and territories. The more important trading nations are given deeper coverage—a brief sketch of the history, economy, political situation, imports, exports, major industries and resources, plus invaluable details such as entry requirements, holidays, health precautions, travel information. Included are addresses and phone numbers of public officials, hotels, airlines, interior transportation.

Business Guide. For Singapore, China, Hong Kong, and Japan. Longman Publications, World of Information. Price: $5.95.

The Pacific Basin: An Economic Handbook. Euromonitor Publications, Ltd. London. Distributed in North America by:

Gale Research Company
Penobscot Building
Detroit, Michigan 48226
Price: $80
204 pages

Explores the economic, social, and political developments affecting the countries of this region: Japan, Hong Kong, South Korea, Singapore, Taiwan, Indonesia, Malaysia, the Philippines, Australia, and New Zealand. Does not cover China. Topics include political and economic issues, commodity and commodity trade, energy, banking and capital markets, social issues, manufacturing, trade, problems, and opportunities.

Foreign Trade and Investment: Economic Growth in the Newly Industrializing Asian Countries. Edited by Walter Galenson. University of Wisconsin Press, 1985. Price: $30. 390 pages. Fourteen authors, many of them Asians, have contributed to this study of trade and investment and their roles in the development of the "four dragons": Taiwan, Korea, Singapore, and Hong Kong.

Encyclopedia of the Third World by George Thomas Kurian. Facts on File, 3rd edition, 1987. Three volumes. $175. The third edition of this outstanding reference work on the 126 countries of the developing world carries updated articles on each of them, their politics, culture, geography, economics, and many more details. There are feature articles, charts, maps, glossaries, statistics, and bibliographies—all made readily accessible by an exhaustive index.

Publications for Specific Pacific Rim Nations

American Chamber of Commerce Publications. Many of the AMCHAMS in Pacific Rim nations publish a journal on the political, economic, and business environment in their country. It would be worthwhile subscribing to the journal for your target markets. For example, *AMCHAM Hong Kong: ACCJ—The Journal of the American Chamber of Commerce in Japan.*

ASEAN

ASEAN Financial Cooperation: Developments in Banking, Finance and Insurance by Michael T. Skully. (St. Martin's Press, 1985.) Price: $29.95. 269 pages. Regional cooperation among the ASEAN countries (Indonesia, Malaysia, Philippines, Singapore, and Thailand) is examined at the inter-governmental, private-industry association, and individual firm level. The study gives consideration to the differences in development of each member nation's financial sector.

A Business Guide to ASEAN: How to Succeed in ASEAN Markets. Best prospects by country. Published by the Department of Commerce.

Australia

Australia Business. Published fortnightly on Thursday by Australian Consolidated Press Ltd. Head Office:

Park House
54 Park Street
Sydney, Australia
Telephone: 282-8300

North American address corrections to:

Australian Consolidated Press Ltd.
25 Van Dam Street
New York, N.Y. 10013

Subscription rates: USA, Canada, Middle East countries: 1 year for $A150.

Australian Consolidated Press
GPO Box 5252
Sydney, NSW 2001, Australia

China

Beijing Review: A Chinese Weekly of News and Views. Distributed in U.S. by:

China Books & Periodicals
2929 24th Street
San Francisco, Calif. 94110

Published weekly. A subscription costs $24 per year. Current events, editorials, and policy changes in political, cultural, social, economic, and foreign relations. Good background source for firms doing business in China.

International Business and Management. China's first international business magazine. Published in Chinese: Your ads are translated into Chinese, and inquiries are translated into English before being forwarded to you. Published by McGraw-Hill. Call (212) 512-3867.

China Takes Off: Technology Transfer and Modernization by E. E. Bauer. (University of Washington Press, 1986.) Price $20.00. 227 pages. The author, an advisor sent to China by Lockheed, gives a behind-the-scenes look at CAAC, airline of the People's Republic of China. He describes his experience in the workplace, as well as the pains and pleasures of residence at the Peking Hotel for four years.

China: Economic Handbook. (Euromonitor, Gale Research, 1986.) Price: $80. 246 pages. Part of an excellent series on the economies of various countries, this volume covers such topics as agriculture, industry, transport, foreign trade, and finance. Useful names and addresses are included, especially for the businessperson interested in exploiting this market.

The China Investment Guide. (Longman Group and China Informational Economic Consultant, Gale Research.) Third Edition, 1986. Price; $90. 92 pages. Comprehensive guide for foreign businesses seeking to make direct investments in China. Six sections: (1) information on China in general, (2) profiles of China's regional and industrial sectors, (3) channels for foreign investment, (4) details on procedures and answers to questions, (5) investment protection and taxation measures, and (6) foreign investment laws and regulations. The *Guide* answers virtually every question on the subject of investment in China.

China's Development Strategies and Foreign Trade by James T. H. Tsao. (Lexington Books D.C. Health, 1987.) Price: $32. 10 pages. China's membership in the International Monetary Fund and the World Bank has resulted in more reliable statistics on her economy. Dr. Tsao has applied sophisticated macroeconomic techniques to these data, thus providing a valuable analysis of the economy and its growth potential.

China Urban Statistics 1986. Compiled by the Chinese State Statistical Bureau, Longman Group and China Statistical Information & Consultancy Service Center (Gale Research), Second Edition, 1987. Price: $80. 492 pages. The third book in this reference group cites comprehensive statistical data and detailed background information on the major cities of China.

Directory of Chinese Foreign Trade 1986. Compiled by China Council for the Promotion of International Trade, Longman Group. (Gale Research, 1985.) Price: $95. 294 pages. Complementing *The China Investment Guide,* this volume provides details on more than 1,000 Chinese economic and trade organizations, agencies, and enterprises that serve as contacts and information sources.

China Express. This data service, which is maintained by London-based 21st Century Publishing and is accessed by any personal computer via NEWSNET, features comprehensive listings of current project opportunities in China (about 3,000 listings divided among 100 industrial categories).

Advertising Directory of China. Published by The National Administrative Bureau of Industry of Commerce, The People's Republic of China, and China United Advertising Corporation (CUAC). A directory of the various media for advertising or publicizing different products, trades, and professions for national, regional, local, and industrial markets. Lists advertising agencies, professional publications, newspapers, radio stations. Lists the audience of each, but not necessarily the circulation or the size of the audience reached. Published in 1985. To see a copy, contact the Chinese Embassy or Consulate.

Annals of China's Enterprise Register. Special edition of National Corporations. Published and updated each year. Lists all national corporations, import and export corporations, and other corporations that do business with foreign countries. Lists basic facts, functions, names and addresses for each company, including branch offices. Categories include finance and commerce, industry, transportation and communications, construction contracting, foreign cooperation, import and export, economic consultancy, tourist service, and others.

Almanac of China's Foreign Economic Relations and Trade. Published by the editorial board of the *Almanac*. Summarizes trade statistics and laws and regulations for trade and investment. The laws and regulations sections cover foreign trade, foreign investment, customs and taxation, inspection and quarantine, financing and foreign exchange, insurance, arbitration, special economic zones, transportation, and environmental protection. Statistical sections include foreign trade, utilization of foreign capital, and foreign economic cooperation. Section three: profiles of areas, special economic zones, coastal cities, Hainan Island, Chong Qing.

A Directory of Resident Offices of Foreign, Overseas Chinese, Hong Kong and Macao Enterprises. This is a directory of all the foreign enterprises in China from every country in the world including overseas Chinese. It is classified by country and area, lists addresses, phone numbers, telexes, and representative scopes of business and office. Compiled by State Administration for Industry and Commerce.

China International Trust and Investment Corporation (CITIC)

19 JIANG GUO MENWAI DAJIE
Bejing, P.O. Box 6200
Bejing, China
Telephone: 502255
Telex: 22305 CITIC CN

Magnificent China: A Guide to It's Cultural Treasures by Petra Häring Kuan and Yu-chien Kuan. (Publishing Co. Hong Kong, copyright 1987.)

Queen Victoria Street
Hong Kong

This book started out as an extended travel article by a Chinese professor and his German wife, and turned into a thorough introduction into the country and culture of China. An excellent introduction for the newcomer. Covers the history, description of the country, language and literature, religion. Contains travel information, description of city and provinces, illustrations and color photographs, and listings of hotels and restaurants.

Japan

Journal of Japanese Trade and Industry. Bimonthly. Published by Japan Economic Foundation. U.S. subscriptions:

Elsevier Science Publishers
52 Vanderbilt Avenue
New York, N.Y. 10017
Price: $65 a year

This is like the Japanese version of *Business Week*. It is printed in English.

The Japan Economic Journal. Distills and analyzes information from *The Nihon Keizai Shimbun* and other leading Japanese business papers.

> 1221 Avenue of the Americas,
> Suite 1802
> New York, N.Y. 10020
> (212) 512-3600
> $99 per year

Establishing a Business in Japan.

> U.S. and Foreign Commercial Service
> American Embassy
> Tokyo, Japan.

Setting Up Enterprises in Japan.

> Japan External Trade Organization
> McGraw-Hill Building
> 44th Floor
> 1221 Avenue of the Americas
> New York, N.Y. 10020

Japan Trade Directory 1987–88. JETRO (Japanese External Trade Association). (Gale Research, 1987.) Price: $265. About 1,400 pages. This voluminous directory provides detailed information on 2,400 Japanese companies and their 14,000 products and services. An import list gives companies interested in importing specific products into Japan, while the export list indicates the companies having specific products to export from Japan. There is also a section on Japan's forty-seven geographic regions or "prefectures," giving information of interest to businesspeople for each one. A mine of business information!

Sources of Information in Japan by David Baskervill of the American Electronic Association Office in Japan. Summarizes the sources of information in Japan available in English. You can purchase the book for $60 from:

> AEA
> Nambu Building 3F
> Kioicho 3-3
> Chiyoda-Ku
> Tokyo, Japan 102
> Phone: (813) 237-7195
> Fax: (813) 237-1237
> Telex: 2322854

Korea

Korea Business World. Monthly economic journal. Order from:

Korea Business World
Yoido
P.O. Box 720
Seoul 150 Korea
Subscription rate: $50 monthly

Tracks Korea's overall economic development, Korea's major business issues, and political and social coverage. Also Korean views on other global events.

Doing Business in Korea, edited by Arthur M. Whitehill. (Nichols Publishing, 1987.) Price: $33.50. 121 pages. South Korea is now a major participant in international trade. "In a little more than twenty years, per capita GNP has risen from $87 to over $2,000, and exports have rocketed from $55 million to more than $30 billion." For the U.S. businessperson interested in the Korean market, this is an essential book.

Business Korea. Department of Commerce Library.

Taiwan

Trade. Published by AIT, The American Institute in Taiwan, in Taipai. Published bi-monthly. Sent free of charge to any company requesting it. Feature articles in both English and Chinese, announcements of trade shows and missions in Taiwan, and product announcements of U.S. firms wishing to sell everything from microprocessors to hardware to produce.

Other Pacific Rim Nations

Trade and Investment Guide to Cook Islands, Fiji, Kiribati, Nauru, Niue, Papua, New Guinea, Solomon Islands, Tonga, Tuvalu, Vanuatu, and Western Samoa. Published by South Pacific Bureau for Economic Cooperation in association with the University of the South Pacific, Suva, Fiji, copyright 1982. Edited by Anthony Haas. About 200 pages. Contact:

The Director of South Pacific Bureau for Economic Cooperation
Suva, Fiji

The guide for each country includes country profile, political profile, economy, economic plans and objectives, trade and investment policy, commerce and industry, labor, infrastructure, information sources and bibliography, statistics, maps, and photos.

The Pacific Islands Buyer's Guide, 1986/87. Products and services, manufacturers and suppliers, importers and exporters. Published by:

Pacific Magazine Corporation
P.O. Box 25488

Honolulu, Hawaii 96825
(808) 377-5335
Price: $5.00
124 pages.

This is a "yellow pages" type directory with many ads showing products and services sold and available in the islands and nations of Micronesia, Polynesia, and Melanesia.

Computer Data Bases

Computer data bases and related services for international trade and investment are multiplying rapidly. Rather than trying to put out a comprehensive list, we will show one example of several different types of services. You should thoroughly investigate a database service because they vary tremendously in quality, comprehensiveness, up-to-dateness, ease of use, and cost.

Conduct your own search. If you have access to any business or personal computer, a telephone, and a modem—plus the willingness to use computer database searches—the best way is to tap into databases on your own. There are many databases you can access directly. Some are listed here.

Center for Japanese Economy and Business Database of Statistics and Market Research.

Columbia University Business School
Broadway and 116th Street
New York, N.Y. 10027
212-280-3497

OLIADS (On-Line Intelligence and Decision Support for International Trade). Published by:

Intellibank Corporation
2214 Torrance Boulevard
Suite 101
Torrance, Calif. 90501
(213) 618-9597

OLIADS brings together data from many sources on foreign trade and investment, and is available to anyone with a personal computer and modem. Very comprehensive, up-to-date, and inexpensive. Easy to use. Organized into five areas: world environment, intelligence service, overseas planning update service, U.S. business conditions, and international trade lead system and world communications. Will soon cover *all* the Pacific Rim countries. Sign up fee: $195. Usage charge: $37.50 per hour.

World Trade Center NETWORK. Electronic message system for worldwide buying and selling opportunities. Users can post any message, through their own computer, and read the messages entered by others. To respond to a message, just type in your response, using the sender's electronic address. The NETWORK ties together 800 cities in sixty-four nations. Very inexpensive: local phone call rates, no charge to browse, 25¢ to read a full message on the network, and $24 to post a ten-line message for two weeks. You must first join the World Trade Centers Association, which is located in most major cities worldwide, or some other affiliated organization such as your Chamber of Commerce. Contact:

World Trade Centers Association
One World Trade Center
55th Floor
New York, N.Y. 10048.

Data Base Search Services

If you do not wish to dig through computer databases on your own, you can hire an expert to conduct a search for you. You tell them what you need; they will conduct a thorough search of computer databases for you, and then send you the data uncovered either as a document or over phone lines to your computer, for you to print out.

LM Warren, Inc. Information Services. Conducts research for you by searching databases all over the world. Retrieves information and transmits it to you through your computer. Data on competitors, distributors, and customers. Identifies potential affiliates and acquisitions. Obtains market research data—often brand-new data that have not yet been incorporated into published reports—trade data on imports and exports, technology transfer opportunities, data on upcoming trade shows and tender offers, long before the official notices are published. By using an expert database searcher, you can tap into data that are much newer than you might be able to find on your own. A search might cost $100 to over $1,000.

LM Warren, Inc.
402-1200 West Pender Street
Vancouver, BC, V6E 2S9, Canada
Phone (604) 683-4446

Information on Demand. Conducts computer and manual searches to find market and technical information. Sends data over computers or delivers copies of the documents to you. Data on competitors, market research, industry surveys, patent or trademark searches, technology reviews, investment information, "electronic clipping service," mailing lists, catalogs, conference proceedings, government reports, consumer surveys, corporate publications, product brochures, technical reports, standards and specs, SEC filings. Cost of a search is typically from $300 to $600. Contact:

Information on Demand, Inc.
P.O. Box 1370
Berkeley, Calif. 94701
Phone: (800) 227-0750, (415) 644-4500

State Export Assistance Programs

Energy Technology Export Program
California Energy Commission
1516 Ninth Street, MS 45
Sacramento, Calif. 95814
(916) 324-3029

Aims to help small and medium-size alternative energy businesses promote their goods and services worldwide. These technologies include solarthermal, photovoltaic, wind, geothermal, small hydroelectric, cogeneration, biomass, and energy conservation.

A State Government Export Directory

Alabama

Fred Denton
Alabama Department of
  Economic Affairs
Box 2939
Montgomery, Ala. 36105
(205) 263-0048

Programs:
1. Education
2. Export Finance Referral
   List
3. Missions
4. Small Business
   Development

Alaska

Dan Dixon
Department of Commerce
Office of International Trade
3601 C St.
Anchorage, Alaska 99503
(907) 561-5585

Programs:
1. Education
2. Missions
3. Research: Alaska Center
   for International Business
   (University of Alaska)
4. Foreign Offices: Tokyo,
   Seoul

Finance:
Greta Anderson
Alaska Industrial Finance
  Authority
P.O. Box D
Juneau, Alaska 99811
(907) 465-2590

1. Legislation Passed. No
   funding as yet
2. Guarantees

Arizona

James C. Ferguson
Arizona Department of
  Commerce

1700 West Washington,
  Fourth Floor
Phoenix, Ariz. 85007
(602) 255-5371

Programs:
1. Education
2. Counseling

Arkansas

Maria Haley/Bill Wilson
Arkansas Department of
  Economic Development
One State Capital Mall
Little Rock, Ark. 72201
(501) 371-7678 or 3545

(Just beginning new
  programs)

California

Robert de Martini
California World Trade
  Commission

413

1121 L Street
Sacramento, Calif. 98814
(916) 324-5511

Programs:
1. Education: Seminars and Counseling
2. Shows
3. Missions
4. Foreign Offices: Tokyo, London

Finance:
Fargo Wells
California Export Finance Authority
1075 South Broadway
Los Angeles, Calif. 90012
(213) 620-2433

1. Legislation Passed
2. Funding
3. Guarantees, Pre- and Post-Export
4. Umbrella
5. Insurance
6. Exim Loan Guarantee Packages

Colorado

Lisa Wheeler
International Trade Office
1313 Sherman St.
Denver, Colo. 80203
(303) 866-2205

Programs:
1. Trade Fairs, Missions, and Seminars
2. Education
3. Literature
4. Counseling
5. Foreign Offices: Taiwan, Japan

Finance:
Jan Sandhouse Hurst
Colorado Finance and Housing Authority
777 Pearl St.
Denver, Colo. 80203
(303) 861-8962

1. Legislation Passed
2. Insurance

Connecticut

Dawn Rodriguez
Department of Economic Development
210 Washington St.

Hartford, Conn. 06106
(203) 566-3842

Programs:
1. Education
2. Trade Shows, Missions
3. Foreign Offices: Tokyo, Frankfurt

Finance:
Gary Miller
Department of Economic Development
210 Washington St.
Hartford, Conn. 06106
(203) 566-3842

1. Legislation Passed
2. Exporters Revolving Loan Fund
3. Guarantee: New-to-Export, Pre- and Post-Export, up to 5 years.
4. Direct Loans: up to $350.000

Delaware

Dr. Dale E. Wolf
Delaware Development Office
Box 1401
Dover, Del. 19903
(302) 736-4271

Programs:
1. Some Counseling
2. Some Export Promotion
3. Missions

Florida

Tom Slatery, Acting Director
Florida Department of Commerce
401 Collins Bldg.
Tallahassee, Fla. 32301
(904) 488-6124

Programs:
1. Missions
2. Education: Seminars and Counseling
3. Foreign Offices: London, Frankfurt

Georgia

James Steed
Georgia Department of Industry and Trade
Box 1776

Atlanta, Ga. 30301
(404) 656-3577

Programs:
1. Education, Literature, Business Visitations, Seminars, Counseling
2. Missions
3. Export Trading Company
4. Foreign Offices: Tokyo, Seoul, Brussels, Toronto

Hawaii

Kenneth Kwak
Department of Business and Economic Development
P.O. Box 2359
Honolulu, Hawaii 96804
(808) 548-3048

Programs:
1. Participate in Trade Fairs and Missions
2. Foreign Trade Zones
3. Local Business Assistance

Idaho

Ron Hershey
Idaho Department of Commerce
State House
Boise, Idaho 83702
(708) 334-2470

Programs:
1. New plan as yet unapproved.

Illinois

Hendrik Woods
Department of Commerce: International
100 West Randolph St.
Chicago, Ill. 60601
(314) 917-7164

Programs:
1. Promotion
2. Missions
3. Export Trading Company
4. Foreign Offices: Brussels, Hong Kong, Osaka, Shenyang [China], Sao Paulo

Finance:
John Kerwitz
Illinois Export Development Authority

100 Randolph St.
Chicago, Ill. 60601
(312) 917-3401
1. Legislation Passed
2. Funding
3. Loans, Guarantees,
   Insurance
4. Maximum: $500,000

Indiana

Phil Grebe
Indiana Department of
   Commerce
One North Capital St., Suite
   700
Indianapolis, Ind. 46204
(317) 232-8846
Programs:
1. Missions
2. Education: Counseling
   and Business Visitations
3. Foreign Offices: Tokyo,
   Amsterdam;
   Representatives in
   Republic of Korea and the
   People's Republic of
   China

Iowa

Mike Doyle
Iowa Development
   Commission
200 Grand St.
Des Moines, Iowa 50309
(515) 281-3581
Programs:
1. Trade Shows and Missions
2. Education
3. Foreign Offices:
   Frankfurt, Hong Kong,
   Tokyo

Kansas

Molly Kirk
Department of Economic
   Development
503 Kansas Ave., Sixth
   Floor
Topeka, Kan. 66603
(913) 296-4027
Programs:
1. Education
2. Trade Shows, Fairs,
   Missions
3. Foreign Offices: Tokyo,
   Stuttgart

Kentucky

Bill Savage
Kentucky Commerce Cabinet
Capital Plaza Tower, 24th
   Floor
Frankfurt, Ken. 40601
(502) 564-2170
Programs:
1. Education: Seminars and
   Counseling
2. Missions
3. Foreign Offices: Tokyo,
   London

Louisiana

Stan Fulcher
Office of International Trade,
   Finance, and Development
Louisiana Department of
   Commerce
P.O. Box 94185
Baton Rouge, La. 70112
(504) 342-5891
Programs:
1. Foreign Offices: Tokyo,
   South Hampton
2. Move into investment
3. Support outreach through
   World Trade Council
Finance:
James Gil
Louisiana Import-Export
   Trust Authority
Box 4407
Baton Rouge, La. 70821
(504) 928-6800
1. Legislation Passed 1979
2. Funding: $150 million
   from taxable bonds
3. Direct Loans
4. Guarantees

Maine

Michael Naylor-Davis
Maine World Trade
77 Sewell St.
Augusta, Maine 04330
(207) 622-0234
Programs:
1. Full promotion
2. Missions
Finance:
Karen Lazareth
Maine Finance Authority
P.O. Box 949

Augusta, Maine 04330
(207) 623-3263
1. Umbrella Policy
2. Insurance
3. SBA and Exim referrals

Maryland

Harold Zassenhaus
Maryland Office of
   International Trade
401 East Pratt St.
Baltimore, Md. 21202
(301) 333-4295
Programs:
1. Education: Seminars and
   Counseling
2. Missions
3. Foreign Offices: Tokyo,
   Brussels
Finance:
Marie Torres
Maryland Finance Authority
401 East Pratt St.
Baltimore, Md. 21202
(301) 333-4262
1. Legislation Passed
2. Funding: $1 Million
   Appropriation
3. Umbrella Policy
4. Insurance up to $1 million

Massachusetts

Andrew Bagley
Massachusetts Office of
   International Trade
100 Cambridge St.
Boston, Mass. 02202
Programs:
1. Full Education
2. Missions

Michigan

Del Willis
Michigan Department of
   Commerce
Box 30017
Lansing, Mich. 48909
(517) 373-9709
Programs:
1. Education
2. Counseling
3. Foreign Offices: Brussels,
   Tokyo

Minnesota

Michael Olson
Minnesota Trade Office
100 World Trade Center
St. Paul, Miss. 55101
(612) 297-4222

Programs:
1. Education
2. Export Trading Company
3. Missions
4. Counseling
5. Foreign Offices: Oslo,
   Stockholm, liaison with
   London

Finance:
Noor Doja/Devin Rice
Minnesta Export Finance
   Authority
100 World Trade Center
St. Paul, Minn. 55101
(612) 297-4659

1. Guarantee: Pre-Export
   $250,000
2. Umbrella

Mississippi

Bill McGinnis
Department of Economic
   Development
Box 849
Jackson, Miss. 38205
(601) 359-3444

Programs:
1. Education: Seminars and
   Counseling
2. Missions

Missouri

Glen Boos
Missouri International
   Development Office
P.O. Box 118
Jefferson City, Mo. 65102
(314) 751-4855

Programs:
1. Export Trading Company
2. Education
3. Trade Shows
4. Foreign Offices:
   Dusseldorf, Seoul, Tokyo

Montana

John Maloney
Montana Department of
   Commerce

State Capital
Helena, Montana 59620
(406) 444-4380

Programs:
1. State Export Trading
   Company
2. Education: Seminars and
   Counseling

Nebraska

Susan Rouch
Department of Economic
   Development
Box 94666
Lincoln, Nebr. 68509
(402) 471-4668

Programs:
1. Trade Clearinghouse of
   Information
2. Referals

Nevada

Julie Wilcox
State Economic
   Development Commission
600 East Williams, Suite 203
Carson City, Nevada 89710
(702) 885-4325

Programs:
1. Export Trading Company
2. Education: Counseling
3. Foreign Office: Tokyo

New Hampshire

James Parks
Department of Resources and
   Economic Development
105 Loudent Road Building
   Two
Concord, N.H. 03301
(603) 271- 2591

Programs:
1. Education

New Jersey

Ming Hsu
Division of International
   Trade
744 Broad St.
Newark, N.J. 07102
(210) 648-3518

Programs:
1. Education: Seminars and
   Counseling

2. Missions
3. Foreign Office: Japan

Finance:
John Walsh
Economic Development
   Authority
200 South Warren St. CN990
Trenton, N.J. 08625

1. Direct Loan: $100,000,
   one year 180 days
2. Guarantee Program: 90%,
   $600,000

New Mexico

Cheri Tillman
Department of Economic
   Development & Tourism
Montoya Building
Santa Fe, N.M. 87503
(505) 827-0300

Programs:
1. Shows, Missions
2. Limited Counseling

New York

Christopher Finn
New York Department of
   Commerce
230 Park Avenue
New York, N.Y. 10169
(212) 309-0503

Programs:
1. Missions
2. Counseling
3. Market Research
4. Foreign Offices: London,
   Wiesbaden, Tokyo,
   Toronto, Montreal

North Carolina

Gordon McRoberts
Director, International
   Marketing International
   Division
Department of Commerce
430 North Salisbury St.
Raleigh, N.C. 27611
(919) 733-7193

Programs:
1. Counseling
2. Education: Business
   Visitations
3. Trade Shows, Fairs,
   Missions

4. Foreign Offices:
   Dusseldorf, Liaison in
   Tokyo

North Dakota

Jack Minton
International Trade Division
Liberty Memorial Bldg.
State Capital Grounds
Bismarck, N.D. 58505
(701) 224-2810
Programs:
1. Export Trading Company
2. Education (limited)
3. Missions, Shows

Ohio

Cindy Cole
Department of Economic
   Development
30 East Broad St.
P.O. Box 1001
Columbus, Ohio 43266
(614) 466-2480
Programs:
1. Education
2. Missions, Shows
3. Foreign Offices: Brussels,
   Tokyo, Lagos

Oklahoma

J. C. Johnson
Oklahoma International
   Export Services
402 North Lincoln Boulevard
Oklahoma City, Okla. 73105
(405) 521-3501
Programs:
1. Education
2. Fairs, Missions
3. Foreign Offices: New
   Delhi, Hong Kong,
   Singapore, Japan, London

Oregon

Amy Galloway
Oregon Department of
   Economic Development
International Trade Division
1500 South-West First Ave.,
Suite 620
Portland, Ore. 97201
(503) 229-5625 or 1-800-
   452-7813

Programs:
1. Foreign Office: Tokyo
2. Export Trading Company
3. Education
4. Shows and Missions

Pennsylvania

Anthony Amorosi
Pennsylvania Department of
   Commerce
489 Forum Bldg.
Hershey, Pa. 17120
(717) 787-7190
Programs:
1. Education
2. Shows, Fairs, Promotion
3. Foreign Offices: Brussels,
   Frankfurt, Tokyo

Rhode Island

Gerry Lessuch
Department of Economic
   Development
7 Jackson Walkway
Providence, R.I. 02903
(401) 277-2601
Programs:
1. Limited Education
2. Shows, Missions
3. Foreign Office: Antwerp

South Carolina

Dr. James A. Kauhlman
Associate Director
International Business
   Development
P.O. Box 927
Columbia, S.C. 29202
(803) 734-1400
Programs:
1. Education
2. Export Trading Company
3. Fairs, Seminars, Missions
4. Foreign Office: Brussels

South Dakota

Nancy Bradley
Office of International Trade
School of Business,
   University of South
   Dakota
Vermillion, S.D. 57069
(605) 677-5287
Programs:
1. Promotion only

Tennessee

David Weber
Economic and Community
   Development
Rachel Jackson Bldg.,
   Eighth Floor
320 Sixth Avenue North
Nashville, Tenn. 37219-5308
(615) 741-5870
Programs:
1. Education
2. Missions, Fairs, Seminars

Texas

Roger Wallace
International Trade
   Department
Box 12728
Austin, Tex. 12728
(512) 472-5059
Programs:
1. Education: Counseling
2. Foreign Office: Mexico
   City

Utah

Greg Gullet
International Business
Economic and Industrial
   Development Division
6150 State Office Bldg.
Salt Lake City, Utah 84114
(801) 533-5325
Programs:
1. Promotion
2. Foreign Office: Tokyo

Vermont

Graham Freeman
Department of Economic
   Development
Pavilion Office Bldg.
Montpelier, Vt. 05602
(802) 828-3221
Programs:
1. Education
2. Trade Shows, Missions
3. Foreign Offices: Japan,
   Canada

Virginia

Ronald Renchard
Department of Economic

Development and
International Trade
1000 Washington Bldg.
Richmond, Va. 23219
(804) 786-3791

Programs:
1. Education
2. Trade Shows, Missions
3. Export Trading Company
4. Foreign Offices: Brussels,
   Tokyo, Hong Kong, Sao
   Paulo

Washington

Steve Odom
Department of Commerce
   and Economic
   Development
312 First Avenue North
Seattle, Wash. 89109
(206) 464-6282

Programs:
1. Promotion
2. Counseling
3. Export Assistance Center
4. Foreign Office: Tokyo

West Virginia

Steve Spence
Governor's Office of
   Community and Industrial
   Development
State Capital, Room B-517
Charleston, W. Va. 25305
(304) 348-0400

Programs:
1. Missions, Shows
2. Limited Education

Wisconsin

James Sindt
International Division

Department of Development
123 West Washington Ave.
Madison, Wis. 53702
(608) 266-1018

Programs:
1. Education: Seminars
2. Literature
3. Foreign Offices: Frankfurt
   and Hong Kong

Wyoming

Peter Cunningham
Department of Economic
   Planning
Herscher Bldg., Third Floor
Cheyenne, Wy. 82002
(307) 777-7285

Programs:
1. Some Trade Missions

Banks and Other Financial Institutions

World Bank. If you wish to register with World Bank, you must fill out the "Guide to Completing the Consulting Firm Registration Form" which you can get from:

The World Bank
1818 H Street, NW
Washington, D.C. 20433
(202) 477-1234

Asian Development Bank (ADB)

The Office of U.S. Director
Asian Development Bank
P.O. Box 789
Manilla, Philippines 2800

U.S. Banks With International Departments

American Asian Bank
500 Montgomery St.
San Francisco, CA 94111
(415) 788-4700
Contact: John Wang, vice
president/

American Fletcher National
Bank
111 Monument Circle
Indianapolis, IN 46277
(317) 639-7940
Telex: 27324
Contact: William M. Stow-
ring, senior vice president
and manager

American National Bank &
Trust Co. of Chicago
33 N. LaSalle St.
Chicago, IL 60690

(312) 661-5000
Telex: 25229
Contact: Scott M. Baranski,
vice president and general
manager

American Security Bank
1501 Pennsylvania Ave.,
N.W.
Washington, D.C. 20013
(202) 624-4000
Telex: 197721
Contact: Clement Geitner,
senior vice president

Banco Popular de Puerto
Rico
Banco Popular Center Bldg.
Avenue Ponce de Leon 208
Hato Rey, P.R. 00936

(809) 759-8900
Telex: 3450033
Contact: Kenneth Groff, vice
president

Bank of America
555 California St.
San Francisco, CA 94104
(415) 622-1234
Contact: Robert Frick, vice
chairman and head of
world banking division

Bank of Boston
23 Third Ave.
Burlington, MA 01803
(617) 270-3300
Contact: Joe Grimaldi, vice
president and deputy divi-
sional manager

419

Bank of Hawaii
111 S. King St.
Honolulu, HI 96813
(808) 537-8111
Telex: RCA 7238434
Contact: William S. Bailey,
    senior vice president

Bank of New England
28 State St.
Boston, MA 02109
(617) 742- 4000
Telex: 940191
Contact: Arthur H. Meehan,
    executive vice president
    international treasury ad-
    ministration

Bank of New York
48 Wall St.
New York, NY 10015
(215) 530-1784
Contact: Jeffrey Lamia, vice
    president

Bankers Trust Co.
280 Park Ave.
New York, NY 10017
(212) 850-3000
Telex: Burroughs 8501704
Contact: David K. Sias Jr.,
    executive vice president

Barnett Bank of South
    Florida
800 Brickell Ave.
Miami, FL 33131
(305) 350-7100
Contact: C. Royce Hough,
    executive vice president
    corporate and international
    banking

Baybanks Inc.
175 Federal St.
Boston, MA 02110
(617) 482-1040
Contact: Paul Godfrey, as-
    sistant vice president

Capital Bank & Trust Co.
1885 Wooddale Blvd.
Baton Rouge, LA 70806
(504) 927-1220

Centerre Bank
One Centerre Plaza

St. Louis, MO 63101
(314) 554-6000
Telex: 447389
Contact: Clyde F. Wendel,
    vice president, and man-
    ager

Chase Manhattan Bank
One Chase Manhattan Plaza
New York, NY 10081
(212) 552-2222
Telex: RCA 232163 CMB
    UR
Contact Donald L. Boud-
    reau, executive vice presi-
    dent

Chemical Bank
277 Park Ave.
New York, NY 10172
(212) 310-7066
Telex: 422803
Contact: Robert J. Callander,
    president world banking
    group

Citibank
399 Park Ave.
New York, NY 10043
(212) 559-7608

Citizens and Southern Na-
    tional Bank
35 Broad St.
Atlanta, GA 30303
(404) 581-2121
Telex: 542346
Contact: Camillo Bozzolo,
    senior vice president

Comerica Bank
211 W. Fort St.
Detroit, MI 48226
(313) 222-3300
Telex: 4320034 COMBKITL
    DET
Contact: Charles F. Turner,
    senior vice president

Community Bank
3124 San Fernando Road
Los Angeles, CA 90065
(213) 258-8100
Contact: Bryan Tardivel,
    vice president and man-
    ager

Connecticut National Bank
777 Main St.

Hartford, CT 06115
(203) 728-2000
Telex: 221086
Contact: John F. Harreys,
    senior vice president

Continental Bank
1500 Market St.
Philadelphia, PA 19102
(215) 564-7433
Contact: James Lynch, exec-
    utive vice president

Continental Illinois National
    Bank & Trust
Co. of Chicago
231 S. LaSalle St.
Chicago, IL 60697
(312) 828-2345
Contact: Alfred F. Miossi,
    executive vice president

Cullen-Frost Bankers
100 W Houston St.
San Antonio, TX 94104
(512) 220-4011

Equibank
2 Oliver Plaza
Pittsburgh, PA 15222
(412) 288-5423
Contact: Tony Adamchik,
    manager

European American Bank
10 Hanover Square
New York, NY 10015
(202) 437-4300
Telex: ITT 420771
Contact: Homer M. Bying-
    ton, executive vice presi-
    dent

Fidelity Bank
Broad and Walnut Sts.
Philadelphia, PA 19109
(215) 985-6000
Telex: 834480
Contact: Claude Roy, vice
    president

Fidelity International Bank
520 Madison Ave.
New York, NY 10022
(212) 715-4967

First City National Bank of
  Houston
First City Tower
1001 Fannin St.
Houston, TX 77001
(713) 658-6011
Telex: 762429
Contact: Robert C. Howard,
  executive vice president

First Commerce Corp.
210 Baronne St.
New Orleans, LA 70112
(504) 561-1371

First Fidelity Bank
550 Broad St.
Newark, NJ 07192
(201) 565-3200

First Florida Bank
111 E. Madison St.
Tampa, FL 33602
(813) 224-1111

First Hawaiian Bank
King & Bishop Streets
Honolulu, HI 96847
(808) 525-7000
Telex: (723)-8851
Contact: John D. Nielsen, in-
  ternational credit officer

First Interstate Bank of-
  Oregon
1300 S.W. Fifth Ave.
Portland, OR 97208
(503) 225-2517
Telex: 360188
Contact: Kenneth L. Stoutt,
  senior vice president and
  manager

First Jersey National Bank
One Exchange Plaza
Jersey City, NJ 07302
(201) 527-7000
Contact: Josh Chapatwala,
  vice president

First Maryland International
  Banking
309 E. Market St.
York, PA 17405
(717) 848-2265
Contact: Ronald T. Teather,
  vice president

First Michigan Bank
101 E. Main St.
Zealand, MI 49464
(616) 396-9000
Contact: Virginia Leffew,
  marketing executive

First National Bank of Atlanta
Two Peachtree St., N.W.
Atlanta, GA 30383
(404) 588-5680
Anthony L. Furr, executive
  vice president

First National Bank of Boston
100 Federal St.
Boston, MA 02110
(617) 434-2200

First National Bank of Chicago
One First National Plaza
Chicago, IL 60670
(312) 732-4000
Telex: 4330253 FNBC UI,
  190201 FNBC UT
Contact: E. Neal Trogden,
  executive vice president
  international

First National Bank in Dallas
1401 Elm St.
Dallas, TX 75283
(214) 744-8000

First National Bank of Louisville
101 South Fifth St.
Louisville, KY 40202
(502) 581-4200
Telex: WUT 6802090
  SWIFT FNBLUS33
Contact: Randolph T. Goode,
  senior international banking officer

First National Bank of Maryland
25 S. Charles St.
Baltimore, MD 21201
(301) 244-4000
Contact: Mary Ann Smith,
  vice president European
  division

First National Bank of Minneapolis

120 S. 6th St.
Minneapolis, MN 55480
(612) 370-4141

First National Bank of St.
  Paul
332 Minnesota St.
St. Paul, MN 55101
(612) 291-5000
Telex: 297027
Contact: A. Wali Naibi, in-
  ternational division head

First National Bank & Trust
  Co. of Oklahoma City
120 N. Robinson St.
Oklahoma City, OK 73125
(405) 272-4000
Contact: John Robin, vice
  president

First National Bank of Oregon
1300 S.W. Fifth Ave.
Portland, OR 97201
(503) 225-2111

First National Cincinnati
425 Walnut St.
Cincinnati, OH 45202
(513) 632-4000

First Pennsylvania Bank
15th and Market Sts.
Philadelphia, PA 19101
(215) 786-5000
Contact: Joseph T. Drennan,
  senior vice president

First Tennessee Bank
Main St.
Jonesboro, TN 37659
(615) 753-3182

First Union National Bank
First Union Plaza
Charlotte NC 28288
(704) 374-6161
Contact: David H. Dormi-
  ney, senior vice president
  and manager

First Union National Bank of
  Florida
200 W. Forsyth St.
Jacksonville, FL 32231
(904) 632-6767
Contact: William C. Ott,
  vice president

Fleet National Bank
111 Westminster St.
Providence, RI 02903
(401) 278-6000

Florida Commercial Banks,
Inc.
960 S.W. 57th Ave.
Miami, FL 33144
(305) 266-2600

Florida National Bank
169 E. Flagler St.
Miami, FL 33131
(305) 545-3154
Telex: 56337.FLANB
Contact: Louis Petrillo, vice
president and director international

Fulton Bank
One Penn Square
Lancaster, PA 17602
(717) 291-2411
Contact: Linda Lee Morrow,
manager

Hamilton Bank
100 N. Queen St.
Lancaster, PA 17604
(717) 569-8731
Contact: Pierre Debbaudt,
vice president

Horizon Bank
225 South St.
Morristown, NJ 07960
(201) 285-2000
Telex: 275144 HRZN
Contact: Douglas F. Judah,
senior vice president

Hospital Trust Bank
One Hospital Trust Plaza
Providence, RI 02903
(401) 278-7154
Telex: 927619
Contact: John Borek, vice
president

Huntington National Bank
41 S. High St.
Columbus, OH 43287
(614) 476-8300
Telex: 245475
Contact: Dieter Heren, senior
vice president

The Indiana National Bank
One Indiana Square
Indianapolis, IN 46266
(317) 266-6000
Telex: 6876025 INDBNK
Contact: Linda Shireman, as-
sistant vice president

InterFirst World Trade
901 Main St.
Dallas, TX 75283
(214) 977-4000
Telex: 73353 IFBD
Contact: Vijay J. Fozdar,
general manager

Irving Trust
51 W. 51st St.
New York, NY 10015
(212) 635-1111
Telex: ITT 420268 IRV UI
Contact: Laurdes Falls vice
president

Jefferson National Bank
123 E. Main St.
Charlottesville, VA 22901
(804) 292-1100
Contact: Bruce Toms, vice
president

Key Bank
60 State St.
Albany, NY 12207
(518) 447-3500
Telex: 4947102
Contact: William G. Harper,
vice president and man-
ager

MBank Dallas
1704 Main St.
Dallas, TX 75201
(214) 698-6360
Telex: 732625
Contact: C. Jeff Pan, senior
vice president and general
manager

Manufacturers Hanover Trust
Co.
270 Park Ave.
New York, NY 10017
(212) 286-6000
Contact: John Simone, executive vice president

Manufacturers National Bank
of Detroit
Manufacturers Bank Tower
Detroit, MI 48243
(313) 222-4000
Telex: 235796
Contact: Robert Herdoiza,
executive vice president

Marine Bank
111 E. Wisconsin Ave.
Milwaukee, WI 53202
(414) 765-3000
Telex: 26835
Contact: M. Straka, executive vice president

Maryland National Bank
2 N. Charles St.
Baltimore, MD 21203
(301) 244-6483
Telex: 197637 MNBINTAD

Mellon Bank
One Mellon Bank Center
Pittsburgh, PA 15258
(412) 234-5000
Telex: 812367
Contact: Deborah Schneider,
vice president global trade
management division

Mercantile Trust Co.
Mercantile Tower
St. Louis, MO 63101
(314) 425-2525
Telex: 4312015
Contact: Richard A. Murray,
vice president

Merchant Bankers Group
280 Park Ave., Ste. 4 East
New York, NY 10017
(212) 557-2610
Telex: 277099, HFCUR
Contact: Robert E. White-
head, president

Merchants National Bank &
Trust Co.
One Merchants Plaza
Indianapolis, IN 46255
(317) 267-7000
Telex: 27411 MERCH
BANK
Contact: Robert J. Schindler,
vice president and director
international

Meridian Bank
17th and Arch Streets
Philadelphia, PA 19101
(215) 320-2000
Contact: Hennk Ersbak, international banking officer and manager

Midlantic National Banks
Metro Park Plaza
Edison, NJ 06818
(201) 321-8000
Telex: 844382, 844389
Contact: John A. Pell, senior vice president

Morgan Guaranty Trust Co. of New York
23 Wall St.
New York, NY 10015
(212) 483-2323
Contact: Alessandro Fusina, senior vice president

National Bank of Detroit
611 Woodward St., Ste. 3
Detroit, MI 48226
(313) 225-1000
Telex: 2252371
Contact: Dennis Nicholas, vice president

National Bank of Georgia
2000 RiverEdge Parkway
Atlanta, GA 30328
(404) 951-4000
Telex: 5841604
Contact: Roy Carlson, president

NCNB National Bank of North Carolina
101 S. Tryon St.
Charlotte, NC 28255
(704) 374-5000
Telex: 3747441
Contact: Mark Paden, senior vice president

National Bank of Washington
4340 Connecticut Ave N.W.
Washington, DC 20006
(202) 537-2000

National City Bank
1900 E. Ninth St.
Cleveland, OH 44114
(216) 575-2000

Contact: Richard Vanderwerf, senior vice president

The National Commercial Bank
245 Park Ave.
New York, NY 10167
(212) 916-9000
Telex: 422037
Contact: Lawrence G. Smith, executive vice president

The National State Bank
68 Broad St.
Elizabeth, NJ 07207
(201) 354-3400
Telex: 138872
Contact: Gregory P. Diefenbach, assistant vice president international

New Jersey National Bank
307 Scotch Road
Pennington, NJ 08534
(609) 771-5700
Telex: 219963 NJBUR
Contact: Glenna Spicer, manager

Northeastern Bank of Pennsylvania
Penn Ave. & Spruce St.
Scranton, PA 18503
(717) 961-7222
Telex: 831819
Contact: Kathleen White, international service officer

Northern Trust Co.
50 S. LaSalle St.
Chicago, IL 60675
(315) 630-6000
Telex: FTC824183
Contact: Dennis Regan, manager international trade division

Norwest Bank
Minneapolis
8th St. and Marquette Ave.
Minneapolis, MN 55479
(612) 372-8123
Telex: 290734
Contact: B.J. Neubeck, vice president

Old Kent Bank and Trust
One Vandenberg Center

Grand Rapids, MI 49503
(616) 774-5000
Telex: 226 373 OLKDKEN BK GDA
Contact: George A. Rabic, assistant vice president

Peoples Bank
899 Main St.
Bridgeport, CT 06601
(203) 579-7171
Contact Mr. Maccio

Peoples Ban Corp.
1414 Fourth Ave.
Seattle, WA 98111
(206) 344-2300

Peoples Bank & Trust
130 S. Franklin St.
Rocky Mountain, NC 27801
(919) 977-4811
Contact: Marshall Tetterton, president

Philadelphia National Bank
Broad and Chestnut Streets
Philadelphia, PA 19101
(215) 629-3100
Telex: 4990118 PNBCOMA
Contact: Harry G. Hayman III, senior vice president

Pittsburgh National Bank
Fifth Ave. and Wood St.
Pittsburgh, PA 15222
(412) 355-2000
Telex: 866533
Contact: Lee Cotrone, senior vice president and manager

Provident National Bank
Broad & Chestnut Streets
Philadelphia, PA 19101
(215) 585-5000
Contact: Edward Casselle, vice president and manager

Puget Sound National Bank
1119 Pacific Ave.
Tacoma, WA 96402
(206) 593-3600
Telex: 327421
Contact: K. Cobb, vice president

Rainier National Bank
1301 Fifth Ave.
Seattle, WA 98101
(206) 621-4111
Telex: 4740137
Contact: Mr. Emery, vice
president and general
manager

Republic National Bank of
Dallas
1707 Pacific and Erbay
Streets
Dallas, TX 75265
(214) 922-5000

Republic National Bank of
New York
452 Fifth Ave.
New York, NY 10018
(212) 930-6000
Telex: 234967
Contact: Michael Shemmer,
senior vice president

Republican International
Bank of New York
1451 Brickell Ave.
Miami, FL 33133
(305) 379-4000
Telex: 07020
Contact: Manlu Biac, presi-
dent

Riggs National Bank of
Washington, D.C.
800 17th St., N.W.
Washington, D.C. 20074
(202) 835-6000

Seattle First National Bank
Seattle First National Bank
Bldg.
Seattle, WA 98124
(206) 583-3131
Contact:

Security Pacific National-
Bank
333 Baudry Ave.
Los Angeles, CA 90071
(213) 613-6211
Contact: Mounir Hamaoui,
vice president

Shawmut Bank of Boston
One Federal St.

Boston, MA 02211
(617) 292-2360
Telex: WUI 6817133
Contact: Ron Gueitin, vice
president

Signet Banking Corp.
7 N. (th St.
Richmond, VA 23260
(804) 747-2000
Telex: 828321
Contact: John Jourdan, vice
president

Society National Bank
800 Superior Ave.
Cleveland, OH 44114
(216) 344-3000
Telex: 985517, 980174
Contact: Kevin J. McGinty,
senior vice president

Southeast Bank
One Southeast Financial
Center
Miami, Fl 33131
(305) 375-6940
Telex: 6811519 SEMIA UW
Contact: Richard J. Uss. vice
president and manager
project finance

Sovran Bank
111 E. Main Streets
Richmond, VA 23219
(804) 788-2000
Telex: 823468
Contact: William E. Riche-
son, international execu-
tive officer

State Street Bank and Trust
Co.
225 Franklin St.
Boston, MA 02110
(617) 786-5000
Telex: 940238
Contact: Kenneth Mc-
Graime, vice president

Sun Bank
200 S Orange Ave.
Orlando, FL 38202
(305) 237-4141
Contact: Carlos M. Gon-
zales, vice president and
manager trade finance

Texas Commerce Bank-
Houston
712 Main St.
Houston, TX 77002
(713) 236-4865

Trust Corp, Inc.
Three Seagate
Toledo, OH 43603
(419) 259-8498
Telex: 2598153
Contact: T. O. Metcalf, vice-
president

Union Bank
445 S. Figueroa St.
Los Angeles, CA 90071
(213) 236-5000
Telex: 4999030 UNIONBK
Contact: John O. Fox, Jr.,
senior vice president

Union Bank and Trust Co.
200 Ottawa Ave., N.W.
Grand Rapids, MI 49503
(616) 451-7000
Telex: 810273 6996
Contact: David C. Hatt, assistant vice president

Union Trust Co. of Maryland
7 St. Paul St.
Baltimore, MD 21203
(301) 332-5777
Telex: 87638
Contact: Elias M. Shomali,
senior vice president

United Jersey Bank
210 Main St.
Hackensack, NJ 07602
(201) 646-5240
Contact: Vaino A. Ahonen,
senior vice president and
manager

Union States National Bank
2201 Market St.
Galveston, TX 77550
(409) 763-1151
Contact: James Selig, assistant vice president

United Virginia Bank
919 E. Main St.
Richmond, VA 23219

(804) 782-5000
Telex: 827420
Contact: John Shibut, senior
   vice president

U.S. Bancorp.
111 S.W. Fifth Ave.
Portland, OR 97204
(503) 225-6111
Telex: 360549
Contact: Bill Carver, manager

Valley National Corp.
241 N. Central St.

Phoenix, AZ 85001
(602) 261-2900
Telex: 667371
Contact: Will Rapp, manager

Wells Fargo Bank
420 Montgomery St.
San Francisco, CA 94104
(415) 983-2000
Telex: 17613 CROCK
   DOMESTICA
Contact: Will C.
   Wood,executive vice pres-
ident

Whitney Holding Corp.
228 Saint Charles Ave.
New Orleans, LA 70130
(504) 586-7272
Contact: Roy Caronna

Wilmington Trust Co.
100 W. 10th St.
Wilmington, DE 19899
(302) 651-1169
Contact: Roy Faville, senior
   operations manager

Pacific Rim Banks in the United States

Asian Development Bank
P.O. Box 789
Metro Manila, Philippines 2800

Australia

Australia and New Zealand Banking Group
120 Wall Street
New York, N.Y. 10005
(212) 820-9800
Telex: 420686
Contact: Rodney Doyle, First Vice President

Commonwealth Bank of Australia
299 Park Avenue
New York, N.Y. 10171
(202) 599-1000
Contact: Adrian T. Walker, Executive Vice President

National Australia Bank
200 Park Avenue
New York, N.Y. 10066
(212) 916-9500
Telex: 424725
Contact: Robert B. Miller, Executive Vice President

State Bank of New South Wales
529 Fifth Avenue
New York, N.Y. 10017
(212) 682-1300
Contact: John M. Bartholomew, Senior Vice President and Chief Manager

State Bank of Victoria
250 Park Avenue
New York, N.Y. 10177
(212) 984-5100
Contact: John Winders, Senior Vice President

China

Bank of the Orient
233 Sansome Street
San Francisco, Calif. 94104
John Barclay, President

Hong Kong

The Bank of East Asia
450 Park Avenue
New York, N.Y. 10022
(212) 980-0510
Telex: 276640
Contact: Roderick Richards, Executive Vice President

Chekiang First Bank Ltd.
360 Pine Street
San Francisco, Calif. 94104
(415) 434-0738
Telex: 171748

The Hong Kong and Shanghai Banking Corp.
5 East 59th Street
New York, N.Y. 10022
(212) 839-5000
Contact: John Hosley, Vice President

Marine Midland Bank
One Marine Midland Center
Buffalo, N.Y. 14240
(716) 839-2424
Telex: 6854314
Contact: W. James Tozer, Jr., Sector Executive, Corporate, Institutional, and International Banking

Indonesia

Bank Central Asia
535 Madison Avenue
New York, N.Y. 10022

(212) 750-1300
Telex: 276633 BCANY
Contact: Guy B. Meeker, General Manager

Bank Dagang Negara
45 Broadway Atrium
New York, N.Y. 10006
(212) 809-8600
Telex: 226690
Contact: K. C. Komala, General Manager

Bank Ekspor Import Indonesia
100 Wall Street
New York, N.Y. 10005
(212) 809-5059
Telex: 423567
Contact: Edward Fishman, Assistant Vice President and Operations Manager

Bank Negara Indonesia
One Exchange Plaza
New York, N.Y. 10006
(212) 943-4750
Telex: 235 638 BNI UR
Contact: H. Willem Tehumijuluw

Japan

Bank of California
400 California Street
San Francisco, Calif. 94104
(415) 765-0400
Telex: RCA 278766
Contact: Magan Patel, Executive Vice President

The Bank of Tokyo Ltd.
100 Broadway
New York, N.Y. 10005
(212) 766-3400
Telex: 222967
Contact: Tomonori Naruse, President

Bank of Tokyo Trust Co.
100 Broadway
New York, N.Y. 10005
(212) 766-3100
Telex: 420742
Contact: Tamotsu Yamaguchi, Chairman

Bank of the West
180 Montgomery Street

San Francisco, Calif. 94104
(415) 765-4800
Telex: 278607
Contact: Greg Philip, Division Executive

The Bank of Yokohama
44 Wall Street
New York, N.Y. 10005
(212) 943-5800
Contact: Toshiharu Okubo, General Manager

The Chuo Trust & Banking Co. Ltd.
One World Trade Center
Suite 7923
New York, N.Y. 10048
(212) 938-0200
Telex: WT 1607
Contact: Hiroshi Katoh, General Manager

The Dai-Ichi Kangyo Bank of California
One World Trade Center
Suite 4911
New York, N.Y. 10048
(212) 466-5200
Telex: 420720
Contact: Yuko Oana, Managing Director and General Manager

Daiwa Bank
140 Broadway
New York, N.Y. 10005
(212) 480-0300
Telex: 4300335
Contact: Nobu Ninomiya, General Manager

Fuji Bank Ltd.
One World Trade Center
Suite 6011
New York, N.Y. 10048
(212) 839-5600
Telex: 420626
Contact: Mr. Tachioka, International Finance Department

Fuji Bank & Trust Co.
One World Trade Center
New York, N.Y. 10048
(212) 839-6800
Telex: 425777

Golden State Sanwa Bank
300 Montgomery Street
San Francisco, Calif. 94104
(415) 772-8200

J. Henry Schroder Bank & Trust Co.
One State Street
New York, N.Y. 10015
(212) 269-6500
Telex: 420477
Contact: Paul Wan, Senior Vice President

The Hokkaido Takushoku Bank Ltd.
One World Trade Center
Suite 3841
New York, N.Y. 10048
(212) 524-9771
Telex: 232230
Contact: Hiokichi Mizutani, Director and General Manager

The Hokuriku Bank Ltd.
One World Trade Center
Suite 8643
New York, N.Y. 10048
(212) 524-9771
Contact: Nobuo Hashigaki, General Manager

The Hyakujushi Bank
2 Wall Street
New York, N.Y. 10005
(212) 513-0114
Telex: 141388
Contact: Masaoki Morita, Chief Representative

The Industrial Bank of Japan Trust Co.
245 Park Avenue
New York, N.Y. 10167
(212) 557-3535
Telex: 425754 IBTC UY
Contact: Hiroshi Nakamura, President

The Kyowa Bank Ltd.
One World Trade Center
Suite 4673
New York, N.Y. 10048
(212) 432-6440
Contact: Junichi Yoshioka, General Manager

The Long Term Credit Bank of Japan Ltd.
140 Broadway
New York, N.Y. 10005
(212) 248-2000
Telex: 425722
Contact: Koji Hirao, General Manager

The Mitsubishi Bank Ltd.
One World Trade Center

Suite 8527
New York, N.Y. 10048
(212) 524-7000
Telex: 232328
Contact: Mr. Titanka, Director and General Manager

The Mitsubishi Trust & Banking Corp.
520 Madison Avenue
New York, N.Y. 10022
(212) 838-7700

The Mitsui Bank Ltd.
One Chase Manhattan Plaza
New York, N.Y. 10005
(212) 269-9750
Telex: 420637
Contact: Yoshisuke Mohri, General Manager

The Mitsui Trust & Banking Co. Ltd.
One World Trade Center
Suite 2365
New York, N.Y. 10048
(212) 938-2750
Telex: 222401 NBCO UR
Contact: Hiroshi Nishiki, General Manager

Nippon Credit Bank Ltd.
Two Wall Street
New York, N.Y. 10005
(212) 984-1200

The Norinchukin Bank
One World Trade Center
Suite 8025
New York, N.Y. 10048
(212) 432-6886
Telex: 6720068
Contact: Hinsuke Sato, General Manager

The Saitama Bank Ltd.
44 Wall Street
New York, N.Y. 10005
(212) 248-2690
Telex: 233410
Contact: Masaaki Saito, General Manager

Sanwa Bank
200 Park Avenue
New York, N.Y. 10166
(212) 949-0222
Telex: 232423
Contact: M. Takeda, Vice President

Sumitomo Trust & Banking Co. Ltd.
40 Wall Street, 9th Floor
New York, N.Y. 10005
(212) 785-3920
Telex: 222049
Contact: Ray Kochler, Assistant Vice President

The Taiyo Kobe Bank Ltd.
350 Park Avenue
New York, N.Y. 10022
(212) 750-1050
Telex: 411242
Contact: Osamu Nishimura, General Manager

The Tokai Bank Ltd.
One World Trade Center
Suite 8763
New York, N.Y. 10048
(212) 432-2600
Contact: Saburo Shinoda, General Manager

Tokyo Trust and Banking
437 Madison Avenue
New York, N.Y. 10022
(212) 371-3535
Telex: TT BCUR
Contact: Mr. Taguchi, General Manager

The Yasuda Trust & Banking Co., Ltd.
One World Trade Center
Suite 8871
New York, N.Y. 10048
(212) 432-2300
Contact: Toshio Hiratsuka, General Manager

Korea

Bank of Pusan L.P.D.
126 East 56th Street
New York, N.Y. 10022
(212) 355-2005
Telex: 238598
Contact: Syung Woong Chang, Chief Representative

Bank of Seoul
280 Park Avenue
New York, N.Y. 10017
(212) 687-6160
Telex: 238288
Contact: Nam Seog Song, General Manager

Cho Hung Bank
535 Madison Avenue
New York, N.Y. 10022
(212) 935-3500
Telex: 662314
Contact: Dyung Yu, General Manager

Commercial Bank of Korea
245 Park Avenue
New York, N.Y. 10167
(212) 949-1900
Contact: Mr. Imm, Assistant Manager

Daegu Bank
29 West 30th Street
New York, N.Y. 10001
(212) 868-1075

Export-Import Bank of Korea
460 Park Avenue
New York, N.Y. 10002
(212) 355-7280

Hanil Bank
299 Park Avenue
New York, N.Y. 10171
(212) 355-6440
Telex: 237208
Contact: Kwang Hyung Oh, General Manager and Agent

Korea Exchange Bank
460 Park Avenue, 12th Floor
New York, N.Y. 10022
(212) 838-4949
Telex: 223533, 12976
Contact: S. J. Cho, General Manager

Korea First Bank
410 Park Avenue
New York, N.Y. 10022
(212) 832-7200
Telex: 661572
Contact: Tai Wan Hong, General Manager

The Small and Medium Industry Bank
375 Park Avenue, Suite 2608
New York, N.Y. 10152
Telex: 237144
(212) 980-3353
Contact: Mr. Hunter, Representative

Malaysia

Bank Bumiputra Malaysia Berhad
900 Third Avenue
New York, N.Y. 10022
(212) 644-1280
Contact: Mahfudz Muhamad, General Manager

Malayan Banking Berhad
400 Park Avenue
New York, N.Y. 10022
(212) 303-1300
Contact: See Inn Ong, General Manager

New Zealand

Bank of New Zealand
575 Fifth Avenue
New York, N.Y. 10017
(212) 984-1400
Contact: Rovert F. Hirten, Executive Vice President and Manager

Philippines

Philippine Commercial International Bank
One World Trade Center
Suite 4621
New York, N.Y. 10048
(212) 466-0960
Contact: Lucrica Panlilio, International Banking Officer

Singapore

The Development Bank of Singapore Ltd.
One World Trade Center
Suite 9057
New York, N.Y. 10048
(212) 839-9031
Telex: 235607 RCA
Contact: Hean-Beng Ong, Agent

Overseas Chinese Banking Corp. Ltd.
One World Trade Center
Suite 2569
New York, N.Y. 10048

(212) 524-9494
Telex: 661656
Contact: Sian-Chee Ban, Agent and Manager

Overseas Union Bank
One World Trade Center
Suite 1201
New York, N.Y. 10048
(212) 775-0560
Telex: 424385
Contact: Raymond Seah, Agent

United Overseas Bank
130 Liberty Street 26th Floor
New York, N.Y. 10006
(212) 775-0560
Contact: Lye Soon Teo, Agent and Chief Manager

Taiwan

International Commercial Bank of China
40 Wall Street
New York, N.Y. 10005
(212) 943-5000
Telex: 232640
Contact: L. C. Shu, Executive Vice President and General Manager.

Thailand

Bangkok Bank Ltd.
40 Wall Street
New York, N.Y. 10005
(212) 422-8200
Telex: 666297
Contact: Chansak Fuangfu, Vice President and Manager

Bangkok Metropolitan Bank
555 Montgomery Street, Suite 1000
San Francisco, Calif. 94111
(414) 392-1580
Telex: 278529
Contact: Sukich Patavivatana, Vice President and Agent.

Krung Thai Bank Ltd.
452 Fifth Avenue
New York, N.Y. 10018
(212) 704-0001
Telex: 237903
Contact: Kovit Rojanasomsit, Vice President and General Manager

Siam Commercial Bank
99 Wall Street, 14th Floor
New York, N.Y. 10005
(212) 344-4101
Telex: 233443
Contact: Pratib Yongvanich, Vice President and Agent

Thai Farmers Bank Ltd.
One World Trade Center
Suite 8373
New York, N.Y. 10048
(212) 432-0890
Telex: 645303
Contact: Paul J. Foley, Senior Vice President and General Manager

Venture Capital Firms

U.S. Venture Capital Firms That Finance Pacific Rim Investment

Advent International (a subsidiary of P.A. Associates), Boston
Churchill International, Weston, Massachusetts, and San Francisco
Hambrecht & Quist, San Francisco
InterPacific Capital Corporation, Los Angeles
Ventura Venture Capital Group, Irvine, California

Pacific Rim Venture Capital Firms That Finance Investment by U.S. Firms

Hong Kong

Arral & Partners Ltd.
ChinaVest
Techno-Ventures Ltd.
David Mathew
Baring Brothers (of UK)
Hong Kong Venture Investment Trust

Singapore

Venture Capital Group, (under Economic Development Board) co-invests in desired
 new technologies
Elders PICA Growth Fund Pte. Ltd.
Singacon Investments Pte. Ltd.
Southeast Asia Ventures Pte. Ltd. (SEAVIC)
Transtech Venture Management Pte. Ltd.
H & Q Singapore
K. H. Ang, Tang Keng Boon (Advent/Technoventure sister funds)

Taiwan

H & Q Taiwan Ltd.
Bank of Communication (Taiwan's development bank)
Taiwan Venture
Global (joint venture with Wang Laboratories and other local partners)
China Venture Management Company (CVM)
International Capital Investment Incorporated (IVTIC) (joint venture with Walden of San
   Francisco)
Ho-Tung (joint venture between local and Japanese partners)

Japan. There are 80 venture companies in three categories: security houses,
banks, and independents.

Venture Enterprise Center (non-profit info clearing center; guarantees bank loans)
Orient Capital in Tokyo.
Techno-Ventures Co Ltd (Advent International) Seeks U.S. ideas, ASEAN manufactur-
   ing, with market in Japan and U.S.)
Nippon Investment & Finance Co Ltd (NIF) (under Daiwa Securities)
JAFCO (under Nomura Securities)
Pacific Technology Ventures Co. Ltd.
Japan Venture Fund (under Schroder PTV Partners KK)
Kangyo Kakumaru Investment Co Ltd (KKI) (under NKK Securities)

Korea

The Technology Fund
Korea Investment Finance Corporation (KIFC)
Korea Technology Development Corp. (KTDC) (government plus private backing)
Korea Development Investment Corp. (KDIC) (private backing)

Thailand

Business Venture Promotion Ltd.
Industrial Finance Corporation of Thailand
Siam Commercial Bank (ADB facility)
Thai Agribusiness Venture Capital Company
H & Q

Malaysia

Malaysian Veentures Sdn. Bhd.

Philippines. There is a lot of capital available, and the institutional venture capital market will become more active when political stability and confidence in economic
stability returns.

First Philippines Capital Fund.
Inter-Pacific Capital Philippines Corporation.
H & Q

Indonesia

Industrial Development Finance Corporation (UPPINDO)
Private Development Finance Corporation of Indonesia (PDFCI.)

Australia.   The Development Finance Company has a representative in the Ausutralian Consulate in Los Angeles.

Numerous Management Investment Companies (MICs)

New Zealand

Development Finance Company of New Zealand

China

CITIC (China International Trade and Investment Company)
Firms such as Techno-Ventures or Baring Brothers of Hong Kong do ventures into China.

Glossary

ACCJ American Chamber of Commerce in Japan. *See also* AMCHAM.

ADB *See* Asian Development Bank.

ADS Agent/distributor service offered by the Department of Commerce, to identify suitable overseas agents or distributors for a company's product or line.

agent One who represents and sells a company's services in a foreign market. Sometimes used interchangeably with *representative*. An agent sells on commission.

AID *See* USAID.

AIST Agency for Industrial Science Technology.

AIT *See* American Institute in Taiwan.

AMCHAM American Chamber of Commerce. Private organizations in each nation composed of companies doing business there. In some countries it is called the American Business Council, and in Japan it goes by ACCJ.

American Institute in Taiwan (AIT). The organization that has fulfilled the role of embassy and trade representative for the United States since the Republic of China was derecognized in favor of the People's Republic of China.

ASEAN Association of Southeast Asian Nations: Singapore, Indonesia, Malaysia, the Philippines, Thailand, and Brunei

Asian Development Bank (ADB) Provides funding for development projects in developing Asian nations. ADB-funded project contracts are awarded under international bidding. It is headquartered in Manila.

aussie Colloquial term for a citizen of Australia.

back translation After text material is translated from English to a foreign languuage, an independent retranslation back from the foreign language to English to check its accuracy and adequacy. Particularly important for idiomatic material such as advertising slogans.

baht Currency of Thailand.

bumipatras Indigenous Malay people.

business culture The unwritten rules, behaviors, taboos, and protocols specific to doing business in a particular culture. Ignorance of business culture is a major cause of failure of international business.

CCNAA Coordination Council for North American Affairs. The CCNAA has been Taiwan's unofficial embassy in the United States and Canada since the United States derecognized the Republic of China in favor of the People's Republic of China.

439

COCOM   Coordinating Committee for Multilateral Export Control. Sixteen industrialized Western trading partners (Japan plus NATO members) that jointly regulate trade of technological items with Communist countries.

commercial risk   Normal risks of doing business with another company, such as non-payment by the buyer or goods not received as ordered by the seller.

compensation   Form of countertrade in which payment for a product or material is delayed until it is used to manufacture another value-added product. That product is then re-exported to obtain foreign exchange from which payment is made for the original product.

countertrade   An international transaction in which a company accepts other products as payments for its products or services. Can be barter of one commodity for another, but more often it is a complex transaction.

critical factors   Events beyond obvious market factors that may influence a company's performance in a market. Examples include political, social, and demographic trends; broad economic shifts or cycles; and structural changes in an industry.

dango **system**   The designated bidder system (Japan) in which potential Japanese bidders decide among themselves who will respond to bid tenders. This tends to keep out foreign bidders.

direct exporting   Selling in a foreign country through a trading company, distributor, agent, or through a company's own sales force. The seller is involved in export documentation, shipping, overseas collections, and market research. Contrasts with *indirect exporting*.

direct investment   Establishing an overseas operation that requires capital outlays. Distinct from investment for purely financial purposes in another business or in securities.

distributor   One who buys goods on discount and resells in the local market. Differs from a larger trading company in that the distributor specializes in one market and one product line and provides a broader range of services and assistance.

documentation   All the essential paperwork that accompanies an order being shipped overseas with information essential to customs, shippers, bankers, government inspectors, and—last but not least—the customer. Documents may include copies of the commercial invoice, packing list, export license, letter of credit, bill of lading, quality certifications, insurance coverage, routing and shipping documents, and import licenses.

economic risk   The possibility of a decrease in the book value of overseas assets resulting from shifts in currency values.

EEC   European Economic Community, or Common Market. EEC coordinates economic, trade, and financial policies among most Western European nations. *See also* 1992.

EMC   *See* export management company.

ETC   Export trading company. Handles specialized export services for member companies: market research, transportation and warehousing, legal and financial assistance. ETCs were made legal in the United States by the 1982 Export Trading Act. They are exempt from antitrust laws and can be owned by bank holding companies.

Eximbank   The Export-Import Bank of the United States, a government institution that finances and backs foreign business transactions by American companies.

expatriate   One who lives and works overseas. The term applies in particular to professionals from Western countries and their family members.

exportize To refine a product, service, packaging, or applied technology for export, thus making the product more appropriate to sell in a target Pacific Rim market

export management company (EMC) A company that handles the exporting for several businesses with related noncompeting product lines and that specializes in a narrow range of products. An EMC sometimes buys goods for resale and sometimes sells goods on commission

FAS United States Foreign Agricultural Service. FAS officials are stationed in many U.S. embassies and consulates, along with foreign service commercial officers, and assist American agricultural producers in selling overseas.

FCS officer *See* United States Foreign Commercial Service officer.

flight capital Funds sent by individuals or companies out of their country for investment in a country that is deemed safer.

foreign exchange Financial transaction between parties in different countries involving exchange of one currency for another, usually through a financial institution.

foreign exchange reserves Currency reserves available in one country in the currency of another country (especially in hard currencies), for the import of goods or services, repayment of debts, or the repatriation of profits or capital by a foreign company operating there.

foreign exchange risk Possibility of commercial loss caused by financial events such as shifts in exchange rates or loss of currency convertibility.

franchising A method of setting up multiple retail outlets for a product or service. A franchise is a contractual right to market goods, services, or trade secrets in a particular territory. It includes the right to use a retail concept, product or service, or specifications and the obligation to retain quality factors and supply requirements.

freight forwarder A company that arranges shipping, documentation, insurance, packing, customs, and related functions for exporters.

FX *see* foreign exchange.

GATT General Agreement on Trade and Tariffs, signed by over one hundred trading nations around the world. GATT specifies fair and unfair trade and tariff policies and prescribes acceptable remedies for unfair practices.

G-7 Group of seven: the finance ministers and central bankers of seven leading industrial nations (the United States, Canada, Japan, West Germany, Britain, France, and Italy). Its purpose is to maintain a stable international economic environment by coordinating national financial and monetary policies.

hard currency Currency from one of the leading industrial and trading nations that is freely convertible on world financial markets. Includes the U.S. dollar, the Japanese yen, the British pound, and the West German deutschmark.

IMF International Monetary Fund.

inconvertibility (1) The inability to convert the currency of one country to other currencies because of that nation's policies or restrictions; (2) the lack of an acceptable exchange rate.

indirect exporting Selling to a trading company or other entity in the United States for resale overseas. By relying on another company to handle its export function, the seller avoids dealing with export documentation, international shipping, foreign exchange, or overseas market research. *See also* direct exporting

intellectual property Property rights to things developed by intellectual effort. These rights are owned by companies, individuals, or other entities. There are two classes of intellectual property: (1) industrial property (inventions, patents, industrial designs, trade secrets, technologies and techniques, trademarks and service marks); (2) copyrights (protection of written, programmed, literary, musical, artistic, photographic, and cinematographic works).

intellectual property protection A nation's laws and enforcement policies for protecting intellectual property from misuse or misappropriation. Inadequate or inconsistent protection of intellectual property is a major concern of international business.

JETRO Japan External Trade Organization. Assists Japanese and foreign companies that wish to trade with or invest in Japan.

JIS Japanese industrial standards. Set by MITI and AIST, JIS is an official set of standards for products manufactured or sold in Japan, used to ensure the high quality of those products. JIS certification is comparable to the Underwriters Laboratory (UL) seal in the United States. Some of these standards differ from those in other industrialized nations.

joint venture A new business enterprise legally separate from the parent companies that share in its ownership, management and control, and profits.

kiwi Colloquial term for a citizen of New Zealand. The term comes from the flightless, nocturnal bird native to New Zealand

Korea Almost always South Korea, the Republic of Korea.

letter of credit A method of payment for international transactions. This financial instrument is obtained by the buyer through its local bank. The buyer's bank guarantees payment to the seller when specified terms are met. The buyer's bank thus substitutes its credit for that of the buyer, thereby virtually guaranteeing payment to the seller.

licensing A method of business whereby one company sells to another company the right to manufacture and distribute a unique product, design, technology, process, or service within a specified market in return for a fee or a royalty.

market partner An informal term for any person or business with which a company must closely cooperate in order to succeed in a market. A market partner may be a joint venture partner, franchisee, contract manufacturer, distributor, or agent.

MITI Japan's Ministry of International Trade and Investment. This influential government agency helps set and administer industrial policy for Japan's industries, and promotes investment and export incentives.

MOFERT China's Ministry of Foreign Economy Relations and Trade. MOFERT coordinates major transactions with outside companies including countertrade. It also administers the import licensing system.

neibu gu-ding. Unpublished internal rules (China) regulating foreign companies.

New Economic Program (NEP) Malaysia's economic development plan, which sets out priorities and policies for investment and trade.

NICs The newly industrialized countries (Hong Kong, Taiwan, South Korea, and Singapore). These countries are also called the Four Tigers or Four Dragons.

NIE Newly industrialized economy (pronounced *knee*). Often used in place of the term

NIC, on the grounds that Taiwan and Hong Kong are separate economies but not separate countries.

1992 The year that EEC will integrate economically. Asian trading nations are concerned that a unified European community will erect barriers to hinder their products.

1997 The date (July 1, 1997) that Hong Kong will revert to Chinese rule from British colonial status. Uncertainty about how China will treat Hong Kong (despite strong guarantees of continued freedom) is already having an impact on Hong Kong business.

OECD Organization for Economic Cooperation and Development. Representatives of the industrialized nations of Western Europe, North America plus Japan, Australia, and New Zealand. Korea and Taiwan are potential new members. *G-7* is a subset of this group.

OEM Original equipment manufacture. Products manufactured to the specifications of a customer, which markets them under their better known brand names.

offset requirements An agreement to spend a certain proportion of the contract amount in the local economy, whereby a company buys local components or services or transfers technology in order to obtain certain government contracts. In the United States, these are called local content requirements.

offshore operations Manufacturing or assembly facilities set up outside the home country in order to obtain proximity to customers or lower labor and operating costs.

OPIC *See* Overseas Private Investment Corporation.

overseas Chinese Ethnic Chinese individuals or communities located outside of mainland China and Taiwan. There are major overseas Chinese communities in Singapore and other Southeast Asian nations, as well as in North America. In Taiwan, the term refers to Taiwanese who have gone overseas, especially to the United States, for education or employment.

Overseas Private Investment Corporation (OPIC) U.S. government-funded organization that offers financial assistance to American companies making direct investments overseas.

Pacific Rim The nations surrounding the Pacific Ocean, including those covered in this book, plus Indochina, North America, and the west coast of Latin America. Also called the Pacific Basin.

political risks Potential commercial losses caused by actions of governments that are beyond buyer or seller, such as those caused by unforeseen changes in policy or regulations, political unrest, expropriation, and government interference.

pribumis Ethnic Indonesian people.

repatriation (1) The transfer of profits, dividends, or capital by a company or individual from operations in a foreign country back to the home country. Repatriation is sometimes limited in nations with foreign exchange controls or shortages. (2) The return of citizens to their home country after a long absence of living and working overseas. Often follows an improvement in domestic economic or political conditions.

representative A sales or manufacturer's rep. An independent person or company that sells a company's manufactured products in a foreign country, usually selling on commission.

ringgit   Currency of Malaysia.
rupiah   Currency of Indonesia.

senmosha   Japanese term for a smaller trading company that is more specialized than *sogoshosha*.

sogoshosha   Large Japanese trading companies set up to export Japanese products, but increasingly used to import products to Japan and provide other, related services as well.

technology transfer   Arrangement by which nations seek to expand their industrial base and develop more sophisticated products by attracting companies to set up operations for manufacturing high-tech products. Local companies and workers thereby gain familiarity with these technologies and learn how to apply them in other ways.

United States Foreign Commercial Service officer (FCS officer)   Officer stationed at the embassy or consulate of a particular nation. FCS officers and their staff members provide several services for American companies doing business in the country where they are stationed: business counseling; help in finding local distributors, agents, or joint venture partners; reports on major projects, opportunities, and trade leads; liaison with local governments.

Uruguay round of GATT negotiations   The current ongoing round of negotiations that began at a meeting in Uruguay. These negotiations seek to expand GATT agreements to cover services, intellectual property protection, and more agricultural commodities.

USAID (also *AID*)   United States Agency for International Development.

won   Currency of Korea.

World Traders Data Report (WTDR)   Report published by the Department of Commerce. Key data on overseas companies that are potential representatives.

WTDR   *See* World Traders Data Report.

yen   Currency of Japan.

yuan   Basic unit of Chinese currency. The currency itself is called *Renminbi* (RMB), which means "people's currency."

zaibatsu   The powerful, informal industry groups (Japan) that encourage cooperation among member companies

zaitech **financial engineering**   The act of taking a global perspective on a company's financial transactions, including obtaining the best terms for trade or investment and currency hedging to reduce risk.

Index